ASPEN PUBl

Calculating Construction Damages
Second Edition

by William Schwartzkopf and John J. McNamara

Calculating Construction Damages, Second Edition, provides practical guidelines for the calculation and preparation of damages in construction claims and sets forth the legal basis for recovery. Organized by type of damages rather than type of claim, the book analyzes each type of damages, such as labor loss or material costs, and reviews numerous sample calculations, all taken from actual claims. Although concisely calculated damages, which reference cost accounting data, can (and, the authors hope, will) aid in the early and amicable resolution of construction claims, the analysis in the book is presented as being done in anticipation of litigation.

Highlights of the 2010 Cumulative Supplement

Supplement prepared by William Schwartzkopf

The 2010 Cumulative Supplement to *Calculating Construction Damages* brings you the most recent developments, ensuring that your book is up-to-date and accurate. It includes:

- New subsection on Apportionment of Damages **(Chapter 1)**.
- Analysis of *Traco Steel Erectors v Comtrol* and its application to the determination of wage rates **(Chapter 2)**.
- New cases discussing loss of bonding capacity **(Chapter 5)**.
- New cases discussing home office overhead **(Chapter 6)**.
- Discussion of *Boro Construction v. Ridley School District*, among others, and its applicability to attorneys' fees **(Chapter 10)**.
- Increased coverage of Liquidated Damages as seen through case decisions in 2009 and 2010 **(Chapter 13)**.

Wolters Kluwer
Law & Business

The Table of Cases and Index have been updated to reflect all the changes to the text.

8/10

For questions concerning this shipment, billing, or other customer service matters, call our Customer Service Department at 1-800-234-1660.

For toll-free ordering, please call 1-800-638-8437.

ASPEN PUBLISHERS

CALCULATING CONSTRUCTION DAMAGES

Second Edition

2010 Cumulative Supplement

William Schwartzkopf
John J. McNamara

Supplement Prepared by
William Schwartzkopf

This supplement supersedes all previous supplements.

Wolters Kluwer
Law & Business

AUSTIN BOSTON CHICAGO NEW YORK THE NETHERLANDS

1 2 3 4 5 6 7 8 9 0

Printed in the United States of America

ISBN 978-0-7355-9281-0

About Wolters Kluwer Law & Business

Wolters Kluwer Law & Business is a leading provider of research information and workflow solutions in key specialty areas. The strengths of the individual brands of Aspen Publishers, CCH, Kluwer Law International and Loislaw are aligned within Wolters Kluwer Law & Business to provide comprehensive, in-depth solutions and expert-authored content for the legal, professional and education markets.

CCH was founded in 1913 and has served more than four generations of business professionals and their clients. The CCH products in the Wolters Kluwer Law & Business group are highly regarded electronic and print resources for legal, securities, antitrust and trade regulation, government contracting, banking, pension, payroll, employment and labor, and healthcare reimbursement and compliance professionals.

Aspen Publishers is a leading information provider for attorneys, business professionals and law students. Written by preeminent authorities, Aspen products offer analytical and practical information in a range of specialty practice areas from securities law and intellectual property to mergers and acquisitions and pension/benefits. Aspen's trusted legal education resources provide professors and students with high-quality, up-to-date and effective resources for successful instruction and study in all areas of the law.

Kluwer Law International supplies the global business community with comprehensive English-language international legal information. Legal practitioners, corporate counsel and business executives around the world rely on the Kluwer Law International journals, loose-leafs, books and electronic products for authoritative information in many areas of international legal practice.

Loislaw is a premier provider of digitized legal content to small law firm practitioners of various specializations. Loislaw provides attorneys with the ability to quickly and efficiently find the necessary legal information they need, when and where they need it, by facilitating access to primary law as well as state-specific law, records, forms and treatises.

Wolters Kluwer Law & Business, a unit of Wolters Kluwer, is headquartered in New York and Riverwoods, Illinois. Wolters Kluwer is a leading multinational publisher and information services company.

CONTENTS

Sections listed below appear only in the supplement and not in the main volume.

PREFACE

This 2010 Cumulative Supplement covers noteworthy cases published through May 2010. Included are new cases on actual cost, *quantum* meruit, loss of productivity, general conditions costs, loss of profit, prejudgment interest, liquidated damages, and no-damages-for-delay clauses. I would like to thank Kate Krause of my office for her assistance in the preparation of this supplement.

June 2010
Denver, Colorado

William Schwartzkopf
Sage Consulting Group, Inc.

CHAPTER 1
GENERAL PRINCIPLES OF DAMAGE CALCULATION

§ 1.01 INTRODUCTION

Page 6, add at end of section:

In *MacQuesten General Contracting, Inc. v. HCE, Inc.*,[10.1] the court held that there was an adequate basis for an award of $27,000 in punitive damages based on a general contractor's conversion of its subcontractor's equipment. Although some New York case law suggests that when a conversion claim arises out of a breach of contract, punitive damages may only be awarded if the culpable party's conduct was directed at the public. This requirement applies only when there is a close nexus between the alleged tortious conduct and the contract from which it is said to arise, for example, when the contract was fraudulently induced or when a party engages in conduct outside the contract but intended to defeat the contract. In this case, however, the conversion of the subcontractor's equipment was independent of the terms of the contract—it was separate tortious conduct—and so the requirement of public harm as a prerequisite for punitive damages was not triggered. The defendant also argued that there was insufficient evidence of malice to warrant punitive damages. However, New York law permits an exemplary award against a party that engages in self-help by violating the rights of its adversary rather than relying exclusively on its legal remedies. In this case, the defendant had no arguable basis for retaining the subcontractor's equipment, and the jury was entitled to infer that it did so merely to give itself leverage in the contract dispute between the parties. Accordingly, an award of punitive damages was warranted.

The Second Circuit Court of Appeals affirmed the decision of the Magistrate Judge, agreeing that, under the facts of this case—where the general contractor had no colorable right to the subcontractor's equipment and was not acting under the contract—the conversion was a tort separate from the contract claim, and there was no public-aim prerequisite for punitive damages. In addition, the Magistrate Judge did not exceed his allowable discretion in finding that, under the facts presented at trial, the jury was entitled to award punitive damages.

[10.1] 296 F. Supp. 2d 437 (S.D.N.Y. 2003), *aff'd*, 128 Fed. Appx. 782 (2d Cir. 2005).

§ 1.03 GENERAL METHODS OF DAMAGE CALCULATION

[A] Actual Cost Method

Page 11, add at end of note 15:

See also, e.g., Ryco Constr., Inc. v. United States, 55 Fed. Cl. 184 (Ct. Cl. 2002) (the preferred method for calculating an equitable adjustment is the actual cost method; this method requires the contractor to provide the court with specific documentation of the added expenses caused by the government conduct); George Sollitt Constr. Co. v. United States, 64 Fed. Cl. 229 (Ct. Cl. 2005) (once contractor has proven government's liability for the costs of added or changed contract work, actual costs incurred by contractor will provide the measure of the equitable adjustment to contract price, if those incurred costs are "reasonable"; a presumption of reasonableness applies to contractor's incurred costs for changed or added work if FAR 31.201-3 is *not* applicable to the contract; however, if FAR 31.201-3 *is* applicable, a cost will be determined reasonable "if, in its nature and amount, it does not exceed that which would be incurred by a prudent person in the conduct of competitive business"; what is reasonable depends upon a variety of considerations, including: (1) whether it is the type of cost generally recognized as ordinary and necessary for the conduct of the contractor's business or the contract performance; (2) generally accepted sound business practices, arm's-length bargaining, and federal and state laws and regulations; (3) the contractor's responsibilities to the government, other customers, the owners of the business, employees, and the public at large; and (4) any significant deviations from the contractor's established practices); Orlosky Inc. v. United States, 68 Fed. Cl. 296 (2005), *appeal dismissed*, 180 Fed. Appx. 928 (Fed. Cir. Apr. 17, 2006) (the court noted that a court may employ several different methods to calculate delay damages, but calculations based on actual costs to the plaintiff are preferred; the alternative methods of calculating damages—the total cost method, and the jury verdict method—may be used only when the actual cost method is not feasible); Carr Business Enters., Inc. v. City of Chowchilla, 2006 WL 619349 (Cal. App. 5th Dist. Mar. 14, 2006) (unpublished), *reh'g denied* (Apr.13, 2006), *review denied* (June 28, 2006) (the correct method for determining damages when there is an alleged breach of a public works contract is the actual cost method; in the instant case, the court affirmed an award of compensation to a contractor of actual damages for extra work caused by the breach of contract by a public agency; Safeco Ins. Co. of Am. v. S & T Bank, 2010 WL 786257 (W.D. Pa. Mar. 3, 2010) (quoting this treatise (which the court noted both parties referenced as an authoritative treatise on the question) and the author to the effect that the Actual Cost Method of calculating damages is the method preferred by most courts).

Page 12, insert after first sentence of first full paragraph:

The reason is that the actual cost method "[p]rovides the court or contracting officer, with documented underlying expenses, insuring that the final amount of the equitable adjustment will be just that—equitable—and not a windfall for either the government or the contractor."[15.1] Courts will employ the actual cost method if:

1. Clear proof of injury appears;
2. No more reliable method for computing damages exists;
3. The evidence is sufficient for court to make a fair and reasonable approximation of the damages.[15.2]

Page 12, insert after first full paragraph:

The claimant must have good records to succeed using the actual cost method. Detailed documentation should be provided showing that the additional costs incurred have been separated from the costs incurred performing the original contract requirements to permit the evaluation of the reasonableness of the added costs. Such recordkeeping can be "cumbersome" as observed by the court in *United States v. Service Eng'g Co.*[15.3] When the records exist and appropriately segregate the costs, the contractor can effectively prove its damages. This was demonstrated in *ACE Constructors, Inc. v. United States*[15.4] in which the contractor was successful in pursuing a claim for additional overtime costs and had the detailed documentation showing the additional cost of the premium time.

In *Beta Analytics International, Inc. v. United States,*[15.5] the court found sufficient documentation to support the majority of actual bid preparation and proposal costs claimed against the government. The court found that the contractor did not need to provide contemporaneous records as detailed as an attorney's billing records, but required sufficient documentation to determine the nature of the tasks performed, the date performed and the person performing the tasks. The court disallowed certain costs incurred by a consultant where there was no basis to segregate bid preparation work from unrelated work, noting a basis for apportionment that was established subsequent to performance of the work would have been acceptable.

[15.1] Dawco Constr. v. United States, 903 F.2d 872 (Fed. Cir. 1991), *rev'd on other grounds by* Reflectone, Inc. v. Dalton, 60 F.3d 1572 (Fed. Cir. 1995).

[15.2] *See Dawco*, 903 F.2d at 880, *citing* WRB Corp. v. United States, 183 Ct. Cl. 409 (1968).

[15.3] 1994 U.S. Dist. Lexis 13596 (N.D. Cal. 1994).

[15.4] 70 Fed. Cl. 253 (Mar. 31, 2006), *aff'd*, 499 F.3d 1357 (Fed. Cir. 2007).

[15.5] 75 Fed. Cl. 155 (2007).

In *Subcrete Construction, Inc. v. Mehrabian,*[15.6] the court noted that a contractor on a cost-plus contract has an obligation to keep fair and accurate records of accounts for costs, charges and expenditures, and to promptly and accurately report such costs to the owner. The court held that the contractor in this case satisfied its obligations by preparing and submitting to the owner monthly detailed progress expense statements summarizing the invoices incurred each month and listing vendors paid, date paid, and check posting dates. The expense statements and actual invoices were admitted into evidence at trial, along with testimony of the contractor's office manager regarding preparation of the expense statements, and expert testimony of another experienced contractor that the plaintiff's record-keeping was excellent. Based upon the contractor's detailed records of actual costs incurred, the contractor was awarded judgment.

The court held that the contractor could not disavow its own cost records in *Woodman Construction, Inc. v. Roy Rogers, Inc.*[15.7] The contractor, Rogers, sought to recover for extra work performed prior to termination. Rogers' job cost report, produced on compact disc during discovery and validated by a Rogers' representative as the only job cost report maintained by Rogers, reflected that Rogers' total costs incurred on the project were $1.2 million, which Woodman established was less than the amount previously paid Rogers. Although Rogers argued that its job cost report did not include all labor costs, its representative testified in discovery that the job cost report should include all labor burden and other labor costs. Since Rogers failed to provide specific facts rebutting the evidence presented by Woodman, including Rogers' own job cost report, Woodman's motion for summary judgment on Roger's claim for extra work was properly granted.

The contractor's cost records were insufficient to establish damages in *Tri-Tech Co., Inc. v. Landis.*[15.8] Tri-Tech entered into a fixed-price contract to perform mold remediation and repair of earthquake damage on the Landis home. Upon completion of the work, Tri-Tech sued Landis for $50,000 allegedly due on the contract, and Landis counterclaimed for defective and incomplete work. A jury awarded Tri-Tech $165,000, and Landis appealed. The appellate court found that there was no evidence of "extra work" justifying an award that exceeded the contract balance, and that Tri-Tech failed to maintain adequate cost records documenting that Tri-Tech performed all of the work required by the contract, including the temporary shoring work, installation of a three-ply roof, or traffic control work required by the contract. The court therefore reversed the judgment as not supported by substantial evidence and remanded for a new trial on Landis' counterclaim for breach of contract.

[15.6] 2007 WL 4376059 (Cal. Ct. App. Dec. 17, 2007) (unpublished), *reh'g denied* (Jan. 15, 2008), *review denied* (Feb. 27, 2008).

[15.7] 142 Wash. App. 1027 (Jan. 14, 2008).

[15.8] 2008 WL 186929 (Cal. Ct. App. 2008) (unpublished).

Page 12, add after last full paragraph:

A subcontractor that had been improperly terminated was precluded from recovering damages due to lack of proof in *Alliance Excavating, Inc. v. Triangle Real Estate Services, Inc.*[15.9] The trial court awarded the subcontractor, Alliance, the total balance due on the four contracts that Triangle breached. However, the appellate court noted that Alliance was only entitled to recover "the further compensation plaintiff would have received under the contract if it had been performed, *less the value to plaintiff of his being relieved of the obligation of completing performance.*" [Emphasis in original.] The court found that there was nothing in the record that would indicate the costs Alliance would have incurred had it completed performance. Alliance's principal testified at trial that Alliance bid the project with a planned profit margin of five percent, and Alliance argued that the foregone costs could be calculated by subtracting this project margin from the bid price. The court rejected this argument, finding that "a contractor's planned profit margin prior to commencing a project is far too speculative a basis upon which to establish actual costs to completion." The court held that Alliance could not recover damages because it failed to introduce sufficient evidence to support its measure of damages.

In *Continental Air Conditioning, Inc. v. Keller Construction Co.*,[15.10] the court noted that the actual cost method requires a determination of the true increased labor costs incurred as a direct result of each incident of delay and disruption, and it is the preferred method to calculate increased labor costs because it provides the court with documented underlying expenses. The expert in this case testified that in applying the actual cost method to determine lost hours of labor for each disruption and delay, he compared the number of hours it actually took laborers to perform certain tasks to the number of hours the expert thought (based on his experience) each task should consume. The court rejected this method on the grounds that the expert's calculations were speculative and unreliable, because the expert erroneously assumed that the contractor would be entitled to perform all of its work without disruption, he had never made such calculations before, he did not compare instances where the contractor worked without disruption to instances where it performed similar work with disruptions, and his calculations always assigned the same number of lost hours for each worker for each day of disruption and delay.

Page 13, add at end of note 21:

See also, e.g., Abra Constr. Corp. v. 112 Duane Associates, LLC, 59 A.D.3d 263, 873 N.Y.S.2d 574 (1st Dept. Feb. 19, 2009) (the trial court properly rejected

---

15.9 2009-Ohio-2761, 2009 WL 1653542 (Ohio App. June 11, 2009), *appeal not allowed*, 123 Ohio St. 3d 1472, 915 N.E.2d 1254, 2009-Ohio-5704 (Ohio Nov. 4, 2009).

15.10 2003 WL 22120886 (Cal. Ct. App. 2003) (nonpublished).

plaintiff's completion-percentage method for calculating the value of work plaintiff performed under the contract until it was wrongfully terminated; the percentage-of-completion was not an accurate indicator of plaintiff's alleged damages, since plaintiff failed to establish substantial completion of the contract as a whole; the contract was terminated in the early stages and plaintiff had only been on the job for approximately two months; the completion-percentage method was also inaccurate because plaintiff sought to obtain the benefit of the percentage-of-completion of work performed by other subcontractors, for which plaintiff did not pay; the trial court thus properly calculated the value of the work performed by using plaintiff's payroll records, adding reasonable percentages for labor burden, overhead and profit, and adding to that figure the amount of proven cost of plaintiff's materials that had been stipulated by the parties, to reach a total of $120,000).

[B] Estimated Cost Method

Page 14, add at end of subsection:

In a recent case, the Federal Board of Contract Appeals rejected use of the contractor's historical profit margin in calculating damages, allowing recovery of a higher profit percentage. In that case, *Appeal of Marshall Associated Contractors, Inc. & Columbia Excavating, Inc.*,[21.1] the government was found to have misrepresented site conditions, causing the contractor to incur additional costs in performing the work. The contractor sought recovery of a 30 percent profit margin on its costs, and the government argued that it should be limited to the contractor's 10 percent historical profit margin. The court held that 30 percent was a "fair and reasonable profit" in light of the contractor's "truly remarkable production rate . . . under the most difficult and adverse of circumstances."

In *Appeal of Beyley Construction Group Corp.*,[21.2] the contractor sought to recover additional costs allegedly incurred in restoring terrain at certain locations damaged by the government. The contractor submitted handwritten calculations which were prepared prior to the work being performed. A different calculation was provided for each of the locations at which additional costs were claimed to have incurred. The Board found that no evidence was provided regarding who prepared the estimates, his or her competency to do so, and whether the calculated amounts reasonably reflect the additional work allegedly performed. As such, the evidence lacked "the necessary foundation to support a conclusion that the amounts claimed are commensurate with the damages suffered," and the contractor's claim was therefore rejected.

[21.1] IBCA No. 1901 (Mar. 22, 2002).

[21.2] ASBCA No. 55692, 2008 WL 4857941, 08-2 BCA P 33999 (Oct. 21, 2008).

[C] Total Cost Method

Page 15, add at end of note 22:

See also Doninger Metal Prods. Corp. v. United States, 50 Fed. Cl. 110 (Ct. Cl. 2001) ("[b]ecause the total cost method provides less assurance that the plaintiff is being precisely compensated for the exact amount of damage suffered, '[t]his theory has never been favored by the court and has been tolerated only when no other mode was available and when the reliability of the supporting evidence was fully substantiated' "); McKie v. Huntley, 620 N.W.2d 599 (S.D. 2000) (court, citing the first edition of this treatise, noted that some courts and commentators criticize the total cost method because it assumes that the breaching party bears responsibility for any extra costs); Ryco Constr., Inc. v. United States, 55 Fed. Cl. 184 (Ct. Cl. 2002) (a trial court must use the total cost method with caution and only as a last resort); Trafalgar House Constr., Inc. v. United States, 73 Fed. Cl. 675 (2006) (a trial court must use the total cost method with caution and as a last resort; the reason for this concern is that bidding inaccuracies and performance inefficiencies on the part of the contractor can skew accurate computation of damages. As a result, the total cost method of computing damages should only be used when there are extraordinary circumstances and there is no other way to compute damages; in this case, because there were sufficient records to show the specific cost impacts, the contractor's bid was unrealistic as shown by its own cost estimates since it misstated quantities and was unable to perform unaffected phases of the work for the amounts bid, and the contractor completely ignored its own inefficiencies, as indicated in its as-bid and as-built charts and the government's findings on entitlement, use of the total cost method of damage calculation was precluded); City of Gillette v. Hladky Constr., Inc., 2008 WY 134, 196 P.3d 184 (Wyo. Nov. 14, 2008) (the total cost method is disfavored primarily because it attributes all responsibility to the owner without establishing a clear causal connection between the owner's breach and the increased costs; however, when a precise itemization of costs is not possible, use of the total cost method is permissible if the breach "pervaded substantial areas of performance" or "substantially affected performance," and the contractor proves the requisite elements regarding bid accuracy, reasonableness of actual costs, etc.).

Page 15, add at end of note 23:

See also Lighting & Power Servs., Inc. v. Roberts, 354 F.3d 817 (8th Cir. 2004) (appellate court held that the acceptability of the total cost method hinges on proof that: (1) the nature of the particular losses make it impossible or highly impracticable to determine them with a reasonable degree of accuracy; (2) the plaintiff's bid or estimate was realistic; (3) its actual costs were reasonable; and (4) it was not responsible for the added expenses; a subcontractor can recover delay damages against a Miller Act payment bond regardless of the lack of fault on the part of the prime contractor; thus, the trial court erred in the present case by requiring the jury to find that the prime contractor had some responsibility in causing the subcontractor's losses, instead of requiring the jury to find that the subcontractor was not responsible for the added expenses); Jackson Constr. Co., Inc. v. United States, 62 Fed. Cl. 84 (Ct. Cl. 2004) (Federal Circuit is generally skeptical of total cost method because that method assumes that contractor is not responsible for any bidding inaccuracies or performance inefficiencies; thus, contractor can recover damages under total cost method only if it can show that: (1) it was impracticable to prove actual losses directly; (2) its bid was reasonable; (3) its actual costs incurred were reasonable; and (4) it was not responsible for any of the additional costs that it incurred. In this case, contractor failed to meet burden of proving these elements: First, contractor did not prove that its work was disrupted by government's changes, and it did not prove that it was impracticable to quantify losses resulting from this disruption; second, contractor offered no evidence to prove that it was not responsible for any added costs on the contract; third, contractor did not properly calculate its total cost claim, that is, it did not subtract the amount of its bid from the amount of its actual costs, as is required under the total cost method. If it had performed this calculation correctly, contractor would apparently have incurred no damages because its total costs were actually less than its bid estimate; therefore, if contractor had properly calculated its damages under the total cost method, it would have shown a profit of approximately $220,000—not a loss—on the contract); Mergentime Corp. v. Washington Metro. Area Transp. Auth., 2006 WL 416177 (D.D.C., Feb. 22, 2006) (four-part test quoted; the court noted that in assessing whether a contractor has met this burden, a court should dismiss the applicability of the total cost basis if the contractor has failed to maintain or sort documentation in a manner that segregates the costs of change orders or otherwise identifies specific costs attributable to a change; in addition, the contractor must have retained records reflecting the amount of additional work and must show that these claimed costs are realistic; the total cost approach is appropriate only when the costs claimed were all directly related to a single changed condition or change and when the government entity is clearly responsible for the damages; thus, a contractor must show that the governmental entity was responsible for the excess costs in question while eliminating its own inefficiencies from its claim; in the instant case, the contractor met none of the requisite criteria of the total cost test with regard to one of its claims for relief, in that: (1) the contractor failed to show that the discrete impacts of certain specified delays to the project could not be quantified with reasonable precision; (2) the contractor's bid was not realistic in several respects, including failure to fully account for warnings of unstable soil conditions that would require extra stabilization efforts; (3) the contractor failed to prove the reasonableness of its costs; and (4) the contractor did not show that its claimed cost overruns were caused by the owner's changes rather than by its own well-documented mismanagement and inefficiencies, including poor performance and turnover of subcontractors, equipment shortages and breakdowns, safety violations, lack of quality control and need for costly rework, and manpower cutbacks, resulting in schedule slippages); Alstom Power, Inc. v. RMF Indus. Contracting, Inc., 418 F. Supp. 2d 766 (W.D. Pa. Mar. 2, 2006), *reconsid. denied*, 2006 WL 1580254 (W.D. Pa. June 5, 2006) (the general contractor's motion in limine to preclude references to the total cost method for proving damages relating to a subcontractor's scaffolding costs was denied. The subcontractor used a reasonable methodology for calculating the difference between the scaffolding as-bid and as-built; there was insufficient evidence to determine the loss under other damages calculation methods because the subcontractor did not maintain construction time and production logs. The original bid and actual costs were reasonable. The increase in costs was allegedly attributable to the general contractor); Cleveland Constr., Inc. v. Ohio Public Emps. Ret. Sys., 2008-Ohio-1630, 2008 WL 885841 (Ohio Ct. App. May 21, 2008), *reconsid. denied*, 118 Ohio St.3d 283, 888 N.E.2d 1068, 2008-Ohio-2337 (Ohio May 21, 2008), *cert. denied sub nom.* City of Cincinnati, Ohio v. Cleveland Constr., Inc., 129 S. Ct. 921, 173 L. Ed.2d 111 (Jan. 12, 2009), *cert. denied*, 129 S. Ct. 925 (Jan. 12, 2009) (sufficient evidence supported the jury's award of damages pursuant to the "total cost method," which requires proof: (1) that it was impossible or highly impracticable for the contractor to prove its actual losses directly; (2) that the contractor's bid was reasonable; (3) that the actual costs sought from the owner were reasonable; and (4) that the owner's breach(es) were the sole cause of the contractor's damages).

Page 15, add at end of note 24:

See also, e.g., Ryco Constr., Inc. v. United States, 55 Fed. Cl. 184 (Ct. Cl. 2002) (if a plaintiff cannot prove all of the elements of the four-part test employed to determine if the total cost method may be used, it cannot benefit from this approach; in this case, plaintiff contractor's books and records were more than sufficient to assemble a claim based upon actual costs, thus defeating the first element; plaintiff also failed to prove that its bid was reasonable, defeating the second element; thus, the total cost method could not be used by the contractor); Best Western Paving, Inc. v. Granite Constr., Inc., 2002 WL 31682370 (Cal. Ct. App. 2002) (nonpublished), *review denied* (2003) (subcontractor failed the four-part test "across the board"; in particular, there was no evidence the contract bid was reasonable; with regard to self-caused damages, the subcontractor's expert did not even attempt to quantify and deduct such losses; he simply applied a standard general inefficiency percentage figure from some pricing guides, without reference to the events that actually occurred on the project); Net Constr., Inc. v. C & C Rehab & Constr., Inc., 256 F. Supp. 2d 350 (E.D. Pa. 2003) (the subcontractor could not recover under a total cost theory where the subcontractor alleged that the general contractor's mismanagement had caused its lost productivity damages, but also conceded that the work had been hampered by the discovery of asbestos, unstable soil conditions, inclement weather and the subcontractor's own problems with a supplier and a bad concrete pour; subcontractor had failed to establish a reasonable allocation of its extra costs as a result of the particular delays caused by the contractor, and was therefore precluded from recovering on its productivity claim); City of Westminster v. Centric-Jones Constructors, 100 P.3d 472 (Colo. App. 2003) (not released) (although the four-part test has not specifically been adopted in Colorado, the fourth element (that the injured party is not responsible for the added costs) has been found applicable; here, the City terminated Centric-Jones due to defects and delays in completing the work, and then sought to recover the total cost of removing, redesigning, and rebuilding the defective construction; the court rejected the City's claim, finding that some of the costs were attributable to the re-design and not to any breaches by Centric-Jones, and that the City failed to offer any evidence to provide a reasonable basis upon which to apportion the costs); Propellex Corp. v. Brownlee, 342 F.3d 1335 (Fed. Cir. 2003) (total cost recovery not permitted where the contractor was unable to prove that it was impossible or impracticable to segregate damages more precisely); United States *ex rel.* Angelo & Co. v. Brimhall-Palmer Constr., Inc., 62 Fed. Appx. 141 (9th Cir. 2003) (applying Arizona law) (same).

Page 15, add at end of note 25:

See also Orlosky Inc. v. United States, 68 Fed. Cl. 296 (2005), *appeal dismissed,* 180 Fed. Appx. 928 (Fed. Cir. Apr. 17, 2006) (the total cost method may be used only when the actual cost method is not feasible).

Page 15, add to last full paragraph on page:

Any of the four elements can be challenged in an attack upon the use of the total cost method. In *In re Environmental Safety Consultants, Inc.,*[25.1] the government unsuccessfully attacked the use of the total cost method by claiming that the Board's use of the bid unit prices was not appropriate without consideration of the contractor's actual planned or estimated costs. The Board found that the contractor's prebid direct cost estimates were realistic and included a markup for overhead and profit, and therefore it was appropriate to compare the actual performance costs with the bid prices to compute the increased performance cost. The government also challenged the equipment rental expenses for which there were no invoice supports. The Board sided with the contractor, finding that although the invoices had not been placed in evidence, there were documents and evidence, including correspondence and suppliers' listings of invoice numbers and amounts, to substantiate the charges.

[25.1] ASBCA No. 53485, 2005 WL 2249078 (Sept. 15, 2005), *motion dismissed,* 2009 WL 2951388 (Nov. 1, 2005).

Page 16, add at end of note 26:

See also McKie v. Huntley, 620 N.W.2d 599 (S.D. 2000) (once liability is established by a preponderance of the evidence, the total cost method of calculating damages may be appropriate for those disputes where it is difficult or impractical to quantify losses from changed conditions: "Although the 'total cost' method must be used with caution, the method should be applied where the nature of the particular loss has made it impossible or highly impracticable to determine damages with a reasonable degree of accuracy and where the loss is substantiated by reliable evidence."); A.G. Cullen Constr., Inc. v. State Sys. of Higher Educ., 898 A.2d 1145 (Pa. Commw. Mar. 15, 2006) (although the total cost method must be used with caution, the method may be applied when the nature of the particular loss renders it impossible or highly impracticable to determine damages with a reasonable degree of accuracy and when the loss is substantiated by reliable evidence. In this case, the evidence was sufficient to support application of the total cost method as the contractor's vice president testified that the contractor contemporaneously recorded the costs of implementing a lead paint abatement program in 14 different categories, and the contractor compared the costs actually incurred over the period the project actually ran with the amount budgeted for the period the project was supposed to run); Eaton Elec., Inc. v. Dormitory Auth. of State of N.Y., 21 Misc. 3d 1135(A), 2008 WL 5005264 (N.Y. Sup. Ct. Kings Co. 2008) (a contractor sought to recover delay damages allegedly resulting from substantial errors in the drawings and specifications issued by the owner, which required substantial corrections, redesigns, and modifications and resulted in out-of-sequence work; the owner moved for partial summary judgment, seeking an order dismissing the complaint on grounds that the contractor had calculated its claimed damages on a total cost basis, so there was no way to distinguish between aspects of its claim that were not barred by lack of notice, change orders, and a no-damage-for-delay clause; the court rejected this argument, noting that delay damages are customarily calculated and proven on a *quantum meruit* total cost basis, that the contractor was not required to prove its claimed damages in response to a motion for partial summary judgment, and that the extent to which its claims were permissible would be determined at trial); City of Gillette v. Hladky Constr., Inc., 2008 WY 134, 196 P.3d 184 (Wyo. Nov. 14, 2008) (the evidence, reviewed in the light most favorable to the contractor, supported submission of the total cost method of calculating damages to the jury; the evidence included testimony of an expert that the City's change essentially resulted in a different project than the contractor bid, the cumulative effect of which was difficult to calculate; this circumstance made the total cost method the only appropriate method of figuring financial damage, as it was not possible to accurately calculate productivity after a major disruption like what occurred on this project using any other method).

Page 17, add to note 34:

; McKie v. Huntley, 620 N.W.2d 599 (S.D. 2000); Safeco Ins. Co. of Am. v. S & T Bank, 2010 WL 786257 (W.D. Pa. Mar. 3, 2010) (stating that "Pennsylvania allows the use of the method where there is no other reasonable means of making a reasonably certain calculation, and the plaintiff has presented reasonably accurate evidence to support the damages claim").

Page 20, add after first full paragraph:

In *Amelco Electric v. City of Thousand Oaks*,[46.1] the contractor sought to use the total cost method to recover increased costs arising from more than 32 contract modifications that increased the contract price by 17 percent. The jury had found in favor of the contractor on its claim, and the City appealed, arguing that Amelco had not presented sufficient evidence to support instructing the jury on the total cost method of recovering damages. The court first noted that the City did not argue that total cost damages are never appropriate against a public entity, and that the court therefore would only determine whether such damages were properly submitted to the jury in this case. The court referenced the four-part test that must be met in order to proceed on a total cost theory: (1) the impracticability of proving actual losses directly, (2) the contractor's bid was reasonable, (3) its actual costs were reasonable, and (4) it was not responsible for the added costs. The court held that Amelco failed to meet the fourth part of the test. Amelco conceded at trial that it had been responsible for some of the added costs, but that its cost records did not distinguish between the inefficiencies caused by Amelco and those caused by the City. The court stated that since Amelco was unable to link its damages to particular breaches by the City, the jury should not have been instructed to calculate Amelco's loss under a total cost measure of damages. The court remanded the case to the trial court for retrial on the issue of damages.

Page 20, add at end of subsection:

A contractor was not allowed to use the total cost method in *Appeal of Management Resource Associates, Inc.*[48.1] because it could not prove either the reasonableness of its bid price or its own lack of contribution to the cost overrun. The contractor's bid was 23 percent below the government cost estimate and 31 percent below the second bid. The bidder, at the request of the government, reviewed its bid and confirmed its accuracy before being awarded the contract. During the hearing on its claim, the contractor did not offer evidence in support of the reasonableness of its bid price. The government asserted that the bid price

[46.1] 27 Cal. 4th 228, 115 Cal. Rptr. 2d 900, 38 P.3d 1120 (2002), *reh'g denied* (2003).
[48.1] ASBCA No. 49457, 2003 WL 139508 (Jan. 16, 2003).

was suspect in light of both the large spread between the contractor and the second bidder and the contractor's lack of experience with this type of work. The government put on evidence of mismanagement by the contractor, which was not refuted by the contractor. As a result, the Board disallowed use of the total cost method, both because of failure to prove the reasonableness of the bid and failure to refute assertions of contributions to the cost overrun.

Similarly, in *Continental Air Conditioning, Inc. v. Keller Construction Co.*,[48.2] Continental, the HVAC subcontractor on the project, sought damages from the general contractor, Keller, asserting Keller delayed and disrupted Continental's work. Continental calculated its damages under several theories, including the total cost method. Continental's expert calculated damages by comparing Continental's bid on the project with the amount of manhours actually expended, then subtracting the number of hours compensated through change orders and hours he attributed to problems caused by Continental. Keller's expert testified that Continental's bid was not a reasonable estimate of the work to be performed. Continental's expert responded that he thought the bid was sufficient, but he had not performed an independent estimate of the work required by the contract documents and therefore could not verify the bid estimates. The court noted that the total cost method is "disfavored and used only as a last resort," and then rejected Continental's calculation of damages utilizing that method on the grounds that Continental's expert testimony was based upon guesswork and assumptions.

One of the elements required for use of the total cost method is that no other method is possible. In the case of *Appeal of TPS, Inc.*,[48.3] a contractor was denied the use of the total cost method on the basis that the performance on the contract was not complicated, the workers employed were few, and the contractor failed to show it was impracticable to prove directly the actual costs incurred. This matter involved a fixed-price contract for structural repairs and roof replacement on nine buildings at the Key West Naval Air Station in Key West, Florida. After the work began on one building, the government suspended work on seven-and-a-half of the remaining buildings. Eventually the suspended work was terminated for the convenience of the government. The contractor completed the work on the buildings that had not been terminated and then submitted a claim for the total costs of all changed and delayed work. This claim was denied. In reviewing this claim the Board determined that the government's unilateral modification, which had been issued in an attempt to settle the claim in the amount of $98,218, was overstated and reduced the payment to the contractor from $98,218 to $367.

In *E. E. Cruz, NAB Construction Corp. & Frontier-Kemper Construction, Inc., Joint Venture v. Coastal Caisson Corp.*,[48.4] an arbitration panel awarded a subcontractor $791,000 in damages against the prime contractor for failure to

[48.2] 2003 WL 22120886 (Cal. Ct. App. 2003) (nonpublished).

[48.3] ASBCA No. 52421, 2004 WL 691781 (Mar. 26, 2004).

[48.4] 346 Fed. Appx. 717 (2d Cir. (N.Y.) Sept. 23, 2009).

provide certain services to aid the subcontractor's work, but refused to award delay damages which had been calculated using the total cost method. On appeal, the district court vacated the award on the basis that the panel had manifestly disregarded New York law, which accepts the total cost method. The arbitration panel thereafter awarded the subcontractor an additional $1.1 million in delay damages, which was confirmed by the district court. On appeal, the Second Circuit reversed the district court's vacatur of the original award, finding that the panel did not disregard the law in failing to award total cost damages. The Second Circuit noted that the panel specifically found that the total cost method was an acceptable method of calculating damages under New York law. The panel instead based its refusal to award delay damages upon its finding that determining costs attributable to the alleged delay was impossible because the subcontractor failed to produce records of delay, submitted calculations that were inaccurate and unreliable, and failed to submit adequate proof as to what delay, if any, it suffered. The panel therefore did not improperly apply New York law, which requires a definite and logical connection between the improper acts and the damages sought to be recovered.

[D] Modified Total Cost Method

Page 21, replace note 49 with:

Biemann & Rowell Co. v. Donohoe Co., Inc., 556 S.E.2d 1 (N.C. Ct. App. 2001) (the modified total cost method is the total cost method with adjustments for any deficiencies in plaintiff's proof in satisfying the four requirements of the total cost method [(i) the impracticability of proving actual losses directly, (ii) the reasonableness of the contractor's bid, (iii) the reasonableness of its actual costs, and (iv) the lack of responsibility for the added costs]; the modified approach assumes the elements of a total cost claim have been established, but it permits the court to modify the test so that the amount plaintiff would have received under the total cost method is only the starting point from which the court will adjust the amount downward to reflect the plaintiff's inability to satisfy the test); Boyajian v. United States, 423 F.2d 1231, 1240 (Ct. Cl. 1970). *See also* Steiny & Co., Inc. v. J.A. Jones Constr. Co., 2002 WL 596800 (Cal. Ct. App. Apr. 18, 2002) (nonpublished) (award of damages upheld where subcontractors calculated their damages through a modified total cost approach, taking into account particular elements of work, trades or skills, facility areas, and job aspects; they compared what their expected costs should have been against what those costs actually were, and *only* in specific work that was impacted by delay and disruption; the claims for damages were carefully culled from the records, not simply obtained by an undifferentiated, rote mathematical formula); McKie v. Huntley, 620 N.W.2d 599 (S.D. 2000) (noting that many courts have approved a modified total cost approach that allows for the deduction of the cost of all problems ascribed to the contractor); G.M. Harston Constr. Co., Inc. v. City of Chicago, 371 F. Supp. 2d 949 (N.D. Ill. 2005) (although the total cost methodology has often been described as not favored, it is necessary to use that methodology when the contractor is entitled to an adjustment but cannot prove the increased costs to which it is entitled to a mathematical certainty; the modified total cost method assumes that the bid was accurately computed, that the costs were reasonable, and that the contractor was not responsible for the increases; but that is only the starting point, and the contractor, in a modified total cost methodology, must strictly exclude any costs it cannot justify and must prove the reasonableness of the assumptions to convince the trier of fact that the amount claimed fairly represents the increased costs the contractor directly suffered from the defendant's actions; thus, it is not enough for the contractor to say, "these are our total costs. Pay them, together with a reasonable profit"; rather, some proof of reasonableness is required; nor is it enough for the owner to say, "tie each cost to a specific revision of plans or schedule, or we will not pay"; the owner must also make its own analysis of what increased costs are reasonably attributable to its own conduct); KGM Contractors, Inc. v. Cass County, 2006 WL 1605178 (Minn. App. 2006), *review denied* (2006) (the appellate court affirmed the trial court's use of the modified total cost method to determine a contractor's damages. The trial court adjusted the contractor's damages by deducting $80,000 for an improper dewatering bid and $7,700 for repair to a severed line, thus increasing the accuracy of the damage award by including consideration of performance inefficiencies); Koga Eng'g & Constr., Inc. v. State, 120 Haw. 256, 203 P.3d 676 (Haw. Ct. App. Mar. 13, 2009), *judgment vacated on other grounds*, 122 Haw. 60, 222 P.3d 979 (Haw. Jan 14, 2010) (court upheld the use of the modified total cost method to calculate contractor's damages resulting from owner's breach of the superior knowledge doctrine and the implied duty of good faith and fair dealing where the contractor demonstrated: (a) the impracticability of proving actual losses directly; (b) the reasonableness of its bid; (c) the reasonableness of its actual costs underlying the awarded damages; and (d) lack of responsibility for the added costs that were awarded as damages).

Page 21, add at end of note 51:

; Baldi Bros. Constructors v. United States, 50 Fed. Cl. 74 (Ct. Cl. 2001) (the modified total cost method allows the court to adjust a claim when a contractor's initial bid is found unreasonable by substituting a reasonable bid amount into the calculations; however, both types of total cost claims, modified or not, are "not favored and should only be resorted to when 'actual costs' cannot be determined"); Sunshine Constr. & Eng'g, Inc. v. United States, 64 Fed. Cl. 346 (2005) (a modified total cost method adjusts for a contractor's lack of proof in the requirements of the total cost method; however, a total cost method is not favored and should not be used when another more reliable method is available by which to compute a contractor's damages; under a modified total cost approach, a contractor still has the burden of proving the four requirements of the total cost method—(1) the impracticability of proving its actual losses directly, (2) the reasonableness of its bid, (3) the reasonableness of its actual costs, and (4) lack of responsibility for the added costs—although that burden is eased; in this case, plaintiff did not sustain the predicate for a recovery for loss of productivity by showing that the owner was responsible for the underlying causes of delay due to defective plans and specifications); In re Electric Mach. Enters., Inc., 416 B.R. 801 (Bankr. M.D. Fla. Aug. 28, 2009) (the court found the modified total cost approach was the only available method to calculate damages incurred by an electrical subcontractor in a convention center construction project when multiple concurrent factors impacted the subcontractor's work, including trade stacking, the building not being dried-in to support electrical work, haphazard scheduling, and lack of coordination by the construction manager; the contractor argued that since the subcontractor could have used the measured mile approach, it was precluded from recovering based on a modified total cost calculation; the court rejected this argument, accepting the testimony of the subcontractor's damages expert that a baseline for the measured mile could not be found because each area and each specific type of electrical work was impacted by the multiple factors; the court went through a detailed discussion of the application of the modified total cost approach to the particular facts of this case); Dillingham-Ray Wilson v. City of Los Angeles, 182 Cal. App. 4th 1396, 106 Cal. Rptr. 3d 691 (Mar. 18, 2010), *as modified on denial of reh'g* (Apr. 16, 2010), *review filed* (Apr. 27, 2010) (trial court granted the City's motion in limine to exclude three of DRW's damages claims: (1) additional costs for change order work when the parties had not agreed on a price; (2) additional payments due from the City as a result of the City's breach of the implied warranty of correctness of the plans; and (3) the cost of inefficient labor caused by the City's breach of that same warranty, based on court's finding that the contract required documentation of actual costs, whereas DRW calculated its damages using the modified total cost method supported only by engineering estimates; the appellate court reversed, first finding that the contract was ambiguous and DRW was therefore entitled to a trial on contract interpretation as to whether documentation of actual costs was required; the court noted that the common law requires only that DRW present the "best evidence available," and found that the best evidence may be the engineering estimates that DRW proferred; the court also held that based upon the *Amelco* case, the modified total cost method of calculating damages is available in California, such that granting the City's motion in limine as to that issue was also reversible error).

§ 1.04 *QUANTUM MERUIT*

Page 23, add at end of note 61:

See also Intermetal Fabricators, Inc. v. The Losco Group, Inc., 2000 WL 1154249 (S.D.N.Y. 2000) (under New York law, a party who defaults under a construction contract may not recover any damages, either under the contract or in *quantum meruit*, unless it has substantially performed under the contract; because plaintiff in this case abandoned work on the subcontract, and defendant was required to retain other subcontractors to complete the work at substantial cost, plaintiff could not recover any damages for work it actually performed); Erney v. Freeman, 84 S.W.3d 529 (Mo. Ct. App. 2002), (the court found that it is well established that if a contractor is prevented from completing the work on a construction project by the actions of the owners, the owners have breached the contract; if the work has been partially completed at the time of the owners' actions, the contractor is excused from his contractual obligations and may cease work on the project; his failure to complete the work is excused and he has not breached the contract; when the owners prevent the contractor from performing work on the contract, the contractor may either sue on the express contract or in *quantum meruit* for the value of the labor and materials the contractor has furnished; however, it is necessary to determine which, if any, party breached the contract by considering whether the contractor's failure to complete the project, or his ceasing of the work, was due to actions of the owners that prevented him from completing the work (prevention) or to voluntary action of the contractor in walking away from the project (abandonment); the contractor has the burden of proving that the owners breached by preventing the contractor from completing the work, and the owners have the burden of proving that the contractor breached by abandoning the contract and voluntarily failing to complete the work. Furthermore, a party's action must be clear and unequivocal to support a finding of abandonment); Rockwell Roofing, Inc. v. Jan Five Corp., 2007 WL 4248144 (Mass. Super. Ct. 2007) (a subcontractor may recover in *quantum meruit* if he can prove both substantial performance of the contract and an endeavor on his part in good faith to perform fully; the burden of proof is upon him to prove both); United Disaster Response, L.L.C. v. Omni Pinnacle, L.L.C., 569 F. Supp. 2d 646 (E.D. La. Aug. 1, 2008) (court dismissed contractor's *quantum meruit* claim "because it is not a cause of action recognized by Louisiana law"; court indicated that unjust enrichment claim may lie if there was no adequate remedy at law); Kennesaw Flooring, Inc. v. Rector, 291 Ga. App. 704, 662 S.E.2d 808 (May 29, 2008) (subcontractor could not assert claims for breach of implied contract or *quantum meruit* against owner with whom it had no contractual relationship, notwithstanding that the owner directed some of the subcontractor's work; subcontract is limited to the statutory remedies provided by Georgia's lien statute); Mike Bldg. & Contracting, Inc. v. Just Homes, LLC, 2010 WL 457303 (N.Y. Sup. Ct. Kings Cty. Feb. 2, 2010) (under New York law, a plaintiff has the right of electing, on the breach of a contract, to maintain an action on the contract for the work performed and the material supplied and for the damage flowing from the failure of the defendant to permit him to complete the contract, or to abandon any claim on or under the contract and to sue for quantum meruit for the work, labor and services, and materials furnished).

Page 23, add at end of note 62:

See also, *e.g.*, Alstom Power, Inc. v. RMF Indus. Contracting, Inc., 418 F. Supp. 2d 766 (W.D. Pa. Mar. 2, 2006), *reconsid. denied* 2006 WL 3839235 (W.D. Pa. June 5, 2006) (the general rule under Pennsylvania law is that when an express contract exists to define the parameters of the parties' respective duties, the parties may avail themselves of contract remedies, but an equitable remedy for unjust enrichment cannot be deemed to exist. However, the Superior Court of Pennsylvania has recognized an exception to the general rule when both parties contend that the other has breached the contract. Under Pennsylvania law a party who commits a breach of contract should be entitled to recover any benefit conferred in excess of the loss caused by its breach; the federal court thus predicted that the Supreme Court of Pennsylvania would hold that a contractor has a claim for restitution [rather than the claimed unjust enrichment] if the evidence demonstrates that the contractor has breached its contract, but nevertheless has conferred a benefit upon the owner in excess of the loss caused by its own breach); Gentry v. Squires Constr., Inc., 188 S.W.3d 396 (Tex. App.-Dallas Mar. 27, 2006) (a contractor may recover the reasonable value of the services rendered and accepted or the materials supplied under the theory of *quantum meruit* if: (1) the services rendered and accepted are not covered by the contract; (2) the contractor partially performed under the terms of an express contract, but was prohibited from completing the contract because of the owner's breach; or (3) the contractor breached but the owner accepted and retained the benefits of the contractor's partial performance. In this case, the contractor failed to substantially comply with the contract, but there was evidence that it partially performed, and the owner accepted and retained the benefits of the partial performance; thus, the trial court did not err when it concluded that the contractor was entitled to be paid its costs for labor and materials under the theory of *quantum meruit*); Tupelo Redevelopment Agency v. Gray Corp., Inc., 972 So. 2d 495 (Miss. 2007) (the essential elements of recovery under a *quantum meruit* claim are: (1) valuable services were rendered or materials furnished; (2) for the person sought to be charged; (3) which services and materials were accepted by the person sought to be charged, used and enjoyed by him; and (4) under such circumstances as reasonably notified the person sought to be charged that the plaintiff, in performing such services, was expected to be paid by the person sought to be charged; the court held that a subcontractor was entitled to maintain both a *quantum meruit* claim against the contractor for extra work performed outside the contract, and a breach of contract claim based on the contractor's failure to pay the balance due under the contract); Specialized Grading Enters., Inc. v. Goodland Constr., Inc., 181 P.3d 352

(Colo. Ct. App. Nov. 1, 2007), *cert. denied sub nom.* Goodland Constr., Inc. v. Specialized Grading Enters., Inc., 2008 WL 921288 (Colo. Apr. 7, 2008) (subcontractor sued for breach of contract to recover payment due for work performed, and also asserted a claim for *quantum meruit* for delay and dewatering work the subcontractor performed as a result of the contractor's failure to perform the dewatering work; the trial court dismissed the *quantum meruit* claim on the basis that the work was covered by the change order provisions of the subcontract, and the appellate court reversed; the court stated the rule in Colorado, "If an express contract exists, there can be no implied contract covering the same subject matter between the parties because the provisions of the express contract supersede those of the implied contract; however, this rule does not apply if the implied agreement is based upon the conduct of the parties subsequent to, and not covered by, the terms of the express contract. [Citations omitted.]" *Quantum meruit* is an appropriate basis for recovery when substantial changes occur that are not covered by the contract and are not within the contemplation of the parties, and when the effect of such changes is to require extra work or to cause substantial loss to one party; here, the court found that the extra work claimed was not occasioned by changes, errors, or lack of clarity in the plans and specifications, but by a breach of the contractor's contractual obligations which could not have been reasonably anticipated; as such, the subcontractor was entitled to assert a *quantum meruit* claim to recover for the added work that was not within the scope of the subcontractor's work).

Page 23, add at end of note 63:

See also Precision Mech. Contractors v. Metropolitan Dev. & Hous. Agency, 2001 WL 1285900 (Tenn. Ct. App. Oct. 25, 2001) (when an express contract governs, recovery under the doctrine of *quantum meruit, i.e.*, implied contract or quasi-contract, is not permitted); Continental Air Conditioning, Inc. v. Keller Constr. Co., 2003 WL 22120886 (Cal. App. 2003) (nonpublished) (in general, when the parties' relationship is governed by express contract, they are not entitled to seek restitution or claim unjust enrichment; in this case, because the general contractor and the subcontractor sought to define their respective rights and responsibilities on the construction project through an express contract, their remedies for a breach of contract could not encompass those normally available for implied and quasi-contract); Convergent Group Corp. v. County of Kent, 266 F. Supp. 2d 647 (W.D. Mich. 2003) (applying Michigan law) (where an express contract is found to exist, *quantum meruit* damages are not available); Levitt-Ansca Towne Park P'ship v. Smith & Co., Inc., 873 So. 2d 392 (Fla. Dist. Ct. App. 2004) (where contractor sought both damages on the contract and an additional sum for work performed outside the contract under theory of *quantum meruit*, court held that contractor was required to elect between the two legal theories; further, because contract provided the method for obtaining payment for additional work, contractor could not seek equitable relief for additional work at the same time it sought legal relief in the form of lost profits for owner's alleged breach of contract); Grace Indus. v. New York City Dep't of Transp., 22 A.D.3d 262, 802 N.Y.S.2d 409 (1st Dept. 2005) (when a contract contained a valid no damages for delay clause, plaintiff's *quantum meruit* claim was properly dismissed, since the contract expressly governed the disputed subject matter); J. Alvarez Constr., Inc. v. Western Nat. Group, L.P., 2007 WL 2083704 (Cal. Ct. App. 2007) (unpublished) (same); Guy M. Cooper, Inc. v. East Penn Sch. Dist., 903 A.2d 608 (Pa. Commw. July 26, 2006), *appeal denied*, 591 Pa. 706, 918 A.2d 748 (Mar. 1, 2007) (unjust enrichment is inapplicable when the parties' relationship is founded upon a written agreement, regardless of how harsh the provisions of such contracts may seem in light of subsequent events. Although the plaintiff in this case argued that an exception exists when one party performs services wholly outside the scope of the contract, the plaintiff's claim for delay damages was based solely on the additional time needed to complete the project. Thus, the trial court did not err in holding that the contractor provided nothing more than the contract requirements and thus did not furnish services wholly outside the contract terms); Bed Bath & Beyond Inc. v. Ibex Constr., LLC, 860 N.Y.S.2d 107, 52 A.D.3d 413, 860 N.Y.S.2d 107 (1st Dept. June 26, 2008) (letter of intent "subject to" execution of a formal construction agreement was held to be a binding agreement governing the project; as such, plaintiff's claim for *quantum meruit* was properly dismissed); Schipper Constr., Inc. v. American Crystal Sugar Co., 2008 N.D. 226, 758 N.W.2d 744 (N.D. Dec. 16, 2008) (in order to recover in *quantum meruit* based upon rescission of the contract, plaintiff must have provided proper notice of rescission; where letters from the contractor failed to "convey a clear, unambiguous and unequivocal intention to rescind the contracts," the trial court did not err in denying recovery in *quantum meruit*).

Cf. J.A. Jones Constr. Co. v. Lehrer McGovern Bovis, Inc., 120 Nev. 277, 89 P.3d 1009 (Nev. 2004), *reh'g denied* (Aug. 26, 2004), *reconsid. en banc denied* (Nov. 4, 2004) (an action may be based upon *quantum meruit* even though an express contract exists: "The contractor may . . . base his action upon both the contract and upon a *quantum meruit* by setting up the former in one count, and the latter in another in his complaint"; that contract may have been changed or abandoned does not negate assertion that at some point there existed a breachable contract; therefore, subcontractor in this case was not required to elect between suing on the contract or in *quantum meruit* before obtaining a jury verdict; trial court could determine, after trial, if a duplicate recovery was obtained on the two theories of recovery); Jay Cashman, Inc. v. Portland Pipe Line Corp., 559 F. Supp. 2d 85 (D. Me. June 18, 2008), *report and recommendation adopted*, 573 F. Supp. 2d 335 (D. Me. Aug. 25, 2008) (under Maine law, a viable *quantum meruit* claim can co-exist with an express contract; evidence that the owner directed the contractor to perform work outside the scope of the contract may be sufficient to support a *quantum meruit* claim, and may further permit a finding that the owner waived or is stopped from relying on strict compliance with the contract's extra-work provisions; summary judgment in the owner's favor was therefore denied).

Page 23, add at end of note 64:

See also ADP Marshall Inc. v. Brown Univ., 784 A.2d 309 (R.I. 2001) (*Marshall II*) (the proper measure of damages when there was no agreement between the parties but a benefit was conferred on the owner is the fair and reasonable value of the work done).

Page 24, add at end of note 70:

See also, e.g., Acme Contracting, Ltd. v. TolTest, Inc., 2008 WL 1990780 (E.D. Mich. 2008), *aff'd in part, rev'd in part*, 2010 WL 1140997 (6th Cir. (Mich.) Mar. 24, 2010) (the contractor, TolTest, verbally directed the subcontractor, Acme, to perform additional work on a time and materials basis, including increased work to meet a heightened compaction standard; the court found that Acme was entitled to recover for this additional work on a *quantum meruit* basis, based upon its findings that TolTest directed Acme to do additional work that was "outside of the scope of Acme's duties" under the subcontract; TolTest was aware that Acme was performing the additional work, and TolTest was benefited by that work; the court rejected TolTest's contention that *quantum meruit* was unavailable because there was a written contract between the parties (Acme was also seeking different damages for breach of the subcontract), finding that Toltest waived the requirement of a written change order because it was aware of the requirement but nevertheless verbally ordered the changes). Acme's entitlement to *quantum meruit* damages was affirmed on appeal, but the Sixth Circuit reversed and remanded on the limited issue of whether double-counting had occurred with respect to both the delay damages and the *quantum meruit* damages). *But see* Pennsylvania Elec. Coil, Ltd. v. City of Danville, 329 Fed. Appx. 399, 2009 WL 1279757 (4th Cir. (Va.) May 11, 2009) (the contractor sought to recover in *quantum meruit* for additional work performed; court held that under Virginia law, where the contract contained a provision governing change order procedures, *quantum meruit* recovery was not available).

Page 24, add at end of note 71:

In J.A. Jones Constr. Co. v. Lehrer McGovern Bovis, Inc., 89 P.3d 1009 (Nev. 2004), *reh'g denied* (Aug. 26, 2004), *reconsid. en banc denied* (Nov. 4, 2004), the Nevada Supreme Court held that plaintiff subcontractor introduced sufficient evidence to present its theory of contract abandonment to the jury, and therefore the trial court improperly dismissed its contract abandonment claim. The court stated that contract abandonment occurs when both parties depart from the terms of the contract by mutual consent. This consent may be express, or it may be implied by the parties' actions, such as when "the acts of one party inconsistent with [the contract's] existence are acquiesced in by the other." Contract abandonment has been recognized "where there have been so many substantial changes to the special contract that it can no longer be used to determine the value of the work done." The issue of whether contract abandonment has occurred generally presents a question of fact. In this case, plaintiff subcontractor introduced evidence from which a jury could have concluded that by directing the subcontractor to perform its work at an inadequately prepared and maintained site, the general contractor in effect directed the subcontractor to perform work inconsistent with provisions in the parties' contract that specifically described the manner and time frame in which the subcontractor was to perform its work. The subcontractor testified that it nevertheless agreed to perform the changed work, despite incurring significant increases in cost and time, on the belief that it would be paid by the general contractor on terms other than those identified in the contract.

Cf. Best Western Paving, Inc. v. Granite Constr., Inc., 2002 WL 31682370 (Cal. Ct. App., Nov. 27, 2002) (nonpublished), *review denied* (2003) (the abandonment doctrine was inapplicable because the evidence did not indicate that the owner changed the plans and specifications in any materially significant way; *i.e.*, there was no evidence at all of the type of radical redesign of the project such as occurred in other cases in which the abandonment doctrine has been held applicable; similarly, the general contractor did not impose change orders of such magnitude as to alter the scope of the work contemplated by the parties under the subcontract, as occurred in the *C. Norman Peterson Co.* case; thus, there was nothing indicating that "the final product differ[ed] substantially from the original"; accordingly, the subcontractor could not recover damages in *quantum meruit* on an abandonment theory).

Page 25, add before first full paragraph:

The California Supreme Court has held that a contractor cannot use an abandonment theory of liability against a public entity in order to recover in *quantum meruit.* In *Amelco Electric v. City of Thousand Oaks,*[71.1] the City had awarded a contract for more than $6 million to Amelco to perform electrical work for a new civic center. During the course of the project, the City issued more than 1,000 sketches changing every aspect of the electrical work. Amelco requested 221 change orders, and the City ultimately issued 32 contract modifications that increased the contract price by 17 percent. Amelco then filed a total cost claim for an additional $2.2 million, contending that the City had abandoned the project and Amelco was therefore entitled to recover in *quantum meruit.* The trial court held that the City had both abandoned and breached the contract, and it awarded Amelco damages of more than $2 million. The Appellate Court

[71.1] 27 Cal. 4th 228, 115 Cal. Rptr. 2d 900, 38 P.3d 1120 (2002), *reh'g denied* (2002).

affirmed the judgment. The Supreme Court reversed, holding that an abandonment theory of liability does not apply against a public entity, as such theory is fundamentally inconsistent with the purpose of the competitive bidding statutes. Since the City could not be found to have abandoned the contract, Amelco could not recover in *quantum meruit.* Instead, Amelco was limited to seeking damages for breach of contract. The Court further found that Amelco had failed to meet the requirements for recovery under the total cost method, and remanded to the trial court for retrial on the issue of damages.

Page 26, add at end of note 84:

See also, e.g., J.A. Jones Constr. Co. v. Lehrer McGovern Bovis, Inc., 89 P.3d 1009 (Nev. 2004), *reh'g denied* (Aug. 26, 2004), *reconsid. en banc denied* (Nov. 4, 2004) (the cardinal change doctrine "provide[s] a breach remedy for contractors who are directed . . . to perform work which is not within the general scope of the contract," and that is therefore not redressable under the contract; a cardinal change occurs "when the work is so drastically altered that the contractor effectively performs duties that are materially different from those for which the contractor originally bargained"; although the "cardinal-change doctrine was created as a check on the government's ability to circumvent the competitive-bidding process by ordering drastic changes beyond those contemplated in the contract, and has been predominantly discussed in disputes based on government contracts, its underlying premise—that compensation for costs resulting from an abuse of authority under the changes clause should not be limited by the terms of that clause—applies to private contracts that include changes clauses"; whether a change is cardinal is principally a question of fact, determined on the basis of the following factors: (1) whether there is a significant change in the magnitude of work to be performed; (2) whether the change is designed to procure a totally different item or drastically alter the quality, character, nature, or type of work contemplated by the original contract; and (3) whether the cost of the work ordered greatly exceeds the original contract cost; in this case, plaintiff subcontractor presented testimony demonstrating material impact on its contractual scope of work, raising an issue of fact for a jury whether it could recover damages under a cardinal change theory).

Page 27, add at end of note 86:

See also Rockwell Roofing, Inc. v. Jan Five Corp., 2007 WL 4248144 (Mass. Super. Ct. Nov. 15, 2007) (the amount of recovery on a claim based in *quantum meruit* is the fair and reasonable value of material and labor supplied to the party receiving the contractor's services; the question of what is fair and reasonable compensation for the services rendered is a question of fact).

Page 27, add at end of note 87:

Cf. Precision Mech. Contractors v. Metropolitan Dev. & Hous. Agency, 2001 WL 1285900 (Tenn. Ct. App. Oct. 25, 2001) (*quantum meruit* recoveries are limited to the actual value of the goods or services, not their contract price; in the instant case, the trial court properly denied the contractor's claims for *quantum meruit* because the court found that there was no proof as to the actual value of the services rendered); Emerald Pointe Prop. Owners' Ass'n, Inc. v. Commercial Constr. Indus., Inc., 978 So. 2d 873 (Fla. Dist. Ct. App. Apr. 16, 2008), *reh'g granted* (Apr. 16, 2008) (*quantum meruit* was a proper measure of damages for breach of a partially performed contract; *quantum meruit* damages are designed to restore the contractor to the same position he would have been in prior to making the agreement; the contract price generally is the upper limit when the contractor sues in *quantum meruit*, but in the event the owner's breach is willful, the contractor may recover his outlay, i.e., the reasonable value of labor, material and services provided, even if it exceeds the contract price; here, the contractor failed to prove the reasonable value of the work actually performed, since it offered evidence only as to the amount it would have charged a third party; this amount clearly included profit, which is not recoverable under *quantum meruit*; the case was remanded for a new trial on damages). *Cf.* Sea Byte, Inc. v. Hudson Marine Mgmt. Servs., Inc., 565 F.3d 1293 (11th Cir. (Fla.) Apr. 20, 2009) (court found that Florida law does not permit a party to recover in *quantum meruit* where an enforceable contract exists; in this case, a lump sum contract was held to have terminated according to its terms when hurricanes hampered the work effort and the parties could not agree on a revised price, as provided for in the contract; the court found that the contractor could recover the value of the work performed prior to the hurricanes, calculated as the percentage of the project's value that had been performed prior to the hurricanes multiplied by the total contract price; as to work the contractor performed after the hurricanes, recovery could be had in *quantum meruit* because no enforceable contract existed at that time; Eldeco, Inc. v. LPS Constr. Co., 2009 WL 4586003 (U.S. Dist. Dec. 1, 2009) (court held recovery under *quantum meruit* was unavailable "because it is undisputed that the relationship and work out of which the claim arises is the result of an express contract between Eldeco and LPS. Not only is that contract express and binding, but it is detailed and written and purports to be the complete agreement of the parties.").

Page 29, add to note 95:

Cf. D.A. Zuluaga Constr. v. Spokane Airports Bd., 102 Wash. App. 1026 (Ct. App. 2000), *review denied*, 143 Wash. 2d 1006, 20 P. 3d 944 (2001) (damages in *quantum meruit* are not liquidated and therefore do not earn prejudgment interest).

Page 29, add before subsection [A]:

In *Barry v. Pacific West Construction, Inc.*,[95.1] the court noted that some courts do not differentiate between claims for unjust enrichment and *quantum meruit*, allowing a *quantum meruit* claim to be brought both to enforce a contract implied in fact based on the parties' conduct and also to enforce an illegal, invalid, or void express contract. The Idaho court held, however, that a claim in *quantum meruit* does not lie when there is an express contract. Rather, such a claim must be one for unjust enrichment or restitution. Unjust enrichment, or restitution, is the measure of recovery under a contract implied in law. A contract implied in law, or quasi-contract, "is not a contract at all, but an obligation imposed by law for the purpose of bringing about justice and equity without reference to the intent of the agreement of the parties, and, in some cases, in spite of an agreement between the parties." In this case, the contract between a subcontractor and the general contract was express, but failed because of illegality—the subcontractor was not properly licensed to perform public works contracts. Thus, the court held that any recovery was limited to restitution, with the subcontractor required to prove that the contractor was unjustly enriched. A party seeking recovery under an unjust enrichment theory must present evidence not only of the value of the services it rendered, but also "the amount of the benefit which, if retained by the [defendant], would result in their unjust enrichment."

In *Encore Construction Corp. v. SC Bodner Construction, Inc.*,[95.2] the court allowed a subcontractor to recover from the owner under *quantum meruit* after the owner terminated the general contractor. Encore was the developer of the hotel project, and SC Bodner was the general contractor. Imperial Marble Corp. entered into a subcontract with SC Bodner to supply materials for the project, and Summit Construction Company was SC Bodner's subcontractor for installation of those materials. On February 4, 1998, Encore gave SC Bodner notice of termination for default under the prime contract, which required 10-days written notice of termination. Imperial shipped the first installment of materials to the site on February 4th, before it learned of the termination. At Encore's request, Imperial made five additional shipments of materials, and Summit installed the materials. Neither Imperial nor Summit was paid by Encore for the materials and labor furnished. At trial, Encore conceded that it was responsible for payment of materials and labor provided after termination of the general contractor, but argued that termination was not effective until February 14, 1998, based on the contract requirement of 10 days notice of termination. The trial court held that termination was effective February 4th, and Encore became responsible for payment to the subcontractors on that date. Encore appealed, and the court of appeals affirmed, stating that regardless of the effective date of termination, Encore was liable to the subcontractors commencing on February 4th under a theory of unjust enrichment.

[95.1] 140 Idaho 827, 103 P.3d 440 (2004).

[95.2] 765 N.E. 2d 223 (Ind. Ct. App. 2002).

Encore requested that the subcontractors provide the materials and labor, and would be unjustly enriched if it retained the benefits without paying.[95.3]

[A] Jury Verdict Method

Page 30, add at end of note 100:

See also, e.g., CEMS, Inc. v. United States, 59 Fed. Cl. 168 (Ct. Cl. 2003) (the "jury verdict" method is most often employed when damages cannot be ascertained by any reasonable computation from actual figures, but it "is not favored and may be used only when other, more exact, methods cannot be applied"; the jury verdict method's primary peril is the risk that unrealistic assumptions will be adopted and extrapolated, greatly multiplying an award beyond reason, and rewarding preparers of imprecise claims based on undocumented costs with unjustified windfalls; thus, the jury verdict method is resorted to only when the plaintiff has shown: that (1) clear proof of injury exists; (2) there is no more reliable method for calculating damages; and (3) the evidence is sufficient for a court to make a fair and reasonable approximation of the damages); Doninger Metal Prods. Corp. v. United States, 50 Fed. Cl. 110 (Ct. Cl. 2001) (same); Orlosky Inc. v. United States, 68 Fed. Cl. 296 (Fed. Cl. 2005), *appeal dismissed*, 180 Fed. Appx. 928 (Fed. Cir. Apr. 17, 2006) (the jury verdict method is not favored and may be used only when other, more exact, methods cannot be applied; to use a jury verdict method of damages, the court must make three findings: (1) that clear proof of the injury exists; (2) that there is no more reliable method for computing damages; and (3) that the evidence is sufficient for a court to make a fair and reasonable approximation of the damages).

Page 30, add at end of subsection:

In *Appeal of Jim Phillips Contracting, Inc.*,[100.1] the contractor was awarded a contract by the Bureau of Land Management (BLM) for road repairs in Idaho. The contract covered a base year and four option years, with a minimum dollar value of services of $655,000 over the life of the contract. BLM issued only one task order during the first year, and then issued a winter suspension order before the contractor commenced work. When BLM issued an order to resume work, the

[95.3] *See also* MCK Building Assocs., Inc. v. St. Lawrence Univ., 754 N.Y.S.2d 397 (N.Y. 2003) (although *quantum meruit* recovery is generally barred where the work is covered by a written contract, the rule does not apply where the contract has been wrongfully terminated prior to completion, and the terminated party has elected to recover *quantum meruit* damages in lieu of breach of contract damages); Universal/MMEC, Ltd. v. Dormitory Auth. of State of New York, 50 A.D.3d 352, 856 N.Y.S.2d 560 (1st Dept. 2008) (a plaintiff is precluded from recovery on a theory of unjust enrichment by the existence of a contract).

[100.1] IBCA Nos. 2000, 4319 and 4320, 04-1 BCA (CCH) ¶ 32,416 (2003).

contractor refused to accept the order on the grounds that the base year period had expired and BLM had failed to properly exercise its option for a second year. The contractor filed a claim for the entire $655,000 guaranteed amount, and subsequently modified its claim to recover approximately $200,000, the amount of profit its expert testified the contractor would have earned on the guaranteed minimum amount. BLM's expert testified that the contractor's anticipated profit would have been no more than $60,000, based upon BLM's cost guides. The Board found that BLM had not timely renewed the contract, and that the contractor was therefore entitled to refuse the resumption order and to recover its anticipated profit on the guaranteed minimum amount of work. Although the Board found that the contractor's expert's methodology was more persuasive than BLM's cost guides, it determined that the contractor's anticipated profit margin might be applicable if the contract was for only year, but not if it had extended over the full five years, when the contractor's prices would likely be substantially higher. The Board therefore applied the jury verdict method and held that the contractor was entitled to 35 to 40 percent of the amount calculated by the contractor, or $75,000.

Appeal of States Roofing Corp.[100.2] was one of eleven appeals arising from a contract for the repair and related work on the roof cells at a building on the Naval Operating Base in Norfolk, Virginia. The Navy issued a modification deleting the majority of work on Roof Cells D and F from the contract work, and the parties could not agree on the value of the labor for installing tapered installation that was included in the deductive change order. The Board found that the contractor's work was obviously impacted by the differing site conditions it encountered and the contract changes made by the Navy. Because of the Board's concerns regarding the contractor's adjusted bid price, the Board was unwilling to adopt the contractor's proposed modified total cost approach to calculating disruption damages. The Board found that there was ample evidence in the record for it to make a fair and reasonable approximation of the labor costs using the jury verdict approach, and that there was no more reliable method of computing these costs. The contractor estimated 1,919 manhours, whereas the Navy initially estimated 4,567 manhours, which was later reduced to 2,940 manhours. The Board concluded that 2,700 manhours represented the reasonable cost for installing the tapered insulation.

[100.2] ASBCA No. 55508, 2008 WL 4467182 (May 5, 2009).

[B] Economic Loss Rule

Page 31, add at end of subsection:

In *City of Westminster v. Centric-Jones Constructors*,[106.1] the City asserted a negligence claim (along with a claim for breach of contract) against Centric-Jones after the City terminated the contractor for alleged defects and delays in constructing a clearwell and pumping station. The court noted that under the economic loss rule, a party suffering only economic loss from the breach of an express or implied contractual duty may not assert a tort claim for such a breach absent an independent duty of care under tort law. Since a commercial contractor owes no independent duty to the owner merely by virtue of the parties' relationship, the City was precluded from asserting a tort claim to recover the cost of rebuilding the defective structures that were the subject of the contract and consequential damages allegedly caused by the same construction practices that contributed to those defects. The City contended that the damages caused by Centric-Jones to neighboring lands should be recoverable notwithstanding the economic loss rule, but the court held that since those damages could only have been caused by Centric-Jones' mishandling of the fill, these damages were merely consequential to the defective construction practices. The City's costs of defending a third-party claim against it would be covered by the indemnification clause in the Centric-Jones contract, and the court found no exception to the economic loss rule for costs incurred by the City to remediate the risk of personal injury created by certain defects.

A number of courts have held that an architect or engineer preparing plans or specifications for a project owes an independent duty of care to the contractor or subcontractors performing work on the project, and that the economic loss rule therefore does not preclude a negligence claim by the contractor or subcontractors.[106.2] For example, in *Bilt-Rite Contractors, Inc. v. Architectural Studios*,[106.3] the project architect's plans represented that the curtain wall system could be constructed using normal and reasonable construction means and methods. The contractor had to use special means and methods, and brought a claim against the architect based upon negligent misrepresentation to recover purely economic damages of increased construction costs. The court held that the economic loss

[106.1] 100 P.3d 472 (Colo. App. 2003) (not released).

[106.2] *See* Tommy L. Griffin Plumbing & Heating Co. v. Jordan, Jones & Goulding, Inc., 463 S.E.2d 85 (S.C. 1995) (design professionals owe a professional duty of care to the contractor not to design or supervise the project negligently); Mayor v. Clark-Dietx & Associates-Engineers, Inc., 550 F. Supp. 610 (N.D. Miss. 1982) (same).

[106.3] 581 Pa. 454, 866 A.2d 270 (Pa. Jan 19, 2005). *But see* Excavation Techs., Inc. v. Columbia Gas Co. of Pennsylvania, 985 A.2d 840 (Pa. Dec. 29, 2009) (court refused to extend the *Bilt-Rite* decision to a utility marking subsurface utility lines, finding the utility owed no duty to the contractor to accurately mark the utility lines; the contractor was precluded from asserting a negligent misrepresentation claim for purely economic loss).

rule did not bar a claim for negligent representation against design professionals whose information may be relied on by others, even though there is no privity of contract between the design professional and the contractor.

In *McElwee Group, LLC v. Municipal Authority of the Borough of Elverson*,[106.4] a general contractor asserted the owner of the project and its engineering firm fraudulently misrepresented the project's complexities. The engineering firm moved to dismiss the contractor's claims, contending that the economic loss rule barred tort claims since the engineering firm and the contractor were not in privity of contract and the contractor was seeking only economic damages. Relying upon the Pennsylvania Supreme Court's decision in the *Bilt-Rite Contractors* case, the court found that a claim for intentional misconduct could similarly be brought.

The New Hampshire Supreme Court held that the economic loss rule barred plaintiff's negligence claim in *Plourde Sand & Gravel Co. v. JGI Eastern, Inc. f/k/a Jaworski Geotech, Inc.*[106.5] Plourde supplied gravel for a roadway project, and was required to remove and replace the gravel when JGI tested the gravel on behalf of the owner and determined the gravel did not meet the contract specifications. JGI's test results were later determined to be inaccurate, and Plourde asserted a negligence claim against JGI to recover the additional costs incurred in removing and replacing the original gravel. The court held that the economic loss rule precluded Plourde's claim because there was no privity of contract between the parties. The court found that neither of the two exceptions to application of the economic loss rule applied: there was no special relationship between the parties similar to an intended beneficiary relationship, and a negligent misrepresentation claim could not be asserted because no reliance could be imputed to Plourde.

Similarly, in *BRW, Inc. v. Dufficy & Sons, Inc.*,[106.6] a subcontractor, Dufficy, sued the project engineer, BRW, and the engineer's inspector to recover economic loss suffered by the subcontractor as a result of the defendants' negligence and negligent representations in preparing the design drawings and specifications and

---

[106.4] 476 F. Supp. 2d 472 (E.D. Pa. 2007).

[106.5] 154 N.H. 791, 917 A.2d 1250 (2007).

[106.6] 99 P.3d 66 (Colo. Oct. 4, 2004). *See also* Affordable Hous. Ltd. P'ship v. Design Alliance, Inc., (Ariz. Feb. 12, 2010) (Arizona Supreme Court reversed the appellate court's holding that the economic loss rule did not bar recovery in a negligence action against an architect for defects in design, as opposed to defects in construction; owner's negligence claim against architect for strictly economic losses was barred by the economic loss rule; court indicated that the economic loss rule would not bar negligence claims where the parties have no contractual relationship with each other); Excel Constr., Inc. v. HKM Eng'g, Inc., (2010 WY 34; 228 P.3d 40 (Wyo. 2010)) (engineer could be liable for economic losses under a fraud theory of recovery, as long as the damages arose from the violation of a duty "independent of contract"); Davencourt at Pilgrims Landing Homeowners Ass'n v. Davencourt at Pilgrims Landing, LC, 2009 UT 65, 221 P.3d 234 (Oct. 2, 2009) (court held that a developer owed an independent duty of care to the homeowners association in maintaining the common areas and disclosing material facts affecting the condition of the common areas during the early period when the developer had control of the association; the economic loss rule did not bar negligence claims relating to those duties).

in inspecting the work on the project. The trial court held the economic loss rule barred Dufficy's tort claims, but the appellate court reversed, holding that an engineer and an inspector owe an independent duty of care under tort law when performing their work. The Colorado Supreme Court reversed, holding that although Dufficy and the defendants did not contract directly with each other, the defendants' duties of care arose from interrelated contracts, and contract law provided any remedies between the parties. Since the duty of care asserted by Dufficy was the same duty memorialized in the defendants' contracts, there was no "independent" duty and the economic loss rule therefore barred Dufficy's tort claims, notwithstanding that Dufficy had not contracted directly with either of the defendants and therefore had no contract claims to assert.

In *Hamon Contractors, Inc. v. Carter & Burgess, Inc.*,[106.7] the contractor, Hamon, not only sued the owner under the contract, but also sued the owner, the engineer, and the construction manager for fraud and negligence, alleging the defendants knew or should have known prior to and after the execution of Hamon's contract that the drainage design was defective, and that they concealed and misrepresented that the design was the true cause of the drainage problems that caused Hamon delays, disruptions and additional work. Considering first Hamon's claims of fraud and negligence that allegedly occurred after Hamon executed its contract (the "post-contractual" claims), the court held that whether a tort is intentional or not is irrelevant to application of the economic loss rule. Instead, the test is whether the duties that are the subject of the claim arose from one or more contracts between or among the parties. Where, as here, the tort duty is the same as the contractual duty, the economic loss rule bars a tort claim. As to the pre-contractual claims, which were based on a failure to disclose, the court held that Hamon had not alleged any special relationship between the defendants and Hamon that would give rise to a duty to disclose, and those claims were also properly dismissed.

Although the economic loss rule does not apply to consumer contracts, including home construction contracts for individual homeowners,[106.8] it does apply to contracts between commercial entities, even if those entities are not "sophisticated."[106.9] The economic loss rule bars subsequent home buyers from asserting negligent or intentional misrepresentation claims against the builder for purely economic losses, although it does not preclude fraudulent concealment

---

[106.7] 2009 WL 1152160 (Colo. App. Apr. 30, 2009), *as modified on denial of reh'g* (June 11, 2009), *cert. dismissed* (Aug. 14, 2009). *See also* Ledcor Builders, Inc. v. Janez Dev., LLC, 2010 WL 925876 (Cal. App. Mar. 16, 2010) (unpublished) (construction manager owed no independent duty of care to general contractor, such that contractor's negligence claims against the construction manager for purely economic losses were barred by the economic loss doctrine).

[106.8] *But cf.* Akbani v. TRC Eng'rs, Inc., 2009 WL 2614473 (N.D. Tex. Aug. 25, 2009) (a homeowner's negligence claim against an engineering company was barred by the economic loss rule when all of the plaintiff's alleged damages stemmed, either directly or indirectly, from the contract to prepare a plat and design a retaining wall).

[106.9] Franklin Grove Corp. v. Drexel, 936 A.2d 1272 (R.I. Dec. 20, 2007).

claims.[106.10] Where a subsequent purchaser of an apartment building sued the owner for negligence in defective construction that resulted in dry rot, seeking more than $300,000 in repair costs, the court held that the economic loss rule did not bar the claim, since the owner alleged physical damage to their real property, and not just economic loss.[106.11] Where an architect sued the general contractor for indemnity in connection with the owner's claim for damages arising from water leaks, the court held that the economic loss rule barred the architect's claim for indemnity relating to the owner's alleged loss of use of the property, but did not bar its claim relating to the owner's damages incurred for repairs and to replace water damages items, as that claim related to property and not solely economic loss.[106.12] A Wisconsin court held that since the architectural contract was solely for services, and the subsequent construction contract included services, the contracts were primarily for services, rather than products, and the economic loss rule therefore did not apply.[106.13]

Citing the *Waynesborough* case, the court in *American Stores Properties, Inc. v. Spotts, Stevens & McCoy, Inc.*[106.14] rejected the owner's contention that the economic loss rule should not apply where the parties are not in privity of contract. In *American Stores*, the owner sued the general contractor and a number of other entities, including five companies that either subcontracted with the general contractor or with a subcontractor to perform work relating to the construction of gabion retaining walls that were failing. Those five defendants moved for summary judgment to dismiss the owner's claims under the economic loss rule. The court stated "the economic loss rule provides that 'no cause of action exists for negligence that results solely in economic damages unaccompanied by physical injury or property damage.' " The court held that since the retaining walls were the "product" for which the owner bargained, the owner's negligence claims were barred by the economic loss doctrine since they did not allege "property damage."

A Washington court examined the "property damage" exception to application of the economic loss rule in *Stieneke v. Russi*.[106.15] A purchaser of a home from a prior owner sued for negligent misrepresentation relating to the condition of the roof, and the trial court awarded the purchaser damages, finding that the claim was for "property damage to property *other than the defective product or*

[106.10] Carlile v. Harbour Homes, Inc., 147 Wash. App. 193, 194 P.3d 280 (Div. 1 Oct. 20, 2008), *reconsid. denied* (Nov. 20, 2008), *appeal dismissed* (Sept. 30, 2009), *review granted in part* (166 Wash. 2d 1015, 210 P.3d 1019 (July 8, 2009).

[106.11] Harris v. Suniga, 344 Or. 301, 180 P.3d 12 (Mar. 20, 2008).

[106.12] Waynesborough County Club of Chester County v. Diedrich Niles Bolton Architects, Inc., 2008 WL 687485 (E.D. Pa. Mar. 10, 2008).

[106.13] Stuart v. Weisflog's Showroom Gallery, Inc., 2008 WI 22, 746 N.W.2d 762 (Mar. 28, 2008).

[106.14] 648 F. Supp. 2d 707 (E.D. Pa. Aug. 13, 2009).

[106.15] 145 Wash. App. 544, 190 P.3d 60 (July 1, 2008), *review denied,* 165 Wash. 2d 1026, 203 P.3d 381 (Feb. 4, 2009). *See also* Poulsbo Group, LLC v. Talon Dev., LLC, 2010 WL 1207220 (Wash. App. Mar. 30, 2010) (confirming that the economic loss rule applies to claims for both negligent and intentional misrepresentation).

property," and not for economic losses that would be precluded by the economic loss rule. On appeal, the court rejected the purchaser's argument that the roof was the "defective product" that caused damage to "other property" consisting of the sheetrock and paint, flooring, and storage in the interior of the house. The court reasoned that the purchaser bought a finished home, not component parts, such that there was no "other property" that was damaged, and the damages were solely economic loss barred by the economic loss rule.

An Arizona court held that the economic loss rule might not preclude a tort claim even if only the defective product is damaged in *Valley Forge Insurance Co. v. Sam's Plumbing, LLC.*[106.16] The defendant, Sam's, had performed work on a gas line for a tenant of a shopping center, and the gas line exploded, causing damage to other portions of the shopping center. The insurance company for the owner of the shopping center asserted a subrogated negligence claim against Sam's, which the lower court held was barred by the economic loss rule. The appellate court reversed, finding that under Arizona law, three separate issues are to be considered in determining the applicability of the economic loss rule: (1) whether quality or safety concerns primarily caused the loss; (2) whether the loss resulted from a slow deterioration or a sudden accident or calamity; and (3) whether the loss resulted from damage solely to the defective product or to other property. The court held that where, as here, the damage occurred suddenly and accidentally and the defect posed an unreasonable risk of damage to people or other property, the claim will sound in tort, even if the only property damaged is the defective product itself. Thus, the economic loss rule did not bar the insurance company's claim.

In South Carolina, the economic loss rule does not apply if a contractor owed a duty of care to the plaintiff separate and distinct from any contractual duties, the contractor breached that duty of care (which may be evidenced by a breach of industry standard), and the breach of duty create a serious threat of physical harm. The "serious threat of harm" requirement was discussed more fully in *Potomac Constructors, LLC v. EFCO Corp.*,[106.17] 530 F. Supp. 2d 731 (D. Md. 2008). Potomac was the general contractor on the $2.5 billion project to replace the Woodrow Wilson Bridge, and subcontracted with EFCO to engineer and supply the concrete formwork for the project. Potomac brought suit against

---

[106.16] 220 Ariz. 512, 207 P.3d 765 (Ariz. App. Mar. 19, 2009). *See also* Hughes Custom Bldg., LLC v. Davey, 2009 WL 1260171 (Ariz. App. May 7, 2009), *affirmed in part, reversed in part on other grounds, remanded* 2010 WL 1407999 (Ariz. App. Apr. 8. 2010) (lower court held that the economic loss rule did not bar a tort claim brought by a home builder against the soils engineer who failed to disclose problems with the soil which resulted in damage to the houses built by the builder, since the defective product was the soil, and the houses were therefore "other property"; cause was remanded by the Arizona Supreme Court to reconsider the ruling in light of the decision in the *Flagstaff* case; on remand, lower court held that the economic loss rule did not bar the home builder's tort claim because the builder had no contractual relationship with the soils engineer).

[106.17] 530 F. Supp. 2d 731 (D. Md. Jan. 9, 2008). *See also* Colleton Preparatory Acad., Inc. v. Hoover Universal, Inc., 379 S.C. 181, 666 S.E.2d 247 (2008).

EFCO, alleging late deliveries and defective design of the formwork, and asserting claims for breach of contract and negligence. The court noted that under Maryland law, a party may recover the cost of correcting negligently created defects if they produce "a substantial and unreasonable risk of death or personal injury." The court held that the damages allegedly caused by late delivery were barred by the economic loss rule, as the late delivery did not create any risk of death or injury. In contrast, the repair of the defective formwork posed a substantial threat to the safety of the workers performing the repair work, based upon evidence that the defective formwork was buckling, moving, and sometimes blew out. As such, Potomac was not precluded from recovering damages stemming from the repair of the defective formwork.

In *RLI Ins. Co. v. Indian River School Dist.*,[106.18] the contractor's surety asserted a claim against the architect (BMGI) and the construction manager (EDis) for negligent representation based upon their approving payments to the contractor that exceeded the work actually performed. BMGI and EDis brought a motion for summary judgment on the grounds that the economic loss rule precluded the surety's claim, and the surety defended by asserting the applicability of the exception in Section 552 of the Restatement (Second) of Torts that allows negligence claims against defendants who supplied information to the plaintiff for use in business transactions with third parties and who are in the business of supplying information. The court rejected the surety's argument, finding that although BMGI and EDis provided information to the owner for use in the owner's business transactions with the contractor, information was not the "end and aim" of BMGI's or EDis' work, but was merely ancillary to the services they were retained by the owner to provide. As such, the exception did not apply, and the surety's negligence claims were dismissed.

Although recognizing that not all states have adopted the economic loss rule, the Nevada Supreme Court held the economic loss rule prevented negligence claims in Nevada against design professionals for purely economic losses absent personal injury or property damage in *Terracon Consultants Western, Inc. v. Mandalay Resort Group.*[106.19] Terracon provided geotechnical engineering advice about the subsurface soil conditions and recommended a foundation design for construction of the Mandalay Resort and Casino in Las Vegas. The amount of settling beneath the foundation exceeded Terracon's projections, and Mandalay was required by the county to repair and reinforce the foundation before proceeding with construction. Mandalay sued Terracon for professional negligence to recover economic losses incurred, and Terracon moved for partial summary judgment on the basis that the economic loss doctrine barred Mandalay's claim. The trial court certified to the Nevada Supreme Court the question of

---

[106.18] 556 F. Supp. 356 (D. Del. June 3, 2008), *reargument denied*, 2008 WL 2686242 (D. Del. 2008).

[106.19] 2009 WL 790364 (Nev. Mar. 26, 2009).

whether the economic loss doctrine applied to bar a negligence claim against design professionals when plaintiff seeks to recover purely economic losses. The court noted that courts adopting the economic loss rule have recognized exceptions to allow recovery in certain types of cases, such as negligent misrepresentation and professional negligence actions against attorneys, accountants, real estate professionals, and insurance brokers. After a lengthy discussion of the purposes of the economic loss rule, including addressing policy concerns about administrative costs and a disproportionate balance between liability and fault, the court held that those purposes would not be furthered by creating an exception to allow negligence-based claims against professionals who provide design-related services in the commercial property development or improvement process.

Applying Vermont law, a federal district court reached a similar result in *Hunt Constr. Group, Inc. v. Brennan Beer Gorman/Architects, P.C.*[106.20] Hunt was the general contractor retained to construct a resort hotel in Stowe, Vermont. The owner contracted with certain architects and engineers to provide the project plans and specifications. After completion of construction, Hunt sued the architects and engineers to recover damages for cost overruns and schedule delays due to defendant's negligence and negligent misrepresentations in failing to timely provide the plans and specifications, providing plans with numerous errors and omissions, and failing to respond promptly to Hunt's requests for information and corrected drawings. The defendants' motion to dismiss the claims was granted on the basis of the economic loss rule. Hunt argued that although the economic loss rule had been adopted in Virginia, the Virginia Supreme Court had indicated that an exception to that rule might exist in a limited class of cases involving violation of professional duty. The court found that this exception would apply only if there was a "special relationship" between Hunt and the defendants, which required the existence of a duty of care owed by the defendants to Hunt "independent of any contractual obligations." The court held Hunt's allegations of negligence and negligence misrepresentation were based solely upon actions required of defendants under their contracts with the owner, which precluded the necessary finding that the defendants owed a special duty of care beyond the terms of the construction contracts.

§ 1.05 LINKING CAUSATION AND DAMAGES

Page 31, add new footnote 106.21 at end of first paragraph of section:

[106.21] *See* U.S. *ex rel.* Belt Con Constr., Inc. v. Metric Constr. Co., Inc., 314 Fed. Appx. 151, 2009 WL 458795 (10th Cir. (N.M.) Feb. 25, 2009) (contractor was not entitled to recover damages for subcontractor's failure to provide roofing warranty, notwithstanding that district court determined contractor was liable to

[106.20] 2008 WL 4870993 (D. Vt. Nov. 3, 2008).

the owner for future warranty work; appellate court held there was insufficient evidence that subcontractor's breach would result in damages, since there was no evidence related to the probability that the owner would hold the contractor liable for the roof warranties; contractor's only evidence of value of the roof warranties was hearsay evidence that another roofer would provide substitute warranties for $118,000, whereas there was evidence that the subcontractor had responded to each of the owner's requests for roof repairs).

Page 32, add at end of page:

In *VIV Electric Co., Inc. v. STR Constructors, Inc.*,[107.1] the general contractor sought to use the critical path method (CPM) to establish that the subcontractor was responsible for a 126-day delay in completing the contract. (CPM is a method of organizing and scheduling a complex project that consists of numerous interrelated separate work activities; some work activities may be performed at any time without any effect on the completion of the project, whereas other work activities must be performed on schedule or the entire project will be delayed; the latter items are on the "critical path.") The subcontractor complained that the contractor had used an "as planned" critical path schedule, without introducing any evidence of an "as-built" critical path schedule, which would reflect extensions and delays as they occurred during the construction process. The subcontractor argued that without a comparison of the two schedules, there was no evidence that the initial schedule was reasonable or achievable. The appellate court rejected this contention, holding that because the trial court did not award the contractor the entire amount of damages it sought for delay, and the record reflected some evidence of specific days on which the subcontractor caused delays, the trial court's award was neither unsupported nor manifestly unjust.

In *George Sollitt Construction Co. v. United States*,[107.2] the court stated that in order to prevail on claims for the additional costs incurred because of late completion of a fixed-price government construction contract, the contractor must show that the government's actions affected activities on the critical path of the contractor's performance of the contract. The determination of the critical path is crucial to the calculation of delay damages because only construction work on the critical path had an impact on the time in which the project was

[107.1] 2000 WL 854857 (Tex. App. 2000).

[107.2] 64 Fed. Cl. 229 (Ct. Cl. Feb. 23, 2005). *See also* Mactec, Inc. v. Bechtel Jacobs Co., LLC, 346 Fed. Appx. 59 (6th Cir. (Tenn.) Sept. 25, 2009) (the court discusses use of the critical path method, defined as "the longest path in the schedule on which any delay or disruption . . . would cause a day-for-day delay to the project itself. . . . Those activities must be performed as they are scheduled and timely in order for the project to finish on time . . ."; the court indicates that because a project's critical path continues to evolve even after work has commenced, in order to grasp accurately the delays that a project takes on, the critical path should be updated regularly; the court also indicates that the CPM approach "has been accepted by the United States Court of Federal Claims as the most accurate way to calculate delay damages in complex construction projects").

completed. One established way to document delay is through the use of Critical Path Method (CPM) schedules and an analysis of the effects, if any, of government-caused events on the critical path of the project. A government delay that affects only activities not on the critical path does not delay the completion of the project. However, the critical path of construction activities may change as a project is actually built, and "activities that were not on the original critical path subsequently may be added." Accurate CPM schedule updates are required during the course of construction to reflect delays and shifts in the critical path. If the CPM is to be used to evaluate delay on the project, it must be kept current and must reflect delays as they occur. Accurate CPM schedule updates produced during actual construction are better evidence of the critical path than the baseline CPM schedule provided at the beginning of the project.

The importance of CPM schedule analysis in determining causation was further highlighted in *Appeals of Fox Construction Inc.*[107.3] In that case, the contractor contended that the Navy delayed the contractor's work through a 30-day delay in the required partnering and pre-construction meetings, delays in submittal approvals and responses to RFIs, and changes in the work. The contractor sought to recover delay damages for home office and job site overhead, and lost productivity damages based upon the extended duration of the work. With respect to the delay in the partnering and pre-construction meetings, the Board found that the contractor could not have commenced work prior to the actual date of the meetings because its quality control plan had not yet been approved. As to the remaining alleged delays, the Navy's expert prepared a CPM analysis which demonstrated that none of the subject submittals or RFIs, and none of the changed work, affected the critical path of the project. The contractor did not dispute this testimony, and the Board held that the contractor had failed to establish that any conduct of the Navy delayed the contractor's work. Further, since the contractor tied its loss of productivity claim to the number of days it was allegedly delayed by the Navy, the contractor's failure to prove that the Navy was responsible for any of the delays was similarly fatal to its lost productivity claim.

Similarly, in *Appeal of AEI Pacific, Inc.*,[107.4] the court rejected AEI's methodology for determining the amount and cause of acceleration of the work. AEI's expert testified that his critical path analysis was a "modified windows analysis" which utilized the following steps: (1) develop a baseline schedule; (2) remove open ends and constraints by adding predecessor and successor activities; (3) identify all Corps of Engineers delaying events and develop fragnets; (4) insert fragnets into the baseline schedule to obtain the impact schedule; (5) "update" the impact schedule for progress; and (6) repeat steps (1) through (5) for each period selected for analysis ("window"); the court quoted from an unpublished paper prepared by the expert emphasizing the importance of the claimant's accounting for its own schedule delay events and consequences and found that the expert's

---

[107.3] ASBCA No. 55266, 2008 WL 698478 (Mar. 5, 2008).
[107.4] ASBCA No. 53806, 2008 WL 436928 (Feb. 8, 2008).

methodology in this case was flawed because it did not take into account any of the delays that the evidence established were caused by AEI and its subcontractors, and because the use of fragnets was an unaccepted method of yielding reliable evidence of acceleration; in contrast, the court approved the CPM methodology utilized by the Corps' expert, which was a "Time Impact Study" comparing the as-planned schedule to the as-built schedule and chronologically identifying each event on the critical path that started late; based upon the Corps' analysis, the court found that AEI was delayed 16 days due to deficiencies in the plans and specifications.

In *Tennessee Gas Pipeline Co. v. Technip USA Corp.*,[107.5] an action brought to recover damages caused by delays in making improvements to a gas pipeline, the trial court erred in granting the contractor's motion for judgment notwithstanding the verdict, thus overturning the jury's award of delay damages. Although conflicting evidence was introduced with regard to who was responsible for certain delays in the project, the evidence in support of the verdict rose "to a level that would enable reasonable and fair-minded people to differ in their conclusions," making a JNOV inappropriate.

Page 33, add at end of note 108:

See **Section 1.05[D]**, below, for a more detailed discussion of concurrent delay and apportionment of damages.

Page 33, add before subsection [A]:

In *Alamo Community College District v. Browning Construction Co.*,[109.1] the jury found that the owner breached its contract with Browning, the general contractor for construction of a new community college campus, by (1) failing to provide complete and accurate drawings; (2) failing to obtain building permits in a timely manner; (3) failing or refusing to correct design errors; or (4) providing inaccurate or incomplete information in response to the contractor's requests for information. The jury awarded Browning delay damages in excess of $2.5 million for additional jobsite costs, additional home office overhead costs, additional management costs, liability to subcontractors, additional and changed work, and change negotiation support costs. On appeal, the owner argued that the evidence supporting Browning's claim was legally insufficient because the contractor failed to provide any evidence showing that its damages were caused by the owner's alleged breach of the contract. The appellate court disagreed. The contractor's critical path and damages expert testified extensively at trial about design

---

[107.5] 2008 WL 3876141 (Tex. App.-Hous. Aug. 21, 2008), *review denied* (2 pets.) (Sept. 25, 2009).

[109.1] 131 S.W.3d 146 (Tex. App. 2004), *petition for review filed* (2004).

defects and incomplete specifications that caused the contractor delay. These included defects in roof geometry, ceiling design, and window installation plans, as well as incomplete specifications for pier caps, beams, electrical services, and draft stops. Other witnesses testified in further detail about these same problems and how they caused the contractor delay. Thus, the contractor presented more than a scintilla of evidence that the owner's breaches caused delay, supporting the award.

In In re *Regional Building Systems, Inc.*,[109.2] a subcontractor sought to recover damages from the general contractor for labor and equipment that were idled when the general contractor, unable to provide the subcontractor with materials to perform because of the owner's failure to pay, suspended its obligations under the subcontract. A bankruptcy court denied the subcontractor's claim for delay damages, holding that New York law prevents such a recovery when the contractor is not responsible for the delays. The appellate court affirmed. Although the subcontractor argued that the contractor's financial difficulty does not excuse performance under a contract and that delay damages are proper, the appellate court reiterated that established New York law provides that when the cause of a delay is not the fault of the general contractor, i.e., the delays are not caused by some agency or circumstance under the prime contractor's direction or control, the subcontractor has no remedy against the general for delay damages absent a contractual commitment to the contrary. Thus, a subcontractor unhappy with this rule "should bargain for the inclusion in its subcontract of a provision" to the contrary.

In *Appeal of Jerry Dodds & Associates*,[109.3] the Board held that a contractor could not recover damages for isolated incidences of government-caused delay. The prime contract provided that the government was not to use an existing loading dock during construction of a steel shelter to cover the dock. The contractor alleged that its performance had been delayed on several occasions when the government used the dock before completion of the shelter. The Board held that occasional, incidental acts of government-caused delay did not constitute a compensable suspension of work or a breach of the implied duty to not hinder or interfere with performance. Even though the government might have "inconvenienced or temporarily slowed [the contractor] here and there," the contractor was not entitled to additional compensation.

The owner was found not to be responsible for the contractor's increased costs in *Appeal of The Ryan Co.*[109.4] The contract required drilling three effluent injection wells, and the government directed the contractor to drill a fourth well. The Board denied the contractor's request for additional compensation, on the grounds that the need for the fourth well arose from the contractor's failure to drill the required three wells with 300 feet of well screen as specified (the contractor provided only 250 feet of well screen). Since the government could have

---

[109.2] 320 F.3d 482 (4th Cir. (Md.) 2003).

[109.3] ASBCA No. 51682 (Apr. 19, 2002).

[109.4] ASBCA No. 53385 (Nov. 6, 2002).

directed the contractor to drill three new wells that met the contract requirements at no cost to the government, its decision to mitigate its damages by adding a fourth well did not give rise to an obligation to pay the contractor additional compensation.

In *Keeney Construction v. James Talcott Construction Co., Inc.*,[109.5] the subcontractor, Keeney, was denied recovery of delay damages based on subcontract language that required the subcontractor to work "as directed" by the general contractor. During the project, the general contractor, Talcott, and the owner negotiated an expanded scope of work and an extended completion schedule. Although the changes did not alter Keeney's scope of work, they did affect the timing of Keeney's work. Keeney asserted a claim against Talcott for damages for delay, arguing that the "as directed" language could not be construed as a disclaimer of Talcott's responsibility for its own breach of contract or negligence, as such a provision would be contrary to Montana law. The Montana Supreme Court disagreed. The court noted that the subcontract did not incorporate any schedule or completion deadline for Keeney's work, and held that the "as directed" language gave Talcott full discretion to schedule Keeney's work, thereby precluding a claim for delay damages. The court said the provision was not contrary to Montana law, as it did not relieve Talcott of all liability.[109.6]

In *RPR & Associates, Inc. v. University of Northern Carolina*,[109.7] the contractor's recovery for delays was reduced by the amount of a settlement the contractor had reached with the project architect. The contractor sued the owner and the architect in separate lawsuits for increased costs incurred during the extended performance period that allegedly resulted from a defective design and improper management. The contractor settled with the architect for $200,000. The court in the owner lawsuit awarded the contractor damages of $850,000, reduced by a credit of $200,000 for the settlement proceeds. The contractor appealed, arguing the trial court failed to make specific factual findings that the recovery against the architect was for the same damages awarded against the owner. The appellate court held that the trial court did not need to make specific factual findings, as the allegations of the complaints demonstrate that the contractor was suing for the same injuries arising from the same delay.

[109.5] 45 P.3d 19 (Mont. 2002), *reh'g denied* (2002).

[109.6] *But see* Blake Constr. Co., Inc. v. C.J. Coakley Co., Inc., 431 A.2d 569 (D.C. App. 1981) (court held that an "as directed" provision did not give the contractor the right to direct out-of-sequence work or to otherwise actively interfere with the subcontractor's performance).

[109.7] 570 S.E.2d 510 (N.C. Ct. App. 2002), *cert. dismissed* (N.C. 2003), *review denied* (N.C. 2003).

[A] Bid and Estimating Errors

Page 34, add at end of note 110:

See also Baldi Bros. Constructors v. United States, 50 Fed. Cl. 74 (Ct. Cl. 2001) (expert's finding of 191 compensable delay days as a result of differing site conditions could not be accepted, because, regardless of plaintiff's confidence that it would have completed its work well ahead of the contract completion date, the government should not be liable when plaintiff's predictions were untested; the court found neither credible documentary nor testimonial evidence to support plaintiff's ambitious schedule and thus held that plaintiff was entitled to no more than 97 compensable delay days); Orlosky Inc. v. United States, 64 Fed. Cl. 63 (Ct. Cl. 2005), *appeal dismissed*, 180 Fed. Appx. 928 (Fed. Cir. Apr. 17, 2006) (plaintiff made erroneous assumptions when bidding on a construction project with the Navy as a result of its failure to conduct a pre-bid site inspection; plaintiff thus could not recover damages under the differing site conditions clause of the contract because such a claim requires the contractor to show that the conditions actually encountered were reasonably unforeseeable based on all the information available to the contractor at the time of bidding); Gillingham Constr., Inc. v. Newby-Wiggins Constr., Inc., 142 Idaho 15, 121 P.3d 946 (2005) (in order to recover damages for errors in a bid, the contractor must show: (1) that it relied on the plans and specifications in making its bid, (2) that it encountered conditions that were unforeseeable and varied substantially from the anticipated conditions, and (3) that it performed extra work; the reason for this rule is that if unanticipated conditions not reasonably foreseeable are actually encountered in the work and vary substantially from anticipated conditions reasonably foreseeable by the parties at the time they entered into the contract, the contractor is performing a contract entirely different from the one agreed upon, and in such case is entitled to the reasonable value of his additional services; thus, in the instant case, where the contractor was required to perform extra excavation work as a result of the higher elevation encountered, it was entitled to recover additional compensation for the extra work, plus the time its equipment sat idle, and the costs of moving its equipment back and forth onto the site).

[B] Productivity Claims

Page 34, add new note 110.1 after second sentence of section:

[110.1] Southern Comfort Builders, Inc. v. United States, 67 Fed. Cl. 124 (2005) (a loss of productivity claim is based upon the theory that individual compensable changes to a contract, taken as a whole, can have such a disruptive effect on the contractor's performance that the contractor has a compensable claim for costs in addition to the amounts of its individual change orders; the government has a duty not to act in a way that will hinder or delay the contractor's performance; in order for the government to be found liable, however, a plaintiff must demonstrate that the government *caused* the plaintiff a compensable injury, *i.e.,* the government is not liable for breach of contract, or causes of action that rely upon "severe defects" in contract drawings, or government hindrance of performance, unless the contractor proves that the alleged defects, changes, or hindrances negatively affected costs and performance of the contract; in this case, however, the contractor never provided the contracting officer or the court with a critical path analysis of the alleged government-caused hindrances and their effect upon the critical path or productivity of this project, nor did the contractor prove that the alleged delays in completing the project were the fault of the government; thus, recovery for loss of productivity was denied). *See also* Appeals of Fox Construction Inc., ASBCA No. 55266 (2008) (where the contractor asserted a loss of productivity claim based upon alleged government-caused delays, and the government's uncontroverted CPM analysis demonstrated that the government's conduct did not impact the critical path of the work, the contractor failed to establish the necessary "causal link or relationship between the affected work and the increased costs due to loss of productivity").

Page 35, add new subsection after end of subsection [C]:

[D] Apportionment of Damages

Linking causation and damages becomes more complicated when more than one party is responsible for delays to the project. Where one party and then the other cause different delays seriatim or intermittently, the delays are considered "sequential."[113] In contrast, "concurrent" delays exist when the delays caused by each party occurred during the same time period, even if the delays are not of the same duration but merely overlap for some period of time.[114] Some jurisdictions treat these two types of delay differently, but most will allow apportionment of concurrent and sequential delays for purposes of calculating delay damages or liquidated damages.

The differing treatment of sequential and concurrent delays in some jurisdictions was discussed in detail in *R.P. Wallace, Inc. v. United States.*[115] Wallace, the general contractor, was assessed $50,000 in liquidated damages for failing to complete renovations of a building by the appointed date. Wallace sought remission of the damages for "excusable delay," allegedly resulting from the contractor having been provided with defective window specifications. The court noted that when a contractor seeks an extension of contract time for excusable delay, which

[113] R.P. Wallace, Inc. v. United States, 63 Fed. Cl. 402 (Ct. Cl. 2004).

[114] *Id.*

[115] *Id. See also* Sunshine Constr. & Eng'g, Inc. v. United States, 64 Fed. Cl. 346 (Mar. 4, 2005).

will relieve it from the consequences of having failed to complete the work within the time allowed for performance, it has the burden of establishing by a preponderance of the evidence not only the existence of an excusable cause of delay, but also the extent to which completion of the contract work as a whole was delayed thereby. The court found that when there are concurrent delays, in that both parties are responsible for the same period of delay, the law is clear that the contractor may be entitled to a time extension but is not entitled to recover any delay damages. In contrast, the court indicated that the law regarding the treatment of sequential delays is unsettled, with some cases allowing apportionment of liquidated damages and others not. The court held that sequential delay could be apportioned and, after a detailed discussion of the evidence, found that the contractor was entitled to remission of liquidated damages for only 21 days, which, at $200 per day, amounted to a recovery of $4,200. The court further held that the contractor was not entitled to delay damages for the 21 days of delay, because there was a clear indication that during the three-week period in which the contractor had difficulty in identifying a window supplier, there was concurrent delay. Among other things, when the contractor encountered the delay, it failed to meet a number of contract deadlines, including that for submitting at least a dozen administrative and material submittals. Moreover, during the same period, delay occurred because of the death of the contractor's grandmother. Accordingly, the contractor could not recover damages for this period because "prosecution of the work as a whole would have been delayed regardless of the government's act."

The *Wallace* court's statement that no-delay damages are available for concurrent delays would be accurate if two delays are considered "concurrent" only if they caused the exact same period of delay. Most courts consider delays to be concurrent even if they are of different durations and overlap just for some portion of the delay period, and they will allow delay damages or an apportionment of liquidated damages as long as there is sufficient evidence upon which to allocate the delay period between the two (or more) causes of delay. For example, in *GASA, Inc. v. United States*,[116] plaintiff contractor alleged that but for delays by the Army Corps of Engineers, it would not have been assessed liquidated damages for 54 days; i.e, that it would have completed the contract within the contractually mandated 180 days (plus any extensions for weather-related delays beyond those contemplated in the contract) had the Corps issued the notice to proceed 53 days earlier. The court noted that delay damages can be recovered by a contractor when delays are concurrent or intertwined if the contractor satisfies its burden of separating its delays from those chargeable to the government. In this case, the court found that a genuine issue of material fact existed as to whether the Corps delayed the

[116] 79 Fed. Cl. 325 (2007). *But see* United States *ex rel.* Belt Con Constr., Inc. v. Metric Constr. Co., Inc., 314 Fed. Appx. 151, 2009 WL 458795 (10th Cir. (N.M.) Feb. 25, 2009) (in dicta, the Tenth Circuit indicated that California case law suggests that California would not apportion concurrent delays, as opposed to sequential delays).

contractor on one part of the contract for 31 days, and whether this delay caused the contractor to work beyond the 180-day period mandated by the contract. Thus, the government's motion for summary judgment was denied, and the contractor would be permitted to show that its liquidated damages assessment should be reduced by 31 days.

In *Hutton Contracting Co., Inc. v. City of Coffeyville,*[117] the court adopted the "modern view" that liquidated damages may be apportioned when there is evidence of delays by both parties and the damages are in fact divisible. The court therefore rejected the contractor's contention that the City's breach of its duty of good faith and fair dealing in requesting unneeded repairs and failing to facilitate completion of cleanup-related tasks precluded it from any award of liquidated damages under Kansas law, and upheld the trial court's determination to reduce the amount of liquidated damages by the number of days the jury attributed to the City's breach.

In *George Sollitt Construction Co. v. United States,*[118] the court held that if the evidence shows that the contractor, along with the government, caused concurrent delays to the critical path of a project, the contractor must apportion the delays affecting the completion of the project to be able to recover delay damages. With respect to liquidated damages, the court held that when apportionment of critical path delays is not possible in a government construction project, the court cannot uphold retention of any liquidated damages by the government. In this case, critical path delays could *not* be apportioned between the contractor and the government with any certainty, and thus the trial court erred in assessing liquidated damages.

Apportionment of delay damages caused by concurrent delays was allowed in *Appeal of ADT Construction Group, Inc.*[119] The draft RFP for the project to design and build a munitions maintenance facility at Nevis Air Force Base, Nevada, allowed the contractor to fast track the construction, whereby the contractor can begin on those portions of the work for which the design is complete while other portions are still under design. The government determined that approval of the Department of Defense (DOD) was based on 100 percent construction documents, such that fast track construction would not be permissible.

---

[117] 487 F.3d 772 (10th Cir. 2007) (Ct. Cl. 2004). *See also* Sauer Inc. v. Danzig, 224 F.3d 1340 (Fed. Cir. 2000), *on remand sub nom.*, In re Sauer Inc., 01-2 BCA (CCH) ¶ 31,525 (2001) [(where the plaintiff-contractor was only able to prove that the government was responsible for two days of excusable delay, the government was entitled to an award of liquidated damages for the delay period, with the exception of the damages attributable to those two days)].

[118] 64 Fed. Cl. 229 (Ct. Cl. 2005).

[119] ASBCA 55307, 2009 WL 2139063 (July 9, 2009). *See also* PCL Constr. Servs., Inc. v. United States, 53 Fed. Cl. 479 (2002) (the court refused to award delay damages to the contractor or liquidated damages to the government on the basis that there was insufficient evidence to permit an apportionment of the concurrent delays, as neither party had provided credible evidence of how the delays and changes had affected other activities).

The government revised the draft RFP to delete references to fast track construction, but the final RFP still contained language permitting fast track construction. The contractor, ADT, interpreted the RFP as permitting either a fast track or a conventional design build, and ADT based its bid on fast tracking the construction, as reflected in ADT's proposal. ADT was awarded the contract in June 2003, the contract completion date of October 1, 2004 was based upon fast track construction, and the government never challenged ADT's plan to use the fast-track method of construction. In July, the contracting officer's representative (COR) became aware that ADT intended to fast track construction, but said nothing and allowed the design to continue. In a design review meeting in October 2003, ADT stated its intention to commence excavation in November when the 100 percent civil and lightning protection drawings were approved by the DOD. Again, no government represented indicated that fast track would not be permitted. The design process continued throughout early 2004, with the government making significant changes that required re-design of the plans. ADT submitted 100 percent construction documents in May 2004, reiterating its intent to fast track the project and requesting approval to start site work and foundations. Such approval was not granted and, in August 2004, the government sent a show cause letter to ADT threatening termination for default due to ADT's failure to perform with the time required. During the extended time period of design, construction cost escalation was occurring in Nevada, and the government was aware that ADT would be submitting a request for equitable adjustment to cover that escalation. When ADT stated its concern about the government delays to the design phase and the cost escalation, a government representative told ADT to "suck it up or default. . . ." The government decided to allow ADT to continue performance, and the DOD approved the 100 percent construction documents in September 2004. ADT was issued the necessary excavation permit after another period of delay and commenced construction, but was terminated for default in February 2006, at which time ADT's surety took over completion of the project. ADT submitted a claim seeking $826,725 for preconstruction delays and requesting a time extension of 278 days, based upon a total delay of 340 days, of which 44 days were deducted for earthwork concurrent delays and 18 days were deducted for earthwork float in ADT's baseline schedule. The Board determined that the government was responsible for 218 days of delay, of which 60 days were concurrent with delays caused by ADT. As such, ADT was entitled to recover delay damages and a time extension for 158 days of government-caused delay.

In *Wayne Knorr, Inc. v. Pennsylvania Dept. of Transportation*,[120] the project owner, PennDOT, was found to have caused delay and disruption to the contractor, Knorr, on a roadway construction project as a result of five categories of active interference: (1) missing and incorrect grades and elevations in the plans; (2) PennDOT's delay in providing missing grades and elevations around the box culvert; (3) PennDOT's delay in addressing slope failures encountered by Knorr;

[120] 973 A.2d 1061 (Pa. Commw. May 14, 2009).

(4) changes to the method of widening the roadway shoulder; and (5) delay in confirming certain changes in construction methodology. The Board also determined that Knorr caused delay through "self-inflicted" problems, including Knorr's own mistakes in construction of the roadway and adjacent structures, ongoing problems with equipment breakdown, flawed work procedures, multiple changes in supervisor and foremen, and work being redone or corrected. The Board determined that of the total 116-day delay, 87 days were caused both by PennDOT's five categories of interference and Knorr's self-inflicted problems. The Board noted there was no "surgically precise way to apportion the remaining 87 days of delay among these six enumerated causes," but each cause was of significant import. The Board then held that five-sixths of the 87 days of delay were attributable to PennDOT's five categories of interference, and one-sixth was attributable to Knorr's self-inflicted causes. On appeal, PennDOT argued that since Knorr could not establish that the government was the "sole proximate cause" of the delay, Knorr was precluded from recovering any damages attributable to delay. The court rejected this argument, finding that Pennsylvania law does not require proof of damages to a mathematical certainty, and that the Board found sufficient evidence to apportion the delay.

The *Wayne Knorr, Inc.* court found that Knorr failed to link causation and damages with respect to Knorr's claim that Knorr incurred increased costs for maintenance and protection of traffic (MBT) due to disruptions caused by PennDOT. The Board found that PennDOT was responsible for 83 percent of the delays and disruptions on the project, but held that Knorr failed to prove that any of PennDOT's actions materially altered Knorr's ability to maintain two lanes of traffic, which was the alleged cause of the material increase in MPT costs. The Board's findings were upheld on appeal. Although Knorr established that its paving work was disrupted by PennDOT, resulting in recoverable increased costs, the court found there was a "lack of evidence establishing a clear causal connection between the 'piecemeal fashion' in which it performed its paving work and an increase in its MPT costs above that contemplated by the Contract."

Chapter 2
LABOR COSTS

§ 2.01 INTRODUCTION

Page 39, add at end of note 1:

; Miller v. Mills Constr., Inc., 352 F.3d 1166 (8th Cir. 2003) (subcontractor was entitled to recover consequential damages, including $9,000 in wages and payroll costs, for "down-time charges" incurred from the date it ceased working on the contract because of commercial impracticability through the end of the contract term; subcontractor did not have other work scheduled for this period because it was scheduled to work on the project, and, as a result, it did not have a stream of income to cover its expenses); Trucco Constr. Co., Inc. v. Columbus, 2006 WL 3825262 (Ohio Ct. App. 10th Dist. Dec. 29, 2006) (there was a genuine issue of material fact, precluding summary judgment in favor of defendant city, whether the plaintiff-contractor was entitled to recover increases in the cost of wages due to the city's delayed commencement of two construction projects; the contractor's claim sought compensation for "premium time," or overtime, in the amount of $23,730, that it allegedly expended in order to maintain the projects' post-delay schedules; the city, on the other hand, had refused to pay any delay damages other than those associated with increased prevailing wages and materials escalation costs).

§ 2.02 DIRECT LABOR OVERRUN

[B] Determination of Wage Rates

Page 40, add new paragraph at end of subsection:

In *Traco Steel Erectors, Inc. v. Comtrol, Inc.*, 2009 UT 81, 222 P.3d 1164 (Utah Dec. 11, 2009), a steel erection subcontractor, Traco, sued the general contractor, Comtrol, to recover monies owed on two construction projects Traco had left unfinished, and Comtrol counterclaimed for its costs to complete the work. The subcontracts provided that Comtrol would be entitled to recover "actual costs incurred" in finishing Traco's work after Traco's breach of contract. Judgment was entered in favor of Comtrol, and Traco challenged the award on the grounds that the trial court used an average hourly rate from the R.S. Means Building Construction Cost Data index to determine Comtrol's cost to complete, rather than requiring Comtrol to produce evidence of its actual labor costs. The Utah Supreme Court held that this was a factual question, and Traco was therefore required to "marshal the evidence surrounding the damages award" in order to appeal, which it did not do. A dissenting justice argued that the question was an issue of law, and that since Comtrol was required to provide the best evidence of what it actually spent in completing Traco's work, its failure to submit actual cost records should have foreclosed its claim to damages as a matter of law.

§ 2.03 LABOR BURDENS

Page 40, add at end of note 8:

; A.A. Beiro Constr. Co., DCCAB No. D-822, 2002 WL 273519 (2002) (contractor incurred $238,020 for labor burden, comprising indirect labor costs for FICA, FUTA, SUTA, workmen's compensation insurance, and a cost item called "Union Burden" for additional fringe benefits required by the Davis Bacon Act, 40 U.S.C. § 276a; the labor burden costs were determined by calculating the ratio of direct labor costs to labor burden from the contractor's job cost report, which yielded a burden rate of 30.12 percent, and multiplying that rate by the supported labor costs of $790,285); ACE Constructors, Inc. v. United States, 70 Fed. Cl. 253 (2006), *aff'd*, 499 F.3d 1357 (Fed. Cir. 2007) (in addition to increased direct labor cost, the plaintiff contractor sought to recover for "labor burden," consisting of various factors applied to direct labor including FICA, unemployment taxes, and workers' compensation insurance. Although plaintiff's construction expert testified that this labor burden should be 40%, the court credited the testimony of a government auditor, who testified that he calculated the contractor's labor burden based on its general ledger, and on that basis the contractor's labor burden was 31.8%; the figure claimed by plaintiff's construction expert, said the court, was partially based on estimations and also included some improper items).

[A] Common Labor Burdens

Page 42, note 17, change cite for Anderson Dev. Corp. to:

543 S.W.2d 402 (Tex. App. 1976), *writ refused n.r.e.* (1977).

Page 42, add at end of note 17:

Cf. L & A Contracting Co., Inc. v. Ram Indus. Coatings, Inc., 762 So. 2d 1223 (La. Ct. App. 2000), *writ denied* (La. 2000) (general contractor sought to recover delay damages from a subcontractor based on expenses incurred to maintain personnel on-site to supervise work of replacement subcontractor; the court denied recovery based on evidence in the record indicating that during the time the replacement was completing subcontract work, the general contractor had other operations ongoing and the same supervisory personnel were responsible for overseeing that work as well; there was no evidence presented to prove that the defendant's actions hindered the general contractor from completing its work within the extended time period granted by the owner, and the general contractor was not charged any liquidated damages for failure to timely complete the project).

§ 2.05 CALCULATION OF WAGE ESCALATION

Page 43, add at end of note 19:

See also, e.g., Vicari v. United States, 53 Fed. Cl. 357 (Ct. Cl. 2002) (contractor contended that delay caused it to have to pay higher rates for carpentry labor than it originally expected; "Due to many interruptions and delays in framing of the UPH Barracks, we experienced a higher than normal labor cost. We were not able to maintain a crew of sufficient size and we were forced to do this work during the summer months in lieu of the winter as planned"; because the extent to which the government caused the delay was a genuine issue of fact, whether plaintiff was entitled to additional direct costs for delayed carpentry work was an issue for trial); George Sollitt Constr. Co. v. United States, 64 Fed. Cl. 229 (Ct. Cl. 2005) (contractor may recover as delay damages labor costs that escalated after projected completion date of project when, as a result of government-caused delays, project was shifted into a period of higher wages for laborers; however, contractor must prove extent of delay and amount of harm caused by that delay to recover on its equitable adjustment claim for increased labor costs; in this case, delays of critical path activities were caused both by contractor and government, and contractor was unable to apportion the delays between the parties; thus, court could not award contractor its claimed costs for labor escalation); El Dorado Irrigation Dist. v. Traylor Bros., Inc., 2007 WL 1113547 (E.D. Cal. 2007) (an award was made by the district court for escalation of labor costs and utility power surcharges due to the passage of time while the project was delayed). *But see* S&B Eng'rs & Constructors, Ltd. v. Progress Energy Florida, Inc., 2010 WL 457439 (11th Cir. (Fla.) Feb. 11, 2010) (contractor's creative argument for recovering the costs of escalated wages under a firm, fixed price contract was rejected by the court; S&B contended that since the contract's *force majeure* provision precluded the contractor from recovering additional costs "resulting from such Force Majeure delays," it did not prevent the contractor from recovering escalated wages that resulted from force majeure events, including seven hurricanes during the course of constructing two electric generating plants in Florida where there was no resulting delay in project completion).

§ 2.06 LOSS OF PRODUCTIVITY

Page 47, add at beginning of note 33:

See, e.g., Clifford R. Gray, Inc. v. City Sch. Dist. of Albany, 716 N.Y.S.2d 795 (App. Div., 3d Dept. 2000) (court affirmed an award of damages to the general contractor for loss of labor productivity, as well as various other expenses incurred as a result of delays caused by the owner; the evidence indicated that the delays were caused by the owner's failure to timely obtain easements for electrical and drain sewer installations; the failure of the owner's construction manager to adequately supervise and coordinate the work of the various contractors, including the failure to prepare the coordinated construction schedules and drawings; the termination of both the construction manager and the general contractor; and the owner's decision to hire 30 subcontractors instead of replacing the general contractor).

[A] Overtime

Page 49, add at end of note 36:

See, e.g., ACE Constructors, Inc. v. United States, 70 Fed. Cl. 253 (2006), *aff'd,* 499 F.3d 1357 (Fed. Cir. 2007) (to estimate its loss of productivity, the plaintiff contractor relied on the Business Roundtable Report, which purports to show the reduction in productivity that results from long-term scheduled overtime on construction projects. The Report includes examples that calculate the productivity rate that results from working a 50-hour week vs. a 40-hour week, as well as the productivity rate that results from working a 60-hour week vs. a 40-hour week, both as a percentage of productivity that results from working a 40-hour week. The expert in this case "interpolated" between the 50-hour and 60-hour productivity figures to arrive at an estimated productivity rate that results from working a 58-hour week vs. a 50-hour work week; the court found no errors in the expert's interpolation of the data in the Business Roundtable Report to apply those data to the contractor's actual circumstances, and the court thus awarded the contractor its projected lost productivity of labor of $12,561.23).

Page 49, add after first full paragraph:

The premium cost of overtime is a well-recognized element of recovery in claims for acceleration. An overtime premium claim normally can be precisely calculated, since the additional costs will be well documented within a contractor's payroll and cost accounting. Despite the normal ease in determining the precise amount of additional costs resulting from the premium costs of overtime, contractors sometimes fail to properly present their damages. In *John F. Harkins*

Co., Inc. v. School District of Philadelphia,[37.1] the contractor used a total cost method to calculate overtime costs by simply comparing its bid estimate for labor costs with actual labor costs. The court rejected this technique for obvious reasons, since any additional labor costs resulting from working additional hours or paying higher wage rates or other factors, in addition to the premium costs of overtime, would be captured. In *J&K Plumbing and Heating Co., Inc. v. State of N.Y.,*[37.2] a contractor's use of a percentage of total labor costs to calculate overtime premium expenses was rejected on the grounds that there was no effort to segregate labor costs incurred during the period of accelerated performance from those incurred during the non-accelerated period. Further, the percentage used by the contractor did not correspond to the contractor's legal obligations for the payment of overtime.

[B] Disruption

Page 51, add at end of subsection:

In *Sherman R. Smoot Co. of Ohio v. Ohio Department of Administrative Services,*[42.1] the prime contractor for masonry work was awarded damages for the productivity losses that were caused by disruption resulting from delays by the prior contractor. Smoot was the contractor for the general trades contract for Phase 3 of a correctional facility project for the state of Ohio. Smoot was later awarded a contract for the general trades work on Phase 4, a separate area of the project. The prime contractor for heating and cooling work on Phase 3 was Power City Plumbing and Heating, and much of Power City's work was precedent to Smoot's masonry work. Because Power City did not complete its work in accordance with the project's schedule, Smoot's masonry crews were unable to complete the work as planned and often were unable to complete tasks that they had started. As a result, Smoot was often forced to move crews between tasks prior to finishing a task. This reduced labor efficiency and caused Smoot to increase the ratio of mason helpers to masons to maintain the schedule. Smoot filed a claim for both increased mason costs and increased cost of mason helpers, and the court held that Smoot was entitled to recover all such costs. Smoot also had pursued claims for impacts on the adjoining contract, Phase 4, as a result of the problem created in Phase 3 by Power City. Smoot's claims for increased labor costs on Phase 4 were denied on the basis that such costs could not be foreseeable at the time Phase 3 was entered into because Phase 4 was bid and awarded months after Phase 3.

[37.1] 460 A.2d 260 (Pa. Super. 1983).

[37.2] 652 N.Y.S.2d 369 (App. Div. 1997).

[42.1] 136 Ohio App. 3d 166, 736 N.E.2d 69 (2000).

In *Bell BCI Co. v. United States*,[42.2] the Federal Circuit Court of Appeals held that the following language in a number of modifications executed by the parties effected an accord and satisfaction of the contractor's cumulative impact claims relating to those modifications:

> The modification agreed to herein is a fair and equitable adjustment for the Contractor's direct and indirect costs. This modification provides full compensation for the changed work, including both Contract cost and Contract time. The Contractor hereby releases the Government from any and all liability under the Contract for further equitable adjustment attributable to the Modification.

The Circuit Court reversed the Federal Court of Claims' award of disruption and delay damages to the contractor, and remanded for a determination of which delays and disruptions, if any, were attributable to modifications that did not include the release language of Modification 93.

In a strong dissenting opinion in the *Bell BCI* case, Circuit Judge Newman emphasized that Modification 93, which added an entire floor to the five-story project and which was the first modification that contained this release language, was executed at a time when the government represented that very few further changes would be made. However, 279 additional Extra Work Orders and 113 additional formal Modifications followed Modification 93, causing cumulative disruptions and delays that could not have been anticipated at the time of execution of Modification 93, and therefore could not be released by the terms of that modification.

[C] Weather

Page 52, add at end of note 44:

See also, e.g., GASA, Inc. v. United States, 79 Fed. Cl. 325 (2007) (although the contractor contended that the Army Corps of Engineers' delays caused it to have to work during January through April when it was faced with inclement winter weather, resulting in increased costs, the plain language of the contract indicated that the project could be affected by bad weather and that the length of the time for contract completion would be extended for any time exceeding the contract estimates; the contractor received a time extension for adverse weather delays, and the contract does not allow for any additional compensation).

[42.2] 81 Fed. Cl. 617 (2008), *aff'd in part, vacated in part, remanded*, 570 F.3d 1337 (Fed. Cir. June 25, 2009), *reh'g and reh'g en banc denied* (Oct. 9, 2009), *on remand*, 72 Fed. Cl. 164 (Feb. 24, 2010).

Page 52, replace note 45 in its entirety with:

[45] Anderson Dev. Corp. v. Coastal States Crude Gathering Co., 543 S.W.2d 402 (Tex. App. 1976), *writ refused n.r.e.* (1977). *Cf.* Ronald Adams Contractor, Inc. v. City of New Orleans, 777 So. 2d 649 (La. Ct. App. 2000), *reh'g denied* (2001) (contractor was delayed in completing its project as a result of abnormal weather conditions, including a hurricane, and it contended that had the defendant issued its notice to proceed earlier, the work would have been completed before the onset of the abnormal weather conditions; recovery was denied because there was no evidence that the delay in issuing the notice to proceed was due to an action or a failure to act on the owner's part; rather, the delay was caused by another city's failure to allow the contractor to use its roads; also, the severe abnormal weather that occurred in this case was not anticipated or expected by any of the parties; further, the special provisions section of the contract clearly provided that time extensions granted for abnormal weather were not compensable); Fraser Constr. Co. v. United States, 57 Fed. Cl. 56 (2003) (contractor was dredging a section of river in Minnesota when high water overwhelmed the contractor's diversion system and forced a suspension of operations; the Army Corps of Engineers refused to grant the requested extension of time, and the contractor was forced to accelerate its performance to complete the work on time; the court denied the contractor's claim for acceleration costs, finding that the peak flow that overwhelmed the diversion system could be expected once every five years (based upon hydrological records), which "falls well within the two- to ten-year event frequency range that experts for both sides testified represents the industry standard for anticipating risk"; since the peak flow was not unforeseeable, the resulting delay was not excusable, the contractor had not been entitled to a time extension, and the Corps therefore did not constructively accelerate when it insisted on project completion within the original contract deadline); George Sollitt Constr. Co. v. United States, 64 Fed. Cl. 229 (Ct. Cl. 2005) (court acknowledged that contractors may sometimes recover for compensable delays when government-caused unreasonable delays push construction activities into the winter months, when these activities were originally scheduled for a different time of year; further, apportionment of additional costs incurred by working in the winter months, when there have been concurrent delays caused by government and contractor, is appropriate, and may be achieved by awarding a proportion of winter-related costs based on a mathematical formula derived from the amount of delay attributable to each party).

Page 52, add at end of note 46:

See also Baldi Bros. Constructors v. United States, 50 Fed. Cl. 74 (Ct. Cl. 2001) (general rule is that the risk of severe weather in a particular region is not shifted to the government via a Differing Site Conditions clause; however, when severe weather interacting with an undisclosed property of the construction site delays construction, the government may be held responsible).

Page 53, add new paragraph at end of subsection:

In *Bechtel Power Corp. v. Athens Generating Co., L.P.*,[51.1] a three-member arbitration panel issued a detailed decision discussing the calculation of labor productivity losses due to weather conditions. In that case, Athens issued a $522 million EPC contract to Bechtel in March 2001 to design and build a power plant in Athens, New York, including three gas turbines. The contract substantial completion date was August 12, 2003, but the project suffered weather delays and significant changes required due to the untested nature of the Siemens gas turbines. Bechtel asserted claims against Athens for more than $94 million, including several loss of productivity claims related to adverse weather conditions. Bechtel sought to recover for 77,196 hours of lost labor productivity resulting from adverse weather from December 2002 through March 2003 under the contract's force majeure provision, which entitled Bechtel to both a time extension and compensation for "inclement weather conditions atypical for the location and/or season." The arbitration panel found that the winter weather conditions during that season were atypical in the amount of snowfall, the number of snowfalls exceeding nine inches (the average number of such snowfalls was 1.4, and the actual number was 3), the average low temperature, and the number of days of below-average temperature. Bechtel claimed 28,414 hours of lost labor productivity incurred over the five days of the three major snowstorms. The panel found that Bechtel suffered a loss of productivity for only three days with an average loss of 50 percent efficiency. However, since the average number of snowfalls was 1.4, Bechtel had to provide a credit to Athens for those days, resulting in a total loss of productivity of 5,993 for the three major snowstorms. Bechtel also sought to recover for a loss of efficiency for the entire period from December 2002 through March 2003 due to the combination of cold weather and snow on the ground, claiming 23,536 hours for "loss of efficiency," 17,645 hours for "rewarming," and 4,901 hours for increased travel time. The panel found that rewarming time was subsumed in the loss of efficiency claim, based upon the NECA study relied on by Bechtel that noted that rewarming time was included within the time assumed to be affected by lack of productivity. As to the increased travel time, the panel found there was insufficient evidence to establish that increased travel time is not also subsumed within the loss of efficiency claim. Thus, the additional hours for rewarming and travel time were disallowed. The loss of efficiency claim of 23,536 hours was reduced to 15,404 hours, based upon the following factors: (1) the evidence established that the cold weather impacted only fine motor skills, yet Bechtel included hours spent performing tasks that consisted of gross motor skills; and (2) Bechtel included all hours spent by persons working inside the unheated turbine building, but it was

[51.1] Arbitration Case No. 6085-08 (Aug. 17, 2009) (can be accessed at constructionclaims.com).

Bechtel's decision not to heat the building. The final number of hours allowed for Bechtel's loss of efficiency claim was based on the testimony of Athens' two experts, including the author of this treatise, who testified that 15,404 hours were an appropriate calculation of the Bechtel's loss of efficiency based upon the hours worked. The panel awarded Bechtel approximately $1 million for this loss of efficiency.

[E] Change in Sequence

Page 54, change cite for Anderson Dev. Corp. in note 56 to:

543 S.W.2d 402 (Tex. App. 1976), *writ refused n.r.e.* (1977).

Page 54, add at end of note 57:

See also James Corp. v. North Allegheny Sch. Dist., 938 A.2d 474 (Pa. Commw. Nov. 30, 2007), *reargument denied* (Jan 30, 2008) (acceleration of the schedule caused by the owner's delays and its refusal to grant time extensions resulted in the contractor's having to perform work out of sequence, which caused inefficient use of labor); Appeal of Webb Elec. Co. of Florida, Inc., ASBCA No. 54293, 2007 WL 4179156 (Nov. 6, 2007), *aff'd sub nom.* Webb Elec. Co. of Florida, Inc. v. Griffin, 299 Fed. Appx. 958 (Fed. Cir. Nov. 10, 2008) (contractor was entitled to recover inefficiency costs resulting from the government's requirement during performance that the contractor install the transformers sequentially, rather than simultaneously as the contractor had planned; the contract's Suspension of Work clause required an adjustment in the contract price if the performance of "all or any part of the work is, for an unreasonable period of time, suspended, delayed, or interrupted . . ." by the government; the court found that the government constructively partially suspended the contractor's work for a total of 40 days, and remanded for a determination of the increased performance costs attributable to that suspension); In re Redondo Constr. Corp., 411 B.R. 89 (Bankr. D.P.R. Aug. 31, 2009), *amended in part on other grounds,* 424 B.R. 29 (Bankr. D.P.R. Feb. 11, 2010), *stay pending appeal granted*, 2010 WL 1286849 (Bankr. D.P.R. Mar. 30, 2010) (plaintiff contractor was entitled to be compensated more than $1.7 million for inefficiency, caused by "numerous changes of sequence in the execution of the work all over the seven kilometers of the project, causing inefficiency throughout the time of the project, due to circumstances that could not be foreseen, among others, different site conditions," numerous change orders and extra work orders resulting from deficient drawings, problems with utilities, and the owner's delays in solving the problems; the degree of changes resulted in a different concept from what the contract originally intended, which affected the sequence of the work, causing inefficiency). *Cf.* Acme Contracting, Ltd. v. TolTest, Inc., 2008 WL 1990780 (E.D. Mich. May 05, 2008), *aff'd in part, rev'd in part*, 2010 WL 1140997 (6th Cir. (Mich.) Mar. 24, 2010) (contractor was properly awarded "delay" damages calculated based upon additional costs of being on the job when no work was being performed, where the delay was comprised of both down time and work inefficiencies; evidence established the contractor was required to perform certain work out of sequence and to change the methods it employed to perform its work; the court states that other courts "have recognized that delay may also occur through lost efficiency, such as having to perform work out of sequence or to perform work in ways that use workers inefficiently).

[F] Trade Stacking

Page 55, add at end of note 65:

See also P.J. Dick, Inc., VABCA No. 5597, 01-2 BCA ¶ 31,647 (2001), *aff'd in part, rev'd in part, vacated in part, and remanded*, P.J. Dick, Inc., v. Principi, 324 F.3d 1364 (Fed. Cir. Apr. 7, 2003) (government's acceleration of the work resulted in the contractor directing a subcontractor to work on floors concurrently in an attempt to make up the time the government had delayed completion; as a result, the subcontractor was forced to assign multiple crews on each floor that were required to perform all aspects of branch circuit installation, causing labor inefficiencies because it made the subcontractor's crew training efforts more difficult and prevented it from realizing the learning curve benefits of sequential circuit installation by task-dedicated crews; also, having its crews working on all floors concurrently affected the ability of the subcontractor to properly supervise the work, a factor that also contributed to labor inefficiency); In re Electric Mach. Enters., Inc., 416 B.R. 801 (Bankr. M.D. Fla. Aug. 28, 2009) (the evidence clearly established that the plaintiff, an electrical subcontractor, was severely impacted and damaged by the trade stacking that resulted from the lack of coordination of the trade contractors; trade stacking on the Project resulted because the time sequences for work were compressed without regard to the inability of trade contractors to simultaneously perform necessarily sequential work; the plaintiff was often unable to proceed because it was blocked by predecessor trade contractors, such as the mechanical, dry wall, roofing, and painting subcontractors); Mecca Constr. Corp. v. All Interiors, Inc., 2009 WL 3416426 (Mass. Super. Ct. Oct. 16, 2009) (damages allegedly caused a subcontractor as a result of hindrances caused by the general contractor's lack of coordination of various subtrades were recoverable and were not barred by the "no damages for delay" clause of the contract, which prohibited "money damages or additional compensation for delay, no matter how caused"; the lack of coordination allegedly caused the subcontractor's materials to be crushed, and the contractor allowed other subcontractors to complete their work before the subcontractor, which caused hindrance to the subcontractor's work, and prevented the subcontractor from completing the job "on budget").

[G] Restricted Site Access

Page 56, add at end of note 68:

See also, e.g., DuBaldo Elec., LC v. Montagno Constr., Inc., 119 Conn. App. 423, 988 A.2d 351 (Feb, 23, 2010) (appellate court upheld award of inefficiency damages of 20% to an electrical contractor whose work was disrupted by the store owner fixturing while the subcontractor was performing its work; the testimony of the subcontractor and two other subcontractors it hired to accelerate the work that they suffered a 30%-50% loss of productivity as a result of several hundred people stocking the store while electrical work was ongoing was sufficient for the court to calculate the lost efficiency; court did not address the contractor's claim that the award was improper because it was not based on the measured mile approach, because the contractor did not raise that argument in the trial court).

Page 56, add at end of subsection:

A highway contractor recovered for lost productivity due to the state department of transportation's refusal to allow overnight lane closures in *State of Texas v. Mid-South Pavers*.[71.1] In that case, the contract did not specifically allow or prohibit overnight lane closures, but certain contract language referenced the re-opening of lanes and stated that the work would be accomplished with no more than one lane closure on each lane at the same time. When the contractor commenced work, the Texas Department of Transportation refused to allow any overnight lane closure, contending that the contract did not permit such closure. The contractor expended additional time each day setting up traffic control and equipment, resulting in a loss of efficiency. An administrative law judge determined that the Texas DOT committed error by refusing to extend the length of the project to accommodate the change in work conditions, and recommended an award of $610,000. The executive director of the Texas DOT reviewed the recommendation, as permitted by statute, and reduced the award by 50 percent based on his determination that the contractor contributed to the delay by failing to seek clarification regarding overnight lane closures at the pre-construction conference. The trial court reversed the executive director's change in the

[71.1] 246 S.W.3d 711 (Tex. Ct. App. Dec. 19, 2007), *reh'g overruled* (Feb. 21, 2008), *review denied* (Sept. 26, 2008).

administrative law judges findings, since there was no evidence regarding the 50 percent reduction, and remanded for further proceedings on this issue of operational delays.

Page 58, add new subsection:

[J] Acceleration

Acceleration of a construction project occurs when the schedule under which the work is performed for all or a portion of the project is shorter than that which would be required to complete the work using normal sequences of construction on a normal schedule. Projects can be bid and performed on accelerated schedules. Claims for damages as a result of acceleration arise when a contractor is directed or otherwise required to accelerate all or a portion of the work. Simply put, acceleration claims arise when a contractor is requested to perform its work in a shorter time than it believes it should be allowed under the terms and conditions of the contract. Acceleration can either occur expressly when the contractor is directed to accelerate the work or constructively when it believes it is accelerated by actions of the owner. Express acceleration often occurs when the contractor is behind schedule as a result of its own actions or the owner believes it to be behind schedule as a result of the contractor's own actions. Projects are also expressly accelerated as a result of an owner who, for its own reasons, wants or needs the project completed earlier than the contractor is entitled to complete it under the terms of the contract. Such acceleration may be the result of the need to recover time lost as a result of delays by third parties, late delivery of owner furnished material, late permits, design or late delivery of owner furnished material. Acceleration may also occur when additional work is added through contract changes but time extensions are not granted.

Acceleration can cause productivity losses and other types of labor overruns. The productivity losses may occur from working overtime, from working shifts, from compressing the work schedule which can lead to trade stacking, can come from having larger crews. Cost increases related to labor can come from the premium cost of the overtime even when there are no productivity losses. The types of additional costs that can occur as a result of acceleration are not only productivity losses. Accelerated schedules require accelerated support services. There may be a need for additional supervision and additional support, such as cleanup, scaffolding, additional equipment operators and additional field engineers, surveyors and other types of support services. The failure to either grant a time extension or failing to grant such an extension in a timely manner may result in a contractor claiming it is constructively accelerated. The requirements for a constructive acceleration claim were set forth in *In re Commercial Contractors Equipment, Inc.*,[73.1] wherein it states:

Acceleration Claim

> Government liability for acceleration of work requires proof by preponderant evidence of traditional elements of acceleration. First there must be excusable delay. Second, the contractor must give notice of excusable delay and specifically request a time extension accompanied by sufficient supporting information to allow the Government to make a reasonable determination concerning how to proceed. Third, the Government must fail or refuse to grant the requested time extension within a reasonable time. Fourth, the Government must order the contractor to accelerate the work, either expressly or by implication, without regard to excusable delay. The contractor must give notice to the CO that the alleged order to accelerate constitutes a constructive change so that the CO is afforded the opportunity to assess the circumstances and take appropriate action to avoid the added costs of the acceleration order. Fifth, the contractor must actually undertake reasonable efforts to accelerate and incur added costs. *Fermont Division, Dynamics Corp. of Am.*, ASBCA No. 15806, 75-1 BCA ¶ 11,139 at 52,999-53,000, *aff'd*, 216 Ct. Cl. 448 (1978). *See The Sherman R. Smoot Corp.*, ASBCA Nos. 52173, *et al.*, 03-1 BCA ¶¶ 32,212 at 159,319 *citing Norair Engineering Eng'g Corp. v. U.S.*, 666 F.2d 546, 548-49, n.5 (Ct. Cl. 1981) (denial of a specific request for an excused delay is "in effect equivalent to the requirement of an order to accelerate").

Acceleration can be a cause of lost labor productivity. To recover for labor productivity losses due to alleged acceleration, it is first necessary to prove that the acceleration occurred. In the case of constructive acceleration—that is, acceleration that results not from an express acceleration directive but from actions that constitute such a directive—it is even more important to show that actions by the owner constituted constructive acceleration. In *Appeal of Phillips Nat'l, Inc.*,[73.2] a contractor's claim for constructive acceleration was denied because it failed to meet the standards for showing constructive acceleration. In *Phillips*, because the contractor failed to prove it encountered excusable delay or had been pressured into overcoming that excusable delay, it could not prove constructive acceleration and therefore the Board did not need to consider whether the acceleration had caused labor productivity losses. In *Fraser Constr. Co. v. United States*,[73.3] the court found that a letter from the government to a contractor urging adherence to the schedule was not enough to be constructive acceleration.

[73.1] ASBCA No. 52932, 2003 WL 22232953 (Sept. 17, 2003).

[73.2] ASBCA No. 53241 (Mar. 16, 2004).

[73.3] 384 F.3d 1354 (Fed. Cir. Sept. 27, 2004).

It should be noted that a contractor need not prove that the owner was responsible for a delay to recover damages for loss of productivity. An equitable adjustment may also be awarded to cover increased costs that are the direct and necessary result of " 'a change or changed conditions, where the condition or the change directly leads to disruption, extra work, or new procedures.' "[73.4] In the *Sauer* case, because the Armed Services Board of Contract Appeals applied the wrong legal standard—the Board required proof of government-caused delay—the court remanded for a determination as to whether the contractor would be entitled to an equitable adjustment due to disruption.

On remand, the Board in *Sauer* emphasized that the contractor has the burden of proving that the change that allegedly caused the disruption in its schedule (in this case, the government's change in another contractor's schedule allegedly disrupted the claimant contractor's schedule) caused the loss of productivity, i.e., proof that the change proximately caused the claimed inefficiency. The evidence offered by the contractor in this case, however, did not satisfy that burden. The Board noted that "the mere expression of an estimate as to the amount of productivity loss by an expert witness with nothing to support it will not establish the fundamental fact of resultant injury nor provide a sufficient basis for making a reasonably correct approximation of damages." The court also noted that the contractor's bid indicated that it anticipated no impact on its work from the presence of other contractors.[73.5]

In *Appeals of Fox Construction Inc.*,[73.6] the contractor contended that the Navy delayed the contractor's work through a 30-day delay in the required partnering and pre-construction meetings, delays in submittal approvals and responses to RFIs, and changes in the work. In addition to delay damages, the contractor sought to recover lost productivity damages based upon the extended duration of the work. The contractor calculated its lost productivity by taking the number of days it contended it was delayed divided by the total number of days it was on the project, multiplied by its total labor costs on the project. Based upon the uncontroverted CPM analysis conducted by the Navy's expert, none of the alleged delays impacted the critical path of the contractor's work. Since the contractor tied its loss of productivity claim to the number of days it was allegedly delayed by the Navy, the contractor's failure to prove that the Navy was responsible for any of the delays was fatal to its lost productivity claim.

In *Murdock & Sons Constr., Inc. v. Goheen Gen. Constr., Inc.*,[73.7] a masonry subcontractor was denied recovery for alleged acceleration damages on the basis

---

[73.4] Sauer Inc. v. Danzig, 224 F.3d 1340 (Fed. Cir. 2000) (*quoting* Elec. & Missile Facilities, Inc. v. United States, 189 Ct. Cl. 237, 416 F.2d 1345, 1359-1361 (1969).

[73.5] In re Sauer, Inc., ASBCA No. 39605, 01-2 BCA ¶ 31,525 (2001). *But see* Appeal of Commercial Contractors Equip., Inc., ASBCA No. 52932 (2003) (where the contractor had not requested an extension of time due to alleged differing site conditions encountered in excavating a streambed, the contractor could not pursue a claim for acceleration costs).

[73.6] ASBCA No. 55266, 2008 WL 698478 (Mar. 5, 2008).

[73.7] 461 F.3d 837 (7th Cir. (Ind.) Aug. 17, 2006).

that no excusable delay existed. Murdock, the subcontractor was claiming that it was entitled to a time extension because its employees were working slower to maximize their earnings. The court denied this claim on the basis that there was no evidence of a labor controversy between the subcontractor and its employees and that under the subcontract for the subcontractor to receive a time extension there had to be a labor dispute.

The court distinguished between acceleration claims and change order requests in *Steel Service Corp. v. Board of County Commissioners of Hamilton County, Ohio.*[73.8] The County directed Steel Service to accelerate the work due to delays for which neither party assumed responsibility. Steel Service submitted a "Claim for Additional Costs" incurred in connection with the acceleration in the amount of $3.2 million, and the parties entered into Change Order #1 whereby the County agreed to make a provisional payment of $700,000 pending determination of Steel Service's claim. During performance of the work, numerous construction change directives were issued by the County, and the parties negotiated Change Orders #2-#8 resolving some of the change directives. After completion of the work, the parties entered into mediation in an attempt to resolve the remaining change directives and Steel Service's acceleration claim. Change Order #9 was executed during the mediation, specifically resolving all claims, demands and causes of action "arising out of or relating to the Changes," with the exception of three listed construction change proposals. Further mediation was unsuccessful, and Steel Service filed an action against the County for breach of contract. The County moved for summary judgment, contending that Change Order #9 constituted a full and final waiver and settlement of Steel Services' acceleration claim. The trial court granted summary judgment, and the Sixth Circuit reversed, holding that Change Order #9 settled only proposals for change orders, which were governed by Article 7 of the standard AIA contract, whereas Steel Service's demand for compensation based upon acceleration was specifically identified as a "Claim" and submitted under Article 4 of the contract. The court found that the acceleration "claim" was not a construction change proposal, either in form or substance, and was therefore not settled or waived in Change Order #9.

§ 2.08 EFFECT OF CHANGES ON LABOR PRODUCTIVITY

Page 63, add at end of section:

In *Hensel Phelps Construction Co. v. General Services Administration,*[88.1] the contractor was awarded $1,518,382 for lost labor productivity on the unchanged work as a result of changed work. The cost of the lost labor impact was

[73.8] 258 Fed. Appx. 825, 2007 WL 4561497 (6th Cir. (Ohio) Dec. 27, 2007).

[88.1] GSBCA No. 14744 (Jan. 11, 2001), *aff'd sub nom.* Perry v. Hensel Phelps Constr. Co., 36 Fed. Appx. 649, 2002 WL 1008622 (2002),

calculated using the MCAA Estimating Manual and various factors from that manual, combined with extensive review of the project requirements by an independent consultant.

§ 2.09 CALCULATING PRODUCTIVITY LOSS

[A] Measured Mile Calculations

Page 64, add at end of note 89:

See also P.J. Dick Inc., VABCA No. 5597, 01-2 BCA ¶ 31,647 (2001), *aff'd in part, rev'd in part, vacated in part, and remanded*, P.J. Dick, Inc. v. Principi, 2003 WL 1793206 (Fed. Cir., Apr. 7, 2003) (use of a "measured mile" analysis developed by a qualified expert is recognized as the most reliable, though not exact, methodology to quantify labor inefficiency; a "measured mile" analysis compares the actual labor costs or labor productivity of performing work during a time period in which the work was not affected by the actions causing labor inefficiency to the actual labor costs or actual productivity rate for performing work during a period that was affected; this analysis generally presumes that the labor costs or productivity rates being compared are for the same work and, ideally, results in a standard (the actual, unaffected productivity of a contractor's labor) against which the effect of the government-caused change to working conditions can be measured); In re W.G. Yates & Sons Constr. Co., ASBCA No. 49398, 01-2 BCA ¶ 31,428 (2001) (for labor inefficiency claims, a "good period vs. bad period" analysis, comparing the cost of performing work during periods both affected and unaffected by disrupted events, "is a well established method of proving damages"; in the absence of a "cogent argument" by the government why the contractor's use of the measured mile methodology was invalid, the Board accepted the contractor's use of this methodology as an acceptable vehicle for determining incurred labor inefficiency costs due to the government's defective specification). *Cf.* Southern Comfort Builders, Inc. v. United States, 67 Fed. Cl. 124 (July 29, 2005) (the contractor's expert's measured mile calculation was deficient in that it did not adequately represent a comparison between the contractor's unaffected work with its affected work; instead, the contractor's calculation compared its work with the work performed by another contractor; although the two companies conducted similar work, even the contractor's own expert indicated that, under a measured mile analysis, comparing two separate companies is fundamentally flawed; also, because the contractor did not provide a basis of its work unaffected by government actions, the court could not properly conclude what the contractor's unaffected work would have been; another flaw in the contractor's measured mile analysis was that in its calculations, plaintiff's final average labor costs under the measured mile analysis was greater than the total cost calculations; this presented a fundamental problem because, as the contractor's expert admitted, a total cost analysis represents the maximum amount a contractor could possibly receive; therefore, it was unreasonable for the contractor's measured mile calculations to be higher than its total cost calculation, which perhaps resulted from comparing the contractor's costs with a different contractor's costs); Daewoo Eng'g & Constr. Co., Ltd. v. United States, 73 Fed. Cl. 547 (2006), *aff'd on other grounds*, 557 F.3d 1332 (Fed. Cir. Feb. 20, 2009), *cert. denied*, 130 S. Ct. 490 (Nov. 2, 2009) (a measured mile approach to damages is a form of total cost calculations that requires subjective judgment calls by the expert, who estimates damages by comparing periods of production that are unaffected by the contractor's alleged government-caused delay, with periods during which delays affected its production adversely; in this case, rain days were used to determine government-caused delay, and the experts merely compared periods affected by rain delay with periods unaffected and presumably efficient, and developed an inefficiency factor; they applied this factor to the project and applied a cost of delay to calculate total costs through completion of the contract; because cross examination showed that the expert's choices of productive and non-productive periods were arbitrary at best, the measured mile approach was not appropriate in this case); James Corp. v. North Allegheny Sch. Dist., 938 A.2d 474 (Pa. Commw. Nov. 30, 2007), *reargument denied* (Jan. 30, 2008) (as a matter of first impression, the court held that a measured mile analysis is a permissible means of determining damages for acceleration, noting that the measured mile approach is the preferred method of computing damages for loss of productivity); Appeal of Bay West, Inc., ASBCA No. 54166, 2007 WL 1342482 (Apr. 25, 2007) (court adopts a measured mile analysis to calculate lost dredging productivity resulting from differing site conditions; the analysis compared a production period that was impacted by the unanticipated stiff clay with a production period that was not impacted; however, certain adjustments to the calculation needed to be made to account for learning curve inefficiencies that extended beyond the normal learning curve period for a project of this type, and to reflect that soft and medium stiff clay should have been anticipated based upon the contract documents).

Page 66, add at end of note 96:

See also P.J. Dick Inc., VABCA No. 5597, 01-2 BCA ¶ 31,647 (2001), *aff'd in part, rev'd in part, vacated in part, and remanded*, P.J. Dick, Inc. v. Principi, 324 F.3d 1364 (Fed. Cir. 2003) (agreeing with the GSA Board of Contract Appeals in *Clark Concrete Contractors, Inc.*, the Board held that a measured mile analysis may be applied even when the work being compared during different time periods is not identical; in this case, the contractor compared the productivity of different crews performing different work, but, on balance, the Board found that the expert's approach to quantification of the government-caused productivity loss was reasonable and valid); Appeal of T & W Edmier Corp., ASBCA No. 53347 (2003) (contractor excavating a flood control reservoir encountered lead contamination in the soil; government suspended work while it devised a remediation plan, and the contractor sought to recover compensation for the impact of the remediation efforts on equipment productivity; board awarded the contractor lost productivity damages based upon the difference between the idle equipment hours rate before the lead contamination was discovered and the idle equipment hours rate after work resumed); Safeco Ins. Co. of Am. v. County of San Bernardino, 347 Fed. Appx. 315, 2009 WL 3157698 (9th Cir. (Cal.) Oct. 1, 2009) (the district court did not commit clear error by accepting an expert's measured-mile analysis and method of identifying impacted and unimpacted days; although the defendant contended that the expert's analysis might have excluded some low-productivity unimpacted days or wrongly attributed decline in production to the fault of the defendant, "once the cause and existence of damages have been so established, recovery will not be denied because the damages are difficult of ascertainment. Liability cannot be evaded because damages cannot be measured with exactness").

Page 66, add at end of subsection [A]:

A measured mile analysis that used labor hours per ton of steel erected prior to design changes with the labor hours per ton of steel erected after the design changes was adopted by the Armed Services Board of Contract Appeals in *Appeal of WG Yates & Sons Construction Co.*[97.1] In this matter, Yates was constructing an aircraft hangar facility to be used by the National Guard in Jackson, Mississippi. After a significant amount of work had been performed, a structural steel truss failed. This caused the government to reexamine the design and determine that there was insufficient splicing in the trusses. A contract modification was issued to Yates that required stiffener bars to be welded to the gusset plates. However, Yates could not agree with the government on a price adjustment for the modification. The government asserted that this additional work was merely value enhancement to the project and not the result of a defective design. Yates asserted that the welding of the stiffener bars disrupted the progress of the steel erection, reducing labor productivity and resulting in increased labor costs in the erection. Yates computed the added erection costs by calculating the labor hours per ton of steel erected for steel work performed prior to the design change with the labor hours per ton of steel erected after the design change. Based upon this analysis, Yates determined it had incurred 7,280 hours of lost productivity as a result of the change. The Board found Yates's methodology persuasive and not refuted by the government. Yates was awarded $161,064 of increased labor costs as a result of the reduced labor productivity.

In *P.W. Construction, Inc. v. United States*,[97.2] the contractor encountered unanticipated subsurface conditions during installation of natural gas lines and pressure stations, and claimed lost labor productivity. The contractor utilized a

[97.1] ASBCA No. 49399 (May 18, 2001).

[97.2] 53 Fed. Appx. 555 (Fed. Cir. 2002) (not selected for publication).

measured mile approach, quantifying its progress and productivity prior to encountering the obstructions and after the disruption, and attributing the increased labor hours during the post-disruption period to the obstructions. The Board accepted the calculation but found that the government was only responsible for 48 percent of the increased labor hours, awarding the contractor 48 percent of the total increased hours during the post-disruption period. The court of appeals reversed, finding that the measured mile calculation was not properly applied because the work before and after the obstructions were encountered was not similar. The pre-obstruction work involved very little trench work, and a small amount of welding that took more than two hours per weld. In contrast, the post-obstruction work involved a great deal of trenching, and a large amount of welding that took only a few minutes per weld. The court vacated the damage award, holding that the rates utilized had to account for the differences in welding and trenching.

A subcontractor in *Bell BCI Co. v. United States*[97.3] successfully utilized a measured mile approach to recover against the owner for productivity losses incurred as a result of extensive changes to the project. The sheet metal subcontractor on the project, Stromberg, compared its productivity rate of 11.23 pounds of duct installed per hour at the beginning of the project to its productivity rate of 5.95 pounds per hour later in the project after the owner began issuing major changes to the duct work. Using the production rate of 11.23 pounds per hour, Stromberg calculated that it should have taken 20,694 hours to perform the changed work. At the production rate actually experienced, 5.95 pounds per hour, Stromberg expended 39,072 hours to complete the change work, reflecting 18,377 inefficient hours. Stromberg applied its average hourly rate of $44.19, including burden and profit, to the total number of inefficient hours to arrive at its claimed inefficiency costs of $812,092. The Federal Court of Claims sustained Stromberg's claim, stating that the measured mile approach used by Stromberg was an accepted method to prove a cumulative impact claim. The Federal Circuit Court of Appeals affirmed.

A measured mile approach to calculating disruption-related damages was approved in *Wayne Knorr, Inc. v. Pennsylvania Dept. of Transportation.*[97.4] The project owner, PennDOT, was found to have caused disruption to the contractor, Knorr, on a roadway construction project as a result of five categories of active interference: (1) missing and incorrect grades and elevations in the plans; (2) PennDOT's delay in providing missing grades and elevations around the box culvert; (3) PennDOT's delay in addressing slope failures encountered by Knorr; (4) changes to the method of widening the roadway shoulder; and (5) delay in confirming certain changes in construction methodology. The Board also determined that Knorr caused disruption to its own work through "self-inflicted"

[97.3] 81 Fed. Cl. 617 (2008), *aff'd in relevant part, vacated in part, remanded*, 570 F.3d 1337 (Fed. Cir. June 25, 2009), *reh'g and reh'g en banc denied* (Oct. 9, 2009), *on remand*, 72 Fed. Cl. 164 (Feb. 24, 2010).

[97.4] 973 A.2d 1061 (Pa. Commw. May 14, 2009).

problems, including Knorr's own mistakes in construction of the roadway and adjacent structures, ongoing problems with equipment breakdown, flawed work procedures, multiple changes in supervisor and foremen, and work being redone or corrected. The Board determined that PennDOT was responsible for five-sixths (83%) of the disruption to the paving and sub-base work. To calculate the inefficiencies in Knorr's paving and sub-base work that resulted from the disruption, Knorr's expert compared an impacted period to performance when PennDOT's actions substantially disrupted Knorr's work with an unimpacted period when the problems had been substantially resolved. The expert compared Knorr's sub-base and paving work in the two periods based on the cost per square yard of paving material placed and the cost per ton of paving material placed, which resulted in a total inefficiency claim of $232,306, plus markup, for total inefficiency damages of $284,276. The Board adjusted the total amount of inefficiency losses to $280,075 based upon a revised markup. The Board determined that PennDOT was responsible for 83 percent of the loss of efficiency suffered by Knorr, and awarded Knorr $232,462. The Board's decision on this issue was upheld on appeal.

In *Safeco Insurance Co. of America v. County of San Bernardino,*[97.5] the appellate court upheld an award of lost productivity damages to the contractor based upon a measured mile analysis, even though the amount may not have been "exact." The County challenged the award by contending that the expert's measured mile analysis might have excluded some low-productivity unimpacted days or wrongly attributed decline in production to the fault of the County. The appellate court noted that "liability cannot be evaded because damages cannot be measured with exactness." The appellate court noted the district court's finding that delays caused by the contractor were "insignificant" in light of the County's own delays. Since the contractor's surety "presented a reasonable estimate of lost-productivity damages," the County's argument that the damage amount is not exact is insufficient to establish clear error.

[B] Comparison with Similar Projects

Page 66, add at end of first paragraph of subsection:

For example, in *Bell BCI Co. v. United States,*[97.6] Bell was the contractor to construct a new laboratory on the National Institutes of Health in Bethesda, Maryland. The original contract price was $63 million, with a planned duration

[97.5] 347 Fed. Appx. 315, 2009 WL 3157698 (9th Cir. (Cal.) Oct. 1, 2009).

[97.6] 81 Fed. Cl. 617 (2008), *aff'd in part, vacated in relevant part, remanded,* 570 F.3d 1337 (Fed. Cir. June 25, 2009), *reh'g and reh'g en banc denied* (Oct. 9, 2009), *on remand,* 72 Fed. Cl. 164 (Feb. 24, 2010).

of 27 months. Nine months into construction, the NIH added a sixth floor to the building, and subsequently required massive design changes resulting in more than 730 extra work orders, which increased the contract price by 34 percent to $85 million, and added more than 19 months to the project duration. Bell asserted that the changes caused disruptions which resulted in a loss of labor productivity of more than $2 million. To calculate the cumulative effect of the changes, Bell's expert analyzed Bell's earned and unearned hours expended each week during the project. The court noted that it had been Bell's practice for many years to track productivity rates by recording the amount of units installed on a project each week, allowing Bell to compare the actual time to install units against its estimates for a given project. On this project, Bell completed a significant portion of the base contract work before most of the changes had been directed, and incurred a non-productive work rate of eight percent. Bell's expert attributed one-half of the non-productive hours to Bell for this period, and set Bell's reasonable productivity level at 104 percent of the originally planned productivity. The court found that Bell's original estimate for the project was reasonable, based on the fact that Bell was not the low bidder on the project. Bell's expert then compared actual hours incurred on the project against 104 percent of the originally planned hours to calculated unearned hours attributable to NIH changes, and determined that about 25 percent of Bell's total hours were attributable to labor productivity loss caused by changes. As such, 25 percent of the 320,703 total hours expended on the project, or 80,317 hours, were lost due to the impact of the NIH changes. Applying Bell's fully burdened average hourly rate of $33.50, the total labor productivity loss attributable to NIH changes was $2,690,649. The expert deducted $632,193 for hourly field supervision that was already included in Bell's claim for delay damages, for a total productivity claim of $2,058,456. The court found the expert's estimate to be reasonable "when considering the number of changes, the amount of replacement of previously completed work, and the overall deteriorated project environment, and sustained Bell's cumulative impact claim of just over $2 million. On appeal, the Federal Circuit Court reversed the award in favor of Bell on the cumulative impact claim, finding that Bell had waived cumulative impact claims as to certain modifications, and remanded to the Federal Court of Claims to determine which cumulative impacts, if any, are attributable to modifications that did not include the release language. It is important to note that the Circuit Court found no error in the lower court's methodology for calculating cumulative impact damages.

[C] Industry Standards

Page 68, add at end of subsection:

In *Hensel Phelps Construction Co. v. General Services Administration,*[104.1] the General Services Board of Contract Appeals held that the use of MCAA labor factors from the MCAA Estimating Manual was an appropriate method of measuring lost labor productivity. This matter involved construction of an office and laboratory for the National Oceanic and Atmospheric Administration (NOAA). During construction, NOAA directed the general contractor, Hensel Phelps, to have its mechanical contractor, Trautman and Shreve, Inc., install vibration isolation on a portion of the piping and plumbing in the project. This extra work caused the contract work to fall behind schedule, and NOAA then ordered Hensel Phelps to accelerate the work. After project completion, Hensel Phelps successfully pursued its claim that the extra work constituted a constructive change to the contract. Hensel Phelps and Trautman and Shreve pursued a separate claim for lost labor productivity on the unchanged portion of the work as a result of the extra work. The contractors calculated the lost labor productivity by having a consultant adjust the originally estimated labor hours using, as a starting point, the labor inefficiencies factors published in the MCAA estimating manual. The factors utilized included stacking of trades, reassignment of manpower, and dilution of supervision. The consultant did not merely take the factors and mechanically apply them. Instead, he conducted detailed analyses of the scope of work and the as-planned and as-built schedules and interviewed numerous personnel who had worked on the site. Using this extensive knowledge of the project requirements and methods of execution, the consultant then applied the factors based on his judgment. Based on this analysis, the Board awarded the contractor and its subcontractor more than $1.5 million for lost labor productivity.

The use of the MCAA labor factors to calculate labor inefficiencies was rejected in *Appeal of AEI Pacific, Inc.*[104.2] The contractor, AEI, sought recovery of more than $680,000 in lost productivity costs resulting from impacts to the work caused by deficiencies in the plans and specifications and changes to the work. AEI's expert utilized the MCAA labor factors, and assigned a percentage of loss to each factor he deemed existed on the project during each of the impacted weeks to arrive at a total percentage of loss for each week, multiplied that by the total labor hours worked during the week on both base contract and changed work, and multiplied the resulting total lost manhours by the composite wage rate. The court found that this methodology was unacceptable for a number of reasons: the expert had no apparent basis for the assignment of particular loss percentage to the various factors, and in many cases AEI's own witnesses

---

[104.1] GSBCA No. 14744 (Jan. 11, 2001), *aff'd sub nom.* Perry v. Hensel Phelps Constr. Co., 36 Fed. Appx. 649, 2002 WL 1008622 (2002).

[104.2] ASBCA No. 53806, 2008 WL 436928 (Feb. 8, 2008).

directly contradicted the expert's conclusions regarding the factors that actually impacted the project at various points in time; the expert applied the percentages for all MCAA factors to both base contract and change order work, whereas the MCAA Manual states that all except three of the factors should be applied to change order work only; the court noted with approval the testimony of the Corps' expert that the MCAA Manual is not intended to quantify damages, but is meant to assist in preparing original estimates and change orders, that the MCAA's percentages of loss are extremely generous, unsupported by studies of actual projects, and result in an inflated value of impact, and that a 2% inefficiency factor would be appropriate on this project rather than the 48% inefficiency rate that AEI claimed; the court held that AEI was entitled to recover 2% of its direct labor hours during the impacted period, or $24,570, for labor inefficiency.

[E] Total Labor Method

Page 70, add at end of note 116:

See also, e.g., City of Gillette v. Hladky Constr., Inc., 2008 WY 134, 196 P.3d 184 (Wyo. Nov. 14, 2008) (although use of the total cost method is disfavored, primarily because it attributes all responsibility to the owner without establishing a clear causal connection between the owner's breach and the increased costs, use of the method is permissible when the breach or unexpected conditions pervade substantial areas of performance; the evidence in this case included expert testimony that the City's change essentially resulted in a different project than the contractor bid, the cumulative effect of which was difficult to calculate; this circumstance made the total labor method the only appropriate method of calculating financial damage, as it was not possible to accurately calculate productivity after a major disruption like what occurred on this project using any other method).

[G] Productivity Analysis

Page 73, add at end of note 129:

See also Homer J. Olsen, Inc. v. Santa Clara Valley Transp. Auth., 2005 WL 3462739 (Cal. Ct. App. Dec. 19, 2005) (unpublished) (the trial court did not err in denying an award of damages for lost productivity when the contractor's evidence in support of its claim was speculative and did not meet the required burden of proof; the contractor prepared a list of field personnel who were required to work 17 straight weeks of overtime, but made no attempt to identify the actual productivity achieved by these workers over that period; instead, the contractor assumed that, based upon an efficiency chart, they were less productive because of the long hours; the contractor then estimated that the company experienced lost productivity in the range of 12 to 25 percent; however, there was no evidence that these workers experienced an actual productivity loss; further, the speculative nature of the claim was underscored by the fact that the contractor originally submitted the claim for the amount of $682,957, but at trial, the amount claimed was $270,243; on appeal, the contractor argued that it was "common sense" that a person doing physically demanding construction work who is required to work extensive overtime will become tired and lose efficiency, and while the court agreed that this might support the contractor's claim, under the substantial evidence rule the question is not whether there was some evidence to support the claim, but rather whether there was evidence to support the trial court's ruling; here, the trial court found that the contractor failed to meet its burden of proof because its evidence was speculative, and the contractor's arguments on appeal did not supply the necessary evidence and therefore did not compel any different result).

CHAPTER 3

EQUIPMENT AND SMALL TOOL COSTS; ADDITIONAL EQUIPMENT COSTS

§ 3.01 INTRODUCTION

Page 77, add at end of note 2:

Cf. Appeal of C.R. Pittman Construction Co., Inc., ASBCA No. 54901 (2008) (Board held that timber mats used on an elevated work platform were "material," and not "equipment"; the contractor was therefore entitled to recover weather delay costs in connection with the timber mats as indirect field overhead, rather than as direct costs priced according to the applicable government equipment schedule).

Page 78, add at end of note 5:

See also Missouri Dep't of Transp. v. Safeco Ins. Co. of Am., 97 S.W.3d 21 (Mo. Ct. App. 2002) (claim of paving subcontractor for delay damages affirmed, including cost to company of specialized equipment forced to remain idle during standby period; president of subcontractor testified, based on his experience, about what amounts company had been able to earn in the past using its various items of equipment, and on what subcontractor could have earned had that equipment, especially the paving equipment, not been committed to the project due to delays that prevented subcontractor from working on other construction projects).

§ 3.02 ADDITIONAL EQUIPMENT USAGE

[B] Standby Versus Operating Costs

Page 80, add at end of note 8:

See also Complete Gen. Constr. Co. v. Ohio Dept. of Transp., 94 Ohio St. 3d 54, 760 N.E.2d 364, 370 (2002), *reconsid. denied,* 94 Ohio St. 3d 1489, 763 N.E.2d 1186 (2002), (the appellate court held that the contractor was unable to recover where it presented no evidence to establish a casual link between a delay in the construction of three bridges and the presence of several pieces of heavy equipment that one of the company's project engineers testified were idle during the suspension period—there was no evidence introduced to show that the equipment was on the job site due to the bridge delay, as opposed to some other cause such as a scheduling decision by the contractor); the Ohio Supreme Court reversed, holding that whether a contractor's equipment remained on the job site because of the owner's delay is a question of fact that generally is best left to the trier of fact; thus, the Court of Appeals in this case erred in rejecting the trial court's characterization of the contractor's witness's testimony on this issue and substituting its own; Missouri Dep't of Transp. v. Safeco Ins. Co. of Am., 97 S.W.3d 21 (Mo. Ct. App. 2002) (paving subcontractor could recover for cost to company of specialized equipment forced to remain idle during standby period).

Page 81, add to text at end of page:

In *Quality Asphalt Paving, Inc. v. State Department of Transportation and Public Facilities*,[9.1] a case in which the State exercised a public works contract's termination-for-convenience clause, the contractor argued that it was entitled to compensation for equipment standby during the period between its receipt of the State's notice of intent and its receipt of the notice to proceed, arguing that the contract terms allowed recovery for standby once the state accepted the contractor's bid. The State responded that the contractor should only be entitled to compensation for standby if the state "took some action that subsequently forced [the contractor's] equipment to be idle," and also asserted that the terms of the contract did not support the contractor's claim. The court agreed with the State. The contractor also argued that it should be entitled to recover for equipment standby through October 31, rather than through August 17, the approximate date that the contractor admitted it was back to work in full force (and the date used by the hearing officer), because some equipment allegedly had remained unassigned months past August 17. The court again agreed with the hearing officer, noting that the contractor was attempting to equate "idle" time with recoverable expense. Although the State was obliged to compensate the contractor for standby costs due to the State's termination of the contract, it was not the contractor's insurer for equipment that remained idle after August 17, when the contractor was back to work in full force.

In *Appeal of T & W Edmier Corp.*,[9.2] the contractor excavating a flood control reservoir encountered lead contamination in the soil. The government suspended work while it devised a remediation plan, and the contractor sought to recover compensation for idle equipment costs during both the suspension period and the subsequent period of altered excavation methods. The Board denied the

[9.1] 71 P.3d 865 (Alaska 2003).

[9.2] ASBCA No. 53347 (2003).

contractor's claim, finding that the government had expressly authorized the contractor to demobilize its equipment from the site during the suspension period, and that the contractor's own mismanagement was responsible for any idle equipment time after the suspension period.

Page 82, add new subsection [C] after subsection [B]:

[C] Idle Equipment Costs

Claims for idle equipment occur when work on a project is suspended or stopped for an indefinite period. On an equipment-intensive project, such claims can quickly represent substantial amounts. The claims are often disputed on the basis that the equipment could have been put to productive use on another project or that there was no use for the equipment on the project.

The calculation of the damages for such claims is difficult for several reasons:

1. If the contractor owns the equipment, there will be significant question about the rate to be charged for that equipment;
2. Even if the equipment is being rented in an arm's-length transaction, there will be arguments about credits or deductions for the reduced wear and tear, and maintenance on the equipment;
3. Arguments are likely about the appropriate hours of use if the equipment is being charged on an hourly rate basis, since equipment is seldom utilized at 100 percent;
4. Arguments are also likely about whether the project owner is responsible for the equipment being idle.

In *Department of Transportation v. Herbert R. Imbt, Inc.*,[12.1] the contractor was denied any recovery for the cost of idle equipment because the contractor removed the equipment from the site at the direction of the owner, even though the contractor was not able to put it all to productive use. The actual demobilization and the partial use of the equipment were found sufficient to deny the contractor's claim. In *In re U.A. Anderson Construction Co.*,[12.2] the contractor was paid for idle equipment costs when the project owner assured the contractor that the suspension would be short and the contractor stood by waiting for that directive. Because the contractor had been assured that the solution was pending, it could not have been expected to remove the equipment and put it to other use. The same logic was applied in *Herman B. Taylor Construction Co. v. General*

[12.1] 157 Pa. Commw. 573 (1993).

[12.2] ASBCA No. 48087 (Apr. 27, 1999).

Services Administration,[12.3] when a stop-work was issued during excavation due to a potential archeological find. Because it was uncertain when work would resume and equipment on site would be needed immediately when work did resume, the contractor was allowed to recover for idle equipment. In *Appeal of Dillon Construction, Inc.*,[12.4] a dredging contract was suspended under a stop-work order that stated the work would resume in one month or shortly thereafter. The short estimated duration of the suspension, combined with the difficulties of demobilizing and remobilizing dredging equipment, justified recovery for idle equipment.

Generally, a contractor can recover for the cost of idle equipment owned by the contractor if:

1. The equipment was idle by a suspension of work for which the owner is responsible;
2. Equipment was necessary for completion of the contract work; and
3. It was impractical to demobilize equipment from the site or put the equipment to other productive use during the period of suspension.

In *RaCON, Inc. v. Tuscaloosa County*,[12.5] the plaintiff-contractor sought to recover $1.5 million in idle-equipment costs allegedly incurred as a result of the defendant county's delays in relocating a gas pipeline. The claim was denied because of a "no damages for delay clause" in the parties' contract. None of the recognized exceptions to enforcement of the clause applied. Although the plaintiff argued that the delay was "not contemplated by the parties," a provision of the contract expressly stated that the "County shall not be liable for damages or cost to [contractor] sustained due to any interference from utilities or appurtenances or from the operations of relocating the same." Further, the contractor provided no evidence that: (1) delays extended such an unreasonable length of time so as to amount to or to justify an "abandonment" of the contract—here, the period of damages under the utility-delay claim extended less than 30 days; (2) the defendant actively interfered with the work—although the contractor alleged that it repeatedly requested the county to relocate a gas pipeline, there were no facts to support a claim that the county "actively" interfered with the contractor's work; and (3) fraud or "bad faith"—there was no evidence to support such a claim).

Idle equipment costs were held not lienable in *Missouri Land Development Specialties, LLC v. Concord Excavating Co., LLC*.[12.6] The grading and excavating subcontractor, Missouri Land (MLDS), stopped work during construction due

[12.3] GSBCA No. 12915 (Aug. 27, 1996).

[12.4] ENGBCA No. PCC-101 (Nov. 21, 1995).

[12.5] 953 So. 2d 321 (Ala. July 28, 2006), *as modified on denial of reh'g* (Sept. 15, 2006).

[12.6] 269 S.W.3d 489 (E.D. Mo. Ct. App. 2008), *reh'g and/or transfer denied* (2008), *transfer denied* (2008).

to nonpayment by the general contractor, Concord. MLDS kept its equipment on site for some period of time, although no operators were on site, and ultimately removed the equipment, performing no further work on the project. MLDS filed a mechanic's lien to recover unpaid amounts for work performed under the subcontract, plus the rental costs of the equipment during the period it sat idle at the site. Although the court recognized that Missouri has found equipment costs to be lienable where both labor and equipment are furnished on a construction site, the issue here was whether "downtime" charges for rental equipment are lienable as "labor and materials." Noting that Kansas, Texas, and Illinois courts had allowed charges for "waiting time" to be included in the lien, the court distinguished those cases because the contracts in those cases specifically provided for an hourly rate to be paid for downtime periods. In contrast, MLDS' subcontract provided only that, if equipment is stopped for insufficient payment, restart or remobilization fees will be paid to compensate MLDS for lost time, movement of equipment, and re-permitting. Thus, the subcontract did not provide for payment of any hourly or daily rates during the actual period of inactivity. In addition, the lien claimants in the other cases resumed work after the period of inactivity, which did not occur in this case. The court held that under these circumstances, MLDS was neither performing "work or labor upon" the property, nor performing a service during the shutdown period that provided a "benefit or improvement" to the property, and the idle equipment costs were therefore not properly lienable.

§ 3.03 COST OF EQUIPMENT

Page 83, add at end of note 14:

See also In re W.G. Yates & Sons Constr. Co., ASBCA No. 49398, 01-2 BCA ¶ 31,428 (2001) (Board determined that percentage of contractor's claim for equipment costs was duplicative, because contractor's owned equipment was verified as being included in its indirect overhead pool expenses, and it charged the equipment to the government contract at a rental rate); Appeal of States Roofing Corporation, ASBCA No. 55506, 2008 WL 4467182 (Sept. 16, 2008) (contractor sought to recover equipment ownership cost of 25-ton crane contractor was required to utilize when the government determined not to permit the contractor to use the elevator for its work; the Board found that the government and the contractor had agreed to a rate of $46.85 per hour for the use of the crane, and that the contractor had been paid $46.85 per hour in previous modifications; however, since the contractor included equipment ownership costs in its field overhead, there was a duplication of costs for the crane; the Board directed the parties to remove crane ownership expense from field overhead and revise the total claim accordingly).

Page 83, add at end of note 15:

See also Orlosky Inc. v. United States, 68 Fed. Cl. 296 (2005), *appeal dismissed*, 180 Fed. Appx. 928 (Fed. Cir. Apr. 17, 2006) (when government-caused delays in contract performance forced an electrical contractor to pay extra rent on the equipment that was idle on the worksite, the contractor was entitled to an award of delay damages measured by the amount of extra rent insofar as it was substantiated by invoices; in this case, the court awarded the contractor $81,554.98 in rental costs).

Page 83, insert before last paragraph on page:

In *Appeal of Safeco Insurance Co. of America*,[16.1] Safeco acquired "all right, title and interest" to the contractor's equipment under a takeover agreement, and Safeco's completion contractor used the equipment to complete the work. The Air Force refused to pay Safeco the cost of contractor-owned equipment, on the grounds that neither Safeco nor the completion contractor ever received certificates of title to the equipment. The Board found that under the Federal Acquisition Regulation, the contractor is entitled to recover the cost of equipment "owned or controlled by" the contractor. Since Safeco had possession, control and use of the equipment, it was entitled to recover the cost of equipment ownership. Although Safeco did not have any actual operational cost data, it was allowed to recover costs computed using the standard rates published by the Army Corps of Engineers. The Board further found that Safeco was entitled to recover standby equipment costs during a government-ordered suspension of the work, even though the takeover agreement limited Safeco's use of the equipment to completion of the bonded project, and Safeco therefore had no other use for the equipment and could not rent it on the commercial market during the suspension.

In *Metric Construction, Inc. v. United States*,[16.2] the contractor sought to recover standby equipment costs for owned equipment during two separate delay periods. The first period was a delay of 65 days attributable to the Navy's requirement that Metric land its barge on a pontoon, instead of on the beach as specified in the contract, and the second period was a delay of 73 days while it was awaiting the Navy's delivery of certain rails required to complete the final portion of the work. The parties agreed that there was no actual cost data, and the court found that Dataquest Blue Book rates were appropriate since those rates had been utilized in change orders on the project. The court found that, with respect to older equipment that was on standby, Metric's expert properly utilized Volume 3 of the Blue Book, which provides rates for equipment between 11 and

[16.1] ASBCA No. 52107 (2003).

[16.2] 81 Fed. Cl. 804 (May 21, 2008).

20 years old. The court held that these rates should be applied even if the equipment had been fully depreciated. Metric also contended that a severity factor of 25% should be applied to increase the Blue Book rates to reflect the difficult conditions on the project, which involved construction of an airfield and roadway on an island off the coast of Southern California. The Navy argued that the regional adjustment factors in the Blue Book for Southern California ranged from .93 to 1.0, which would reduce the rates rather than increase them. Finding that the working conditions on the island exposed the equipment to a corrosive environment, the court held that a severity factor of 10% should be applied to increase the equipment standby rates. The court also determined that certain equipment was not necessary during the 73-day delay period that Metric was waiting to install the rails to complete the project, thereby reducing the average daily standby rate during that period. Finally, the court noted that although the barge was needed to remove the remaining equipment at the end of the job, it was not needed during the actual completion of the final portion of the work and preparations for demobilization, and standby costs for the barge during that period therefore could not be recovered.

§ 3.04 INDUSTRY GUIDES

[C] *Rental Rate Bluebook for Construction Equipment*

Page 88, add at end of note 28:

See also, e.g., ACE Constructors, Inc. v. United States, 70 Fed. Cl. 253 (2006), *aff'd,* 499 F.3d 1357 (Fed. Cir. 2007) (the plaintiff-contractor was reasonable in using the Caterpillar Handbook and the Dataquest Blue Book, two widely used reference guides, for estimating its costs of operating *rental* equipment. The contractor could thus recover its estimated operating costs of $70,839.32 for rented equipment, as well as $1,626.90 for insurance paid on the equipment, as the latter was a cost incident to operating rented equipment that was not included in the rental rate. However, the hourly rate with respect to the contractor's *owned* equipment should be determined by reference to a manual published by the Army Corps of Engineers—the Construction Equipment Ownership and Operating Expense Schedule, Region VI, EP 1110-1-8, Volume 6 (June 1999), as required by FAR 31.105, which was incorporated into the parties' contract); Metric Constr. Co., Inc. v. United States, 81 Fed. Cl. 804 (May 21, 2008) (to calculate standby costs on the contractor's owned equipment during periods of delay under the Federal Acquisition Regulations, the contractor was entitled to use the Dataquest Blue Book rates, at least where actual cost data was not available and the Blue Book rates had been used by the government on change orders for the project; however, due to the severity of working conditions in the location of the construction—the island's relatively remote location in an area frequented by winds and surf, the island's small size, and the facts that the construction work largely took place on the periphery of the island and the staging and storage areas for equipment were also at or near the periphery of the island meant that the contractor's construction equipment was constantly exposed to a corrosive environment—a severity factor should be applied to the *Blue Book* standby rates; the court concluded that a severity factor of 10% was appropriate); Commonwealth v. AMEC Civil, LLC, 54 Va. App. 240, 677 S.E.2d 633 (2009), *appeal granted* ____ (Va. Jan. 28, 2010) (the estimates in the "Rental Rate Blue Book" may be relied upon by the trial court on remand as a basis for determining owner-furnished equipment costs [citing Treatise]).

Page 89, add at end of subsection:

Similarly, in *Quality Asphalt Paving, Inc. v. State Department of Transportation & Public Facilities*,[30.1] the State argued that the hearing officer erred in awarding idle equipment time to the contractor at *Blue Book* rental rates, rather than reimbursing the contractor's actual costs. The court held, however, that the contract provided the hearing officer with broad authority to reach an equitable award, which allowed him, although it did not compel him, to use the *Blue Book* rates. In this case, the hearing officer based his decision to employ *Blue Book* rates on a number of relevant reasons, including: (1) "from the testimony and my own experience . . . contractors, generally, do not keep equipment costs for the purposes of developing claims"; (2) the "difficulty in not using *Blue Book* rates is that contractors with different accounting systems would be treated differently"; and (3) industry custom routinely permits the use of rates such as those found in the *Blue Book*. Because the hearing officer's decision did not rely on an improper interpretation of the contract, and because his decision relied on substantial evidence, it was not error to use *Blue Book* rates in determining the contractor's standby costs.

§ 3.06 COST OF ADDITIONAL SMALL TOOLS

[C] Reasons for Increased Small Tool Costs

Page 92, add at end of note 39:

See also Clifford R. Gray, Inc. v. City Sch. Dist. of Albany, 716 N.Y.S.2d 795 (App. Div. 3d Dept. 2000) (owner-caused delay supported the contractor's recovery of damages for various expenses incurred as a result of such delay, including expenses for small tools and consumables).

[30.1] 71 P.3d 865 (Alaska 2003).

Chapter 4
MATERIAL COSTS

§ 4.03 REASONS FOR MATERIAL CLAIMS

Page 100, add at end of note 11:

See also Appeal of The Sherman R. Smoot Corp., ASBCA No. 52261, 2003 WL 715270 (Feb. 26, 2003) (written change orders required contractor to change floor layout for buildings in connection with renovation and extended the contract completion date by 61 days, resulting in additional $14,166.47 in direct material costs).

[A] Costs Attributable to Owner-Caused Delay

Page 100, add at end of note 12:

Cf. Appeal of C.R. Pittman Constr. Co., Inc., ASBCA No. 54901 (2008) (contractor on drainage canal improvement project incurred weather-related delay of almost one year, and sought to recover additional costs to replace damaged timber mats used on an elevated work platform, along with delay costs relating to the extended use of the timber mats; the Board rejected the contractor's claim for costs of replacement, finding that although the government directed the replacement of the mats, the contractor was required under the contract to maintain a safe working environment and had failed to do so; the Board also held that the timber mats were "material," and not "equipment"; the contractor was therefore entitled to recover weather delay costs in connection with the timber mats as indirect field overhead, rather than as direct costs priced according to the applicable government equipment schedule).

[B] Costs Attributable to Defective Specifications

Page 101, add at end of note 21:

See also MACTEC, Inc. v. Bechtel Jacobs Co., LLC, 346 Fed. Appx. 59 (6th Cir. (Tenn.) Sept. 25, 2009) (affirming an award of $3,010,661.48 to compensate plaintiff subcontractor for costs associated with placing increased contour fill in connection with its subcontract to design and build a hydraulic isolation system for a Solid Waste Storage Area over an area containing unanticipated radiation hot spots; the evidence indicated that the additional fill was not anticipated in the plaintiff subcontractor's bid because the subcontractor was provided inaccurate topographical surveys by the defendant); Ace Constructors, Inc. v. United States, 499 F.3d 1357 (Fed. Cir.), *aff'd*, 499 F.3d 1357 (Fed. Cir. 2007), (the plaintiff contractor was entitled to compensation for unforeseen site conditions requiring 129,000 additional cubic yards of fill, due to defective specifications; the government's specifications indicated the project would be a "balanced project" that would not need such earthwork; the contractor had retained an expert consultant to analyze the excavation and fill requirements based on the Army Corps of Engineers' specifications, and the contractor acted reasonably in concluding that a significant amount of additional fill would not be required based on the expert's analysis); Orlosky Inc. v. United States, 64 Fed. Cl. 63 (Ct. Cl. 2005), *appeal dismissed*, 180 Fed. Appx. 928 (Fed. Cir. Apr. 17, 2006) (there was a triable issue of fact whether defendant Navy provided plaintiff with defective specifications, resulting in increased costs; although defendant asserted that plaintiff's failure to inspect site prior to bidding on job precluded defective specification claim, court held that plaintiff's omission prevented recovery only for a differing site conditions claim; plaintiff's contention that "the mode of installation required by the Navy violates safety regulations and manufacturer's warranties" constituted a disputed fact, requiring a trial); Caddell Constr. Co., Inc. v. United States, 78 Fed. Cl. 406 (2007) (when the government includes detailed specifications in a contract, it impliedly warrants that (i) if the contractor follows those specifications, the resultant product will not be defective or unsafe, and (ii) if the resultant product proves defective or unsafe, the contractor will not be liable for the consequences [citing United States v. Spearin]; a defective specification is one that is so faulty as to prevent or unreasonably delay completion of the contract performance; in this case, the fact that a large number of RFIs were issued was not an indication that the plans were defective, and because the contractor provided nothing beyond the self-serving statements of its witnesses to demonstrate that the cumulative effect or extent of the errors was either unreasonable or abnormal, the government could not be held liable for damages allegedly caused by delay due to defective specifications). *But see* Dugan & Meyers Constr. Co., Inc. v. Ohio Dept. of Adm. Servs., 113 Ohio St. 3d 226, 864 N.E.2d 68 (Apr. 25, 2007), *on remand* 2007 WL 2405923, 2007-Ohio-4141 (Ct. Cl. July 19, 2007) (Ohio courts recognize that the *Spearin* doctrine holds that, in cases involving government contracts, the government impliedly warrants the accuracy of its *affirmative indications regarding job site conditions*; however, the doctrine should not be extended from job-site-conditions cases to cases involving delays due to plan changes; nor does the *Spearin* doctrine invalidate an express contractual provision, such as a valid no-damages-for-delay clause, that precludes an award of damages under such circumstances); Thomas & Marker Constr. Co. v. Wal-Mart Stores, Inc., 2008 WL 4279860 (S.D. Ohio Sept. 15, 2008) (*Spearin* doctrine will not be extended to create an implied warranty of the accuracy of plans, specifications, and soil reports in the case of a non-governmental owner).

[C] Costs Attributable to Owner-Directed Changes

Page 103, add new footnote referent 35.1 at end of second to the last sentence of the subsection, and add note 35.1:

[35.1] *See, e.g.,* Appeal of States Roofing Corp., ASBCA No. 55508, 2009 WL 1464384 (May 5, 2009) (Navy paid for tapered insulation for roof cells that were subsequently deleted from the contractor's scope of work; contractor was unable to return the material, and eventually disposed of it; Board rejected the Navy's assertion that it should receive credit for the full value of the material, finding that the material was a special order and the Navy did not establish that it had any useful value or benefit apart from the deleted work scope).

§ 4.07 MITIGATING FACTORS IN RECOVERING ADDITIONAL COSTS

Page 108, add at end of note 62:

See also, e.g., R.P. Richards Constr., Inc., DOTCAB No. 4019, 01-2 BCA ¶ 31,594 (2001) (the purpose of requiring timely notice of defective specifications is to afford the government the opportunity to investigate the problem and take action to mitigate any claim for excess costs; thus, costs incurred as a result of delay in notifying the contracting officer of defective specifications may be denied); A.G. Cullen Constr., Inc. v. State Sys. of Higher Educ., 898 A.2d 1145 (Pa. Commw. 2006) (in a case involving a contract for the renovation of a state university building in which a contractor sought to recover for certain delay costs, the evidence indicated that the State System of Higher Education knew of a lead-based paint problem and had previously included its remediation in contract specifications but simply failed to incorporate those terms in the instant contractor's contract, possibly inadvertently due to an oversight. This evidence was more than sufficient to demonstrate, under the contract, an unforeseen condition for which the contractor was entitled to recover. Thus, the court affirmed an award of the contractor's direct costs attributable to the defective specifications, including costs required to provide its workers with respirators, protective clothing, air-monitoring, protective enclosures, and blood tests to determine exposure to lead containing material).

CHAPTER 5
BOND AND INSURANCE COSTS

§ 5.06 CALCULATING COSTS OF INCREASED BOND PREMIUMS

[A] Calculating Bond Premiums as a Percentage of the Equitable Adjustment

Page 116, add at end of note 22:

; Appeal of Sherman R. Smoot Corp., ASBCA No. 52261, 2003 WL 715270 (Feb. 26, 2003) (equitable adjustment marked up by 0.48 percent for bond premium increase); *See also, e.g.*, ACE Constructors, Inc. v. U.S., 70 Fed. Cl. 253 (2006), *aff'd,* 499 F.3d 1357 (Fed. Cir. 2007) (the court awarded plaintiff-contractor a bond premium of 0.65% multiplied by direct field costs plus field and home office overheads and profit associated with extra work required as a result of encountering differing site conditions. Although the contractor's expert claimed that a 0.84% rate was appropriate, the government's expert testified that his calculations, based on actual invoices, indicated that 0.65% was the appropriate bond rate; further, a government audit of the contractor's claim verified the 0.65% rate with the bonding insurance agent. The court thus accepted the 0.65% rate.).

§ 5.07 LOSS OF BONDING CAPACITY

Page 119, add at end of note 36:

See also Jeffrey B. Peterson & Assocs. v. Dayton Metro. Hous. Auth., 2000 WL 1006562 (Ohio Ct. App. 2000) (if not for a provision in the contractor's contract limiting recovery of damages resulting from a termination for convenience to certain specified types of losses, the contractor would have been entitled to recover its actual damages, including lost profits and loss of bonding capacity); The Millgard Corp. v. E.E. Cruz/Nab/Frontier-Kemper, 2007 WL 2388902 (S.D.N.Y. Aug. 21, 2007), *adhered to on reconsideration on other grounds*, 2007 WL 4302492 (S.D.N.Y. Dec. 5, 2007), *judgment aff'd on other grounds*, 329 Fed. Appx. 307 (2d Cir. (N.Y.) May 8, 2009) (the contractor could not recover for lost profits due to impaired bonding capacity in the absence of proof of causation; the contractor could not prove that the refusal of its prior bonding company to bond it on a future project was caused by the fact that it was terminated for cause rather than for convenience on the instant project; in addition, the significant time difference between the contractor's termination and the future project for which it could not obtain bonding (five years) indicated that the alleged loss of profits on that project was not a reasonably foreseeable consequence of the events occurring five years earlier); Lewis Jorge Constr. Mgmt., Inc. v. Pomona Unified Sch. Dist., 34 Cal. 4th 960, 22 Cal. Rptr. 3d 340, 102 P.3d 257 (2004) (contractor not entitled to recover, as either general or special damages against a breaching owner, lost profits on unidentified contracts contractor did not get when its bonding was impaired as a result of owner's breach of contract; lost profits were not recoverable as general damages because they were clearly not contemplated as part of the parties' bargain, nor were they recoverable as special damages because profits contractor claimed it would have made on future, unawarded contracts were not actually foreseen nor reasonably foreseeable by owner); K2 Construction, Inc. v. Anjani Investments, Inc., 2007 WL 2269814 (Cal. Ct. App. 2007) (unpublished), *as modified on denial of reh'g* (2007), *review denied* (2007), *appeal after remand on other grounds*, 2009 WL 1664784 (Cal. App. June 15, 2009 (unpublished), *reh'g denied* (July 6, 2009) (although a contractor may be entitled to recover lost profits on other contracts it was prevented from bidding on and performing due to impaired bonding capacity resulting from the owner's wrongful termination of the contractor, the contractor must establish that such consequential damages were foreseeable at the time of contract formation by proving that the owner knew the state of the contractor's finances and the criteria the surety used to evaluate the contractor's bonding limits (citing the *Lewis Jorge* case); it was not sufficient to show that the owner had experience with construction projects in general and knew that a performance bond was used in connection with the current project, and the contractor's claim for lost profits was therefore properly denied); U.S. *ex rel.* Sun Constr. Co., Inc. v. Torix Gen. Contractors, LLC, 2009 WL 3416214 (D. Colo. 2009) (citing the Colorado Supreme Court's holding in *Denny Construction, infra*, the court held that the plaintiff subcontractor, Sun, could not recover damages for lost bonding capacity because (1) although Sun proved the fact that it lost profits, it failed to introduce sufficient admissible evidence that would enable the trier of fact to compute a fair approximation of the loss—Sun failed to refer to any specific projects, or the value of such projects, that Sun was qualified to bid on, but for its inability to bond; and (2) Sun did not show that its losses were the foreseeable result of a breach at the time the contract was made; although Sun asked the court to hold as a matter of law that a material question of fact—specifically, whether lost profits due to impaired bonding capacity were objectively foreseeable by the parties at the time of entering into the contract—will always exist whenever the parties to the contract "are familiar with the bonding requirements of federal projects," such a holding would be inconsistent with Colorado law, as held by the court in *Denny*; since Sun failed to offer any evidence that the general contractor knew or should have known that lost profits due to impaired bonding capacity were foreseeable at the time of contracting, the general contractor's motion for summary judgment was properly granted); Begl Constr. Co., Inc. v. Los Angeles Unified Sch. Dist., 66 Cal. Rptr. 3d 110 (App. 2007), *reh'g denied* (Sept. 18, 2007), *review denied and ordered not to be officially published* (Nov. 28, 2007) (the trial court's award of $506,000 in lost profits due to impaired bonding capacity was affirmed; in this case, the School District terminated the contractor and filed a bond claim with the contractor's surety for completion of the project, the surety hired another contractor to finish the project and brought an action against the contractor, and the contractor was unable to obtain bonding on any public works projects while the dispute was pending; the court found there was unequivocal evidence establishing an industry custom that when there is a dispute between a surety and a contractor, the contractor will not be bonded as long as the dispute remains unresolved, and that there was sufficient evidence to support the jury's finding that the District "knew or reasonably should have known" this industry custom when the parties made the contract; the court distinguished the *Lewis Jorge* case on the basis that the evidence in that case was an "equivocal" showing that the owner's terminating a contract "might or might not cause the contractor's surety to reduce its bonding capacity"); Denny Constr., Inc. v. City and County of Denver ex rel. Bd. of Water Comm'rs, 199 P.3d 742 (Colo. Jan. 12, 2009) (the Board declared Denny in default during construction and filed a claim with Denny's surety; the surety subsequently decreased Denny's bonding capacity, and then stopped underwriting bonds for Denny; the trial court awarded Denny damages for lost profits due to reduced bonding capacity, the appellate court reversed, and the Colorado Supreme Court reversed the appellate court; the supreme court held that the appellate court erred in holding that claims for lost profits due to impaired bonding capacity are never reasonably certain and thus are speculative as a matter of law; instead, claims of lost profits due to impaired bonding capacity, like all claims for lost profits, must be established with reasonable certainty, which standard can be met notwithstanding that there are uncertainties inherent in any estimation of future damages; the court further held the appellate court also erred by applying an incorrect legal standard to determine whether lost profits are reasonably foreseeable; the question is not, as the court of appeals held, whether the defendant *actually knew* that the plaintiff contractor would suffer lost profits due to impaired bonding capacity, but whether it knew *or should have known* that such loss would probably occur; the court reversed and remanded for further proceedings consistent with its opinion); Llamas Group v. Huron Valley Schools, 2008 WL 3349076 (Mich. Ct. App. 2008), *appeal denied*, 483 Mich. 918, 762 N.W.2d 523 (Mich. 2009) (trial court erred in precluding contractor from presenting evidence of lost profits due to impaired bonding capacity; contractor had submitted an offer of proof setting forth the public sector work the contractor would have bid on but for the loss of its bonding capacity, its historical success rate, its historical profit margin, and that the owner was a public entity whose contractors must be bonded; the court found this was sufficient evidence to allow a reasonable trier of fact to determine that the owner knew or should have known that if it committed a breach that resulted in a loss of the contractor's bonding capacity, the contractor would suffer a loss of profits, and a reasonable basis for determining such lost profits); Tempo, Inc. v. Rapid Electric Sales & Service, Inc., 132 Mich. App. 93, 347 N.W.2d 728 (1984) (subcontractor, Rapid, presented evidence that Tempo's actions in improperly terminating Rapid's subcontract caused Rapid to lose its bonding, which prevented Rapid from being able to bid on other jobs; Rapid estimated its lost profits at $26,250, derived by determining which jobs Rapid would have bid on during that period had it had bonding, and estimating that it would have been awarded contracts on one out of every three to four jobs bid, with a profit margin of 3 percent; court held this evidence sufficient to warrant an award of damages for lost profits, finding that while to some degree speculative, this method of calculating lost profits had a reasonable degree of certainty and was not based solely on conjecture and speculation); Granite Re, Inc. v. City of La Crescent, 2009 WL 2982642 (D. Minn. Sept. 11, 2009) (contractor recovered lost profits resulting from loss of bonding capacity due to its wrongful termination in February 2008; the court found it was reasonably foreseeable at the time the contract was executed that termination would result in the contractor losing its bonding capacity, and that lost bonding capacity would cause significant financial harm in the form of lost business, revenues and profits; the court found that while "the City itself may not have actually foreseen such damages, what the City actually foresaw is not relevant. As a municipality that itself requires performance bonds on construction contracts, the loss of bonding capacity and the resulting harm was a *reasonably* foreseeable consequence of wrongful termination"; the calculation of the contractor's lost profits was based upon the testimony of the contractor's President, who provided its actual gross revenues for the years 2005, 2006, 2007, and 2008, and projected what its gross revenues would have been had its business continued growing at the same rate; the contractor then took the difference between the projected annual revenue for 2008 and subtracted actual 2008 revenue to arrive at its lost gross revenue claim for the year, and used its gross profit percentage of 25% to arrive at a figure of $570,317.00 for 2008; for 2009, taking account of the economic slowdown, the contractor assumed no growth from its projected 2008 earnings and also assumed the same actual revenue for 2009 as it actually experienced in 2008, resulting in a claim in the same amount of $570,317.00 of lost revenues for 2009; the court calculated lost profits in a different manner, holding that but for the City's breach, the contractor would have earned profits in 2008 at least as high as in 2007; since the contractor's revenues in 2008 were $1,643,612 less than in 2007 as a result of the breach, and 25% of the contractor's revenue consisted of profit, the contractor was awarded lost profits for 2008 in the amount of $410,903; the court further held that any lost profits in 2009 were "too remote and speculative to be awarded given the passage of time, the volatile nature of the current economic environment, and the lack of information regarding [the contractor's] actual revenues earned thus far in 2009").

Page 119, add at end of subsection:

A contract clause waiving consequential damages may preclude an award of damages for lost bonding capacity. In *Wal-Mart Stores, Inc. v. S.C. Nestel,*

Inc.,[36.1] the contractor alleged that, as a result of the defendant owner's unwarranted termination of a construction contract, the contractor was unable to procure performance bonds from sureties for future construction projects. The owner argued that the contract provision waiving consequential damages, including "damages incurred by the Contractor for principal office expenses including the compensation of personal stationed there, for losses of financing, business and reputation, and for loss of profit except anticipated profit arising directly from the Work. This mutual waiver is applicable, without limitation, to all consequential due to either party's termination of the Contract in accordance with the provisions of the Contract documents . . ." evidenced the parties' intent to waive all claims for consequential damages, including damages from lost bonding capacity. The court agreed. Although the contractor contended that the provision did not apply to lost bonding capacity claims when the owner breached the agreement, as opposed to terminating the agreement, the court found the reference to termination of the agreement was merely a nonexclusive example of situations in which the waiver applied, and that consequential damages for lost profits of any kind resulting from a breach of contract had been waived.

[36.1] 2010 WL 1190534 (S.D. Ind. Mar. 23, 2010).

Chapter 6
HOME OFFICE OVERHEAD

§ 6.02 HOME OFFICE OVERHEAD COSTS DEFINED

Page 124, add at end of note 10:

See also Norment Security Group, Inc. v. Ohio Dept. of Rehab. & Corr., 2003 WL 22890088 (Ohio Ct. Cl. 2003) (home office overhead includes such items as accounting and payroll services, insurance, upper-level management salaries, heat, electricity, taxes, depreciation, etc.; these costs are recovered by the contractor indirectly by allocating them on a proportionate basis among all of the contractor's projects; when performance on a particular project is suspended, the contractor's indirect costs exceed the amount originally allocated to the project; these "unabsorbed" indirect costs are generally recoverable by the contractor in an action against the government entity); Gladwynne Constr. Co. v. Mayor & City Council of Baltimore, 147 Md. App. 149, 807 A.2d 1141 (2002) (ordinarily, overhead costs subject to the *Eichleay* formula include items such as administrative and officers' salaries, rent, payroll, taxes, insurance, depreciation, dues, office expenses, utilities, cleaning, travel, and telephone expenses); Jackson Constr. Co., Inc. v. United States, 62 Fed. Cl. 84 (Ct. Cl. 2004) ("Typical home office overhead costs include salaries of upper-level management, home office rent, general taxes and insurance, accounting and payroll costs, maintenance and utilities, depreciation, and other fixed costs that are necessary to manage a business"; court noted that every contractor relies on receiving a steady stream of income from its various contracts not only to cover direct costs associated with those contracts, but also to cover its overhead costs, and if government disrupts contractor's stream of income on a contract and contractor cannot find replacement work, then government is liable for the contractor's lost overhead).

Page 124, add at end of note 14:

In Quality Asphalt Paving, Inc. v. State Dept. of Transp. & Pub. Facilities, 71 P.3d 865 (Alaska 2003), the contractor argued that its recovery for unabsorbed home office overhead should have been calculated by dividing the amount of claimed overhead costs by a shorter period than a full year to reflect the seasonal nature of the contractor's business, yielding a daily rate that would then be multiplied by the number of calendar days attributed to the state's termination for convenience. The hearing officer, however, divided the amount of the contractor's claimed overhead costs by 365 days, concluding that overhead costs for a seasonal construction business continue over the course of a year even though revenues are generated primarily during summer months. The hearing officer based his decision on the expert testimony and his own expertise. The court concluded that substantial evidence supported this decision.

§ 6.03 EXTENDED AND UNABSORBED OVERHEAD COSTS DISTINGUISHED

Page 125, add at end of note 19:

See also Appeals of Fru-Con Constr. Corp., ASBCA No. 55197, 2007 WL 3265020 (2007) (the issue in the instant case was extended home office overhead, not unabsorbed home office overhead; extended home office overhead is recoverable as a fixed percentage mark-up of costs incurred from a contract time extension due to changed or additional work).

Page 125, add at end of note 24:

See, e.g., MACTEC, Inc. v. Bechtel Jacobs Co., LLC, 346 Fed. Appx. 59 (6th Cir. (Tenn.) Sept. 25, 2009) (an award of $916,300.00 to compensate the plaintiff subcontractor for damages sustained for "extended program costs" or "extended site overhead" for an approximately eight-month period following the planned project completion date was affirmed; the evidence indicated that the defendant general contractor was responsible for various impacts to the schedule, with the result that the plaintiff was forced to perform its originally scheduled work in a different time period, which was hampered by unexpected weather impacts, which, in turn, significantly impacted plaintiff's ability to perform its originally scheduled work).

In contrast, in MBA Constr., Inc. v. Redding Sch. Dist., 2007 WL 1793432 (Cal. Ct. App. June 22, 2007) (unpublished), the court held that MBA could not assert a claim for delay damages based upon MBA's planned early completion date. The court found that the contract completion date could be modified only by a written change order and that nothing in the contract required the District to "approve" MBA's schedule showing early completion, nor did the District do so. The court distinguished the *Howard* case, with no explanation, and found that contrary federal authority was not binding in this case based upon state law. *Cf.* Crown Corr, Inc. v. Wil-Freds Constr., Inc., 2000 WL 1809996 (N.D. Ill. 2000) (in this case the general contractor sought to recover $701,798 from the construction coordinator for the project for extra home office support incurred as a result of delays caused by the coordinator; the defendant argued that the appropriate starting date for calculating such damages was the notice-to-proceed date rather than the contract award date; however, the court held that because part of the plaintiff's claim was premised on the allegation that certain notices to proceed were unreasonably delayed due to the defendant's failure to properly coordinate the project, it would be unreasonable to require the plaintiff to compute damages beginning with its receipt of the notice to proceed).

Page 126, add at end of note 29:

See also, e.g., George Sollitt Constr. Co. v. United States, 64 Fed. Cl. 229 (Ct. Cl. 2005) (when government suspends performance of a contract, contractor's indirect costs, such as home office overhead, often accrue beyond the amount originally allocated to that particular contract; such additional indirect costs may thus be "unabsorbed"; Court of Claims has consistently allowed contractor to recover not only additional direct costs that accrue to a contract when completion of performance is delayed by government, but also any unabsorbed, indirect costs that result).

§ 6.05 *EICHLEAY CORP.:* A SIMPLE APPROACH TO CALCULATING HOME OFFICE OVERHEAD

Page 128, add at end of note 49:

See also Oak Environmental Consultants, Inc. v. United States, 77 Fed. Cl. 688 (2007) (determining the amount of recoverable damages under the "*Eichleay* formula" requires three steps: (1) find the allocable contract overhead by multiplying the total overhead cost incurred during the contract period by the ratio of billings from the delayed contract to total billings of the contractor during the contract period; (2) find the daily contract overhead rate by dividing the allocable contract overhead by the number of days of contract performance; (3) determine the amount recoverable by multiplying the number of days of delay by the daily contract overhead rate).

Page 128, add at end of note 51:

; Complete Gen. Constr. Co. v. Ohio Dept. of Transp., 94 Ohio St. 3d 54, 760 N.E.2d 364, 370 (2002), *reconsid. denied,* 94 Ohio St. 3d 1489, 763 N.E.2d 1186 (2002), ("'recovery under the *Eichleay* formula is an extraordinary remedy designed to compensate a contractor for unabsorbed overhead costs that accrue when contract completion requires more time than originally anticipated because of government-caused delay,'" quoting from West v. All State Boiler, Inc., 146 F.3d 1368, 1377 (Fed. Cir. 1998)).

Page 128, add at end of note 52:

See also, e.g., Gladwynne Constr. Co. v. Mayor & City Council of Baltimore, 147 Md. App. 149, 807 A.2d 1141 (2002) (three elements must be satisfied for a contractor to recover under the *Eichleay* formula: (1) plaintiff must prove that the contract was suspended, delayed, or disrupted by the government; (2) plaintiff must prove that it was forced to "stand by" during the delay; and (3) plaintiff must prove that, while "standing by" during the suspension, delay, or disruption, it was unable to take on other work; when the contractor establishes a prima facie case of entitlement to use the formula, the burden of production as to the third element shifts to the government; at that point, the government must present "rebuttal evidence or argument" to demonstrate that the contractor did not suffer any loss "because it was able to either reduce its overhead or take on other work during the delay"); Orlosky Inc. v. United States, 64 Fed. Cl. 63 (Ct. Cl. 2005), *appeal dismissed,* 180 Fed. Appx. 928 (Fed. Cir. Apr. 17, 2006) (plaintiff contractor's attempt to invoke the *Eichleay* formula for recovery of overhead costs could not proceed until plaintiff proved that: (1) government caused a delay of uncertain duration, (2) delay forced extension of completion date of project or contractor incurred additional costs because it planned to finish earlier, and (3) contractor must have been "on standby and unable to take on other work during the delay period"; periods of alleged delay are non-recoverable when contractor caused a concurrent delay or when contractor was not in standby status; thus, plaintiff was required to distinguish delays caused by government versus those caused by itself; because plaintiff stipulated that it informed government that it "'elected not to demobilize [its] equipment . . . until the Government has had the opportunity to respond to [its] request for information,'" recovery for plaintiff's delay claim associated with defendant's alleged failure to allow plaintiff to remove equipment from site might be precluded unless plaintiff could establish triable issues of fact with regard to its claims that government caused delay because of: dilatory responses to outage requests; failure to timely allow plaintiff access to site and to certain data, as well as its equipment; and failure to allow plaintiff to complete performance); Cleveland Constr., Inc. v. Ohio Public Emps. Retirement Sys., 2008-Ohio-1630, 2008 WL 885841 (Ohio Ct. App. 2008), *appeal not allowed*, 119 Ohio St.3d 1447, 893 N.E.2d 517, 2008-Ohio-4487 (Sept. 10, 2008) (in order to present a valid claim for *Eichleay* damages, the contractor must first demonstrate two important elements, which establish the prima facie case for a damages award for unabsorbed home office overhead: (1) the contractor was on "standby," i.e., (a) work was suspended for a period of uncertain duration; and (b) the contractor was able to return to work immediately; and (2) it would have been impracticable to take on any other work during the time on standby, i.e., the uncertainty of the duration of the delay made it impracticable to commit to working on a different project at the same time; the court found that the trial court erred in refusing to allow the contractor to present evidence of *Eichleay* damages through the testimony of a lay witness, since the relevant questions could be answered by a witness with personal knowledge of the relevant facts, and did not require expert testimony).

Page 128, add at end of note 54:

; Orlosky Inc. v. United States, 68 Fed. Cl. 296 (2005), *appeal dismissed,* 180 Fed. Appx. 928 (Fed. Cir. Apr. 17, 2006) (in order to recover *Eichleay* damages, the contractor "must first prove there was a government-caused delay to contract performance . . . that was not concurrent with a delay caused by the contractor or some other reason"; in this case, plaintiff successfully showed that the government caused four delays, during which plaintiff was unable to proceed with any aspect of the project; plaintiff was subject to a directive from the Navy before it could proceed; moreover, the government-caused delays were not concurrent with delays caused by plaintiff); Complete Gen. Constr. Co. v. Ohio Dept. of Transp., 94 Ohio St. 3d 54, 760 N.E.2d 364, 370 (2002), *reconsid. denied,* 94 Ohio St. 3d 1489, 763 N.E.2d 1186 (2002), (the Ohio Department of Transportation argued against use of the *Eichleay* formula, contending that it allows contractors to recover for breach of contract without establishing causation; the court held to the contrary, noting that before the formula can be applied, a contractor must prove a rather extraordinary set of circumstances that by their very nature demonstrate causation and damages; the court said a contractor may recover only with proof of an *owner-caused* construction delay and with proof that the "standby" character of the delay was also caused by the owner and that it prevented the contractor from finding replacement projects to cover the overhead).

Page 128, add before last full paragraph:

In *In re Appeals of Catel, Inc.,*[54.1] the contractor was denied recovery of unabsorbed home office overhead because the contractor could not show that the owner was solely responsible for the delay or that the contractor's crew was forced to stand by.

Page 128, add at end of note 55:

See also Richmond American Homes of Colorado, Inc. v. United States, 2008 WL 681515 (Fed. Cl. 2008), *appeal dismissed*, 352 Fed. Appx. 421 (Fed. Cir. May 8, 2009) (in order to satisfy the standby requirement, the contractor is not required to show that it ceased all other normal business activities; rather, the ability to perform other normal business activities is irrelevant in determining unabsorbed overhead expenses caused by a delay; a contractor is injured under this theory if it is unable to reallocate the indirect costs to an alternative project,

[54.1] ASBCA No. 54633, 2006 WL 2535622 (Aug. 25, 2006).

causing those costs to become unabsorbed); Oak Envtl. Consultants, Inc. v. United States, 77 Fed. Cl. 688 (2007) (a contractor can still recover *Eichleay* damages even though it continued to perform minor tasks during the one-year period of government suspension of a project prior to termination for convenience; in this case, given the relatively low value of the work done during the suspension (approximately $43,000), the minimal ten-day duration of the post-suspension work compared to that of the total contract work suspended, and the fact that the parties knew in advance of the suspension that this work would have to be accomplished, the standby requirement for *Eichleay* damages was met); Appeal of Packard Constr. Corp., ASBCA No. 55383, 2009 WL 2601247 (Aug. 10, 2009) (to establish "standby," a contractor must show it was precluded from performing much, if not all, contract work; in this case, the record indicated that the contractor, Packard, was performing significant and substantial amounts of contract work during most of the claimed 88-day delay period; Packard contended it was on standby for 71 work days during the delay period because it earned less than 100% of its direct site costs on those days, which was akin to being on standby; however, a review of the contractor's records indicated that Packard was paid roughly 48% of the bid contract value during the claimed delay period, much of which work was necessary and critical; instead, the court found that on only ten days during the delay period, the contractor performed little, if any, contract work while awaiting government direction on water line discrepancies; thus, the contractor made out a *prima facie* case of recovery of unabsorbed overhead for these days).

Page 129, add after quotation and before first text paragraph:

Similarly, in *P.J. Dick, Inc.*,[56.1] the court affirmed the Board's finding that the contractor was not on standby during the suspension period. In that case, the government issued more than 400 change orders that the contractor alleged suspended its work during various time periods. In determining whether the contractor was entitled to recover home office overhead under the *Eichleay* formula, the court set forth the following six-part analysis:

[56.1] VACBCA No. 5597, 01-2 BCA ¶ 31,647 (2001), *aff'd in part, rev'd in part, vacated in part, and remanded,* P.J. Dick, Inc. v. Principi, 324 F.3d 1364 (Fed. Cir. Apr. 7, 2003). *See also* Appeals of Coronet Mach. Corp., ASBCA No. 55645, 2009 WL 4048362 (Nov. 13, 2009) (although the government conceded to questions 1-4, enumerated in *P.J. Dick, Inc.* as prerequisites to the recovery of *Eichleay* damages, the plaintiff contractor construed this concession of steps 1-4 as a complete concession of entitlement by the government; however, all six steps must be considered to determine if a contractor is entitled to recover such damages; the board thus denied the contractor's motion for summary judgment in order to allow the government time to conduct further discovery regarding whether the contractor could have mitigated its damages during the claimed time period and to introduce evidence as to the extent of the period of government-caused delay, during which the contractor remained on standby).

1. Was there a government-caused delay that was not concurrent with another delay caused by some other source?
2. Did the contractor demonstrate that it incurred additional overhead, either because the contract time was extended or the contract was finished on time or early but the contractor would have finished even sooner?
3. Did the government issue a suspension or other order expressly putting the contractor on standby?
4. If not, can the contractor prove there was a delay of indefinite duration during which it could not bill substantial amounts of work on the contract *and* at the end of which it was required to be able to return to work on the contract at full speed and immediately?
5. Can the government satisfy its burden of production showing that it was not impractical for the contractor to take on replacement work (*i.e.*, a new contract) and thereby mitigate its damages? and
6. If so, can the contractor satisfy its burden of persuasion that it was impractical for it to obtain sufficient replacement work?

Applying this analysis, the court found that P.J. Dick was not on standby because it continued to perform substantial amount of work on the project during the suspension periods. The court ultimately awarded the contractor home office overhead based upon a Suspension of Work Contract provision that allowed recovery for delays calculated by multiplying the number of delay days by specified daily rates (including rates for home office overhead) "without the need for future proof of costs or damages. . . ." The court held that this contract provision obviated the need for P.J. Dick to separately prove facts demonstrating entitlement to *Eichleay* damages.

In *Gladwynne Constr. Co. v. Mayor & City Council of Baltimore,*[56.2] the court noted that the *Eichleay* formula compensates contractors who are unable to take on replacement work because the standby status prevents the contractor from doing so. The court found that although the standby status must be attributable to the government, the standby test does not require that the contractor's work force be idle; nor must the work be entirely suspended. A contractor may be unable to take on additional work if the owner causes delay of uncertain duration or the contractor's bonding capacity is limited. Nor is recovery "compromised" merely because the contractor continues "to perform minor tasks throughout the period. . . ." Contractors have been permitted to use the *Eichleay* formula to calculate extended home office overhead in situations where disruption, delay, or outright suspension have cast a cloud of uncertainty over the length of the performance period of the contract. The court stated: "'The *raison d'etre* of Eichleay requires at least some element of uncertainty arising from suspension, disruption

[56.2] 147 Md. App. 149, 807 A.2d 1141 (2002).

or delay of contract performance. Such delays are sudden, sporadic and of uncertain duration. As a result, it is impractical for the contractor to take on other work during these delays.'" (quoting *C.B.C. Enterprises, Inc. v. United States*, 978 F.2d 669 (Fed. Cir. 1992)).

If the contractor is able to perform work during the alleged suspension period, he might not be in a standby mode and therefore may be precluded from using the *Eichleay* formula. In *Appeal of Carousel Development, Inc.*,[56.3] the Armed Services Board of Contract Appeals denied the contractor's attempt to apply the *Eichleay* formula on the grounds that the contractor was performing more than minor work during the alleged suspension period. This case involved a fixed price contract awarded by the Air Force to Carousel for renovation of 24 military family housing units at Eglin Air Force Base, Florida. The contract provided for units to be released to the contractor in groups of four, every 21 days, and the contractor was to complete each group of four units within 75 calendar days. After 12 units had been released, the Air Force became dissatisfied with the work being performed by Carousel and refused to release additional units. Work on the remaining 12 units was suspended for as long as 146 days. Carousel filed a claim for the unabsorbed home office overhead using the *Eichleay* formula. Although the Board found that the government had suspended the work on the 12 units for an unreasonable and uncertain duration of time, it did not find that all work under the contract had been suspended. The Board noted that Carousel was able to work on the first 12 units during the suspension and had completed approximately half of the work on those units. In the Board's opinion, this constituted more than a minor amount of work and, as such, Carousel's work had not come to a standstill. Therefore, Carousel was not entitled to recover unabsorbed home office overhead. The Board did rule that Carousel was entitled to a time extension and hence a remission of liquidated damages.

The contractor in *Appeal of TPS, Inc.*,[56.4] was denied recovery on its claim for unabsorbed overhead calculated using the *Eichleay* formula because it was not required to remain in a "standby" position. The project involved repairs to nine buildings at the Key West Naval Air Station in Florida. After starting work on one building, the contractor was suspended on seven-and-a-half of the buildings, and later the repairs on those buildings were terminated for convenience and removed from the contractor's contract. However, the contractor proceeded with completion of one-and-a-half of the buildings. The Board, in analyzing this claim, determined that there was no evidence that the government had required the contractor to remain on standby position, ready to resume work on short notice, and therefore the contractor was not entitled to recover unabsorbed home office overhead.

[56.3] ASBCA No. 50719 (Jan. 23, 2001).

[56.4] ASBCA No. 52421 (Mar. 26, 2004).

In *Norment Security Group, Inc. v. Ohio Dept. of Rehabilitation and Correction*,[56.5] the court held that a contractor is on standby when work on a project is suspended for a period of uncertain duration and the contractor can at any time be required to return to work immediately. In effect, the contractor is not working on the project, yet remains bound to the project. The contractor must be ready to immediately resume performance at any time. In this case, the contractor contended that the government's failure to adequately schedule and coordinate the project caused delays that extended the date of completion and that the project extensions resulted in reduced income that would otherwise be used to absorb overhead costs. The court found that the government acted reasonably when it removed the construction manager and assigned the scheduling duties to another contractor, and that the delays caused by inadequate scheduling therefore were not "owner-caused delays." Further, although the contractor incurred damages as a result of owner-caused delays in one area of the project, the contractor completed that part of the job in a timely manner through the use of overtime hours, and the evidence did not suggest that the contractor was placed on standby with regard to that phase of the project. Moreover, delay damages awarded by the court included a 10 percent mark-up for profit and overhead, and it would be improper for plaintiff to recover both *Eichleay* damages and overhead costs for those claims.

In *Broward County v. Brooks Builders, Inc.*,[56.6] the contractor's principal testified that the contractor faced delays at "virtually every turn" because "either the plans were deficient and we had trouble getting a response" or "we couldn't get change orders" and "we couldn't get anything we needed in the way of support from either the owner or the architect." However, when the contractor's principal was questioned as to whether work continued anyway, he answered: "We kept working the best we could. Although, I must say it wasn't in a sufficient manner." The court concluded from this testimony that there was not an effective suspension of much, if any, of the work on the contract. In addition, a trial exhibit documented the contractor's substantial monthly invoices, apparently suggesting the exact opposite—that work continued. Accordingly, the trial court erred in awarding *Eichleay* damages to the contractor.

In *Strand Hunt Constr., Inc. v. Lake Washington School Dist., No. 414*,[56.7] the court held that the *Eichleay* formula is "an extraordinary remedy," the use of which is severely limited. Such damages are utilized to compensate a contractor for its indirect costs that cannot be allocated to a particular contract for the period during which the government has made contractual performance impossible, while requiring the contractor to remain available to resume performance on short notice. As long as the contractor is able to continue performing the contract,

---

[56.5] 2003 WL 22890088 (Ohio Ct. C1. 2003).

[56.6] 908 So. 2d 536 (Fla. Dist. Ct. App. 4th Dist. July 27, 2005).

[56.7] 134 Wash. App. 1053, 2006 WL 2536315 (Wash. App. Div. 1 2006), *review denied*, 160 Wash. 2d 1023, 163 P.3d 794 (Wash. July 11, 2007).

although not in the same way or as efficiently or effectively as it had anticipated it could do so, it can allocate a portion of its indirect costs to that contract. There is accordingly no occasion in that situation to resort to recovery under the *Eichleay* formula. In this case, the *Eichleay* formula could not be applied, because the record showed that the contract work was never suspended, and the contractor worked continuously throughout the project.

In *Acme Contracting, Ltd. v. TolTest, Inc.*,[56.8] the court held that the subcontractor could not recover administrative overhead costs using the *Eichleay* formula because the subcontractor had not established it was on standby. The court stated that a finding that a contractor is on standby under Ohio law (the governing law under the subcontract) requires proof that the contractor was ready to immediately resume performance at any time during the suspension of work, and that the contractor was unable to take on other work during this time. In this case, the subcontractor was able to perform some limited contract work and some additional time and materials work during the delay periods. Since the subcontractor failed to present evidence sufficient to allow the court to parse out the periods when the subcontractor was truly on standby, the subcontractor's entire claim for unabsorbed overhead costs was denied.

Page 129, add at end of note 57:

; Complete Gen. Constr. Co. v. Ohio Dept. of Transp., 94 Ohio St. 3d 54, 760 N.E.2d 364, 370 (2002), *reconsid. denied,* 94 Ohio St. 3d 1489, 763 N.E.2d 1186 (2002) (as with any other contract claim, the contractor pressing an *Eichleay* claim has the duty to mitigate damages; central to *Eichleay* is the requirement that, if able, the contractor must take on other work to absorb the overhead allotted to the delayed project). *Cf.* Appeal of Roy McGinnis & Co., Inc., ASBCA No. 49867, 01-2 BCA ¶ 31,622 (2001) (government argued that performance of the contract "was neither suspended nor significantly interrupted during the delay" because the contractor "was able to successfully shift his crews to other activities during the period of delay and managed to earn nearly 100 percent of what it had planned to make during the same time frame"; the Board found, however, that although none of the delaying events caused a complete suspension of work, the delays stretched out the performance period by 110 days); Appeal of Bay Constr. Co., VABCA No. 5526 (Mar. 19, 2002) (contractor unable to recover unabsorbed home office overhead resulting from government-caused suspensions that had affected work on the critical path and delayed project completion; court found that contractor had failed to offer evidence that it had been forced to stand by for an uncertain period of time); Appeal of Huff Sealing Corp., ASBCA No. 53587 (May 3, 2002) (government-ordered work stoppages for brief periods of time on four occasions forced the contractor into a standby position, and entitled the

[56.8] 2008 WL 1990780 (E.D. Mich. May 5, 2008), *aff'd in part on other grounds, rev'd in part on other grounds*, 2010 WL 1140997 (6th Cir. (Mich.) Mar. 24, 2010).

contractor to recover unabsorbed home office overhead; contract provision allowing the government to stop work due to "unforeseen difficulties" arising out of aircraft operations did not prevent contractor's recovery, as the training exercises that caused the work stoppages had already been planned at the time the contract was awarded); United States of Am. for the Use of Poong Lim/Pert Joint Venture v. Dick/Pacific/Ghemm Joint Venture, 2006 WL 436048 (D. Alaska, Feb. 22, 2006) (contractor was not entitled to use the *Eichleay* formula because it failed to offer any evidence that it was "on standby and unable to take on other work" during any delays; the contractor contended that it was effectively suspended from completing its critical path work each time there was a delay to the project, which resulted in indefinite delays to the project because the contractor could not proceed with its planned critical path work; however, this statement only supported the fact that the contractor could not do its *planned* work, not that it was unable to do *other* work; in fact, the contractor also stated that it was forced to perform under winter weather conditions, and that it mitigated its damages and prevented even further and much larger damages to the project by resequencing the project schedule; these and other statements by the contractor clearly suggested that despite alleged delays, the contractor never stopped working, although its work was alleged to be less productive because of weather and other problems caused by the delays).

Page 129, add at end of note 58:

See also Complete Gen. Constr. Co. v. Ohio Dept. of Transp., 94 Ohio St. 3d 54, 760 N.E.2d 364, 370 (2002), *reconsid. denied*, 94 Ohio St. 3d 1489, 763 N.E.2d 1186 (2002) ("Impracticability, rather than impossibility, of other work is the standard that is applied, and the contractor is entitled to damages '*only* if its inability to take on additional work results from its standby status, *i.e.*, is attributable to the government'"; thus, a prima facie case requires the contractor to demonstrate that it has committed a portion of its overhead costs to a particular project and that not only has the project's suspension left those costs unabsorbed, but that the character of the government-caused delay is such that it is impractical for the contractor to obtain other work to fill the gap; once the contractor commits resources to a project, the resources remain committed whether the project moves forward or not—"[t]he contractor is all geared up with nowhere to go"); Gladwynne Constr. Co. v. Mayor & City Council of Baltimore, 147 Md. App. 149, 807 A.2d 1141 (2002) (contractor testified that it was "unable to take on additional work to replace this Project due to bonding restrictions"; contractor said that it had a $3 million bonding capacity, it put up a $500,000 bond on this project, and it had $2.5 million tied up in other jobs, so it was at its capacity; "I have other jobs going, but they total 3 million, and until I complete those jobs and free up bonding, I can't bid anything else. . . ."). *Cf.* Ryco Constr., Inc. v. United States, 55 Fed. Cl. 184 (Ct. Cl. 2002) (a contractor can have some excess bonding capacity and still qualify for *Eichleay* damages; however, when the contractor has reduced bonding capacity, an inference can be drawn that it is impractical for it to take on additional work; thus, in a particular case, whether it was impractical for plaintiff to take on other work during any time it may have been on standby is generally a triable question of fact); Oak Environmental Consultants, Inc. v. U.S., 77 Fed. Cl. 688 (Fed. Cl. 2007) (because the government suspended its contract with its contractor, rather than terminating it, the contractor's bond was not released, in spite of repeated requests to have it released, thus contributing to the indefinite nature of the suspension; as a result, the contractor was forced to remain on standby, without the ability to obtain replacement work; as a small company with limited bonding capacity, the contractor was unable to obtain additional bonding which would have allowed it to take on replacement work).

Page 129, add at end of note 60:

See also Orlosky Inc. v. United States, 68 Fed. Cl. 296 (2005), *appeal dismissed,* 180 Fed. Appx. 928 (Fed. Cir. Apr. 17, 2006) (in determining whether a contractor was on standby and unable to take other work during the period of delay, the Federal Circuit has held that a "court should first determine whether the [government] . . . issued a written order that suspend[ed] all the work on the contract for an uncertain duration and require[d] the contractor to remain ready to resume work immediately or on short notice"; when no written order was issued, as in the instant case, the contractor must make a three-part showing: (1) the government-caused delay was not only substantial but was of an indefinite duration—this analysis hinges on uncertainty; thus, for example, if the government suspended work, but alerted the contractor as to the date upon which work could recommence, the contractor could not be deemed to be on standby; (2) during the delay, the contractor was required to be ready to resume work on the contract, at full speed as well as immediately—this element requires something more than an uncertain delay; the implication is that the contractor must be required to keep at least some of its workers and necessary equipment at the site, even if idle, ready to resume work, but on the other hand, if the government gives a contractor time to reassemble its workforce, the contractor cannot be deemed to be on standby; and (3) the contractor must show effective suspension of much, if not all, of the work on the contract—suspension does not require that the workforce assigned to the contract be standing by, only that work on the contract has ceased or been delayed; government inaction, such as failure to vacate spaces in which the contract was to be performed, can effect a valid suspension); Oak Environmental Consultants, Inc. v. U.S., 77 Fed. Cl. 688 (Fed. Cl. 2007) (the contractor must show that the government-caused delay was not only substantial, but was of an indefinite duration; indefiniteness is the very characteristic that distinguishes a period during which resources can be allocated elsewhere, versus one in which the uncertainty of resumption creates a risk of breach if a contractor does not stand at the ready; the indefiniteness, as related to home office overhead, restricts a contractor from making organizational changes that could otherwise be made, such as "laying off" employees and shifting resources elsewhere).

[A] *Eichleay* Formula Accepted, Criticized, and Modified

Page 130, add at end of note 61:

Complete Gen. Constr. Co. v. Ohio Dept. of Transp., 94 Ohio St. 3d 54, 760 N.E.2d 364 (2002), *reconsid. denied,* 94 Ohio St. 3d 1489, 763 N.E.2d 1186 (2002) (noting that the *Eichleay* formula is *one* way of determining unabsorbed home office overhead damages in public construction delay cases; however, if formula is used, owner must be allowed to dispute items of overhead that did not bestow any benefit on the project at issue, perhaps by considering the Federal Acquisition Regulations' dissection of allowable and unallowable indirect costs); Gladwynne Constr. Co. v. Mayor & City Council of Baltimore, 147 Md. App. 149, 807 A.2d 1141 (2002) (court remanded for trial court to consider whether the *Eichleay* formula was satisfied, and, if so, for what period of time and at what daily rate); Orlosky Inc. v. United States, 68 Fed. Cl. 296 (2005), *appeal dismissed,* 180 Fed. Appx. 928 (Fed. Cir. Apr. 17, 2006) (the *Eichleay* formula is the exclusive formula for calculation of damages for unabsorbed overhead due to government-caused delay in situations in which contract performance has begun).

Page 130, add at end of note 63:

See also, e.g., U.S. *ex rel.* Steel-Fab, Inc. v. Wynn Constr. Co., Inc., 2006 WL 1207621 (E.D. Okla. May 2, 2006) (the court indicated that the *Eichleay* formula is an extraordinary remedy and that the Tenth Circuit and the state of Oklahoma have not yet adopted it; in Oklahoma, the measure of damages for a breach of contract claim is the amount that will compensate the party aggrieved for all the detriment proximately caused thereby, which amount must be ascertainable in some matter other than by mere speculation, conjecture or surmise, and by reference to some definite standard. Although the contractor correctly pointed out that the *Eichleay* formula is a judicially approved standard, such standard is not "definite" as required under Oklahoma law, because the *Eichleay* formula only roughly approximates extended home office overhead. Moreover, use of the *Eichleay* formula generally results in a greater windfall than application of a fixed percentage mark-up formula. The court accordingly granted plaintiff's motion in limine, prohibiting the defendant from introducing evidence or testimony concerning extended home office overhead damages by use of the *Eichleay* formula).

Page 131, add at end of note 72:

Cf. Complete Gen. Constr. Co. v. Ohio Dept. of Transp., 94 Ohio St. 3d 54, 760 N.E.2d 364, 370 (2002), *reconsid. denied,* 94 Ohio St. 3d 1489, 763 N.E.2d 1186 (2002) (the Ohio Department of Transportation argued against use of the *Eichleay* formula, contending that it allows contractors to recover for breach of contract without establishing causation; the court held to the contrary, noting that before the formula can be applied, a contractor must prove a rather extraordinary set of circumstances that by their very nature demonstrate causation and damages; a contractor may recover only with proof of an *owner-caused* construction delay and with proof that the "standby" character of the delay was also caused by the owner and that it prevented the contractor from finding replacement projects to cover the overhead).

Page 133, add at end of note 84:

See also, e.g., Jackson Constr. Co., Inc. v. United States, 62 Fed. Cl. 84 (Ct. Cl. 2004) (when contractor attempts to recover unabsorbed home office overhead on a contract that was completed within the contract's original deadline, but not early as originally anticipated, contractor must "demonstrate that it incurred additional overhead" by satisfying "a three-part test": (1) that it intended to finish early, (2) that it was capable of finishing early, and (3) that it would have actually finished early but for government's actions; although government need not have notice of contractor's intent to finish early, record must contain concrete evidence of contractor's intent, such as a bid, estimate, or any other contemporaneous documentation of its planned early completion; notice to government, while not required, may be sufficient evidence of intent; this three-part test must be satisfied in addition to the other requirements for recovery of *Eichleay* damages; in this case, first, contractor did not substantiate its claim that contract was delayed by 120 days, and its failure of proof left court without any basis to quantify the actual number of days of delay to project's critical path; second, even if contractor had demonstrated a delay to contract's critical path, its claim would still fail because it calculated its *Eichleay* damages using incorrect data that unjustifiably inflated amount of its daily contract overhead; third, aside from contractor's flawed calculation of *Eichleay* damages, contractor also failed to establish a valid early completion delay claim under the three-part test).

Page 136, add after last full paragraph on page:

In *Able Products Co. v. Department of Treasury,*[90.1] the government attempted to rebut the presumption of delay by showing that replacement work

[90.1] GSBCA No. 15167-TD (July 31, 2001).

had been awarded to the contractor. In this matter the contractor, Able, was renovating heating, ventilating, and air conditioning systems in a classroom building in Georgia. After Able found asbestos during the demolition work, work was suspended and a change order issued to Able for the asbestos abatement. Able was prevented from performing any of its original contract work in the affected area of the building until the abatement work was performed. Able was not qualified to perform abatement work and was forced to subcontract the abatement work and suspend its own contract work while waiting for the abatement to be completed. Able filed a claim for unabsorbed overhead during the period its work was suspended. Able calculated the additional overhead costs using the *Eichleay* formula. The government asserted that the change order work for the asbestos abatement was replacement work. Able asserted that it was not replacement work, since Able had to subcontract all of the work and its own crews were forced to stand by while waiting for access to its original contract work. The government moved for summary judgment based upon its contention that replacement work was made available to Able. This motion was denied, with the Board ruling that Able's allegations were sufficient to raise a factual question as to whether the asbestos subcontract work was replacement work.

[B] Standard *Eichleay* Calculation

Page 137, add at end of note 93:

See also Ryco Constr., Inc. v. United States, 55 Fed. Cl. 184 (Ct. Cl. 2002) (Federal Circuit Court of Appeals has approved use of the standard *Eichleay* formula to determine delay damages; court emphasized, however, that *actual* days of contract performance must be used in calculation of daily overhead rate allocable to contract, rather than original number of days of performance in contract); P.J. Dick, Inc., VABCA No. 5597, 01-2 BCA ¶ 31,647 (2001), *aff'd in part, rev'd in part, vacated in part, and remanded*, P.J. Dick, Inc. v. Principi, 324 F.3d 1364 (Fed. Cir. Apr. 7, 2003) (where the contract provided that the "current" schedule "will be" the basis for determining the extent of the delay, the Board was required to analyze the six major changes separately utilizing the most recent monthly update of the CPM schedule, rather than treating the suspension period as the date on which the first change was issued); Richmond American Homes of Colorado, Inc. v. United States, 80 Fed. Cl. 656, 2008 WL 681515 (Mar. 11, 2008), *appeal dismissed*, 352 Fed. Appx. 421 (Fed. Cir. May 8, 2009) (home builders were properly awarded unabsorbed home office overhead calculated under the *Eichleay* formula during the period they were effectively on standby during development of a remediation plan for the former Lowry Air Force Base in Colorado; builders' expert witness first calculated the amount of each builder's home office overhead allocable to the Lowry project by factoring company-wide total revenues/overhead and the company's total revenue for the Lowry project, then calculated daily overhead costs by dividing the Lowry overhead by the projected performance days, and finally calculated the unabsorbed overhead by multiplying the daily overhead by the number of days of delay).

Page 138, add to note 98 after Wickham case and before Appeal of Genisco:

; Complete Gen. Constr. Co. v. Ohio Dept. of Transp., 94 Ohio St. 3d 54, 760 N.E.2d 364, 370 (2002), *reconsid. denied*, 94 Ohio St. 3d 1489, 763 N.E.2d 1186 (2002) (the court modified the *Eichleay* formula for use in Ohio courts; specifically, courts applying the *Eichleay* formula must allow owners the opportunity to dispute particular items a contractor submits in an overall overhead cost presentation; government agencies could consider in this regard the Federal Acquisition Regulations' dissection of allowable and unallowable indirect costs, found at 48 C.F.R. §§ 31.205-1 through 31.205-52, for guidance).

Page 138, add to end of note 98:

; Nicon, Inc. v. United States, 331 F.3d 878 (Fed. Cir. 2003) (the trial court held that the contractor could not recover unabsorbed home office overhead where the contractor never began contract performance, since the contractor had no actual days of performance or actual contract billings as required by the *Eichleay* formula; the appellate court reversed and remanded, holding that the contractor is still entitled to recover unabsorbed home office overhead for the period between the date of the contract award and the government's termination for convenience if the contractor was forced into a standby position and if the contractor can find a reasonable method for allocating its fixed home office expenses during the period of suspension among the suspended contract and the other contracts the contractor was performing during the period of suspension); Appeal of Singleton Contracting Corp., ASBCA No. 51692 (2003) (the Board ruled that the *Eichleay* formula was inappropriate in a situation where notice-to-proceed was never issued, since *Eichleay* relies on a comparison of scheduled days of performance and actual days of performance; instead, the contractor had to provide indirect cost information sufficient to allow for an allocation of fixed home office expenses during the period of suspension among the suspended contract and the contractor's other contracts; here, the contractor failed to provide such cost information, and was therefore unable to recover).

§ 6.06 CALCULATING HOME OFFICE OVERHEAD IN STATE AND PRIVATE CONTRACTS

Page 140, in third sentence of first paragraph, add, Connecticut, Florida, Maryland, Ohio, and Puerto Rico after Virginia:

Page 140, add at beginning of note 105:

Triple R Paving, Inc. v. Broward County, 774 So. 2d 50 (Fla. Dist. Ct. App. 2000), *reh'g denied* (2001) (court noted that the *Eichleay* formula had previously been approved by the court, citing Broward County v. Russell, Inc., 589 So. 2d 983 (Fla. 4th Dist. Ct. App. 1991));

Page 140, add to note 105 after Nebraska Pub. Power Dist. case:

; Complete Gen. Constr. Co. v. Ohio Dept. of Transp., 94 Ohio St. 3d 54, 760 N.E.2d 364, 370 (2002), *reconsid. denied*, 94 Ohio St. 3d 1489, 763 N.E.2d 1186 (2002) (the *Eichleay* formula is *one way* of determining unabsorbed home office overhead damages in public construction delay cases; once it is determined that an owner-caused delay has caused a contractor to suffer unabsorbed overhead costs, then the *Eichleay* formula can be employed, but not necessarily exclusively; thus, for example, a court could use the direct cost formula instead). *But cf.* Continental Air Conditioning, Inc. v. Keller Constr. Co., 2003 WL 22120886 (Cal. App. 2003) (nonpublished) (although subcontractor argued that the *Eichleay* formula is the proper method of calculating extended home office overhead, citing Howard v. G.A. MacDonald Constr. Co., Inc., 71 Cal. App. 4th 38 (1999), for the proposition that the *Eichleay* formula has been accepted by California courts, the court said that the subcontractor misstated the holding in *Howard*; the *Howard* court did not adopt the *Eichleay* formula as the appropriate office overhead formula under California law; rather, it merely mentioned in passing that the parties in that case had agreed to use the *Eichleay* formula as the measure of damages; further, in this case, the trial court observed that although the *Eichleay* formula is the standard method of calculating such damages in federal courts, no California appellate court has approved the use of that formula; moreover, the trial court found that even if the *Eichleay* formula were used, the general contractor met its burden by demonstrating that the subcontractor experienced a steady increase in revenues before, during and after its work on the construction project, negating its claim for delay damages for increased home office overhead).

Page 140, add to note 105 after Fairfax Country case:

; M.J. Daly & Sons, Inc. v. City of West Haven, 1999 WL 793807 (Conn. Super. Sept. 24, 1999), *amended on reconsideration*, 1999 WL 1207130 (Conn. Super.

Dec. 3, 1999); Broward County v. Brooks Builders, Inc., 908 So. 2d 536 (Fla. Dist. Ct. App. 4th Dist. 2005); Gladwynne Constr. Co. v. Mayor & City Council of Baltimore, 147 Md. App. 149, 807 A.2d 1141 (2002); Norment Sec. Group, Inc. v. Ohio Dept. of Rehab. & Corr., 2003 WL 22890088 (Ohio Ct. Cl. Dec. 2, 2003); In re Redondo Constr. Corp., 411 B.R. 89 (Bankr. D.P.R. 2009) *amended in part on other grounds*, 424 B.R. 29 (Bankr. D.P.R. Feb. 11, 2010), *stay pending appeal granted*, 2010 WL 1286849 (Bankr. D.P.R. Mar. 30, 2010) (*Eichleay* formula utilized to calculate extended home office overhead costs awarded to contractor).

Page 141, add at end of note 119:

See also Heckler Elec. Co., Inc. v. City of N.Y., 186 Misc. 2d 77, 715 N.Y.S.2d 619 (Sup. Ct. N.Y. Cty. 2000) (court held that because home office overhead may be difficult to measure, even after the delays have ended, it may be permissible to estimate the overhead increases by use of a mathematical formula, provided that it is shown that overhead increases were in fact incurred as a result of delays but that proof of the actual amount of the increases is unavailable due to the nature of the business (citing *Berley Indus., Inc. v. City of New York*)).

Page 142, add at end of note 127:

But see Alamo Community College Dist. v. Browning Constr. Co., 131 S.W.3d 146 (Tex. App. 2004) (trial court awarded a contractor damages for home office overhead costs, calculated "by the daily rate of overhead allocable to the Contract and multiplying it by the number of days the job was extended"; on appeal, the owner argued that the submission of this instruction was error because Texas law does not recognize the *Eichleay* method of calculating damages, citing *Chilton*, 930 S.W.2d 877 (Tex. App. 1996); the appellate court noted that the *Chilton* court expressly declined to decide that issue, finding it unnecessary to decide the propriety of using the *Eichleay* standard; because the owner thus failed to present authority for its argument that the *Eichleay* formula should not be applied, it waived the issue, and the appellate court accordingly affirmed the trial court's measure of damages).

Page 143, add to end of section:

In *W.B. Construction v. Mountains Community Hospital District*,[127.1] a California Court of Appeal noted that the *Eichleay* formula has not been adopted by any California decisional authority and questioned whether it should be. Quoting from a treatise on California construction law (1 Acret, Cal. Construction

---

[127.1] 2005 WL 1385571 (Cal. Ct. App. June 13, 2005) (unpublished), *review denied* (Sept. 21, 2005).

Contracts and Disputes (Cont. Ed. Bar 3d ed. 1999) Public Works Contracts: Disputes and Remedies, § 4.67, p. 409), the court criticized the *Eichleay* formula for creating a rate for home office overhead and allocating it to projects in a manner independent of causation. For example, contractors that have a large amount of overhead and few projects will generally post a greater daily rate for home office overhead under the formula than will an efficiently run firm with many projects and proportionately lower overhead. As a result, contractors to which the formula is applied could be rewarded for inefficient or extravagant use of home office overhead.

§ 6.07 ESTABLISHING A PRIMA FACIE CASE FOR RECOVERY OF HOME OFFICE OVERHEAD

Page 143, add at end of note 128:

; Continental Air Conditioning, Inc. v. Keller Constr. Co., 2003 WL 22120886 (Cal. App. 2003) (nonpublished) (subcontractor argued that in cases where courts have approved the *Eichleay* formula, the burden shifts to the respondent to show the party seeking such damages could have undertaken other work during the period of delay; court held that no California appellate court has approved use of the *Eichleay* formula, but even if the *Eichleay* formula were used in this case, the general contractor met its burden by demonstrating that the subcontractor experienced a steady increase in revenues before, during, and after its work on the construction project; moreover, despite the shift in the burden of production when applying the *Eichleay* formula, contractor must still establish that it was unable to take on other work; in this case, however, subcontractor was unable to prove that due to the delay it was unable to take on other work; subcontractor claimed that because of its dispute with general contractor, it had to turn to insurance bond "secondary market" to meet its insurance needs, resulting in the subcontractor paying a higher rate for insurance; subcontractor's expert testified that he made no inquiry as to other possible causes for the increase in the bond rate, and in fact was not certain the increase was caused by the project; he also failed to inquire as to whether the subcontractor had in fact reached its bonding limit during the period at issue; subcontractor's expert did not even perform any investigation as to whether the subcontractor obtained new work during the project, or could have taken on other work during that time; further, there was no testimony that subcontractor wanted to bid on other jobs but could not do so because it was on standby).

Page 144, add at end of note 133:

See also Clifford R. Gray, Inc. v. City Sch. Dist. of Albany, 716 N.Y.S.2d 795 (App. Div. 3d Dept. 2000) (plaintiff's request to recover home office overhead expenses was properly rejected by the trial court; in rejecting the plaintiff's argument that proof was not necessary for this item of damages, the court repeated the well-established proposition that "[a] contractor wrongfully delayed by its employer must establish the extent to which its costs were increased by the improper acts because its recovery will be limited to damages actually sustained"; the plaintiff's evidence did no more than approximate such expenses by calculating a proportion of company-wide labor costs over job-specific labor costs for the relevant time period; this was insufficient to establish the requisite causal link between the delays and actual increased costs); Complete Gen. Constr. Co. v. Ohio Dept. of Transp., 94 Ohio St. 3d 54, 760 N.E.2d 364, 370 (2002), *reconsid. denied*, 94 Ohio St. 3d 1489, 763 N.E.2d 1186 (2002) (a prima facie case requires the contractor to demonstrate that it has committed a portion of its overhead costs to a particular project and that not only has the project's suspension left those costs unabsorbed, but that the character of the government-caused delay is such that it is impractical for the contractor to obtain other work to fill the gap; once the contractor commits resources to a project, the resources remain committed whether the project moves forward or not—"[t]he contractor is all geared up with nowhere to go"). *See also* Idela Constr. Co., ASBCA No. 45070, 01-2 BCA ¶ 31,437 (2001) (the Board stated that once Idela had proved: (1) the operations were suspended for a period of uncertain duration; (2) this suspension was caused solely by the government; and (3) the suspension of work extended the overall period of contract performance, then a presumption was created that the contractor had incurred unabsorbed home office overhead; once this presumption has been created, the government has the opportunity to rebut that presumption with evidence that the contractor was able to replace the suspended work with other work; in this case, the Board found that the government did not overcome the presumption of unabsorbed home office overhead).

Page 144, add at end of note 134:

Cf. Ryco Constr., Inc. v. United States, 55 Fed. Cl. 184 (Ct. Cl. 2002) (the court agreed with the government that plaintiff-contractor was not on standby during winter shutdowns of construction—once work was shut down for the winter, plaintiff could not have been on standby until the following season; however, the court did not agree that plaintiff was not on standby during the remaining portions of construction seasons; it was a triable issue whether plaintiff was on standby during those periods in which it was not prevented from working due to the winter shutdown; at trial, both parties would be able to present evidence as to whether this suspension was for an uncertain amount of time, and whether plaintiff was required to remain ready to perform); Triple R Paving, Inc. v. Broward County, 774 So. 2d 50 (Fla. Dist. Ct. App. 2000), *reh'g denied* (2001) (critical factor is not whether the contractor was able to obtain or continue to work on *other* or *additional* projects, but rather its ability to obtain a *replacement* contract to absorb the indirect costs that would otherwise be unabsorbed solely as a result of a government suspension on one contract); Commonwealth v. AMEC Civil, LLC, 54 Va. App. 240, 677 S.E.2d 633 (2009), *appeal granted*, ____ (Va. 2010) (not "every instance of delay," even if attributable to a contractual breach, entitles the contractor to a recovery of home office overhead costs; under Virginia law, the contractor must prove, among other things, that it could not otherwise reasonably recoup its pro rata home office expenses incurred while its workforce was idled by deploying its workforce on other revenue-producing aspects of the project during the delay; since neither AMEC's expert nor any of its fact witnesses addressed this issue, AMEC failed to present a prima facie case for recovery of home office overhead).

Page 145, add after carryover paragraph:

The government can rebut a contractor's prima facie case for unabsorbed overhead damages with evidence that: (1) the contractor actually reallocated all of its unabsorbed overhead to replacement work; (2) the contractor could have reallocated all of its unabsorbed overhead to replacement work, as it was not impracticable for the contractor to obtain such work; or (3) although it was impracticable for the contractor to reallocate its unabsorbed overhead to replacement work, the impracticability of obtaining replacement work was not due to the actions of the government.[136.1]

Page 145, add new note 137.1 at end of first full paragraph:

[137.1] *See also* Sauer Inc. v. Danzig, 224 F.3d 1340 (Fed. Cir. 2000) (citing *Satellite Elec. Co. v. Dalton*, the court said that before a contractor can recover *Eichleay* damages, it must show that a government-imposed delay occurred, that the contractor was required to stand by during the delay, and that while standing by it was unable to take on additional work; in this case, the contractor failed to demonstrate a government-imposed delay, i.e., a compensable delay; rather, the evidence indicated that the government's delay was concurrent with the contractor's own delay). On remand from the Court of Appeals, the Armed Services Board of Contract Appeals again denied the contractor's claim for damages for alleged productivity loss, citing a lack of proof: "The record contains too little evidence on the specifics of how and why productivity was lost." In re Sauer Inc., ASBCA No. 39605, 01-2 BCA ¶ 31,525 (2001).

[136.1] *Complete Gen. Constr. Co. v. Ohio Dep't of Transp.*, 2000 WL 674899 (Ohio Ct. App. 2000), *aff'd in part, rev'd in part*, 94 Ohio St. 3d 54, 760 N.E.2d 364 (2002), *reconsid. denied*, 94 Ohio St. 3d 1489, 763 N.E.2d 1186 (2002).

See also Vicari v. United States, 53 Fed. Cl. 357 (Ct. Cl. 2002) (*Eichleay* damages are recoverable only when work on the entire project is suspended, not when work is stopped on only part, forcing the contractor to work on other aspects of the project; in the latter case, plaintiff is not on standby, with its contract performance delayed indefinitely, thereby causing unabsorbed or extended indirect costs; rather, the plaintiff still receives a steady stream of payments for the direct costs associated with the other aspects of the contract; "[i]f work on the contract continues uninterrupted, albeit in a different order than originally planned, the contractor is not on standby"; indirect costs "are only unabsorbed, and thus only compensable, to the extent they accrue during the extension period because a contractor must continue work on that contract to make up for standing by throughout an unexpected suspension caused by the government"); JCI Int'l, Inc., ASBCA No. 54209 (2003) (as a result of encountering a differing site condition, Navy suspended work on the project until the problem was resolved; JCI was given a time extension and additional compensation for the changed work; Board denied JCI's claim for unabsorbed home office overhead during the suspension; although JCI claimed that the suspension impaired its bonding capacity and prevented it from taking on replacement work during the suspension, Board found that the primary cause of the impaired bonding capacity was two unresolved claims on other contracts).

Page 147, add at end of section:

When a federal contractor asserts a claim for *Eichleay* damages, the Board must itself determine whether the contractor is entitled to such damages, not merely decide whether the auditor's "finding" that the contractor has or has not done so is supported by the record. Thus, for example, the court in *Charles G. Williams Construction, Inc. v. White*,[141.1] reversed a denial by the Armed Services Board of Contract Appeals of a contractor's claim for *Eichleay* damages because the Board did not mention, let alone discuss, whether the contractor satisfied the two prerequisities to application of the *Eichleay* formula: (1) that the contractor was on standby; and (2) that the contractor was unable to take on other work. The court noted that the Board was entitled to give the auditor's evidence and testimony, like that of any other evidence, whatever weight it concluded it should have. However, under the Contracts Disputes Act, it is the function and responsibility of the Board, and not the auditor, to decide the question of entitlement. On the basis of the Board's opinion, the Court of Appeals could not determine whether the Board properly rejected the contractor's *Eichleay* claim, and the court therefore remanded for further proceedings.

[141.1] ASBCA No. 49,775, 00-2 BCA (CCH) ¶ 31,047 (2000), *rev'd and remanded*, 271 F.3d 1055 (Fed. Cir. 2001), 02-1 BCA (CCH) ¶ 31,833 (2002), *aff'd*, 326 F.3d 1376 (2003).

On remand, the Board held that Williams was not entitled to recover *Eichleay* damages because it had not established that it was on standby. Williams continued to work on the project during the extended contract performance period, and there was no reduction in Williams' flow of direct costs on the project. The appellate court affirmed, finding that as long as the contractor is able to continue performing the contract, it cannot recover *Eichleay* damages because it can still allocate a portion of its indirect costs to that contract, even if the contractor cannot perform the work in the same way or as efficiently or effectively as it had anticipated.

§ 6.08 CALCULATION OF HOME OFFICE OVERHEAD COSTS IN CASES OF EXTENDED CONTRACT PERFORMANCE

Page 147, add at end of note 142:

See also MacQuesten Gen. Contracting, Inc. v. HCE, Inc., 296 F. Supp. 2d 437 (S.D.N.Y. 2003) (in seeking damages for a two-month project delay, the subcontractor computed extended home office overhead by taking the total contract overhead carried in its bid for the five-month job, computing a monthly overhead rate, and then applying that rate to the two months of delay; court held this calculation was legally insufficient because the overhead element of the bid price was inherently unreliable, there was no evidence the delay actually increased subcontractor's total overhead costs, and there was no evidence that actual overhead figures were unavailable); The Millgard Corp. v. E.E. Cruz/Nab/Frontier-Kemper, 2007 WL 2388902 (S.D.N.Y. 2007), *adhered to on reconsideration on other grounds*, 2007 WL 4302492 (S.D.N.Y. Dec. 5, 2007), *judgment aff'd on other grounds*, 329 Fed. Appx. 307 (2nd Cir. (N.Y.) May 8, 2009) (the contractor was not entitled to recover home office overhead; it established the amount of home office overhead attributable to the period of contract performance, but not home office overhead costs before it commenced performance or after it was terminated, and therefore did not prove that any conduct for which the owner was responsible increased its home office overhead costs); CAMO Constr. Co., Inc. v. Town of Vidalia, 966 So.2d 796 (La. Ct. App. 2007) (contractor's claim for extended overhead was denied where the court found that executed change orders had compensated the contractor for all costs incurred due to changes in the plans resulting from defective plans and differing site conditions).

§ 6.09 CALCULATION OF HOME OFFICE OVERHEAD COSTS INCURRED AFTER DATE OF SUBSTANTIAL COMPLETION

Page 149, add at end of section:

In contrast, in *Young Enterprises of Georgia, Inc. v. General Services Administration,*[145.1] the contractor was denied home office overhead in part because much of the 82-day delay period claimed by the contractor occurred after substantial completion. The court further found that Young had not experienced any disruption in cash flow from the project.

§ 6.11 SUBCONTRACTOR PASSTHROUGH CLAIMS AND THE *EICHLEAY* FORMULA

Page 151, add at end of note 159:

See also, e.g., Harper/Nielsen-Dillingham, Builders, Inc. v. United States, 81 Fed. Cl. 667 (Apr. 29, 2008), *appeal dismissed*, 2009 WL 981976 (Fed. Cir. Jan. 29, 2009), *reconsid. denied*, 2009 WL 1227719 (Fed. Cir. May 4, 2009) (in determining whether a prime contractor is liable to a subcontractor for purposes of the *Severin* doctrine, damages are not limited to payments actually made to subcontractors but can include potential liability; thus, a passthrough suit to the government may be maintained when the prime contractor has reimbursed its subcontractor for the latter's damages or remains liable for such reimbursement in the future; in this case, however, the prime contractor was immunized from liability to its subcontractor by an "iron-bound" no-damages-for-delay clause in the subcontract, and thus, the prime contractor could not "pass through" the subcontractor's delay claims to the government under the *Severin* doctrine; further, even if California recognized a limited foreseeability exception to enforceability of a no-damages-for-delay clause, the evidence in this case established that the delays arose prior to execution of the subcontract, and therefore were within the contemplation of the parties).

[145.1] GSBCA No. 14437 (Oct. 19, 2000). *See also, e.g.*, In re Redondo Constr. Corp., 411 B.R. 89 (Bankr. D.P.R. 2009) *amended in part on other grounds*, 424 B.R. 29 (Bankr. D.P.R. Feb. 11, 2010), *stay pending appeal granted*, 2010 WL 1286849 (Bankr. D.P.R. Mar. 30, 2010) (no delay damages for extended overhead costs could be recovered for the period of time after the project was substantially completed when all the contract work, except for few very minor details, had been completed; after the project was substantially completed there could be no further delay analysis because the only tasks to complete were the minor items, punch list items or finishes which were not critical for the completion of the project).

§ 6.12 SECONDARY CONSIDERATIONS IN CALCULATING HOME OFFICE OVERHEAD

Page 153, add at end of note 169:

See also, e.g., Complete Gen. Constr. Co. v. Ohio Dept. of Transp., 94 Ohio St. 3d 54, 760 N.E.2d 364, 370 (2002), *reconsid. denied*, 94 Ohio St. 3d 1489, 763 N.E.2d 1186 (2002) (courts applying the *Eichleay* formula must allow owners the opportunity to dispute particular items a contractor submits in an overall overhead cost presentation; government agencies could consider in this regard the Federal Acquisition Regulations' dissection of allowable and unallowable indirect costs, found at 48 C.F.R. §§ 31.205-1 through 31.205-52, for guidance); Wayne Knorr, Inc. v. Pennsylvania Dept. of Transp., 973 A.2d 1061 (Pa. Commw. May 14, 2009) (where the contract provided for a markup on labor, material and equipment for force account work "to cover all administration, general superintendence, other overhead, bonds insurance, anticipated proft . . . ," and those markups were applied to delay damages awarded the contractor, no separate award of extended home office overhead would be allowed, since the markups already include an allowance for extended home office overhead).

§ 6.13 OTHER METHODS OF CALCULATING HOME OFFICE OVERHEAD

Page 153, add new note 170.1 at end of first sentence of section:

[170.1] *See, e.g.*, Metric Constr. Co., Inc. v. United States, 81 Fed. Cl. 804 (2008) (the plaintiff contractor claimed that a home office overhead rate of 8.45% should be applied to its recovery, but the government argued that this rate was excessive; the court agreed, noting that an overhead rate of 5.31% accorded with the overhead rates allowed in other similar cases; the court thus applied that rate here).

Chapter 7
JOBSITE OVERHEAD

§ 7.02 JOBSITE OVERHEAD DEFINED

Page 159, add at end of note 1:

See also Clifford R. Gray, Inc. v. City Sch. Dist. of Albany, 716 N.Y.S.2d 795 (App. Div., 3d Dept. 2000) (owner-caused delay supported contractor's recovery of damages for various expenses incurred as a result of such delay, including expenses for extended jobsite overhead.); P.J. Dick Inc., VABCA No. 5597, 01-2 BCA ¶ 31,647 (2001), *aff'd in part, rev'd in part, vacated in part, and remanded,* P.J. Dick, Inc. v. Principi, 324 F.3d 1364 (Fed. Cir. Apr. 7, 2003) (contractor held entitled to recover additional field overhead necessarily incurred as a result of government's constructive acceleration of work); Appeal of VA Venture Pueblo, VABCA No. 6959 (2003) (contractor was issued several contract modifications increasing the contract price, and the price adjustments included a 10 percent overhead mark-up on direct costs; contractor filed a claim for extended general conditions expenses incurred during the additional time on the project, including project supervision, rented modular space, dumpsters, portable toilets, and temporary utilities; Board held that the 10 percent overhead mark-up included in the modifications compensated the contractor for the added expenses, which were essentially field overhead); George Sollitt Constr. Co. v. United States, 64 Fed. Cl. 229 (Ct. Cl. 2005) (court distinguished between claim for extended field office overhead and unabsorbed home office overhead, noting that an extended field office overhead claim requests damages for costs that are increased due to maintaining a presence at construction site for longer period than originally anticipated in bid and requires different proof from a claim for unabsorbed home office overhead; home office overhead is an indirect cost, whereas field office overhead is a direct cost; plaintiff must prove government liability under the Suspension of Work clause for delay to project completion, and also must prove extent of its increased field office overhead costs; "field office overhead costs . . . , like other direct costs, require specific proof of proximate causation (as well as the quantum of damages)." [Citations omitted.]); ACE Constructors, Inc. v. United States, 70 Fed. Cl. 253 (2006), *aff'd,* 499 F.3d 1357 (Fed. Cir. 2007) (plaintiff-contractor sought an allowance for field overhead reflecting extra work performed by the contractor and the need for field supervision of that extra work. The contractor described this field overhead as "administrative costs to run a project, such things as [a] superintendent, quality control, vehicles associated with those people, clerical staff, [and] office supplies." The contractor requested field overhead equal to approximately 8.2% of direct costs before markups, and the court awarded all of the field overhead requested, resulting in an addition to the award of $29,938.97); Titan Stone, Tile & Masonry, Inc. v. Hunt Constr. Group, Inc., 2007 WL 3232588 (D.N.J. Oct. 31, 2007) (the defendant subcontractor's failure to adhere to the agreed-upon timetable for completion of its work entitled the general contractor to recover for the foreseeable increases in the costs of heating and the cost of construction of a temporary enclosure for the subcontractor's employees, along with overtime costs the contractor was required to pay follow-on subcontractors to accelerate their work as a result of the defendant subcontractor's delay); Appeal of States Roofing Corp., ASBCA No. 55506, 2008 WL 4467182 (Sept. 16, 2008) (contractor sought to recover equipment ownership cost of 25-ton crane contractor was required to utilize when the government determined not to permit the contractor to use the elevator for its work; the Board found that the government and the contractor had agreed to a rate of $46.85 per hour for the use of the crane, and that the contractor had been paid $46.85 per hour in previous modifications; however, since the contractor included equipment ownership costs in its field overhead, there was a duplication of costs for the crane; the Board directed the parties to remove crane ownership expense from field overhead and revise the total claim accordingly).

Page 159, add at end of note 4:

See also, e.g., Gilbane Bldg. Co. v. Two Turners Elec. Co., 2007 WL 582252 (Tex. App.-Hous. Feb. 27, 2007), *review denied* (Sept. 28, 2007), *reh'g of petition for review denied* (Dec. 14, 2007) (an electrical subcontractor was entitled to recover the actual cost of additional time worked by its employees as a result of the general contractor's breach of the contract, which resulted in a compression of the schedule, plus a 20 percent burden rate, consisting of compensation for profit (5%), overhead (10%), and taxes, insurance and supervisor costs (5%). The subcontractor also received a 5% supervisory fee for the work performed by various contract electricians hired by the subcontractor and the general contractor).

Page 160, add at end of section:

When project management costs are not being incurred on the project site, they may not be recoverable. In *Keever & Associates, Inc. v. Randall,*[4.1] the contractor was denied recovery of administrative costs on the basis that these efforts were included in the overhead and profit markup. In this matter, the contractor had a contract to construct a barn and residence and was to be paid the actual cost of labor and materials plus 10 percent for overhead and profit. The contractor charged $55 per hour for time spent by its president administering the project,

[4.1] 129 Wash. App. 733, 119 P.3d 926 (Sept. 20, 2005).

and contended this constituted costs for which it should be reimbursed. The court ruled against the contractor, finding that the percentage markup in the contract included the cost of administering and managing the contract. The court noted that there were no time cards or other documents supporting the administrative efforts of the president and that the claimed amount was based entirely on estimated or averaged hours. It was further noted that such charges had not been made until a dispute arose between the owner and the contractor.

When general conditions costs are incurred on site and are treated consistently as direct costs, they are not part of the markup on subcontractor costs. In *AMEC Construction Management, Inc. v. General Services Administration*,[4.2] the General Services Board of Contract Appeals ruled that extended general conditions costs were a direct cost of contract performance and were not included in the markup on subcontractor costs. In this matter, the contract duration had been extended for additional work, all of which was performed by subcontractors. GSA asserted that it should not have to pay extended general conditions costs during the five-month extended period because those costs would be covered by the 10 percent markup on the subcontracted work. The contract did not define what was covered in the markup on subcontracted work. On earlier change orders, a general conditions allowance had been included in addition to the markup and, based upon that prior practice and the lack of any provision defining what the markup covered, the Board determined that extended general conditions costs were recoverable.

The owner may also incur certain jobsite costs, which might be recoverable in the event of contractor delay. For example, in *Tennessee Gas Pipeline Co. v. Technip USA Corp.*,[4.3] the owner, TGP, brought a breach of contract action against the general contractor, Technip, to recover damages caused by delays in making improvements to a gas pipeline, including "project delay costs" relating to extended administration of the contract. Although Technip argued that a contract clause precluding recovery of consequential damages for such items as loss of profits or revenue and loss of opportunity or use barred TGP from recovering any delay damages, the court held that the clause excluded only delay damages that *also qualified* as consequential damages (damages that result naturally, but not necessarily, from the breach), and did not preclude recovery of delay damages that constituted *direct* damages (damages that result naturally and necessarily from the breach). TGP incurred extended expenses for contract administration, including labor, travel, environmental contractors, TGP inspectors, supply of additional construction consumables, costs for hauling wastewater from the site, and services and utilities. These costs were the "owner's Responsibilities" under the contract, and the parties therefore clearly contemplated that TGP would incur these costs throughout the project and that a delay in contract completion "naturally and

[4.2] GSBCA No. 16233 (Nov. 18, 2005).

[4.3] 2008 WL 3876141 (Tex. App.-Hous. Aug. 21, 2008), *review denied* (2 pets.) (Sept. 25, 2009).

necessarily" would cause these costs to be extended over a longer period of time. The court held these costs were thus direct damages, and not excluded under the consequential damages provision of the contract.

§ 7.03 CALCULATION METHODS

Page 160, add at end of note 5:

See also, e.g., Appeal of Fire Sec. Sys., Inc., VABCA No. 5559-63, 02-2 BCA ¶ 31,977 (2002) (contractor calculated its total site overhead costs for the 300-day contract period at $38,011, resulting in a daily rate of $126.70 ($38,011 ÷ 300) for the period; the court applied that rate to the 16 calendar days of suspension ($126.70 × 16) to calculate total site overhead costs during the suspension periods of $2,027); Bell BCI Co. v. United States, 81 Fed. Cl. 617 (2008), *aff'd in part, vacated in part, remanded*, 570 F.3d 1337 (Fed. Cir. June 25, 2009), *reh'g and reh'g en banc denied* (Oct. 9, 2009), *on remand*, 72 Fed. Cl. 164 (Feb. 24, 2010) (contractor sought to recover extended general condition costs for extended period of construction, including project management, field supervision staff, clerical support, field engineering, office trailer, equipment, supplies, storage facilities, trash dumpsters, pick-up trucks, fuel, temporary toilets, and utilities; contractor's expert calculated these delay damages by determining total general conditions costs for the project of $7,953,857, dividing it by the total duration of the project of 1,410 days to obtain a daily rate of $5,641 (rounded), then multiplying the daily rate by 284 days of delay to arrive at a total of $1,602,053; since the government only disputed that it was responsible for the delay, and did not challenge the calculation of extended general conditions costs, the entire amount was awarded to the contractor); on appeal, the Federal Circuit Court reversed the award on the grounds that the contractor waived its delay claims in connection with certain modifications, and remanded to the lower court to determine which delays, if any, were not waived; however, the Federal Circuit Court found no error in the lower court's methodology for calculating delay damages); Appeal of Packard Constr. Corp., 09-2 BCA ¶ 34234, ASBCA No. 55383, 2009 WL 2601247 (Aug. 10, 2009) (the government had issued a unilateral modification for 66 calendar days of compensable time extension for government-directed changes, with extended field overhead calculated at $308.89 per day, plus markups; the actual daily contract field overhead rate, as audited by the government, was $786.00, and Packard was entitled to recover that amount less the amounts already paid under the unilateral modification); In re Electric Mach. Enters., Inc., 416 B.R. 801 (Bankr. M.D. Fla. 2009) (electrical subcontractor, EME, was severely impacted and damaged by trade stacking resulting from the general contractor's lack of coordination of the trade contractors; EME sought to recover its actual jobsite overhead costs, which totaled 23.88% of EME's total direct costs; the Court instead awarded EME 15% overhead, which was the percentage of overhead upon which EME's bid was based, because there was no evidence that the overrun of EME's overhead resulted from the general contractor's mismanagement).

Page 164, add new note 5.1 at end of second full sentence on page:

[5.1] George Sollitt Constr. Co. v. United States, 64 Fed. Cl. 229 (Ct. Cl. 2005) (contractor sought to recover $115,122 in additional costs for temporary enclosures and heat allegedly made necessary by construction delays that pushed project into winter months; contractor's burden was to prove that work would have been completed before winter months but for unreasonable delays by government; however, contractor did not meet its burden of proof, and even if contractor had proven that unreasonable delays by government pushed the exterior masonry work into winter months, it did not prove that government-caused delays were sole and proximate cause of delayed start to this work; rather, documents showed a delay of at least one-and-a-half months in contractor's procurement of structural steel, which also would have delayed exterior masonry work; contractor bore burden of apportioning any concurrent delays to prove its claim, and because contractor did not apportion delays affecting the exterior masonry work, and record lacked specificity and certainty that would make apportionment feasible, no award could be made).

Page 164, add at end of note 6:

See also Appeal of J.C. Equipment Corp., ASBCA No. 51321, 02-1 BCA ¶ 31,810 (2002) (a claim for additional *salaried* employees' compensation due to changed work will not be granted when the contractor also allocates field and/or home office overhead costs to the same changed work; in this case, a contractor's claim for reimbursement of the salaries of its salaried employees who worked on changed work was disallowed when the contractor also allocated to the same changed work a 10 percent field and/or 3 percent home office overhead costs. There was no evidence submitted that any salaried employee was being paid an amount over and above his or her salary as a result of the changed work).

Page 165, add at end of note 9:

Gladwynne Constr. Co. v. Mayor & City Council of Baltimore, 147 Md. App. 149, 807 A.2d 1141 (2002) (where the trial court found that the contractor was entitled to recover extended field costs for 195 days due to delays occasioned by the city, but the evidence indicated that the delay was actually longer, the appellate court vacated the trial court's judgment and remanded for further proceedings as to the length of delay for which the contractor was entitled to compensation for extended field costs); Appeal of AEI Pacific, Inc., ASBCA No. 53806, 2008 WL

436928 (Feb. 8, 2008) (the contractor was found to be entitled to 16 days of extended field overhead at a rate of $1,641.33 per day to compensate for owner-caused delays and acceleration).

Page 166, add at end of note 13:

Quality Asphalt Paving, Inc. v. State Dept. of Transp. & Pub. Facilities, 71 P.3d 865 (Alaska 2003) (the court affirmed the hearing officer's decision to award the contractor mobilization costs, which cover preparatory work and operations, including movement of personnel, equipment, and supplies to the jobsite, but not demobilization costs, which cover equivalent activities upon completion of the project; the contract's termination-for-convenience clause allowed recovery for "mobilization efforts," and it was the standard practice of the industry—and of the contractor—to charge only mobilization costs to a project, and to charge demobilization costs as part of mobilization for the next project; although the contractor claimed that its normal policy regarding demobilization was inapplicable to this project because the government's termination for convenience left the contractor without a new job to which to charge its demobilization costs, the court held that the industry standard and the contractor's own policy regarding demobilization costs constituted substantial evidence supporting the hearing officer's decision to deny the contractor additional demobilization costs).

Page 166, add at end of section:

The two methods discussed above for recovering project overhead or general conditions costs are the percentage markup on direct costs method and the daily rate method. On projects where the time of performance is not extended but work is added, the percentage markup method is typically used. On a project where the major change is to extend the time of performance, the daily rate method is typically used. With the *Mortenson* decision, the contractor faces a difficult decision in determining which approach it should elect for a project with both significant amounts of added work and delays. In such a case, the contractor risks under-recovery of the additional project overhead costs. To address this problem, there are several possible approaches:

1. Use both methods;
2. Use segregated cost pools; or
3. Use daily rate and daily rate differential to quantify both delay costs and additional costs.

To use both methods, the contractor will need to carefully calculate the additional overhead recovered using the percentage method and when those overhead recoveries occurred based upon when the changes were performed. This overhead recovery can then be credited against the overhead expended during the additional time for performance. This analysis is necessary to prevent double recovery of project overheads. Contractors that maintain sophisticated cost accounting systems can segregate the project overheads into the fixed time-related costs, such as office rental, telephone, and project manager salary, and activity-related costs, such as equipment, tools, consumables, fuel, and similar items. The appropriate cost pool can be assigned to each change and the appropriate calculation method used. The problems with this approach are apparent. Precise definition of what type of cost any particular cost is can be difficult. Further, certain types of costs, such as a superintendent's pickup truck, radios, telephone, etc., can fall into both pools depending upon the circumstances.

By carefully measuring periodic costs of project overhead, increases in project overhead can be identified and potentially allocated to specific events, such as added work or extended periods of performance. In other words, if it is necessary to increase the staff or work more overtime or obtain more office space as a result of a large number of changes, it may be possible to identify that added cost. The added costs can then be segregated from the extended period of performance, and both costs recovered.

On highway or other road projects, provision for traffic control devices and traffic control is a significant cost that is required for performance of the work but does not represent work incorporated into the final product. Recovery of these costs can become a significant issue when projects are delayed or changed in other fashions. In *In re MIG Corporation*,[14] a contractor sought recovery of the unamortized portion of the purchase price of traffic control devices following a partial termination for convenience. The contractor was performing deck repair and paving of the Bourne and Sagamore bridges crossing the Cape Cod Canal in Bourne, Massachusetts, under a fixed price contract. The contract value was broken down into contract line items, one of which comprised traffic control devices such as barriers, drums, cones, and signs. The contractor completed the Bourne Bridge work, but was terminated for convenience for the work on the Sagamore Bridge. MIG sought payment of the unamortized portion of the cost of the traffic control devices as part of its termination settlement proposal. The Corps of Engineers contended that MIG had been paid for the use of the devices through the performance of the work on the Bourne bridge and therefore was not entitled to any payment for these devices as part of the work on the Sagamore bridge. The contractor claimed that the devices were unique to the project, as they did not comply with the requirements for traffic control devices on Massachusetts State Highway Department projects and that they had been purchased exclusively for this contract with the Corps of Engineers. As a result of the government's termination for convenience, a portion of purchase price for the traffic control devices was never recovered. The Board found that the cost of the traffic control devices were part of the preparatory cost of the terminated portion of the work and therefore the contractor was entitled to recover the unamortized portion of the cost.

---

[14] ASBCA No. 54451, 2005 WL 1271522 (May 25, 2005).

CHAPTER 8
PROFIT

§ 8.01 INTRODUCTION

Page 169, add at end of note 1:

See **Chapter 12, Section 12.05**, *infra*, for a discussion of an owner's ability to recover lost profits.

§ 8.02 PROFIT DEFINED

Page 170, add new note 1.1 at end of section:

[1.1] *See, e.g.*, Levitt-Ansca Towne Park P'ship v. Smith & Co., Inc., 873 So. 2d 392 (Fla. Dist. Ct. App. Apr. 14, 2004), *reh'g denied* (June 8, 2004) (developer and contractor executed contract for contractor to perform earthwork; parties agreed to $2 million contract price, which consisted of $1.7 million in cost of performance, profit of $300,000, and a speculative amount for surplus fill that was to be removed from jobsite by contractor; developer terminated contract after contractor had partly performed, and contractor sued, seeking to recover lost profits and also additional damages for "costs" incurred as a result of developer's breach, which allegedly took the form of idle equipment, an added bond premium, and unfunded equipment mobilization (plus a 15 percent markup); court held, however, that if these "costs" were to be recouped, they needed to be deducted from contractor's claim for lost profits; thus, court below committed error in adding these costs as an element of recoverable damages); J. Alvarez Constr., Inc. v. Western Nat. Group, L.P., 2007 WL 2083704 (Cal. Ct. App. July 23, 2007) (unpublished) (lost profits are defined as "the gains made from sales 'after deducting the value of the labor, materials, rents, and all expenses, together with the interest of the capital employed"; a plaintiff must show loss of net pecuniary gain, not just loss of gross revenue; in this case, the only evidence presented by the contractor was the amount of profit margin included in its bid; the contractor failed to present evidence that it accurately assessed the costs of labor when it bid the contract, and it presented no evidence as to the amount of money it expended on labor through the date of termination, or the amount of money it would have cost to complete the project; thus, the contractor failed to prove with reasonable certainty the extent of its lost profits).

§ 8.03 PROFIT ON WORK PERFORMED

Page 171, add at end of note 11:

See also Norment Sec. Group, Inc. v. Ohio Dept. of Rehab. & Corr., 2003 WL 22890088, 2003-Ohio-6572 (Ct. Cl. 2003) (plaintiff asserted that it was unable to install conduit, wiring, and electronic security systems in accordance with its contractual obligations because it did not have timely access to the rooms where the construction was to occur; the court agreed, finding the condition of the rooms at the time that plaintiff was scheduled to perform its work were in such a disruptive state that plaintiff was effectively denied access to the building site; court held that plaintiff was entitled to recover direct damages in the amount of $87,603 and, in accordance with the contract, an additional $8,760, representing a 10 percent "mark-up" profit on its subcontractor's work). *Cf.* Clifford R. Gray, Inc. v. City Sch. Dist. of Albany, 716 N.Y.S.2d 795 (App. Div. 3d Dept. 2000) (owner-caused delay supported contractor's recovery of damages for various expenses incurred as a result of such delay, including lost profit).

Page 172, add at end of section:

In *Intermetal Fabricators, Inc. v. The Losco Group, Inc.*,[14.1] a general contractor sought to recover damages, including lost profit, from a subcontractor who abandoned the project. The court held that the general contractor was entitled to the additional cost incurred for labor and materials, that is, the actual cost of completing the work, but because it hired another steel subcontractor to perform the work, under New York law it was not entitled to include its general requirements, overhead, and profit in the backcharge. In contrast, the court noted that when a contractor uses its own forces to complete work that the subcontractor was obligated to complete under the contract, the general contractor is entitled to add overhead and profit to its backcharge, "since it could otherwise have been using its resources in other profit making activities."

In *Commonwealth of Virginia v. AMEC Civil, LLC.*,[14.2] the general contractor, AMEC, was awarded damages based upon differing site conditions, plus a profit markup under the contract provision regarding extra work on a "force account basis." The appellate court reversed, finding that the differing site conditions provision of the contract expressly excluded "anticipated profits," and the general dispute provision states only "actual costs for materials, labor and equipment will be considered." Since profit is not included in actual costs, either direct or indirect, and AMEC's claims were not based upon the force account provision, the award of a profit markup was reversed.

[14.1] 2000 WL 1154249 (S.D.N.Y. 2000).

[14.2] 54 Va. App. 240, 677 S.E.2d 633 (2009), *appeal granted* _____ (Va. Jan. 28, 2010).

§ 8.04 DETERMINING PROFIT PERCENTAGES ON WORK PERFORMED

Page 172, add at end of note 15:

See also, e.g., ACE Constructors, Inc. v. United States, 70 Fed. Cl. 253 (2006), *aff'd*, 499 F.3d 1357 (Fed. Cir. 2007) (a rate of profit included in an equitable adjustment should fairly reflect the nature of the work and the risks involved [citing Cibinic and Nash, Administration of Government Contracts at 754 (3d ed.1995)]); Metric Constr. Co., Inc. v. United States, 81 Fed. Cl. 804 (2008) (the plaintiff contractor requested that a profit margin of 12% be applied to its equitable adjustment; the government, on the other hand, argued that no profit should be allowed because the contractor had been steadily losing money on the projects at issue—a government expert opined that he had examined the contractor's financial statements over a four-year time period that included the time up to and through the instant claim and had found that the contractor's profitability was "a negative 5 percent"; the court did not doubt the accuracy of the government expert, but held that the conclusion that no profit should be allowed could not be accepted; the court accordingly reduced the claimed profit to ten percent, an allowance the court asserted to be fairly standard [citing Ace Constructors, *supra*, as well as Cibinic and Nash, *supra*]).

Page 172, add at end of note 19:

See also A.A. Beiro Constr. Co., DCCAB No. D-822, 2002 WL 273519 (2002) (Board held that a 10 percent profit factor was reasonable where the government made no showing that there would have been a loss on the contract; applying the 10% rate to the $6,923,663 sum of the contractor's direct costs of $6,294,239 and overhead costs of $629,424, yielded profit of $692,366). *Cf.* United States *ex rel.* Maris Equip. Co., Inc. v. Morganti, Inc., 163 F. Supp. 2d 174 (E.D.N.Y 2001) *aff'd sub nom.* Morganti, Inc. v. Liberty Bond Serv., Inc., 2003 WL 21488807 (2nd Cir. (N.Y.) 2003) (award of 10% profit to subcontractor on *quantum meruit* claim was erroneous when project report indicated that subcontractor anticipated a profit of not more than 6.4 percent, and change orders in the prime contract, although of questionable relevance, indicated a 5 percent profit); ACE Constructors, Inc. v. United States, 70 Fed. Cl. 253 (2006), *aff'd*, 499 F.3d 1357 (Fed. Cir. 2007) (a 10% rate is often treated as standard, although when a modification is of relatively small dollar value and contains basically the same mix of work as the basic contract, many agencies apply the profit rate that pertains to the basic contract; in this case, the contractor sought a markup of 10% for profit, while the government contended that the profit rate should be 8.28% of direct costs plus field and home-office overheads. The court awarded the 10% rate, noting that the government failed adequately to explain how it derived its suggested 8.28% profit rate, that some of the early amendments to the contract incorporated a 10%

profit, and that the extra work at issue was of the same nature as the other work the contractor was performing under the contract).

§ 8.05 PROFIT ON WORK PERFORMED PRIOR TO TERMINATION

Page 176, add after numbered list and before first paragraph:

The rate of profit a contractor is entitled to on a termination for convenience is not necessarily the change order rate specified in the contract. In *Charles G. Williams Construction, Inc. v. White,*[30.1] the Armed Services Board of Contract Appeals ruled that when a contract is terminated for the convenience of the government, profit on performed work should be based on the profit percentage the contractor would have realized on the entire contract had there been no termination. In this matter, the contractor was performing improvements to the Army medical center in Aurora, Colorado. The project was divided into Phase 1, the south half of the building, and Phase 2, the north half of the building. After completion of Phase 1, the government decided to terminate the contract because it was going to make substantial changes in Phase 2 and was unable to reach an agreement with the contractor on the price of those changes. The contractor submitted its termination settlement using a 10 percent markup on the cost of the work, based on the percentage allowed on change orders. The government audited the bid documents and determined that the contractor's bid documents showed a 3.61 percent profit. The court held that the contractor was entitled to the 3.61 percent profit rate rather than the 10 percent change order rate sought by the contractor.

However, if it is determined that the contractor would have incurred a loss on the project if it had completed the work, the contractor is not entitled to recover any profit on a termination for convenience. In *In re Abcon Associates, Inc.,*[30.2] the United States Postal Service's termination for cause was converted to a termination for convenience upon a finding that Abcon had been entitled to time extensions pursuant to Requests for Equitable Adjustment that were denied by the Postal Service. The contractor's claim for lost profit was denied, however, because the contractor's direct costs and overhead incurred to perform the work prior to termination, plus its estimated cost to complete the work, exceeded the adjusted contract price at termination.

Another method for calculating lost profit is by determining the percent complete of the contract and awarding the contractor that percentage of the originally estimated profit. In *Appeal of Quality Seeding, Inc.,*[30.3] it was determined

---

[30.1] ASBCA No. 49775, 00-2 BCA (CCH) ¶ 31,047 (2000), *reversed and remanded on other grounds*, 271 F.3d 1055 (Fed. Cir. 2001), *on remand*, 02-1 BCA (CCH) ¶ 31,833 (2002), *aff'd*, 326 F.3d 1376 (Fed. Cir. 2003).

[30.2] 2008 WL 53123, PSBCA No. 5291 (Mar. 12, 2008).

[30.3] IBCA No. 2297 (Aug. 8, 1998).

that the contractor had completed 85.4 percent of the work as of the date of termination for convenience, and was therefore entitled to 85.4 percent of the project's projected profit.

In *The Millgard Corp. v. E.E. Cruz/Nab/Frontier-Kemper*,[30.4] the court held that the contractor was entitled to an award of $9.1 million in damages for lost profits equal to 62.57 percent of direct costs incurred in performing the work prior to termination; although the contractor had prepared estimates of anticipated profits that were inconsistent with this claim amount, the court found that the testimony of the contractor's president and an expert witness was sufficient to meet the contractor's burden of proving lost profits "with reasonable certainty."

In *Abra Constr. Corp. v. 112 Duane Associates, LLC*,[30.5] the trial court properly rejected Abra's completion-percentage method for calculating the value of work Abra performed under the contract until it was wrongfully terminated; the percentage-of-completion was not an accurate indicator of Abra's alleged damages, since Abra failed to establish substantial completion of the contract as a whole; the contract was terminated in the early stages and Abra had only been on the job for approximately two months; the completion-percentage method was also inaccurate because Abra sought to obtain the benefit of the percentage-of-completion of work performed by other subcontractors, for which Abra did not pay; the trial court thus properly calculated the value of the work performed by using Abra's payroll records, adding reasonable percentages for labor burden, overhead and profit (percentage not specified), and adding to that figure the amount of proven cost of plaintiff's materials that had been stipulated by the parties.

Page 176, add at end of section:

There are situations in which the Loss Position Rule, which prohibits recovery on a termination for convenience if the contractor would have lost money on the entire contract, may not be applicable. For example, in *Appeal of D.E.W., Inc.*,[31.1] the Armed Services Board of Contract Appeals found that when a termination for convenience results from impossibility of performance, the contractor's recovery is not limited to the contract price and is not subject to the Loss Position Rule. In this matter, the contractor had been terminated for default. The Board subsequently determined that the government's design was technically impossible to perform and converted the default to a termination for convenience of the government. The contractor then submitted a termination settlement proposal that was challenged by the government on the grounds that

[30.4] 2007 WL 2388902 (S.D.N.Y. Aug. 21, 2007), *adhered to on reconsideration*, 2007 WL 4302492 (S.D.N.Y. Dec. 5, 2007), *judgment aff'd*, 329 Fed. Appx. 307 (2nd Cir. (N.Y.) May 8, 2009).

[30.5] 59 A.D.3d 263, 873 N.Y.S.2d 574 (1st Dept. 2009).

[31.1] ASBCA No. 507.96 (Sept. 11, 2000).

the contractor would receive performance costs in excess of the contract price and that the contractor had been in loss position at the time of termination. The Board ruled that since the termination for convenience resulted from impossibility of performance, the usual limitations did not apply.

In *Foremost Mechanical Systems, Inc. v. General Services Administration,*[31.2] the Loss Position Rule was not applied because the contractor's loss position was due to numerous government drawing errors for which the contractor should have received price adjustments. The government had refused to authorize the price adjustments, resulting in the contractor being in a loss position. The Board found that the contractor was entitled to recover the full cost of the work performed prior to termination, but was not allowed a profit markup on the costs since it could not show that even with the change orders it would have earned a profit on the project.

In *In re Alfair Development Co. Inc.,*[31.3] the government's application of the Loss Rule was upheld. In this matter, the contractor had been awarded a contract to construction ammunitions maintenance facility at Hurlburt Field in Florida. When the work was approximately 93 percent complete, the government terminated the contractor for convenience. At that time the contractor had incurred $2,575,059 in performance costs and had been paid $2,384,674 of the $2,495,000 contract price. The contractor asserted that all performance costs prior to the date of termination, plus profit on all costs, less amounts paid, should be the amount it was entitled to. The government objected, asserting that the estimated cost to complete the work was $186,990 which should be added to the performance cost for a total cost of $2,762,049, which would make the contract a loss contract when compared to its $2,495,000 contract price. The Board sided with the government and divided the contract price of $2,495,000 by the $2,762,049 of estimated and actual project cost to arrive at a loss ratio of .9033. The contractor was, therefore, entitled to recover 90.33 percent of its total incurred costs and to receive no profit on those costs, since it was a loss contract. When the amount calculated by this formula was added to the $33,635 in allowable settlement expenses, the contractor's total entitlement was less than the contract payments it had received, and therefore it was not entitled to further payments.

§ 8.06 PROFIT ON UNPERFORMED WORK

Page 176, add at end of note 32:

See also, e.g., Tolar Constr., LLC v. Kean Elec. Co., Inc., 944 So. 2d 138 (Ala. 2006) (the "well-settled" rule for calculating damages when one party has prevented another's performance is: "'If the [general contractor] breached an essential and dependent feature of the contract, the [subcontractor] may abandon it

[31.2] GSBCA No. 12335 (Mar. 31, 1998).
[31.3] ASBCA No. 53119 (June 9, 2005).

and . . . sue on the contract and recover an amount equal to a proportion of the contract price which he has earned. . . .'"; when a plaintiff sues on a contract to recover the amount he would have received for the full performance prevented by the defendant's breach, he seeks in effect to recover as damages the profit from performance of the contract which profit defendant's breach prevented him from earning); Millgard Corp. v. E.E. Cruz/NAB/Frontier-Kemper, 2007 WL 2388902 (S.D.N.Y. Aug. 21, 2007), *adhered to on reconsideration*, 2007 WL 4302492 (S.D.N.Y. Dec. 5, 2007), *judgment aff'd*, 329 Fed. Appx. 307 (2nd Cir. (N.Y.) May 8, 2009) (an award of $9.1 million in lost profits was affirmed in favor of a subcontractor that was wrongfully terminated for cause on a contract to construct a sewer overflow facility; although the owner contended that it was not liable due to impossibility of the subcontractor's performance by virtue of the inability to secure city approval for wall designs, such a defense may be raised only when the impossibility is produced by an unanticipated event that could not have been foreseen or guarded against in the contract; thus, the subcontractor was entitled to lost profits measured from the time of contract up to the time when the subcontractor would have been terminated for convenience due to the impossibility of the design).

Page 176, add at end of note 33:

See also, e.g., Levitt-Ansca Towne Park P'ship v. Smith & Co., Inc., 873 So. 2d 392 (Fla. Dist. Ct. App. Apr. 14, 2004), *reh'g denied* (June 8, 2004) (trial court erred in awarding plaintiff contractor lost profits, because the award, which was based on an estimate, was too speculative; parties had agreed to a $2 million contract price, which consisted of $1.7 million in cost of performance, profit of $300,000, and a speculative amount for surplus fill that was to be removed from jobsite by contractor; contract provided no guarantee of the amount of surplus fill that contractor might expect, nor did developer agree to a specified sum; contract defined surplus fill as that which was "not needed for the Project"; because contractor never completed project, its proof came in the form of an estimation, not reality; jury's award was thus too speculative).

Page 176, add at end of note 34:

See also Richmond American Homes of Colorado, Inc. v. United States, 80 Fed. Cl. 656, 2008 WL 681515 (Mar. 11, 2008), *appeal dismissed*, 352 Fed. Appx. 421 (Fed. Cir. May 8, 2009) (in this case of first impression, the court held that indemnification under Section 330 of the National Defense Authorization Act for Fiscal Year 1993, 10 U.S.C. § 2687 note, does not allow for recovery of lost profits; notwithstanding the legislative aim of Section 330 to remove disincentives to private development of former military bases, the remedies available to an indemnitee cannot be expanded beyond those contemplated by Congress; although section 330 spares the transferee of military base property the burdens and risks associated with defending environmental suits or enforcement actions, no authority guarantees that the purchase of military base property will be profitable).

Page 177, add new note 34.1 after certainty in first line of page:

[34.1] Wisch & Vaughan. Constr. Co. v. Melrose Props. Corp., 21 S.W.3d 36 (Mo. Ct. App. 2000) (anticipated profits lost because of a breach of contract are recoverable only when they "are made reasonably certain by proof of actual facts which present data for a rational estimate of such profits"). *See also* Building Materials Wholesale, Inc. v. Triad Drywall, LLC, 287 Ga. App. 772, 653 S.E.2d 115 (Oct. 10, 2007), *on remand sub nom.* Triad Drywall, LLC v. Building Materials Wholesale, Inc., 2008 WL 4905076 (Ga. Super. Aug. 7, 2008), *aff'd sub nom.* Triad Drywall, LLC v. Building Materials Wholesale, Inc., 300 Ga. App. 745, 679 S.E.2d 364 (Nov. 4, 2009) (appellate court reversed an award of lost profits incurred by a subcontractor, Triad, after the supplier, BMW, refused to honor its price quote and Triad lost the subcontract which it had started to perform but had not yet been signed; although the evidence established that BMW breached its contract to supply materials, and that such breach caused Triad to be unable to perform the work, the court found that Triad had failed to meet its burden of proving both anticipated revenues and expenses with reasonable certainty; although anticipated revenues were established by the amount of the proposed subcontract between Triad and the general contractor, Triad offered no evidence as to anticipated expenses; the testimony of Triad's president that the company's average and anticipated profit margin was 30% was relevant to show that it was entitled to some recovery, but the amount of the probable gain and expenses must be shown with "great specificity"; the court remanded for a new trial on the issue of damages; on remand, the lower court held that "the testimony and evidence of anticipated profits presented to the jury by Plaintiff are too incomplete and speculative for the jury to determine what the damages are. The Plaintiff did not present to the jury by way of testimony or evidence, the true profit margin or the total profits that Plaintiff could have realized if it had completed the job. The testimony and evidence as to damages were so indefinite that there is nothing the jury could use to determine damages"; on appeal, the appellate court affirmed, finding that there was insufficient evidence that Triad had a history of profitability during the period relevant to this case; further, Triad failed to provide definite, certain, and reasonable data to ascertain the amount of lost profits on the job; Triad's estimate exceeded the price Triad contended had been agreed upon, and Triad's estimator attributed this to some unspecified amount relating to stucco that was deleted from the parties' agreement).

Page 177, add at end of note 35:

See also, e.g., Lewis Jorge Constr. Mgmt., Inc. v. Pomona Unified Sch. Dist., 34 Cal. 4th 960, 22 Cal. Rptr. 3d 340, 102 P.3d 257 (2004) (contractor is not entitled to recover as general damages lost profits on unidentified contracts contractor did not get when its bonding was impaired as a result of owner's breach, such damages clearly were not contemplated as part of the parties' bargain; full performance by owner would have provided contractor with full payment of contract price, and, while contractor anticipated earning a profit on its contract, that projected profit was limited by contract price and contractor's costs of performance; if contractor's bid accurately predicted its costs, benefit of its contractual bargain for profits was capped by whatever net profit it had assumed in setting its bid price; owner's termination of contract did not directly or necessarily cause contractor's loss of potential profits on future contracts; such loss resulted from decision of contractor's surety at the time of breach, to cease bonding contractor; nor were lost profits recoverable as *special damages* in this case, because such damages were not actually foreseen nor reasonably foreseeable by owner); GASA, Inc. v. United States, 79 Fed. Cl. 325 (2007) (test for recovery of lost profits cited; contractor was unable to recover in this case, however, because the contract's Suspension of Work clause did not permit recovery of lost profits, and thus recovery for lost profits was not within the contemplation of the parties).

Page 177, add at end of note 38:

See also, e.g., Tolar Constr., LLC v. Kean Elec. Co., Inc., 944 So. 2d 138 (Ala. May 19, 2006) (when a contractor is unable to complete his contract because of the defendant's breach, and he sues to recover the amount he would have received but for the breach, i.e., the profit that defendant's breach prevented the contractor from earning, the plaintiff has the burden of alleging and proving not only: (1) what he would have received from the performance so prevented; but also (2) what such performance would have cost him (or the value to him of relief therefrom). Unless the contractor proves both of those facts, he cannot recover as damages the profits he would have earned from full performance of the contract); DeVore Constr. v. Tirapelli, 2009 WL 3246415 (Cal. App. Oct. 9, 2009) (nonpublished) (terminated T&M contractor held not entitled to recover lost profits on remaining unperformed work; contract provided for 15% profit on labor and materials, and the contractor could provide no evidence as to the cost of labor and material that would have been expended completing the project; this was particularly true since the contractor expended $370,000 performing 75% of the work on an estimated $311,000 project, such that future profits could not be estimated with reasonable certainty).

Page 178, add at end of section:

The Federal Circuit recently refused to award anticipatory profits in a requirements contract case in *Rumsfeld v. Applied Cos. Inc*,[39.1] The Defense Logistics

[39.1] 325 F.3d 1328 (Fed. Cir. 2003), *cert. denied*, 124 S. Ct. 462 (2003).

Agency (DLA) issued an RFP for an annual requirements contract for supply of refrigerant storage cylinders, with an estimated quantity of 119,495 units. The DLA determined prior to award that the purchased quantity would be only about 10 percent of the RFP estimate, but failed to notify the contractor, Applied, prior to the award. After the award, the DLA notified Applied of the revised estimate, and ordered 11,000 units. Applied requested a substantial increase in the price per unit, plus more than $600,000 in "under absorbed indirect costs." The parties could not agree on a modification, and the DLA then terminated the contract for convenience before delivery. Applied sued to recover its anticipated profits on the total estimated quantity of 119,495 units. The court held that the DLA had breached the contract by negligently preparing the RFP estimate. Noting that anticipatory profits have been awarded when the government breaches a requirements contract by diverting business to a third party, the court stated that in this case, where the government had ordered all of its requirements from the contractor but had negligently estimated those requirements, anticipatory profits were not recoverable. If the DLA had not negligently estimated its requirements, the RFP would have reflected an estimate of 11,000 cylinders, which is precisely what the DLA ordered. Thus, if the DLA had not breached the contract, Applied would still not have earned profits on anything more than approximately 11,000 units. The court held that Applied was entitled to recover the reasonable value of the work performed, which may include an equitable adjustment to the price per cylinder to reflect the change in quantity, plus reasonable profit.

In *Marut Testing & Inspection Services, Inc. v. General Services Administration,*[39.2] the contractor was awarded the maximum relief under a services contract when the government had failed to order the guaranteed minimum level of service for a contract year. The contractor was paid 10 percent of the total evaluated bid price for that year as compensation for the lost profit in absorbed operating costs as a result of the government not ordering the minimum requirement for the year.

In *Appeal of Jim Phillips Contracting, Inc.,*[39.3] IPhillips was awarded a contract by BLM for road repairs in Idaho. The contract covered the 1999 base year and four option years, with a minimum dollar value of services of $655,000 over the life the contract. The contract was a unit-priced, indefinite delivery, indefinite quantity contract, not a requirements contract: BLM was free to also use other contractors if it chose to do so. The normal construction season for road work in that part of Idaho was May or June through October or November, depending on the weather, but mainly July through September. By the time BLM's October 18, 1999, task order was issued, and Phillips had mobilized at the site, snow already covered the ground. Thus, on December 15, 1999, BLM issued a winter suspension order. A subsequent order to "resume work" (which had not yet begun) was not issued until August 15, 2000. Phillips refused to accept the resumption order,

[39.2] GSBCA No. 16079 (Apr. 11, 2006).

[39.3] BCA Nos. 2000, 4319 and 4320, 04-1 BCA (CCH) ¶ 32,416 (2003).

asserting that the contract had expired because the option to renew it for a second year had not been exercised. Phillips subsequently filed a claim for the entire $655,000 guaranteed amount, despite never having performed any work. Phillips later modified its claim to recover approximately $200,000, the amount of profit its expert testified Phillips would have earned on the guaranteed minimum amount. The Board found that BLM had not timely renewed the contract, and that Phillips was therefore entitled to refuse the resumption order and to recover its anticipated profit on the guaranteed minimum amount of work. Using the jury verdict method, the Board awarded Phillips approximately 40 percent of the $200,000 claimed.

In *Smith Paving & Excavating, Inc. v. Vermillion Shores Development Group, Inc.*,[39.4] a subcontractor was awarded damages for breach of contract and loss of profits on work it was not allowed to perform. In this matter, the Vermillion Shores Development Group, as developer of the project, hired Pinewood Construction Company as its general contractor. Pinewood awarded a $194,861 fixed price subcontract to Smith Paving and Excavating, Inc. At the time of contracting, the drawings and specifications for the project were incomplete and Vermillion had not obtained the permits and approvals necessary to construct the project. Pinewood never gave Smith Paving a commencement date for its work. After some time, a Smith Paving representative visited the jobsite and discovered that the concrete road work had been completed by another company. Smith Paving made a demand upon Pinewood for its profits on the project and then commenced suit for breach of contract. In defense, Pinewood asserted that there was no binding subcontract with Smith Paving and then alternatively argued that if there was a binding subcontract, the actual work performed was significantly different from that work described in the Pinewood/Smith Paving subcontract. The court rejected both arguments, finding that Pinewood had signed a subcontract for a specific scope of work and that even though the work had changed, the changes could have been addressed through the change order process described in the subcontract. As a result, Pinewood was liable for breach of contract and Smith Paving was entitled to a damage award of all anticipated profit. At trial Smith Paving had shown an anticipated profit of $38,385. Pinewood had offered no evidence that those profits were not appropriate or not reasonable, and, therefore, the damage award was upheld.

Sometimes it may not be necessary to prove lost profits to recover them. In *Appeal of Delta Construction International, Inc.*,[39.5] a contractor on an indefinite quantity construction contract was awarded the price difference between the amount actually awarded and the guaranteed minimum without proof of actual damages. In this matter, the Army had awarded an indefinite delivery/indefinite quantity contract to Delta to replace rotten wood at various government facilities throughout Panama. The government guaranteed a minimum of $200,000 in

[39.4] 2005 WL 1491758, 2005-Ohio-3196 (Ohio App. 2005).

[39.5] ASBCA No. 52162 (Nov. 16, 2000).

work orders during the base contract period. Further, Delta was required to maintain the capabilities to accomplish a minimum of $3,000 per day of work. During the contract period, work orders were issued totaling only $86,323. Delta filed a claim requesting the difference between $86,323 and the $200,000 guaranteed minimum. The Army acknowledged liability for lost profits and unabsorbed overhead but contended that the contractor had to prove those elements of damage and could not merely claim the difference between the guaranteed minimum and the actual payments. The Board awarded Delta the difference between the guaranteed minimum and the amount actually ordered, reasoning that when a contract requires the contractor to maintain a certain level of performance, the contractor is entitled to be paid the guaranteed minimum price without further proof of damage.

Many construction contracts allow the owner to terminate the contract for the convenience of the owner. Under a Termination for Convenience provision, the owner has the virtually unlimited right to terminate the contract without establishing a default on behalf of the contractor or being in breach of the contract itself. A Termination of Convenience provision gives the owner the flexibility to stop construction of a project without incurring the liabilities that result from breaching the contract. In a typical Termination for Convenience clause, the contractor is entitled to recover profit on the work performed prior to termination. Unlike a breach of contract claim for damages, lost profits are frequently not allowed in a Termination for Convenience. The general policy that has developed is against the recovery of profit on unperformed work. This policy in government contracts is very strong. In *Appeal of Plaza 70 Interiors, Ltd.*,[39.6] the contractor was denied lost profits on unperformed work when the contract was terminated for convenience prior to the contractor performing the guaranteed minimum quantity of work. It is probable that absent a termination for convenience, the contractor would have been entitled to the profit on the minimum guaranteed quantity. However, the termination for convenience prevented the contractor in this case from recovering any profit on the unperformed work.

When contracts contain unit prices, such as is commonly done with highway and utility contracts, each line item unit price is presumed to carry the proportionate overhead and profit. When a unit price contract is terminated for convenience, if the overhead and profit is not distributed on a pro rata or proportional basis, the terminated contractor may be forced to forgo a substantial amount of profit. In *Appeal of Ideker, Inc.*,[39.7] a contractor who was terminated on a unit priced dredging contract complained that the unperformed work was the highest profit margin work and that it should be compensated for the lost profits. The Board ruled that the unit prices govern, and the contractor was not entitled to the additional profit allegedly carried in the unperformed units of work. The same result, that unit

---

[39.6] HUDBCA No. 94-C-150-C9 (May 2, 1995).
[39.7] ENGBCA No. 4389 (Aug. 31, 1987).

prices govern on the termination for convenience of a unit price contract, occurred in *Appeal of Manis Drilling*.[39.8]

Page 178, add new § 8.06A before § 8.07:

§ 8.06A PROFIT ON CONTRACTS NOT AWARDED

If a contractor is the low bidder on a project and is passed over and the project is awarded to another bidder, and the contractor then appeals the failure to award and is successful on that appeal, the issue arises as to what the appropriate measure of damages is for a contract that was not performed by the contractor but was performed by another bidder. Owners frequently argue that the bid preparation costs are the appropriate remedy since that reflects the costs incurred by the bidder. Bid preparation costs are usually fairly minor in relation to the profit that the bidder anticipated making on a project that it was wrongfully denied. Two divergent views have emerged on the treatment of competitive bidding statutes and, hence, on the damages that can be recovered by the wrongfully denied bidder: (1) that competitive bidding statutes exist to protect the taxpaying public, and (2) that the statutes exist to protect the bidders.

The North Dakota Supreme Court came down on the side that competitive bidding statutes are for the protection of the public. In *Becker Electric, Inc. v. City of Bismarck*,[39.9] that court held that the contractor could not recover damages against the public entity for violation of the competitive bidding statute.

The California Supreme Court, in *Kajima/Ray Wilson v. Los Angeles County Metropolitan Transportation Authority*,[39.10] reversed a ruling that had awarded profit to a low bidder, finding that allowing recovery of lost profits would injure the public twice—once in paying the unjustifiably higher price to the chosen bidder, and again when the lost profits are awarded to the disappointed bidder that did not perform the work.

The New Hampshire Supreme Court in *Marbucco Corp. v. City of Manchester*,[39.11] came down on the side of rejected bidders when it acknowledged that awarding a disappointed bidder its anticipated profit results in the taxpayers paying a profit twice for the same construction work. However, in the court's view, if a public owner is not subject to some sanction, there is no penalty for the manipulation of the competitive bidding system.

[39.8] IBCA No. 2658 (Mar. 11, 1993).

[39.9] 469 N.W.2d 159 (N.D. 1991).

[39.10] 1 P.3d 63 (Cal. 2000).

[39.11] 632 A.2d 552 (N.H. 1993).

The Ohio Supreme Court, in *Cleveland Construction, Inc. v. Cincinnati,*[39.12] denied an award of lost profits to an unsuccessful bidder for a public contract because the defendant city had retained broad discretion to accept or reject bids. Cleveland submitted the low bid on the drywall contract, but failed to meet the 35% requirement for small business enterprises (SBEs), and the City awarded the contract to the next lowest bidder who met the SBE requirement. The court said that a contractor has a property interest in a public contract only when either a bidder is actually awarded a contract and then deprived of it or when a governmental entity has limited discretion in awarding the contract yet abuses that discretion. In this case, the city's bid package, which contained the invitation to bid and the bidding requirements, reserved the right of the city to "reject any and all bids or parts of any bid . . . and not award a contract" and to "consider all elements entering into the question of determining the responsibility of the bidder." In addition, the city municipal code provided that contracts should be awarded to the lowest "and best bidder," and even the lowest and best bid may be rejected if the bid "is not in the best interests of the city." Given the extensive discretion of the city in considering bids, the plaintiff contractor had no property right in the drywall contract at issue in this case, and was therefore not entitled to recover any anticipated profit on the contract.

The other extreme was set out by the Supreme Court of Mississippi in *City of Durant v. Laws Construction Co., Inc.*[39.13] In that matter, the low bidder's bid had an irregularity in that it did not bear the contractor's certificate of responsibility number on the outside of the bid. The project owner waived this irregularity and the contract was awarded. The second low bidder challenged the waiver of the irregularity and was awarded its anticipated profits on the project.

The Wisconsin Court of Appeals refused to award lost profits to an unsuccessful bidder in *DMK, Inc. v. Town of Pittsfield.*[39.14] In this matter, DMK was the low bidder on four roads contracts put out for bid by the town of Pittsfield. Town officials rejected awarding the contracts to DMK after officials expressed concerns about problems with DMK on an earlier project. After negotiations with DMK concerning award of some but not all of the contracts, the town ultimately awarded all of the contracts to other bidders. DMK filed a claim for $216,000 in alleged lost profits. After the town denied its claim DMK filed suit. The trial court granted summary judgment for the town. On appeal the Appeals Court affirmed the summary judgment finding that the Wisconsin Statute stated the determination of the lowest possible bidder implied the exercise of discretion.

[39.12] 2008 Ohio 2337, 118 Ohio St. 3d 283, 888 N.E.2d 1068 (May 21, 2008), *reconsid. denied,* 2008 Ohio 3880, 119 Ohio St. 3d 1416, 891 N.E.2d 773 (Aug. 6, 2008), *cert. denied,* 129 S. Ct. 921, 173 L. Ed.2d 111 (Jan. 12, 2009), *cert. denied,* 129 S. Ct. 925 (Jan. 12, 2009).

[39.13] 721 So. 2d 598 (Miss. 1998).

[39.14] 209 Wis. 2d 474; 711 N.W.2d 672 (Wis. Ct. App. Feb. 28, 2006), *review denied,* 292 Wis. 2d 411, 718 N.W.2d 725 (Wis. May 9, 2006).

In *Clifford R. Gray, Inc. v. LeChase Constr. Services,*[39.15] CRG was an electrical contractor who assisted LeChase in preparing a bid to become the prime contractor for design and construction of an atomic power laboratory. CRG alleged that it promised not to participate with any other general contractors bidding the project in exchange for LeChase's promise that it would use CRG as the exclusive electrical subcontract should LeChase be awarded the prime contract. LeChase was awarded the prime contract, but declined to use CRG as a subcontractor, and CRG sued to recover its costs of bid preparation and its anticipated profit on the theories of breach of contract, promissory estoppel, unjust enrichment, equitable estoppel, and fraud. The court dismissed all claims except for promissory estoppel, at which point LeChase moved to limit CRG's evidence at trial to reliance damages (bid preparation costs) and to preclude CRG from offering evidence of expectancy or benefit-of-the-bargain damages (lost profit). The court held that since it had previously determined that no contract existed between the parties, there was no "bargain" to which CRG was entitled to the benefit. As such, CRG was limited under the promissory estoppel theory to those expenses that CRG incurred in relying on LeChase's alleged promise, such as bid preparation costs.

§ 8.07 MEASURING PROFIT ON UNPERFORMED WORK

Page 178, add at end of note 40:

See Forney v. Missouri Bridge & Concrete, Inc., 112 S.W. 3d 471 (Mo. App. 2003) (the proper measure of damages in a case where an owner breaches a construction contract by preventing the contractor from performing the work is the contract price less the amount it would have cost the contractor to perform the contract; in this case, plaintiff's claim failed because it did not present evidence of the costs to complete the subcontract); The Millgard Corp. v. E.E. Cruz/Nab/Frontier-Kemper, 2007 WL 2388902 (S.D.N.Y. Aug. 21, 2007), *adhered to on reconsideration*, 2007 WL 4302492 (S.D.N.Y. Dec. 5, 2007), *judgment aff'd*, 329 Fed. Appx. 307 (2nd Cir. (N.Y.) May 8, 2009) (the court accepted the testimony of plaintiff's expert that a reasonable way to determine lost profits would be to take the anticipated percentage of profit (62.5 percent) and apply it to the anticipated daily direct costs ($71,000), yielding $44,375/day of expected profit; the subcontractor was entitled to those expected profits from the date the subcontractor's performance would have begun through the time the subcontract would have been terminated for convenience had it not been wrongfully terminated for cause).

[39.15] 51 A.D.3d 1169, 857 N.Y.S.2d 347 (N.Y. App. Div. 3d Dept. May 8, 2008).

Cf. Wisch & Vaughan Constr. Co. v. Melrose Props. Corp., 21 S.W.3d 36 (Mo. Ct. App. 2000) (when the owner breaches a construction contract by preventing the contractor from performing the work, the measure of damages is generally the contract price less the amount it would have cost the contractor to perform; however, the jury may substitute the owner's actual cost to complete the project for the contractor's estimate; it is for the jury to decide which figure is proper).

Page 178, add at end of note 42:

See also Forney v. Missouri Bridge & Concrete, Inc., 112 S.W.3d 471 (Mo. App. 2003) (amount of lost profits incurred when owner has breached contract by preventing contractor from performing work must be shown with reasonable certainty by proof of facts from which anticipated profits can rationally be estimated).

Page 178, add to text after note 42:

In *Butera v. Boucher*,[42.1] the court held that a builder who fails to substantially perform a construction contract is still entitled to recover the contract price minus the cost of completion and correction when the contract has been so far performed that the structure can be used by the owner for its intended purpose or the work is of some value to the owner. In this case, although the jury held that both parties were liable for breaching the contract, it awarded the builder $15,500 for lost profits after concluding that the homeowners prematurely terminated the contract. The jury also awarded the homeowners $1,200 to remedy defects in the builder's performance; namely "cracks in the garage." Thus, a builder can recover for lost profits, even though he has not substantially performed the contract, if the owner has breached the contract by terminating it without justification before the completion date.

The Federal Board of Contract Appeals recently rejected the use of a contractor's historical profit margin in calculating damages and permitted recovery of a higher profit percentage. In *Appeal of Marshall Associated Contractors, Inc. & Columbia Excavating, Inc.*,[42.2] the government was found to have misrepresented site conditions, causing the contractor to incur additional costs in performing the work. The contractor sought recovery of a 30 percent profit margin on its costs, and the government contended that it should be limited to the contractor's 10 percent historical profit margin. The court held that 30 percent was a "fair and reasonable profit" in light of the contractor's "truly remarkable production rate . . . under the most difficult and adverse of circumstances."

[42.1] 798 A.2d 340 (R.I. 2002).

[42.2] IBCA No. 1901 (Mar. 22, 2002).

In *Phillips Contractor's and Management, LLC v. Stealth Group, LLC.*,[42.3] Phillips performed and was paid for the interior water, sewer, and electric work, but refused to perform the exterior work unless the developer, Stealth, issued a change order increasing the contract price due to an owner-directed change in the work. Stealth did not agree to the price increase, Phillips refused to perform the work, and Stealth hired a substitute contractor who performed the work for substantially less than the balance due on Phillips' original contract. Phillips sued to recover the entire balance due on its contract, and the trial court awarded Phillips the total balance due less certain amounts paid directly by Stealth to certain material suppliers. The appellate court reversed, holding that upon Stealth's improper termination, Phillips was only entitled to the net profit it would have made if it had performed the entire contract, rather than the gross amount due. The court identified three methods for calculating lost profits: (1) the balance of the contract price, less the contractor's cost to complete; (2) the profit on the entire contract (total contract price less contractor's total cost of construction, both expended and to be expended) plus the cost of the work actually performed; or (3) for the work done, such proportion of the contract price as the cost of the work done bears to the total cost of doing the job, plus, for the work remaining, the profit that would have been made upon it. Since the trial court had not applied any of the acceptable methods for calculating lost profits, the appellate court reversed and remanded.

In *B & W Supply, Inc. v. Beckman*,[42.4] B & W entered into a contract for $60,000 to remodel several rooms of the Beckman's home. After approximately half of the work had been completed and Beckman had paid $30,000, Beckman asked B & W what its profit was on the job. When B & W responded it was making 30% profit, Beckman was so outraged he insisted upon line-item approval of all future work, which B & W refused to allow. No further work was done on the project, and no further amounts were paid. Beckman sued for breach of contract, conversion, and breach of fiduciary duty, and B & W counterclaimed to recover its lost profit on the balance of the contract. The jury found in favor of B & W and awarded $9,000 in lost profits, but the court granted Beckman's motion for judgment notwithstanding the verdict and denied either party any recover. On appeal, the court found there was sufficient evidence to support the jury's finding that Beckman breached the contract, thereby entitling B & W to its lost profit. As to the calculation of lost profit, the court noted that B & W's president testified at various points that B & W was entitled to recover $9,000, and at other points that the amount was $7,593, based upon a contract amount of $60,000, total estimated expenses of $43,407, and a profit of $16,593 less the $9,000 B & W took out of the $30,000 paid by Beckman. The court found that

---

[42.3] 2007 WL 1373189 (Tenn. Ct. App. 2007).

[42.4] 2009 WL 943792 (Tex. App. (1st Dist.) Apr. 9, 2009), *review denied* (Aug. 7, 2009).

the latter calculation was the proper method for determining lost profits, but that the jury's award of $9,000 profit would be upheld as "within the range of the evidence."

The court rejected the contractor's estimate of lost profit damages in *Abra Constr. Corp. v. 112 Duane Associates, LLC.*[42.5] In seeking lost profit on work not performed after wrongful termination, the contractor's president testified that he estimated between 45% and 60% profit on the contract. The court rejected this testimony on the grounds that the president was never qualified as an expert and his offer of proof was purely speculative. Instead, the court awarded 8% profit on the unperformed work, based on testimony that 8% profit was the industry standard.

Page 179, add at end of note 45:

See also Leon Angel Constructors, Inc. v. Kirk Knott Elec., Inc., 837 So. 2d 743 (La. App. 2003) (Angel was the prime contractor on a courthouse renovation project, and Knott was the electrical subcontractor; Angel terminated Knott, and the arbitrator awarded Knott damages that included lost profit computed as 10 percent of the original subcontract price; on appeal, the court found that Knott had received several progress payments that presumably included a portion of the subcontract profit margin; the court therefore reversed the award, finding that the arbitrator should have subtracted the progress payments before applying the 10 percent margin).

Page 179, add after first full paragraph:

In *Foster Construction Co., Inc. v. Wafer,*[45.1] a contractor agreed to build a restaurant for the owner at a price of $199,516.00. Of this amount, $28,008.50 was designated in the contract as the contractor's overhead and profit. The owner issued a notice to proceed but then breached the contract before work even began. The contractor sued to recover the profits designated in the contract. The trial court awarded the contractor the full amount of $28,008.50, and this judgment was affirmed on appeal. The appellate court noted that under La. Civ. Code Art. 2765, an award for breach of contract may be made not only for "the expense and labor already incurred," but also for "such damages as the nature of the case may require." The court then held that the trial court's determination that the "nature of the case" required the award of lost profits as denominated in the parties' contract was not manifest error.

[42.5] 59 A.D.3d 263, 873 N.Y.S.2d 574 (1st Dept. Feb. 19, 2009).

[45.1] 776 So. 2d 1272 (La. Ct. App. 2000), *writ denied*, 787 So. 2d 320 (La. 2001).

Page 179, add at end of section:

When the quantity of work under a unit price contract dramatically increases, often one party wants to renegotiate the unit price. Many contracts expressly provide for such price modifications when significant quantity changes exist. When parties are unable to agree on the change, the results can be unexpected. In *Spirtas Co. v. Missouri Division of Design and Construction*,[46.1] the contractor, who was awarded a fixed-price contract to demolish a building, did not perform the additional work and did not receive any profit on the additional work. The contract contained a unit price for removing asbestos-containing duct with an estimated quantity of 16,000 square feet and a unit price of $4.75 per foot. The parties discovered asbestos-containing duct in quantities much larger than anticipated—approximately 168,000 feet more than estimated. The contractor asserted that it was entitled to remove all of the duct at $4.75 per foot, its unit price. The owner demanded that the added work be done on a different basis, and ultimately hired another contractor to perform the work. The contractor sued for lost profit on the additional work. The trial court granted summary judgment in favor of the contractor, and the owner appealed. The Court of Appeals of Missouri concluded that the contract, while clearly containing a unit price provision that contemplated a change in quantities, also contained a changes provision that permitted changes to be priced by three methods—lump sum, cost plus, or unit prices—and remanded the matter to the trial court for interpretation of what the court viewed as a latently ambiguous contract provision for the treatment of additional ductwork.

In *Forney v. Missouri Bridge & Concrete, Inc.*,[46.2] the court held, with regard to a claim for lost profits, that when overhead expenses are included in the contractor's total costs saved by nonperformance, they may be deducted from the contract price when the owner proves that such expenses were actually saved by the breach. In the absence of proof that the contractor saved overhead expenses as a result of the owner's breach of contract, overhead expenses are included in the lost profits damages award. The rationale supporting this conclusion is that if the contract had not been breached, fixed business expenses would have been paid from profits remaining after payment of costs directly related to performance of the contract.

[46.1] 131 S.W.3d 411 (Mo. Ct. App. 2004).

[46.2] 112 S.W.3d 471 (Mo. Ct. App. 2003).

§ 8.08 LOST BUSINESS REVENUES

Page 180, add at end of note 48:

See also Granite Re, Inc. v. City of La Crescent, 2009 WL 2982642 (D. Minn. Sept. 11, 2009) (plaintiff contractor was entitled to recover damages for lost profits as a result of lost bonding capacity when the contractor established that its bonding capacity was lost as a direct result of the defendant City's wrongful termination of the contract; the court found that it was reasonably foreseeable, at the time the contract was executed, that termination would result in the contractor losing its bonding capacity, and it was also reasonably foreseeable that lost bonding capacity would cause significant financial harm in the form of lost business, revenues and profits; as a municipality that itself required performance bonds on construction contracts, the loss of bonding capacity and the resulting harm was a reasonably foreseeable consequence of wrongful termination by the City); Denny Constr., Inc. v. City & County of Denver *ex rel.* Bd. of Water Comm'rs, 199 P.3d 742 (Colo. Jan. 12, 2009) (the Colorado Supreme Court held that an incorrect legal standard was applied by the lower court to plaintiff's claim for lost profits due to impaired bonding capacity when the lower court held that such claims are never reasonably certain and thus are speculative as a matter of law; instead, claims of lost profits due to impaired bonding capacity, like all claims for lost profits, must be established with reasonable certainty, which standard can be met notwithstanding that uncertainties will exist as to whether a future bid would have been successful and the amount of future profits; the lower court also erred by applying an incorrect legal standard to determine whether lost profits are reasonably foreseeable; the question is not, as the court of appeals held, whether the defendant actually knew that the plaintiff contractor would suffer lost profits due to impaired bonding capacity, but whether it knew or should have known that such loss would probably occur).

Page 181, add before first full paragraph:

In *M.A. Butters & Associates v. City of Lancaster*,[50.1] a wrongfully terminated contractor was awarded by the trial court, as damages, the full contract amount less the cost of finishing the project plus an additional amount to compensate the contractor for the reduction of profits on later-performed work on other projects. The trial court found that the wrongful termination led to increased costs for the contractor, including higher bond rates and borrowing costs on subsequent projects and decreased revenue in subsequent years, which ultimately forced the contractor out of business. The appellate court allowed recovery of the reduced profit for the period the contractor was still in business, but disallowed anticipated profits on jobs not performed, holding that lost profit damages on

[50.1] 2005 WL 1926546 (Cal. Ct. App. 2005) (unpublished).

potential but presently nonexistent contracts were too remote to be compensable. As the prevailing party in a dispute, under a contract provision, the contractor was also awarded attorneys' fees.

Page 181, add to end of first full paragraph:

RYN, Inc. v. Platte County Memorial Hospital[51.1] is another case denying lost profit from allegedly impaired bonding capacity, the damage being too remote and speculative.

Similarly, the court in *United States ex rel. Sun Construction Co., Inc. v. Torix General Contractors, LLC*, 2009 WL 3416214 (D. Colo. 2009) held that the plaintiff subcontractor, Sun, could not recover damages for lost bonding capacity from the general contractor, Torix, as a result of Torix's alleged breach of the subcontract. The court stated that under *Denny*, lost profits due to impaired bonding capacity are treated like any other lost profits claim—Sun must prove the lost profits with reasonable certainty, and the particular lost profits were objectively foreseeable by the parties at the time of contracting. The court found that the following evidence presented through testimony of Sun's owner and financial statements prepared by Sun's CPA was sufficient to establish the fact of lost profits: Sun was profitable every year between 2002 and 2006, earning an average annual profit of $500,000; Sun had completed more than 200 contracts with the City of Colorado Springs and the Colorado Department of Transportation (CDOT) prior to 2006, with the average Colorado Springs project being worth $2 million; subsequent to losing its bonding capacity in 2006, Sun has been awarded only five Colorado Springs contracts, each worth only $100,000; Sun is no longer allowed to bid on CDOT projects worth more than $600,000, and these projects previously amounted to 90 percent of Sun's work; Sun remains qualified by Colorado Springs to work on projects up to $4 million in size, but can no longer bid on such projects because it is unable to obtain a bid bond. However, the court further found that although Sun proved the fact that it lost profits, it failed to introduce sufficient admissible evidence that would enable the trier of fact to compute a fair approximation of the loss. Sun failed to refer to any specific projects, or the value of such projects, that the contractor was qualified to bid on, but for its inability to bond. In addition, Sun did not show that its losses were the foreseeable result of a breach at the time the contract was made. Sun presented no evidence to support a finding that Torix knew or should have known that lost profits would probably be incurred by Sun if Torix breached the subcontract. The court refused Sun's request to hold as a matter of law that a material question of fact as to objective foreseeability will always exist whenever the parties to the contract "are familiar with the bonding requirements of federal projects," as such a holding would be inconsistent with Colorado law, as noted by the Colorado Supreme Court in *Denny*.

[51.1] 842 P.2d 1084 (Wyo. 1982).

Page 182, add at end of note 56:

See also, e.g., Blue Water Envt'l., Inc. v. Incorporated Village of Bayville, 12 Misc. 3d 1169(A), 820 N.Y.S.2d 841 (Sup. Ct. Nassau County 2006) (to recover lost profits, it must be demonstrated with certainty that such damages have been caused by the breach, and the alleged loss must be capable of proof with reasonable certainty; the lost profits may not be merely speculative, possible or imaginary but must be directly traceable to the breach; in this case, although the plaintiff contractor contended that it was prevented from bidding on and performing other projects because its performance of the contract with the defendant-village was delayed by the village's actions, the contractor failed to submit any proof as to the manner in which a delay in performance caused it to be unable to bid on or perform other projects; thus, the contractor failed to show that its claim for lost profits was capable of proof with reasonable certainty, making its damages claim merely speculative).

§ 8.09 CONTRACTUAL BARRIERS TO RECOVERY OF LOST PROFITS

Page 184, add at end of section:

Recovery for lost profits may not only be *barred* by contract, it may also be *limited* by contract. For example, in *M.J. Paquet, Inc. v. New Jersey Department of Transportation*,[63.1] the contract for bridge repairs required "balanced bidding," that is, bids that reflected under each pay item the "actual cost which the bidder anticipates the performance of that particular item entails, together with a proportional share of the bidder's anticipated profit, overhead and costs. . . ." The contract further provided that the owner "would not consider any claim for additional compensation arising from the bid on an item, or group of items, inaccurately reflecting the cost of such work or containing a disproportionate share of the bidder's anticipated profit, overhead and other costs," and that "[t]he Contractor expressly waives the right to pursue such claims either before the Commissioner or under the terms of the New Jersey Contractual Liability Act." Paquet prepared its 44 line item bid schedule using the lowest subcontractor quotation it had at the time. Immediately prior to turning in the bid, Paquet received a lower quote for the painting. Paquet chose to reduce line items other than the painting line item to reflect this lower quote. As a result, Paquet bid $826,473 for the painting work, although the subcontractor bid it incorporated in its overall bid price was only $450,514. After the contract was awarded, the owner issued a deductive change order to delete the painting work, using as a basis for its deductive change order the $826,473 line item. Paquet complained that the deductive credit was inequitable and should be processed as an equitable adjustment reflecting the actual cost of the work being

[63.1] 794 A.2d 141 (N.J. 2002).

deleted, plus overhead and profit. The contractor brought suit, asserting that individual pay items in the contract "should not be considered sacrosanct," and that the court should undertake a "searching inquiry" into the cost, overhead, and anticipated profit that would have been expended or realized had the contract been fully performed in accordance with its original terms. The appellate court disagreed, holding that when a "contract expressly prohibits unbalanced bids and mandates that pay items accurately reflect the cost, overhead and anticipated profit attributable to the particular portion of work to be performed, and further directs that 'payment will be made at the original unit price for the quantities of work accepted,' we perceive no injustice in effectuating these provisions as written." The New Jersey Supreme Court reversed, finding that Paquet was entitled to an equitable adjustment even though its bid was unbalanced.

Recovery for lost profits may also be barred by a liquidated damages clause. In *El Dorado Irrigation District v. Traylor Bros., Inc.*,[63.2] the contract provided that if the project was not substantially completed by the contractor and fully operational within the contract time, or within any period of extension authorized by a change order, the contractor would be liable to pay the owner, as fixed and liquidated damages, $500 for each calendar day of delay until the project was substantially completed and fully operational. The court held that this liquidated damages provision precluded the owner from recovering for a loss of power sales (alleged to amount to $2.4 million) due to delay.

§ 8.10 PUNITIVE DAMAGES

Page 185, add at end of section:

Punitive damages can also be awarded in arbitration. In *Drywall Systems, Inc. v. ZVI Construction Co., Inc.*,[71.1] the subcontractor was awarded punitive damages equal to twice the direct damages for breach of the subcontracts pursuant to a statutory provision in Massachusetts for trebling damages as punishment for willful or intentional violations of a private contract. Drywall was a subcontractor on five subcontracts with ZVI for gypsum wallboard work at five retail store sites where ZVI was the general contractor. The subcontracts provided for arbitration of disputes pursuant to the construction industry arbitration rules of the American Arbitration Association. Drywall filed a demand for arbitration, asserting claims for delay, disruption, and nonpayment. Drywall also alleged that ZVI had engaged in unfair and deceptive business practices as defined by MGLA Ch. 93A, § 12, which authorizes recovery of treble damages as punishment for willful or intentional violations of a private contract. Drywall was awarded breach damages of $447,365, and additional damages pursuant to the statute of

[63.2] 2006 WL 38953 (E.D. Cal. Jan. 4, 2006).

[71.1] 761 N.E.2d 482 (Mass. 2002).

$894,730. ZVI appealed, asserting that the arbitrators did not have authority to consider claims for punitive damages under the statutory punitive provisions. ZVI asserted such an award could only be made by a court. The Court of Appeals of Massachusetts upheld the award of the punitive damages, finding that nothing within the statute prohibited arbitration of statutory claims or the award by arbitrators of treble damages. On appeal to the Massachusetts Supreme Court, the award of punitive damages was affirmed.

§ 8.11 PROFIT ON DEDUCTIVE CHANGES (BACKCHARGE)

Page 185, add new note 71.2 at end of second sentence in section:

[71.2] *See, e.g.*, Fru-Con/Fluor Daniel Joint Venture v. Corrigan Bros., Inc., 154 S.W.3d 330 (Mo. Ct. App. 2004) (subcontractor argued that trial court erred in assessing backcharges against it, because contractor allegedly breached contract by failing to give subcontractor 72 hours to cure any defective work after a notice of default, as required by the contract; appellate court found that the parties had abandoned the contract, and a contracting party cannot be guilty of a breach of a contract that has been mutually abandoned; trial court did not err, and properly assessed backcharges to reduce the subcontractor's *quantum meruit* recovery by amount needed to correct subcontractor's defective work under contract).

[A] Judicial Interpretations Regarding Overhead and Profit on Backcharges

Page 189, add at end of section:

Different rules apply when a deductive change order results from the deletion of work, rather than the owner's completion of a defaulting contractor's work. In *Appeal of Fru-Con Construction Corp.*,[78.1] the Army Corps of Engineers issued a deductive change order eliminating the commissioning requirements for rehabilitation of a dam in West Virginia, thereby reducing the performance period of the contractor, Fru-Con, and its subcontractor, Noell, by 84 days. The Corps sought a credit of $670,000 in connection with the waiver of the commissioning requirement, comprised primarily of Fru-Con's and Noell's field and home office overhead costs during the 84-day period, plus profit on these costs. The Board noted that when a deductive change is issued, the contractor is to be left in the same financial position it would have been in had the change not occurred. "The contract price adjustment should not be used to reduce or increase profit or loss or convert a loss to a profit or vice versa, for reasons unrelated to the change." Since Noell was in a loss position on the contract, a contract price deduction that reflected a loss of profit

[78.1] ASBCA No. 55197, 55248, 2007 WL 3265020 (2007).

would increase the loss over what it would have been without the change, and was therefore not permitted. Since there was no evidence that Fru-Con was in a loss position on the contract, the Corps was entitled to include Fru-Con's profit in the contract price adjustment.

Relying upon the *Fru-Con* case, the Board reached a similar decision in *Appeal of States Roofing Corp.*[78.2] This was one of eleven appeals arising from a contract for the repair and related work on the roof cells at a building on the Naval Operating Base in Norfolk, Virginia. The Navy issued a modification deleting the installation of wood nailers, or wood blocking, from the contract work, and the parties could not agree on the value of the deductive change order. Apart from a dispute as to the direct labor estimate, the parties also disagreed as to whether the Navy was correct in including profit in the calculation of the credit due. States Roofing argued that since it was in a loss position on this contract, as previously concluded by the Board, no profit should be included in the adjustment. Quoting the *Fru-Con* holding that "the contract price adjustment should not be used to reduce or increase profit or loss," the court found that a contract price deduction reflecting a loss of profit would increase States Roofing's loss over what it would have been without the change, and would therefore be improper.

[78.2] ASBCA No. 55507, 2009 WL 740120 (Mar. 4, 2009). *See also* Appeal of States Roofing Corp., ASBCA No. 55508, 2009 WL 1464384 (May 5, 2009) (same). *Cf.* Peter Scalamandre & Sons, Inc. v. State of New York, 65 A.D.3d 774, 883 N.Y.S.2d 821 (App. Div. Aug. 13, 2009) (public owner would be permitted to delete a substantial portion of the work without compensating the contractor for lost profits on that work if the deletion was "reasonably necessary for the public interest," and the owner's actions were not arbitrary or capricious).

Chapter 9
INTEREST

§ 9.02 PREJUDGMENT INTEREST IN FEDERAL CONTRACTS

Page 196, add at end of note 20:

See also, e.g., Environmental Tectonics Corp. v. United States, 72 Fed. Cl. 290 (July 31, 2006) (FAR 52.233-1 allows a contractor to recover interest on a claim submitted to the Contracting Officer that is found to have merit. This interest is computed from the receipt of the claim by the Contracting Officer and at the rate applicable for each six-month period as fixed by the Treasury Secretary during the pendency of the claim. In this case, the contractor's complaint specifically sought interest in the form of financing costs incurred as a result of the government's delays in making payment and changes to the Contract. The fact that the Contracting Officer denied Plaintiff's Certified Claim was not dispositive of entitlement to interest under FAR 52.233-1, if the court were to determine otherwise; therefore, the court held that it had jurisdiction to award the contractor interest that had accrued on the Certified Claim, if plaintiff were to prevail in the case); Morrison Knudsen Corp. v. Ground Improvement Techniques, Inc., 532 F.3d 1063 (10th Cir. (Colo.) July 8, 2008) (a wrongful termination for default must be treated as a termination for convenience and, although the Federal Acquisition Regulations do not expressly provide for prejudgment interest, they also do not prohibit it except where a "settlement by determination" has been effected; the court held that under both compensatory principles and considerations of fairness, the award of prejudgment interest to the subcontractor on its $15 million judgment against the contractor was proper; the court further held that prejudgment interest would accrue from the date of termination as to those damages that had been incurred at the time the parties stipulated that damages would accrue from the date of termination; however, damages that accrued after the date of the stipulation in the subcontractor's settlement with its subcontractors would not be subject to the stipulation, and prejudgment interest would accrue from the date of each of the settlement agreements; finally, the court rejected the subcontractor's argument that the trial court should have applied the Colorado interest rate, holding that since prejudgment interest is an integral element of compensatory damages, and the governing law under the contract was federal law, the federal interest rate was properly applied).

§ 9.03 FEDERAL JURISDICTION INTEREST STATUTE

Page 176, add at end of note 32:

See also Acme Contracting, Ltd. v. Toltest, Inc., 2008 WL 2782922 (E.D. Mich. 2008), *aff'd in part on other grounds, rev'd in part on other grounds*, 2010 WL 1140997 (6th Cir. (Mich.) Mar. 24, 2010) (the court held that postjudgment interest was properly awarded under 28 U.S.C § (1961), prejudgment interest on the subcontractor's *quantum meruit* claim would be awarded in accordance with Michigan law, but prejudgment interest on the subcontractor's contract claims would be determined by Ohio law, which was the governing law under the terms of the contract).

§ 9.04 PROMPT PAYMENT ACT

Page 197, replace note 33 with the following:

31 U.S.C. §§ 3901-3907.

Page 198, add before last paragraph of section:

A contractor cannot recover interest under the Prompt Payment Act (PPA) when the government withholds progress payments due to a bona fide dispute concerning contractual obligations. In *Appeal of Dillingham Construction Pacific Basin, Ltd.,*[40.1] the contract for renovation of military housing units in Guam provided for on-site storage of uninstalled or undistributed materials. The contractor complained of slow payment for such materials and demanded interest under the PPA. The government argued that payments had been withheld due to questions regarding the materials for which the contractor had requested payment. The Board ruled that since payment was delayed due to an "objectively discernable dispute" concerning entitlement, the contractor was not entitled to recover interest under the PPA.[40.2]

[40.1] ASBCA No. 53284 (Dec. 6, 2002).

[40.2] *See also* George Sollitt Constr. Co. v. United States, 64 Fed. Cl. 229 (Ct. Cl. 2005), in which the court stated that although the Prompt Payment Act provides an interest penalty to businesses for "delivered item[s] of property or service [not paid for by the federal government] by the required payment date," if a payment amount is disputed, contractors are limited to the interest offered by the Contract Disputes Act (*see* 41 U.S.C. § 611: "[i]nterest on amounts found due contractors on claims shall be paid to the contractor from the date the contracting officer receives the claim . . . from the contractor until payment thereof"). Thus, the interest penalty provided by the Prompt Payment Act is not available to a contractor for payments for which the government has disputed its liability.

In *Southern Comfort Builders, Inc. v. United States*,[40.3] the court reiterated that the Prompt Payment Act does not apply when the payment in question is disputed. If a dispute exists, a contractor is not entitled to payment or late payment interest penalties until the dispute is resolved, and if a contractor prevails under its claim filed under the Contract Disputes Act, interest is to be paid pursuant to that act. In the instant case, the court found that the plaintiff was entitled to recover only under two small claims that were not disputed by the government. The court thus awarded interest on those claims and denied any additional interest under the Prompt Payment Act.

In *PCL Constr. Services, Inc. v. United States*,[40.4] the contract for construction of the visitors' center and parking garage at the Hoover Dam provided that interest penalties were not required on amounts temporarily withheld or retained in accordance with the terms of the contract. The court determined that PCL was entitled to the retention held by the government, but the government did not include Prompt Payment Act interest in its retention payment. The court agreed with PCL that there was no requirement that PCL specifically request Prompt Payment Act interest in its complaint. However, since the contract permitted the government to withhold the amount considered adequate protection for incomplete work and delays, and there was sufficient evidence of incomplete and delayed work, the retention was withheld "in accordance with the terms of the contract," even though the court ultimately determined that PCL was entitled to return of the retention. As such, PCL was not entitled to penalty interest under the Prompt Payment Act. The court further held that the Prompt Payment Act applies only in cases in which no disagreement exists over the claim, citing the *George Sollitt* case, among others. Thus, even absent the contract provision, PCL would not be entitled to penalty interest under the Prompt Payment Act.

The requirement of a bona fide dispute to avoid liability under the Prompt Payment Act was discussed in detail in *Appeal of Dick Pacific/GHEMM, Joint Venture*.[40.5] Dick Pacific was the general contractor on a contract with the U.S. Army Corps of Engineers to construct the Basset Hospital Replacement at Fort Wainwright, Alaska. During construction, the Corps withheld significant amounts in excess of the 10% retention from several pay applications, asserting various bases for the withholding, including unsatisfactory progress, unapproved schedule, and various work deficiencies. Dick Pacific objected to the withholding and, although certain funds were released, the Corps continued to withhold most of the funds. Dick Pacific sued to recover $236,674 in interest penalties under the Prompt Payment Act (PPA) based on improper withholding. Dick Pacific also sought to recover $181,171 in interest penalties under the PPA, arguing that the Corps' failure to timely definitize certain unilateral modifications prevented Dick

[40.3] 67 Fed. Cl. 124 (2005).

[40.4] 84 Fed. Cl. 408 (Oct. 16, 2008), *appeal dismissed*, 2009 WL 3489221 (Fed. Cir. Oct. 27, 2009).

[40.5] ASBCA No. 55829, 2008 WL 3832136, 08-2 BCA P 33937 (Aug. 8, 2008).

Pacific from invoicing for the work, and thereby constituted constructive withholding of payments due. The Corps moved for summary judgment on both claims. As to the actual withholdings, the Board found as follows:

> To avoid PPA interest, "there must be, at the time payment of an invoice is delayed, a 'present basis for delaying payment which is related to an objective discernible dispute.' " [Citations omitted.] All that is required to raise a *bona fide* dispute concerning contract compliance is that the government's questions be raised in good faith. That a contractor may ultimately prevail on the merits does not defeat an otherwise proper payment withholding if there is such a good faith dispute. . . . The government has not shown, example by example, how each of the questioned withholdings was allegedly in *bona fide* dispute, or otherwise was exempt from the application of PPA interest penalties and additional interest penalties. Thus, we cannot conclude, on the record currently before us, that the government is entitled to summary judgment regarding any actual withholding.

The Board granted the Corps' motion for summary judgment with respect to the alleged constructive withholdings based upon Dick Pacific's stated inability to invoice under modifications that have not been definitized, stating that the PPA is not the proper vehicle for compensating a contractor for government delays in adjudicating change orders (citing an earlier ASBCA decision which indicated that the Contract Disputes Act was the proper vehicle for compensation in that situation).

Numerous states have enacted their own version of the federal Prompt Payment Act. Not only are there variations in the statutes, there are also differences in how each state interprets similar statutory provisions. It is therefore imperative that owners, contractors, and subcontractors become familiar with the Prompt Payment Acts applicable to their projects. For example, Texas' Prompt Payment Act, Tex. Prop. Code Ann. § 28.002(a), provides that if an owner receives a written payment request from a contractor for an amount that is allowed to the contractor for properly performed work or suitably stored materials, the owner must pay the amount to the contractor, less any statutory offsets, not later than the 35th day after the owner receives the request. The Act has a "good-faith" exception, however, allowing an owner to withhold payment of up to 100 percent of the difference between the amount the contractor claims is due and the amount the owner claims is due when there is a good-faith dispute as to the amount owed. Tex. Prop. Code Ann. § 28.003.[40.6] Similarly, in *RAJ Partners, Ltd. v.*

[40.6] *See also, e.g.*, Reed v. Zurn, 2010 VT 14, 2010 WL 800913 (Mar. 1, 2010) (the trial court did not err in finding that the defendants did not act in good faith in refusing to pay plaintiff contractor the amounts set forth in final invoices submitted after defendants terminated plaintiff, and that plaintiff contractor could thus recover interest, penalty interest, and attorneys' fees under Vermont's Prompt Pay Act (PPA), 9 Vt. Stat. Ann. §§ 4001-4009; the PPA did not condition its application on the contractor submitting monthly invoices; although defendants claimed that they withheld payment based on their engineer's advice and thus, at worst, they merely miscalculated

Darco Constr. Corp.,[40.7] the owner argued that an award of prejudgment interest should not have been made to the plaintiff-contractor because, under Tex. Prop. Code § 28.003(b), there could be no overdue payment when a good faith dispute existed concerning the amount owed and whether the contractor's work was performed in a proper manner. However, the trial court's unchallenged findings were that the owner, acting through its agent, egregiously interfered with the performance of the contract by the contractor, and the owner's agent's invasions and interference caused the project to be more expensive, the scope of work more burdensome, and the project delayed, disrupting the contractor's performance of its contract and the quality of performance by its subcontractors. The trial court also found that the project was substantially completed on or about November 25, 2002, and that the contractor submitted its last pay applications on or about February 18, 2003. Thus, there was no error in the trial court's award of prejudgment interest of 18 percent per year from March 31, 2003 until the date of judgment.

In *ARCO Constr. Co., Inc. v. Americon Services Co., Inc.*,[40.8] the contractor submitted to the subcontractor a check for a portion of the amount withheld, with the proviso that the subcontractor accept the check as payment in full. The subcontractor refused, and was awarded penalty interest under the Texas Prompt Payment Act because the amount submitted was undisputedly owed to the subcontractor, and the contractor improperly made receipt contingent upon a waiver of any claim to the disputed portion still withheld. The court further found that there was sufficient evidence to support the jury's finding that the disputed amount withheld was not the subject of a "good faith" dispute, and upheld the award of penalty interest on that amount as well.

In *Tolar Construction, LLC v. Kean Elec. Co., Inc.*,[40.9] Alabama's equivalent of the "prompt-payment act," Ala. Code § 8-29-6, provides for the payment of prejudgment interest at the rate of 12 percent per annum on any payment unjustifiably withheld in noncompliance with the Act. The court found that although the Act does not specify from when interest is to accrue, the legislature obviously intended prejudgment interest to accumulate as of the time the payment was due under the Act. However, because the Act authorizes a contractor to withhold payment from a subcontractor "if there is a bona fide dispute over one or more" of seven specified circumstances, and the trial court expressly held that

---

what they believed they owed plaintiff, the trial court found that (1) defendants' agents oversaw and authorized plaintiff's work before advising defendants to pay two previous invoices; (2) the agents continued to oversee plaintiff's work on the project until defendants abruptly terminated plaintiff; (3) defendants' agents authorized work that defendants later decided they did not want to pay for; (4) defendants were responsible for most of the misunderstandings that arose between the parties; and (5) the amounts claimed by plaintiff were readily ascertainable, but defendants did not want to pay them).

[40.7] 217 S.W.3d 638, 2006 WL 3542992 (Tex. App.-Amarillo Dec. 8, 2006).

[40.8] 2008 WL 2058214 (Tex. App. 1 Dist. May 15, 2008), *review granted, judgment vacated* (Jan. 9, 2009).

[40.9] 944 So. 2d 138 (Ala. 2006).

the contractor had withheld the payment in question because of a bona fide dispute within the meaning of the Act, the court permissibly concluded that interest at the rate of 12 percent per annum did not begin to accrue until the jury reached its verdict.

In *Fletcher Hill, Inc. v. Crosbie*,[40.10] the trial court awarded interest at the statutory interest rate (12 percent per annum) rather than the rate provided in the "late fees" provision of the parties' construction contract (2 percent per month). The Vermont Supreme Court upheld the award, stating that the trial court did not abuse its discretion in applying the statutory rate because under Vermont law, an owner may "withhold[] payment in whole or in part under a construction contract in an amount equalling [sic] the value of any good faith claims against an invoicing contractor or subcontractor, including claims arising from unsatisfactory job progress, defective construction, disputed work or third-party claims." 9 Vt. Stat. Ann. § 4007(a). In this case, the homeowner had a good-faith basis for withholding payment of the outstanding balance due because the contractor breached the contract by failing to complete its work on the owner's home in a workmanlike manner.

In *New Design Construction Co., Inc. v. Hamon Contractors, Inc.*,[40.11] the court held that penalty interest under the Colorado Prompt Payment Act, C.R.S. § 24-91-103(2), for a contractor's failure to pay its subcontractor runs from seven days after the contractor receives payment from the owner, and not from final completion of the project. In addition, since the Prompt Payment Act does not specifically provide for compounded interest, only simple interest is allowed. Further, although penalty interest continues to accrue after appeal of judgment until the judgment is paid, such interest accrues only on the unpaid contract amount, and not on other portions of the judgment, such as costs and prejudgment interest—the latter would accrue postjudgment interest only.

The owner of a contracting company was held personally liable for violation of Ohio's Prompt Payment Act in *Midwest Curtainwalls, Inc. v. Pinnacle 701, LLC*.[40.12] Gus Georgalis owned and controlled Kostas, LLC, a general contractor on a condominium project. Kostas subcontracted with Midwest to provide the glass curtain wall system for the project. Kostas failed to make timely payments to Midwest, and Midwest filed suit against Kostas and Georgalis, seeking penalty interest under Ohio's Prompt Payment Act and attorneys' fees. The parties agreed to arbitrate the matter, and the arbitrator awarded Midwest $573,512 jointly and severally against Georgalis and Kostas, including $115,090 in attorneys' fees for the bad faith conduct of Georgalis and Kostas. Georgalis challenged the portion of the award entered against him personally, and the court affirmed the award.

[40.10] 178 Vt. 77, 2005 VT 1, 2005 WL 77130 (2005).

[40.11] 213 P.3d 1172, 2008 WL 2522306 (Colo. Ct. App. June 26, 2008).

[40.12] 2008-Ohio-5134, 2008 WL 4444285 (Ohio Ct. App. 8 Dist. Oct. 2, 2008).

The court found that the evidence established that Kostas, through Georgalis, repeatedly submitted pay applications to the bank which certified Midwest's entitlement to be paid, thereby obtaining funds allocated for Midwest by the owner, but then refused to make payment to Midwest and converted the funds to Georgalis' own use. The court held this was sufficient evidence of bad faith to support an award of attorneys' fees under the Prompt Payment Act against an individual who commits fraud such that his company violates the Act.

In *Martin Bros. Construction, Inc. v. Thompson Pacific Construction, Inc.,*[40.13] the court held that under California's Prompt Pay Act, Public Contract Code Section 7107, and Business and Professions Code Section 7108, the general contractor was permitted to retain retention as long as it had a bona fide dispute with the subcontractor regarding payment under the subcontract, even if that dispute related to the value of certain change orders as opposed to a dispute specifically directed to the retention; further, as to progress payments, the court held that the parties were not precluded from waiving the applicability of the fixed payment schedule of not later than ten days of receipt of each progress payment in their subcontract, as they had done in this case by agreeing to a subcontract provision stating that "Subcontractor agrees that payment is not due until Subcontractor has furnished all applicable administrative documentation required by the Contract Documents and the applicable releases pursuant to Civil Code section 3262," which included lien releases, certified payroll, union letters (verifying payment of prevailing wages), and proof of insurance).

§ 9.05 PREJUDGMENT INTEREST UNDER STATE LAW

[A] State Statutes

Page 199, add at end of note 46:

See also Scoccolo Constr., Inc. v. City of Renton, 158 Wash. 2d 506, 145 P.3d 371 (2006) (the contractor was entitled to an award of prejudgment interest because the owner/city failed to challenge the reasonableness of the expenses submitted by the contractor. Although the defendant city argued that the contractor's claim was not liquidated, because the jury did not award either the damage amount requested by the contractor, $935,433.27, or the amount argued by the city, $364,904.00, but rather $425,533.00, and thus the jury exercised some degree of discretion, the court disagreed. A sum may still be liquidated even if the adversary successfully challenges the amount and succeeds in reducing it); Quality Design and Constr., Inc. v. City of Gonzales, 977 So. 2d 87, 2007 WL 4181286, 2006-2211 (La. Ct. App. 1st Cir. Nov. 28, 2007) (under La. Civ. Code

[40.13] 179 Cal. App. 4th 1401, 2009 WL 4456380 (Dec. 4, 2009), *as modified* (Dec. 14, 2009), *review denied* (Mar. 24, 2010).

art. 2000, interest is recoverable from the time a debt becomes due unless otherwise stipulated; thus, the trial court erred in not awarding the plaintiff contractor legal interest from the date of substantial completion of the construction project, which was the date the debt became due); James Corp. v. North Allegheny Sch. Dist., 938 A.2d 474 (Pa. Commw. Nov. 30, 2007), *reargument denied* (Jan. 30, 2008) (under the Pennsylvania Procurement Code, 62 Pa. C.S. §§ 102(a); 3901-3942, the contractor was entitled to prejudgment interest at the rate of 10% on the amount due).

Page 200, add new note 49.1 at end of carryover paragraph:

49.1 *See also* D.A. Zuluaga Constr. v. Spokane Airports Bd., 102 Wash. App. 1006 (Ct. App. 2000), *review denied,* 143 Wash. 2d 1006, 20 P.3d 944 (2001) (damage awards to the contractor that were based on standard rates and formulas were not liquidated; although the standard rates were evidence of what was reasonable, they did not necessarily represent the exact amount the contractor would have gained had the work been part of the Board's original design and specifications; similarly, amounts itemized for the contractor's out-of-pocket expenses, including wages paid to its workers, the cost of extra materials, the amounts paid to subcontractors, and the cost of equipment rentals and other miscellaneous items, were not liquidated because those amounts were disputed by the Board); Hutton Contracting Co., Inc. v. City of Coffeyville, 487 F.3d 772 (10th Cir. (Kan.) 2007) (under Kansas law, damages were not liquidated where the amount was not sufficiently definite, since entitlement to any of the retainage was disputed; further, even if some portion of the damages was liquidated, the district court acted within its discretion in denying prejudgment interest, particularly because the contractor was itself partially at fault and the City made a settlement offer to the contractor of more than the contractor later obtained through its judgment).

Page 200, add at end of note 50:

But see Hawken Northwest, Inc. v. State, Dept. of Admin., 76 P.3d 371 (Alaska 2003) (prejudgment interest may not be assessed against the State unless specifically authorized by legislation; under Alaska law existing at the time of suit, plaintiff could not recover such interest with regard to claims under the state procurement code because the statute did not specifically authorize prejudgment interest on awards under the relevant sections of the Act; although a provision allowing prejudgment interest on awards against the Department of Transportation and Public Facilities was added to the procurement code after plaintiff filed suit, the legislature specified that the prejudgment interest provision would apply only to "[c]ontroversies for which a claim is filed with an agency . . . on or after the effective date of this act").

Page 200, add after reference to note 50 in first full paragraph:

Similarly, a Louisiana statute, La. Civ. Code Art. 1989, allows prejudgment interest to be recovered for a breach of contract, whether or not the claim is liquidated. The statute provides that "[d]amages for delay in the performance of an obligation are owed from the time the obligor is put in default." In *L & A Contracting Co., Inc. v. Ram Industrial Coatings, Inc.*,[50.1] the court held that where the defendant subcontractor breached the subcontract in three respects, the earliest of which was the unauthorized assignment of its subcontract, the trial court erred in ordering interest to run from the date of judicial demand rather than from the date of this first breach.

Page 200, add to the end of note 51:

See, e.g., McCarthy Bldg. Co., Inc. v. Teng Li & Assocs., 2005 WL 1532274 (Cal. Ct. App. June 30, 2005) (unpublished), *reh'g denied* (July 20, 2005), *review denied* (Sept. 21, 2005) (the trier of fact has discretionary authority to award prejudgment interest on unliquidated claims under Cal. Civ. Code § 3287(b), which permits "[e]very person who is entitled under any judgment to receive damages based upon a cause of action in contract where the claim was unliquidated" to "recover interest thereon from a date prior to the entry of judgment as the court may, in its discretion, fix, but in no event earlier than the date the action was filed"; the appellate court reviews a lower court's decision to award prejudgment interest in cases covered by Civ. Code § 3287(b) for abuse of discretion); *See also* Steiny & Co., Inc. v. J.A. Jones Constr. Co., 2002 WL 596800 (Cal. Ct. App., Apr. 18, 2002) (nonpublished) (the court had discretion to make an award of prejudgment interest to subcontractors from the date the general contractor would have received 100 percent of its claim to the date of judgment on subcontractors' claims).

Page 200, add new footnote referent 51.1 at end of quotation in third sentence of first full paragraph and add footnote 51.1:

[51.1] Cal. Civ. Code § 3287(a) provides for prejudgment interest on liquidated claims: "Every person who is entitled to recover damages certain, or capable of being made certain by calculation, and the right to recover which is vested in him [or her] upon a particular day, is entitled also to recover interest thereon from that day. . . ." Thus, in Best Western Paving, Inc. v. Granite Constr., Inc., 2002 WL 31682370 (Cal. Ct. App., Nov. 27, 2002), (nonpublished), *review denied* (2003), the court held that an asphalt supplier for a road construction project was entitled to recover prejudgment interest on its breach of contract claim against a contractor that had failed to pay invoices for materials; however,

[50.1] 762 So. 2d 1223 (La. Ct. App. 2000), *writ denied* (La. 2000).

the trial court, after recognizing that the supplier's figures were not 100 percent accurate, erred in arbitrarily reducing the figure "in an extra effort to be in fairness or to try to get as close to true as possible [to the right amount]. . . ."; rather, by its very nature, prejudgment interest on liquidated claims is subject to precise calculation; the appellate court thus remanded for a recalculation of an appropriate award of prejudgment interest. *See also* Homer J. Olsen, Inc. v. Santa Clara Valley Transp. Auth., 2005 WL 3462739 (Cal. Ct. App. Dec. 19, 2005) (unpublished) (when a claim is brought for breach of contract, interest properly runs from the date upon which the claimant's right to recover vested (Cal. Civ. Code § 3287(a)); in this case, the contractor claimed that the court should have offset judgments in favor of both parties before applying interest and also that interest should run from the date of demand; the court disagreed with both contentions: (1) an offset of awards was not appropriate because the awards arose from a multitude of different claims, and the interest awarded on each claim was specific to the particular details of that claim; and (2) as noted above, under the statute, interest properly runs from the dates upon which the claimant's right to recover vested, not from the date a demand for payment was made); J. Alvarez Constr., Inc. v. Western Nat. Group, L.P., 2007 WL 2083704 (Cal. Ct. App. 2007) (unpublished) (the test for recovery of prejudgment interest under Cal. Civ. Code § 3287(a) is whether the defendant actually knows the amount owed or from reasonably available information could have computed that amount; the statute does not authorize prejudgment interest when the amount of damage, as opposed to the determination of liability, depends upon a judicial determination based upon conflicting evidence and it is not ascertainable from truthful data supplied by the claimant to his debtor; thus, when the amount of damages cannot be resolved except by verdict or judgment, prejudgment interest is not appropriate; here, where the subcontractor submitted invoices in the amount ultimately awarded, the amount of damages was sufficiently liquidated to permit an award of prejudgment interest); Golden State Boring & Pipe Jacking, Inc. v. Colich Constr., L.P., 2007 WL 4532831 (Cal Ct. App. 2007) (unpublished) (contractor that recovered on its claim for the reasonable value of work and labor was not entitled to prejudgment interest; although the trial court used the contract price as a criterion to determine the reasonable value of services provided, it was not required to do so; as such, the amount of contractor's claim was not certain or capable of being made certain by calculation under Cal. Civ. Code § 3287(a); the contractor did not contend that the trial court abused its discretion in denying prejudgment interest under the discretionary provisions of § 3287(b)); DeVore Constr. v. Tirapelli, 2009 WL 3246415 (Cal. Ct. App. Oct. 9, 2009) (nonpublished) (affirming award of prejudgment interest on the amount billed for work and materials that remained unpaid less the owner's setoff amount).

Page 201, add at end of note 59:

; S.D. Comp. Laws § 21-1-13.1 ("Any person who is entitled to recover damages . . . is entitled to recover interest thereon from the day that the loss or damage occurred, except during such time as the debtor is prevented by law, or by act of the creditor, from paying the debt."). *See, e.g.*, Gettysburg Sch. Dist. 53-1 v. Helms & Assocs., 2008 S.D. 35, 751 N.W.2d 266 (Apr. 30, 2008) (prejudgment interest is allowed from the date of the loss regardless of whether the damages were known with certainty under South Dakota statute; moreover, a mere difference of opinion as to the exact amount of damages is not sufficient to excuse a defendant from compensating a plaintiff for loss of the use of its money; school district's loss or damage from faulty construction of outdoor track occurred when district received track, making that the day on which prejudgment interest began to run; fact that district had not incurred the expense of replacing the track did not make district's loss a future damage on which prejudgment interest was prohibited).

Page 201, add at end of note 63:

See also H & B Masonry Co., Inc. v. Davis, 32 S.W.3d 120 (Mo. Ct. App. 2000) (under Missouri law, Mo. Rev. Stat. § 408.020, prejudgment interest is "awarded whenever the amount due is liquidated or, if not strictly liquidated, readily ascertainable by reference to recognized standards").

Page 201, add at end of note 64:

See also United States *ex rel.* Maris Equip. Co., Inc. v. Morganti, Inc., 163 F. Supp. 2d 174 (E.D.N.Y. 2001), *aff'd sub nom.* Morganti, Inc. v. Liberty Bond Serv., Inc., 2003 WL 21488807 (2nd Cir. (N.Y.) 2003) (New York law provides for a 9% per annum rate of prejudgment interest in contract actions, N.Y. C.P.L.R. 5001(a), 5004; further, this statute extends to *quantum meruit* recoveries in quasi-contract actions).

Page 201, add new note 64.1 at end of first sentence in third full paragraph:

[64.1] *Cf.* Intermetal Fabricators, Inc. v. The Losco Group, Inc., 2000 WL 1154249 (S.D.N.Y. 2000) (where the general contractor terminated a nonperforming subcontractor and replaced it with other subcontractors, the court held that New York law required that interest on the damages award run from a date that was the approximate midpoint of the period during which the contractor's damages were incurred by its payment to other subcontractors for work the subcontractor had not properly performed).

Page 202, add new note 65.1 at end of indented quotation:

[65.1] *Id. See also* Norment Sec. Group, Inc. v. Ohio Dept. of Rehab. & Corr., 2003-Ohio-6572, 2003 WL 22890088 (Ct. Cl. 2003) (under Ohio Rev. Code § 2743.18(A)(1), prejudgment interest, at the rate of 10% per annum unless a written contract provides a different rate, runs from the time that a payment on a contract becomes "due and payable"; a government contractor's money becomes due and payable when the contractor substantially completes its work on the project; in this case, the court determined that substantial completion occurred on January 21, 2001, the date when the plaintiff's major subcontractor completed its work on the project, thus entitling the plaintiff to prejudgment interest on the $189,740.42 award from January 21, 2001, to the date of the court's judgment entry); Jeffrey B. Peterson & Assocs. v. Dayton Metro. Hous. Auth., 2000 WL 1006562 (Ohio Ct. App. 2000) (citing *Royal Elec. Constr. Corp*, the court said that in determining whether to award prejudgment interest, a court need only ask one question: Has the aggrieved party been fully compensated? If the answer is no, the trial court must then decide factually when the claim was "due and payable").

Page 202, add after first sentence in first full paragraph:

In contrast, in *Complete General Construction Co. v. Ohio Dept. of Transp.,*[66.1] the court held that, pursuant to Ohio Rev. Code § 2743.18(A)(1), the contractor was entitled to prejudgment interest of 10 percent per annum on all damages awarded by the Court of Claims from the time of the accrual of the claim, *i.e.,* the time that the contractor had substantially completed its work on the project.

Page 202, add at end of note 69:

But cf. Quality Asphalt Paving, Inc. v. State Dept. of Transp. & Pub. Facilities, 71 P.3d 865 (Alaska 2003) (contractor urged the court to follow the holding of the Washington Supreme Court in Architectural Woods, Inc. v. State, 92 Wash. 2d 521, 598 P.2d 1372 (1979), in which the court reversed the trial court's denial of interest to the plaintiff based on sovereign immunity and held that any sovereign immunity possessed by the State was waived by its entry into an authorized contract; the Washington court based its reasoning on principles of fairness and the concept that the state should not expect favorable treatment; the instant court, however, agreed with the State that, in Alaska, the authorization to pay interest may not be implied, but must be specifically and explicitly authorized solely by legislative enactment).

[66.1] 94 Ohio St. 3d 54, 760 N.E.2d 364, 370 (2002), *reconsid. denied,* 94 Ohio St. 3d 1489, 763 N.E.2d 1186 (2002).

Page 202, add at end of subsection:

In addition, a claim for prejudgment interest may be barred by the doctrine of sovereign immunity when sought to be recovered from a governmental entity in the absence of a specific waiver of such immunity in a state statute or in the authorized contract.[69.1]

[B] General Contract Law

Page 202, add at end of note 70:

See also Encon Utah, LLC v. Fluor Ames Kraemer, LLC, 2009 UT 7, 2009 WL 172438 (Jan. 27, 2009), *reh'g denied* (June 24, 2009) (prejudgment interest may be recovered "where the damage is complete, the amount of the loss is fixed as of a particular time, and the loss is measurable by facts and figures"; thus, if the amount due is ascertainable by calculation, prejudgment interest will be awarded, even though the method to be used in making the calculation was uncertain; plaintiff was entitled to prejudgment interest, notwithstanding that plaintiff changed the amount of damages it sought during trial, the court had to choose between conflicting expert testimony to determine several cost categories, and the court reduced the damages award based upon its determination as to the reasonableness of plaintiff's overhead and profit percentages).

Page 203, add at end of note 75:

See also, e.g., Lassonde v. Stanton, 157 N.H. 582, 956 A.2d 332 (Aug. 15, 2008) (a contract provision authorizing prejudgment interest at a rate higher than the statutory rate if final payment were not made to the contractor when required was enforceable; the trial court erred in holding that the contract clause—providing that "[f]inal payment not made as agreed may result in an additional finance charge of 15%-18% per annum added to the outstanding balance"—was ambiguous; the contractor was entitled to insist that the owners pay prejudgment interest at a rate of at least 15%, and, because the contractor failed to demand imposition of an interest rate higher than 15%, that figure would be used on remand of the action).

[69.1] *See, e.g.*, Commonwealth v. AMEC Civil, LLC, 54 Va. App. 240, 677 S.E.2d 633 (2009) *appeal granted* _____ (Va. Jan. 28, 2010) (no contractual or express statutory waiver of sovereign immunity existed for plaintiff contractor's claim for prejudgment interest; the relevant statute authorizes an administrative claim to recover "costs and expenses" under the contract, but does not authorize an allowance of prejudgment interest on contractually recoverable costs and expenses).

Page 203, add at end of note 77:

See, e.g., Tennessee Gas Pipeline Co. v. Technip USA Corp., 2008 WL 3876141 (Tex. App.-Hous. Aug. 21, 2008), *review denied* (2 pets.) (Sept. 25, 2009) (under Texas law, when the interest rate is not specified in a contract, prejudgment interest should be calculated based on the statutory rate provided in Texas Finance Code § 304.003; in the instant case, the parties' contract provided for interest of 9% (annual prime plus two percent) on any late payments due under the contract from the owner, but it did not provide for any rate of interest on damages resulting from a breach of the contract by either party; because an applicable interest rate was thus not specified in the contract, prejudgment interest on the owner's recovery of delay damages was calculated based on the statutory rate provided in Texas Finance Code § 304.003, which, at the time of the final judgment in this case, was 7.75%).

§ 9.06 POSTJUDGMENT INTEREST

Page 204, add at end of note 79:

See also, e.g., RAJ Partners, Ltd. v. Darco Constr. Corp., 217 S.W.3d 638, 2006 WL 3542992 (Tex. App.-Amarillo 2006) (the trial court erred in making no award of postjudgment interest when the plaintiff-contractor was awarded money damages for breach of contract; under Tex. Finance Code § 304.001, a "money judgment of a court in this state must specify the postjudgment interest rate applicable to that judgment". Thus, postjudgment interest was mandated by statute, and was recoverable even if the trial court's judgment failed to mention it); Upper Occoquan Sewage Auth. v. Blake Constr. Co., Inc./Poole & Kent, 275 Va. 41, 655 S.E.2d 10 (Jan. 11, 2008) (the principal distinction between prejudgment and postjudgment interest is that the decision whether to award prejudgment interest is discretionary with the trier of fact, while the application of postjudgment interest for all money judgments is mandatory under Va. Code § 8.01-382; [u]nderlying the distinction is the principle that prejudgment interest is normally designed to make the plaintiff whole and is part of the actual damages sought to be recovered while postjudgment interest is not an element of damages, but is a statutory award for delay in the payment of money actually due).

Page 205, add at end of note 83:

See also, e.g., Upper Occoquan Sewage Auth. v. Blake Constr. Co., Inc./Poole & Kent, 275 Va. 41, 655 S.E.2d 10 (Jan. 11, 2008) (postjudgment interest begins to accrue on the date that a fixed amount of a judgment debt is rendered by the factfinder charged with making that determination; thus, if a jury determines through its verdict that money damages are owed to a plaintiff, without regard to whether the jury has also awarded prejudgment interest, postjudgment interest accrues from the date of the verdict until the judgment is paid; similarly, if a trial court sitting without a jury renders a judgment for money damages, the rendition of that award in an order or decree fixes the date on which postjudgment interest begins to accrue as to that award, even if the order or decree rendering the award does not conclude the cause or otherwise stays an immediate execution on the judgment; thus, the contractor was entitled to postjudgment interest on compensatory damages commencing on the date the jury awarded such damages, even though the court suspended the effective date of the judgment for more than two years; the court rejected the contractor's argument that postjudgment interest should accrue on the prejudgment interest that was part of the jury's award).

§ 9.07 INTEREST ON BORROWED FUNDS

Page 205, add at end of note 84:

Cf. Env't Tectonics Corp. v. United States, 72 Fed. Cl. 290 (July 31, 2006) (under FAR 52.243-1, a contractor may recover interest actually paid on funds borrowed because of the government's delay in payments or because of changes to the contract made by the government. However, the interest expended by the contractor must be on actual borrowings, rather than imputed interest on equity capital. "[f]or a contractor to recover interest under FAR 52.243-1, the government must either delay payments or change the contract, causing the contractor to borrow and use that money to fund the contract." In the instant case, the plaintiff-contractor sought to recover financing costs to fund additional costs incurred to perform the Contract, and the court held that to the extent these costs were interest on actual debt to finance government-initiated changes to the contract pursuant to FAR 52.243-1. The court had jurisdiction to adjudicate the claims. The contractor also was seeking, as financing costs, the costs from borrowing against a line of bank credit incurred because of the government's delay in payment of invoices. To the extent these costs were interest on actual debt to finance the contract because of the government's delay in payment of invoices, the court had jurisdiction to adjudicate these claims as well).

Page 207, add at end of note 95:

See also Tempo, Inc. v. Rapid Electric Sales & Serv., Inc., 132 Mich. App. 93, 347 N.W.2d 728 (1984) (where subcontractor's bank withdrew its line of credit due to dispute with contractor, and subcontractor had to obtain an SBA loan at a higher interest rate, subcontractor was entitled to recover the $90,000 of additional interest; subcontractor also entitled to recover the loss of the 2% discount it would have received if it had been paid by the contractor and thereby could have promptly paid its suppliers); Acme Contracting, Ltd. v. Toltest, Inc., 2008

WL 1990780 (E.D. Mich. 2008), *aff'd in part on other grounds, rev'd in part on other grounds*, 2010 WL 1140997 (6th Cir. (Mich.) Mar. 24, 2010) (subcontractor entitled to recover interest paid on its line of credit used to pay its subcontractors when the contractor wrongfully withheld payment).

§ 9.08 IMPUTED INTEREST

Page 207, add at end of note 96:

See also, e.g., Env't Tectonics Corp. v. United States, 72 Fed. Cl. 290 (July 31, 2006) (under FAR 52.243-1, a contractor may seek to recover interest expended on actual borrowings directly tied to a construction project, but not imputed interest on equity capital).

Page 209, add new note 102.1 at end of section:

[102.1] *See, e.g.*, Tennessee Gas Pipeline Co. v. Technip USA Corp., 2008 WL 3876141 (Tex. App.-Hous. Aug. 21, 2008), *review denied* (2 pets.) (Sept. 25, 2009) (in a breach of contract action brought to recover damages caused by delays in making improvements to a gas pipeline, the owner claimed that it was entitled to damages for the interest that accrued on the total amount the owner invested in the Project during the delay period, i.e., interest the owner theoretically could have earned on its money—generally "ranging from five to six percent"—had it invested the funds it spent on this project in other investments during the delay period; recovery was denied; the lost use of money represented an indirect loss to the owner because any return that might be attributable to theoretical investments it might have made fell outside its contract with the defendant contractor; thus, the owner's interest claim was a consequential "loss of use" claim that was precluded by a clause in the Contract barring recovery for consequential losses).

Page 209, add new sections at end of chapter:

§ 9.09 INTEREST ON RETAINAGE

Contractors are entitled to recover interest penalties from the federal government for late payment of retainage under the Prompt Payment Act. Although interest earned on retainage is otherwise not generally recoverable by the contractor, interest on an escrow fund provided in lieu of retainage has been held payable to the contractor. In *McCarthy Building Cos. v. City of St. Louis*,[103] the contract required

[103] 81 S.W.3d 139 (Mo. Ct. App. 2002), *reh'g and/or transfer denied* (2002).

10 percent retention, but permitted the contractor to establish an escrow account and deposit funds or securities equal to the amount of the retainage. The contractor would be responsible for expenses of the escrow account, and would enter into an escrow agreement that was "satisfactory to the owner." After final payment, the contractor would receive the escrowed assets. The contract was silent as to which party would receive the accrued income generated by the escrowed assets. The trial court held that the contractor had no right to receive the interest on the escrow account absent a specific contract provision.

The Missouri Court of Appeals reversed, finding that if the contract is silent on who should receive interest on escrowed funds, the interest is payable to the owner of the escrowed funds. Since the contractor deposited the funds into the escrow account, the contractor was the owner of those funds and therefore entitled to interest earned on the funds.

Missouri's Prompt Payment Act provides that a contractor must pay subcontractors and material suppliers within fifteen days after the contractor receives payment from the public owner. If the contractor does not make such payment in full within fifteen days after receipt of its payment, and if such payment is withheld in bad faith and without reasonable cause, the contractor is liable not only for the amount of the due payment, but also for penalty interest in the amount of 18 percent annually. Mo. Stat. Ann. § 34.057, subd. 1(7). However, in the absence of a showing of bad faith, interest may be recovered at an annual rate of 9 percent pursuant to the statute that generally allows recovery of interest by creditors "when no other rate is agreed upon, for all moneys after they become due and payable, on written contracts, and on accounts after they become due and demand of payment is made; for money recovered for the use of another, and retained without the owner's knowledge of the receipt, and for all other money due or to become due for the forbearance of payment whereof an express promise to pay interest has been made." Mo. Stat. Ann. § 408.020.[104]

In *Tennessee Gas Pipeline Co. v. Technip USA Corp.*,[105] an action brought to recover damages caused by delays in making improvements to a gas pipeline, the defendant contractor appealed the trial court's failure to award it prejudgment interest on retainage at the rate specified in the contract for late payments as an

---

[104] *See, e.g.*, Jerry Bennett Masonry, Inc. v. Crossland Constr. Co., Inc., 171 S.W.3d 81 (Mo. Ct. App. July 28, 2005), *reh'g and/or transfer denied* (Aug. 22, 2005), *transfer denied* (Sept. 20, 2005) (the trial court made no express determination that the contractor acted in bad faith without reasonable cause in withholding payments from the subcontractor, but there was sufficient evidence supporting the trial court's implicit determination that the subcontractor's failure to provide sufficient manpower contributed to the contractor's delay in completing the project in a timely fashion, and thus the trial court did not err in declining to award prejudgment interest in the amount of 18 percent pursuant to § 34.057; however, the trial court erred in not awarding the subcontractor interest at the rate of 9 percent pursuant to § 408.020 after the contractor was paid its retainage by the government).

[105] 2008 WL 3876141 (Tex. App.-Hous. Aug. 21, 2008), *review denied* (2 pets.) (Sept. 25, 2009).

offset against delay damages awarded the owner. The appellate court held, however, that because the parties had stipulated to the retainage amount that would be an offset against a damages award should the owner prevail, the stipulated amount was conclusive, and interest could not be added. However, the trial court erred by failing to subtract the stipulated retainage prior to calculating prejudgment interest on the judgment; rather, the retainage should have been subtracted from the principal amount of the judgment prior to the calculation of prejudgment interest.

§ 9.10 INTEREST ON EXTRA WORK

Construction contracts frequently have clauses that permit the project owner to require the performance of extra work by the contractor. When the owner issues directives for extra work, the contractor generally will incur added costs. If the contractor is only receiving progress payments for completed work, the contractor may not be receiving payments for the extra work. As a result, the contractor may end up financing the cost of the changed work. Generally, contractors are held to be responsible for having and obtaining capital required prosecuting the work in a contract. When the contractor has agreed to perform extra work as required by the owner, this will typically be true even when the project owner expands the work required. However, there have been some federal contracts cases that may provide an avenue for contractor recovery of the cost of financing change order work.

One way to categorize the costs involved in financing additional unanticipated work is to include a charge for imputed interest within the proposal for the additional work. Imputed interest would be calculated using the contractor's cost of its own equity capital. Determining the value of equity capital may be difficult. Further, the case law has not been kind to contractor's asserting imputed interest. In *Appeal of Dawson Construction Co., Inc.*,[106] the contractor was involved in construction at a Veterans Administration (VA) hospital. During construction, the government redesigned the radiology rooms. These changes were extremely expensive. The government and the contractor were unable to agree on a price for more than a year, during which time the contractor was performing the work. The contractor asserted it should recover, as part of the cost of the change, imputed interest on the equity capital that had been used to finance the change. However, this claim was denied. A similar result is found in *District of Columbia v. C.J. Langenfelder & Son, Inc.*,[107] where a contractor on a highway project incurred increased costs because the government would not permit the use of a designated government-owned waste disposal site. Although the contractor was ultimately given a change order, it was denied any recovery for the cost of the capital tied

[106] VABCA No. 2016 (Sept. 23, 1986).
[107] 558 A.2d 1155 (D.C. 1989).

up in the change while the dispute was being resolved. There is a dissenting opinion in this case that the lost use of equity capital was a legitimate cost to the changed work. Imputed interest on contractor equity can also be difficult to recover because it is extremely difficult to value. The United States Court of Appeals for the Federal Circuit in *Gevyn Construction Corp. v. United States*[108] held that there is a distinction between the recovery of interest on debt versus the recovery of imputed interest on the use of equity capital. The costs of borrowed capital are readily ascertainable, but the costs of equity capital are not. This decision does suggest another path to recovery of capital costs on financing change orders: Assert the costs of borrowing the funds to perform the changed work. Recovering the interest on loans to finance extra work was recognized by the United States Court of Claims in *Joseph Bell v. United States.*[109] The court set forth standards for recovery as follows:

1. Change for extra work resulted from an owner directive.
2. The borrowing of funds was necessitated by the owner directive.
3. The funds were segregated and used only for performance of the extra work.

These are difficult standards to meet.

The first standard—that the extra work must be caused by an owner directive—would disqualify changes caused by unanticipated subsurface conditions. In *Servidon Construction Corp. v. United States*,[110] a contractor with an anticipated subsurface conditions claim was expressly denied interest on money borrowed to perform the extra work necessitated by the subsurface condition.

Proving that the directive necessitated borrowing the funds can be difficult and will require analysis of the contractor's cash flow, borrowings, and the incurring of costs to perform the changes. In addition to proving that the borrowing was a necessary result of the changes, it is necessary to show that the funds borrowed were segregated and used for extra work. For contractors who typically use a revolving line of credit, this may be virtually impossible. In *Appeal of J.W. Bateson Co., Inc.*,[111] the contractor was barred from recovering interests simply because the borrowed money was commingled in general accounts, a typical practice for a contractor. In *Appeal of Ed Goetz Painting Co.*,[112] the Veterans Administration Board of Contract Appeals stated that interest on a loan will be denied as a recoverable cost element if the loan proceeds are not segregated in a separate account used exclusively for performance of the additional work. Federal agencies have attempted to prevent recovery of interest on borrowed

[108] 827 F.2d 752 (Fed. Cir. 1987).
[109] 186 Ct. Cl. 189, 404 F.2d 975 (1968).
[110] 931 F.2d 860 (Fed. Cir. 1991).
[111] VABCA No. 1148 (Dec. 4, 1985).
[112] DOT CAB No. 1168 (Nov. 23, 1982).

funds by inserting contract clauses that expressly preclude recovery of interest. The Department of Defense FAR specifically states, *Interest on borrowings (however represented) . . . [and] costs of financing and refinancing capital are disallowed.* This clause was specifically enforced in *Appeal of Tomahawk Construction Co.*[113] Financing of changed work is a real cost to contractors, but recovering it from federal government and its agencies is extremely difficult.

[113] ASBCA No. 45071 (Aug. 18, 1993).

Chapter 10
ATTORNEYS' FEES AND CLAIM PREPARATION COSTS

§ 10.01 INTRODUCTION

Page 213, add at end of note 4:

See also, e.g., Garrison v. CC Builders, Inc., 2008 WY 34, 179 P.3d 867 (Wyo. Mar. 28, 2008) (the trial court did not abuse its discretion in finding the plaintiffs to be the prevailing party and in awarding their costs, as the central issue [whether the plaintiffs had been overcharged under the "cost plus" construction contract] was determined in their favor; the fact that the final judgment amount was less than what they sought did not mean they did not prevail for the purpose of awarding costs).

Page 213, add at end of note 6:

See also, e.g., TA Operating Corp. v. Solar Applications Eng'g, Inc., 191 S.W.3d 173 (Tex. App. - San Antonio Sept. 28, 2005), *reh'g overruled* (Feb. 8, 2006), *review granted* (Apr. 27, 2007) (contractor that was terminated from a construction project to build a truck stop sued for final payment based on a theory of substantial performance; court entered judgment for contractor in the amount of $392,000, the amount of consideration remaining on the contract less the cost of remediable defects in the work; owner argued on appeal that the $8,000 offset for remediable defects made it a prevailing party on its counterclaim, therefore entitling it to recover its attorneys' fees; court, however, disagreed; the $8,000 offset was something contractor was required to prove under its substantial performance cause of action, rather than a successful recovery proven by owner; further, trial court's judgment specifically denied owner recovery on its counterclaim; to recover attorneys' fees under Texas law, owner had to prevail on its counterclaim and recover damages; a party that is not awarded damages cannot recover attorneys' fees; because owner was not awarded damages under its counterclaim for breach of contract, it was not entitled to recover attorneys' fees); Coral-Tech Assocs., Inc. v. Plumbing Contractors, Inc., 916 So. 2d 958 (Fla. Dist. Ct. App. Dec. 7, 2005), *reh'g denied* (Jan. 19, 2006) (the trial court erred in determining that the subcontractor was entitled to an award of attorneys' fees resulting from an arbitration of the subcontractor's claim against the general contractor and the general contractor's counterclaim, because the arbitrator failed to designate either party as the prevailing party, and it was not clear from the face of the arbitration award which party prevailed; even though the arbitrator awarded the subcontractor $982.07 on its claims, and denied the contractor's $27,000 counterclaim, the arbitrator adopted the general contractor's breakdown and pay schedule; although the proper procedure in such circumstances ordinarily is for the trial court to remand the matter back to the arbitrator for an explanation of the basis for the recovery, the deadline for modification or clarification of the arbitrator's ruling (application must be made within 90 days after delivery of the ruling) had long passed, and, as a matter of law, the arbitrator was without legal basis to revisit its prior award; the court thus ruled that neither party was entitled to an award of attorneys' fees); CJ Building Corp. v. TRAC-10, 368 Ark. 654, 249 S.W.3d 793 (2007) (the court held that the defendant was the "prevailing party" entitled to an award of attorneys' fees under the state statute where the plaintiff was awarded $13,000 of its $56,000 retainage due to backcharges properly asserted by the defendant; the court stated that the prevailing party was "the one with the most points at the end of the contest," based on the entire case and not just particular issues or claims; here, the defendant "scored the most points, as it received three-fourths of the money at issue"); Golden State Boring & Pipe Jacking, Inc. v. Colich Constr., L.P., 2007 WL 4532831 (Cal. Ct. App. 2007) (unpublished) (the contract contained a provision entitling the prevailing party to an award of attorneys' fees and experts' fees, and California Code of Civil Procedure Section 1717 provides that the "prevailing" party in a contract action is the party "who recovered a greater relief in the action on the contract. The court may also determine that there is no party prevailing on the contract for purposes of this section." In this case, Golden State's breach of contract claim was denied, but it was awarded $71,354 for the fair value of its work and services on its common count claim. Colich was awarded $36,500 in liquidated damages on its breach of contract cross-complaint, resulting in a net recovery by Golden State of $34,854. The trial court denied Golden State's request for attorneys' fees, finding that neither party was the prevailing party under Section 1717, and the appellate court affirmed. The court stated that in making this determination, a trial court must compare the relief awarded on the claims with the parties' demands on those claims and their litigation objections as disclosed by the pleadings, trial brief, opening statements, and similar sources, to ascertain the extent to which each party has succeeded and failed to succeed in its contentions. Due to the mixed results at trial, where Golden State had a net recovery but did not prevail on its breach of contract claim, and Colich was awarded a significant setoff on its breach of contract cross-complaint, the trial court could reasonably find that there was no prevailing party); Boro Constr., Inc. v. Ridley Sch. Dist., 2010 WL 759835 (Pa. Commw. Ct. Mar. 8, 2010) (Boro completed a $10 million contract for construction of a school building, and sued the District for $247,829.90, comprised of the balance due of $44,000, delay damages of $40,026.83, and miscellaneous other damages; the District counterclaimed for $38,717 for repairs and credit change orders, and sought attorneys' fees under the no-damages-for-delay provision of the contract, which provided that if the contractor "shall choose to litigate this clause or issue and loses said litigation," the District was entitled to reasonable attorneys' fees and costs; after trial, judgment was entered in favor of the District on Boro's claims based on Boro's breach of the contract by failing to submit the required documentation for final payment, while the District's counterclaims were denied; both sides appealed, and the court upheld that judgment against Boro on its claims; as to the attorneys' fees, the court affirmed the trial court's determination that the District was not entitled to recover its fees and costs on the grounds that since Boro had "prevailed" with respect to the District's counterclaims, the District could not be considered a "substantially prevailing party;" [the court failed to discuss the fact that attorneys' fees were permitted only in connection with a delay claim, as to which claim the District completely prevailed]).

Page 214, add to note 10 after Mission Hardwood case:

; Jenkins, Inc. v. Walsh Bros., Inc., 2001 Me. 98, 776 A.2d 1229 (Me. 2001), *appeal after remand*, 2002 Me. 168, 810 A.2d 929 (2002) (under Maine's prompt payment statute, 10 Me. Rev. Stat. Ann. § 1118(4), in any proceeding to recover a payment under the Act, the substantially prevailing party must be awarded reasonable attorneys' fees in an amount to be determined by the court or arbitrator, together with expenses); Fru-Con/Fluor Daniel Joint Venture v. Corrigan Bros., Inc., 154 S.W.3d 330 (Mo. Ct. App. Oct. 19, 2004), *transfer denied* (Jan. 26, 2005), *transfer denied* (Mar. 1, 2005) (trial court did not err in awarding subcontractor penalty interest and attorneys' fees pursuant to the Missouri Prompt Payment Act, Mo. Rev. Stat. § 431.180; under the statute, a trial court may award litigation costs and interest upon a showing that the parties entered into a contract for construction work, and prime contractor failed to make payments in accordance with contract; trial court's award of damages in *quantum meruit* did not preclude trial court from also awarding interest and attorneys' fees under the Act, because the parties did enter into a contract, and the statute does not require the contract to be in existence throughout the duration of the project; even if trial court found that the contract had been abandoned, parties still entered into it, and contractor still withheld payment to subcontractor for its work done pursuant to the contract; therefore, statute's requirements were met, and trial court was well within its rights to award these additional damages); Tolar Constr., LLC v. Kean Elec. Co., Inc., 944 So. 2d 138 (Ala. 2006) (subcontractor was entitled to attorney's fees under Alabama's Miller Act, Ala. Code § 8-29-6, which provides for such awards to be made to the prevailing party. Contrary to the defendant's contention, the statute provides for awarding attorney fees irrespective of whether a party is entitled to interest under the Act for failure to comply with its prompt payment provisions); Gentry v. Squires Constr., Inc., 188 S.W.3d 396 (Tex. App.-Dallas Mar. 27, 2006) (under Tex. Civ. Prac. & Rem. Code Ann. § 38.001, a prevailing party may recover reasonable attorney's fees in a suit for *quantum meruit*, in the trial court's discretion. Because the trial court erroneously made the legal conclusion that the plaintiff contractor was not entitled to recover fees, and thus did not make any finding of fact that the plaintiff should not recover attorney's fees, the appellate court remanded for a factual determination to be made by the trial court); Quality Design & Constr., Inc. v. City of Gonzales, 977 So. 2d 87, 2007 WL 4181286, 2006-2211 (La. Ct. App. 1st Cir. Nov. 28, 2007) (under La. Rev. Stat. § 38:2191(B), "[a]ny public entity failing to make any final payments after formal final acceptance and within forty-five days following receipt of a clear lien certificate by the public entity shall be liable for reasonable attorneys fees"; in this case, the mayor of the defendant city executed a "Certificate of Substantial Completion" for the project, which was effective as a "formal final acceptance" for all purposes; the contractor was thus entitled to an award of attorney's fees based on the City's failure to submit final payment within 45 days).

Page 214, add at end of note 10:

Cf. Barry v. Pacific W. Constr., Inc., 140 Idaho 827, 103 P.3d 440 (2004) (reasonable attorneys' fees may be awarded under Idaho Code § 12-120(3) to "prevailing party" in actions on contracts or "commercial transactions"; however, when alleged contract or commercial transaction is illegal, "neither party should be permitted to claim the benefit of [the statute]"; in this case, there was an illegal contract, because plaintiff subcontractor did not have public works license required to do work; thus, although subcontractor was permitted, on a theory of unjust enrichment, to recover some damages for work performed, attorneys' fees were not available).

§ 10.02 CONTRACTUAL PROVISIONS

Page 214, add at end of note 12:

See also, e.g., Intercontinental Group P'ship v. KB Home Lone Star L.P., 295 S.W.3d 650 (Tex. Aug. 28, 2009) (KB sued IGP for specific performance and breach of a written contract to sell KB a subdivision, and IGP counterclaimed alleging that KB had orally agreed and then refused to purchase other subdivisions as part of the written contract; the contract mandated attorney's fees to the "prevailing party," a term undefined in the contract; at trial, the jury found in favor of KB on its claim and on the counterclaim, awarded KB $0 damages, and further awarded KB $66,000 in attorneys' fees; the court of appeals found that under Texas law, "a "prevailing party" is a party who successfully prosecutes the action or successfully defends against it, prevailing on the main issue, even though not to the extent of its original contention," and that since the central concern is "success on the merits, and not whether damages were awarded," KB was properly considered the prevailing party; the Texas Supreme Court reversed, held that a claimant must obtain actual and meaningful relief, something that materially alters the parties' legal relationship, in order to be the "prevailing" party; thus, a plaintiff must prove compensable injury and secure an enforceable judgment in the form of damages or equitable relief—"there must be a showing that the plaintiff was actually harmed, not merely wronged"; a finding by the jury that the defendant breached the contract was not sufficient in the instant case to support an award of attorneys' fees when the jury awarded $0 in damages); Scoccolo Constr., Inc. v. City of Renton, 158 Wash. 2d 506, 145 P.3d 371 (2006) (the plaintiff contractor was entitled to an award of attorneys' fees pursuant to a contract provision allowing such fees to the prevailing party in an action to enforce the provisions of the contract. Although the defendant city argued that the contractor was not the prevailing party, the contractor successfully secured a verdict against the city for breach of contract and on the question of the city's liability for delays. Under these circumstances, an award of attorneys' fees was warranted); Gettysburg Sch. Dist. 53-1 v. Helms and Assocs., 2008 SD 35, 751 N.W.2d 266 (Apr. 30, 2008) (the trial court did not err as a matter of law or abuse its discretion in awarding attorneys' fees and expert witness costs when the parties' contract contained two separate provisions allowing for recovery of such costs and fees: (1) if the contractor's work was found to be defective, as defined within the contract, the contractor was responsible for all costs and disbursements, including attorneys' fees, spent by the plaintiff owner in bringing a civil action; and (2) the owner may have defective work removed and replaced, and the contractor will be paid all costs, including attorneys' fees and all court or arbitration costs, relating to such removal or replacement; because the contract permitted the award of attorneys' fees and other costs, the plaintiff merely had to establish, by a preponderance of the evidence, the basis for such an award); City of Gillette v. Hladky Constr., Inc., 2008 WY 134, 196 P.3d 184 (Wyo. Nov. 14, 2008) (the trial court properly awarded plaintiff contractor attorneys' fees pursuant to a clause in the contract allowing recovery of fees by the prevailing party in a suit to enforce rights under the contract; plaintiff's claim for breach of the implied covenant of good faith and fair dealing was a suit to enforce rights under the contract, contrary to the defendant city's contention, because the covenant is implied in every contract; because the plaintiff prevailed, it was entitled to recover reasonable attorneys' fees).

Page 215, add at end of note 15:

See also Steiny & Co., Inc. v. J.A. Jones Constr. Co., 2002 WL 596800 (Cal. Ct. App. Apr. 18, 2002) (nonpublished) (general contractor was contractually obligated to pay attorneys' fees and costs to subcontractors; however, court erred in making undifferentiated lump sum awards of $185,000 and $135,000, without articulating basis for awards; because awards bore no rational relationship to evidence, court remanded for reconsideration of factors delineated in earlier case, taking into account all relevant circumstances; court noted that items on verified cost bills would be *prima facie* evidence that the costs, expenses, and services listed were necessarily incurred, including legal fees and expert witness fees); Sooner Builders & Investments, Inc. v. Nolan Hatcher Construction Services, L.L.C., 2007 OK 50, 2007 WL 1752788 (2007) (Sooner asserted claims of more than $100,000 against Hatcher on six separate contracts for the balance due and additional work performed; the arbitrator awarded Sooner $92,000 on its claims, less $25,000 paid by Hatcher to others, for a net recovery of $67,000, plus prejudgment interest on a $46,000 excessive offset withheld by Hatcher; the subcontract provided that "the prevailing party shall be entitled to recover reasonable attorney's fees, costs, charges and expenses," but the arbitrator denied Sooner's request for attorneys' fees and expenses, finding that Sooner and Hatcher each prevailed on some of their claims; the Oklahoma Supreme Court affirmed the district court's decision modifying the arbitration award to grant Sooner attorneys' fees and expenses, finding that the arbitrator exceeded his authority when he ignored the prevailing party attorneys' fee provision in the subcontract; the court found that the applicable subcontract clause was not ambiguous, that Sooner was the "prevailing party" because it was the "successful party who has been awarded some relief on the merits of his or her claim" and had been awarded prejudgment interest, and that an award of attorneys' fees and expenses was therefore mandatory under the subcontract).

Page 215, add new note 15.1 at end of first paragraph:

[15.1] *See also* L & A Contracting Co., Inc. v. Ram Indus. Coatings, Inc., 762 So. 2d 1123 (La. Ct. App. 2000), *writ denied* (La. 2000) (award of attorneys' fees to the general contractor and against the subcontractor and its surety was proper when the contract allowed for imposition of fees if the contractor was forced to take over the subcontract because of the subcontractor's failure to take corrective action with regard to a complaint for a need to increase job progress or because of a failure of the subcontractor to pay and discharge all claims for payment of supplies, materials, or equipment).

Page 215, add at end of note 16:

See also City of Westminster v. Centric-Jones Constructors, 100 P.3d 472 (Colo. App. 2003) (not released) (the court held that the City could not recover attorneys' fees and costs in a breach of contract action against the prime contractor where the trial court directed a verdict against the City and refused to allow the jury to award nominal damages; the City was not the prevailing party, since it could have recovered no more than $1 in nominal damages, whereas the contractor was awarded more than $900,000 on its counterclaim; the trial court's award of costs to the contractor was upheld, as the contractor was properly deemed a "prevailing party" under the state statute); Fletcher Hill, Inc. v. Crosbie, 2005 VT 1, 2005 WL 77130 (Vt. Jan. 14, 2005) (court similarly held that a contractor could not recover attorneys' fees from a homeowner when contractor itself had breached the parties' contract; in this case, parties had negotiated and agreed to a "late fee" provision that provided for attorneys' fees in the event of a balance overdue more than 30 days from the invoice date; court noted that under Vermont statutes, owner is generally obligated to pay a contractor strictly in accordance with the terms of the construction contract; however, owner may "withhold[] payment in whole or in part under a construction contract in an amount equalling [sic] the value of any good faith claims against an invoicing contractor or subcontractor, including claims arising from unsatisfactory job progress, defective construction, disputed work or third-party claims" (9 Vt. Stat. Ann. § 4007(a)); in this case, trial court did not abuse its discretion in refusing to invoke the "late fee" provision concerning attorneys' fees because the homeowner had a good-faith basis for withholding payment of the outstanding balance for two reasons: (1) the contractor breached the contract by failing to complete the work in a workmanlike manner (the homeowner's counter-claim described a list of substantial deficiencies); and (2) "there was an adequate basis in the record, had [the jury] chosen to do so, to provide more relief to the defendant," and, as a result of the "issues of poor workmanship" and "the substantial deficiencies in the construction," the homeowner "was within her rights to withhold funds under the circumstances").

Page 215, add at end of note 17:

See also, e.g., O & G Indus., Inc. v. All Phase Enters., Inc., 112 Conn. App. 511, 963 A.2d 676 (Feb. 10, 2009) (in a third-party action brought by a general contractor against its subcontractor to recover attorneys' fees that the general contractor incurred in defense of the first-party action filed against it and for the attorneys' fees that it was ordered to reimburse to the plaintiff, the general contractor was entitled to full indemnification of the fees on the basis of the clear language of the subcontract).

Page 216, add at end of section:

In *Adams Builders & Contractors, Inc. v. York Saturn, Inc.*,[18.1] the appellate court held that the trial court erred in declining to award attorneys' fees to the owner pursuant to a clause in the contract providing that the owner "shall be entitled to collect from the Contractor all direct, indirect, and consequential damages suffered by the Owner on account of the Contractor's default, including, without limitation, . . . attorneys' fees incurred by the Owner on account of such default." The trial court had ruled that the owner was not entitled to recover the

[18.1] 60 Mass. App. Ct. 1101, 798 N.E.2d 586 (2003).

attorneys' fees it incurred in pursuing its claims of defective performance against the contractor because the owner itself had breached the payment provisions of the contract by "unjustifiably failing to timely pay [the contractor's] Requisition No. 9 in full." The appellate court disagreed. Generally, when both parties commit a breach of the agreement, each party has the right to claim damages. In this case, the trial court had found that both parties breached the agreement. Having awarded the owner its damages for the contractor's departure from the contract documents, there was no basis for the judge's denial of the owner's attorneys' fees, which the contractor had contracted to pay as part of the owner's damages in the event of the contractor's default. The court accordingly remanded the case for determination of such fees.

An award of attorneys' fees in arbitration was upheld even though the underlying contractor arbitration agreement did not specifically provide for the award of attorneys' fees. In *Drywall Systems, Inc. v. ZVI Construction Co., Inc.*,[18.2] an arbitration award of $146,000 to Drywall Systems for attorneys' fees was overturned by the Massachusetts Court of Appeals. The appellate court ruled that the Massachusetts Arbitration Act expressly prohibited the award of attorneys' fees in arbitration unless the underlying arbitration agreement provided for the award of fees. Since the underlying agreement did not provide for the awarding of attorneys' fees, the award was vacated. On appeal, the Massachusetts Supreme Court reversed, finding that the Massachusetts statute mandating an award of attorneys' fees upon a finding of unfair practices took precedence over the Arbitration Act.

§ 10.03 EQUAL ACCESS TO JUSTICE ACT

Page 216, add after second sentence of first paragraph, ending, ". . . unless it is determined that the position of the government in the litigation was 'substantially justified.' ":

In order to recover attorneys' fees under the EAJA, the following must be shown: (1) the claimant was a "Prevailing party"; (2) the government's position was not "substantially justified"; (3) no special circumstances make the award unjust; and (4) the fee application was submitted within 30 days of final judgment and was supported by an itemized statement.[19.1]

[18.2] 747 N.E.2d 168 (Mass. App. Ct. 2001).

[19.1] Baldi Bros. Constructors v. United States, 52 Fed. Cl. 78 (Ct. Cl. 2002).

Page 216, add new footnote referent 20.1 at end of first sentence of second paragraph:

[20.1] Al Ghanim Combined Group Co. Gen. Trad. & Cont. W.L.L. v. United States, 67 Fed. Cl. 494 (Fed. Cl. 2005) (status as a "party" for purposes of the EAJA cannot be established by introduction of a "conclusory, self-serving, and non-probative" affidavit that the statutory requirements have been met, *i.e.*, that the applicant: (1) had a net worth less than $7 million at the time the action was filed, (2) did not have in its employ more than 500 persons at the time the action was filed, and (3) was the prevailing party in the underlying action; in order to establish the financial requirements, the applicant must provide "an integrated balance sheet reflecting a systematic analysis of the assets and liabilities of" the business; because the plaintiff in the instant case submitted only a self-serving, non-probative affidavit, providing nothing resembling a balance sheet and with no documentation to support this appraisal of its net worth, it was not eligible to recover attorneys' fees and costs).

Page 217, add at end of note 22:

See also Karcher Envtl., Inc., PSBCA No. 4085, 02-1 BCA ¶ 31,787 (2002) (paralegal fees are recoverable under EAJA, but only at the actual cost of the paralegal services to the attorney, even if the rate billed to the client is higher; similarly, fees for a staff forensic engineer are recoverable only at the actual cost to the attorney; on the other hand, work performed by a document clerk that is clerical in nature typically is included in the overhead rate included within the attorney's per-hour rate, rather than billed separately on an hourly basis, and thus is not allowed as a separate recovery; also, expenses related to the attendance of a lay witness at a deposition are not recoverable); *In re* Appeal of Haselrig Constr. Co., Inc., PSBCA No. 4609, 2003 WL 21757162 (2003) (holding that paralegal fees can be recovered under the EAJA only at the actual cost to the attorney (including benefits paid to or on behalf of the paralegal), not the attorney's hourly billing rate to the contractor; the Board noted this position is consistent with that of the Armed Services, Interior, and Agriculture Boards, but contrary to that of the Department of Veterans Affairs and General Services Boards).

Page 217, add after second full paragraph on page:

Proof that the government's position is "substantially justified" does not mean that the government is required to be "justified to a high degree." Rather, the standard is analogous to the one requiring a "reasonable basis in law and fact," which means that the government must be "justified to a degree that could satisfy a reasonable person." It has been held, however, that the fact that a particular plaintiff is able to recover only a percentage of the damages sought does not necessarily prove that the government's position was substantially justified. Thus, in *Baldi Bros. Constructors v. United States*,[25.1] the government asserted that because plaintiff ultimately recovered only 55 percent of the amount of damages sought, the substantial justification of the government's litigation position was self-evident. The court said, however, that this argument missed the point that the court is "required to rule on the EAJA application 'independent from the merits phase.' The fact the plaintiff recovered only 55 percent of its monetary claim is not of itself sufficient to discharge defendant's burden of proving substantial justification of its position before the actual litigation, especially given that plaintiff's diminished recovery represents failure to prove specific damages, rather than exoneration of the Government." Because the government in this case made no attempt to provide a "defense, explanation, or substantiation" for its action, either before or during the litigation phase, defendant could not prove that the government's conduct was substantially justified.

In contrast, in *Application of Environmental Safety Consultants, Inc.*,[25.2] the Board refused to allow the prevailing party to recover attorneys' fees under the EAJA, based upon its finding that the government's position was substantially justified. ESCI entered into a contract with the U.S. Naval Facilities Engineering Command (NAVFAC) to remove and dispose of sludge on two lagoons in Pennsylvania. The contract represented the density of solids contained in each lagoon and stated that only lagoon #2 contained hazardous waste. During performance, ESCI determined that each lagoon had a higher density of solids than represented, and that lagoon #1 also contained hazardous waste, which was more expensive to remove. ESCI submitted a request for equitable adjustment in the amount of $150,000 for the additional costs of removal, which was denied by NAVFAC on the grounds that the contract adequately disclosed the materials at the site and that ESCI's sampling methods were not supportable. ESCI filed an appeal, asserting claims for differing site conditions, government-caused delay, and changed work. The Board determined that there was a change in the physical characteristics of the sludge at the lagoons and that the government should have disclosed the presence of hazardous waste in lagoon #1. The Board awarded ESCI $94,000 for additional costs of sludge removal and denied ESCI's remaining claims. ESCI then sought an award of its attorneys' fees under the EAJA. The Board found that although ESCI was the "prevailing party," NAVFAC's position with respect to the original request for equitable adjustment and the appeal proceedings was "substantially justified," thereby precluding an award of attorneys' fees. The Board found that NAVFAC made a good-faith effort to analyze the issues as they were known at the time of the original claim, and that NAVFAC spent considerable time trying to assist ESCI in its performance of the contract and "had no plan to injure [ESCI] or cause [ESCI] to fail in performing the contract." The Board further found that NAVFAC's position in the appeal proceedings was reasonable, that ESCI recovered less than 50 percent of the

[25.1] 50 Fed. Cl. 78 (Ct. Cl. 2001).

[25.2] ASBCA No. 47498, 2007 WL 2427975 (Aug. 9, 2007).

amount claimed in its Statement of Costs, and that ESCI failed to cooperate in providing cost documents to NAVFAC during the quantum phase of the hearing. Based upon these factors, the court held that NAVFAC's position was substantially justified.

In *Metric Construction Co., Inc., v. United States*,[25.3] Metric was awarded $1.3 million on its claim for $2.1 million against the government relating to the government's design errors that resulted in Metric having to replace the roof it had constructed on a warehouse project. Metric then sought more than $100,000 in attorneys' fees under the Equal Access to Justice Act, and the government defended by asserting that its position was "substantially justified." The court stated that the government's position must have been reasonable in both law and fact, and that such reasonableness must be shown in this case with respect to the government's treatment of Metric's certified claim, the government's litigation of Metric's suit through the time of the court's decision on the government's summary judgment motion, and the government's conduct throughout trial activities until judgment was entered. Although the government did not respond to Metric's certified claim, the court found that this "deemed denial" does not indicate that the government's position was not substantially justified and that, given the complicated and highly factual nature of the dispute and the fact that the contractor has the burden of proving entitlement to an equitable contract adjustment, the government's deemed denial of Metric claim was not unreasonable. The court also found that the government's motion for summary judgment had a reasonable basis in both fact and law, even though it was ultimately denied. Finally, the court determined that the government's arguments and presentation of evidence at trial were reasonable, noting that the government was successful in reducing the damages award which, although not dispositive of the "substantial justification" question, provides additional support that the government's position at trial was more than tenuous, and reasonable. The court therefore denied Metric's request for attorneys' fees and other litigation expenses.

In *Appeal of Abcon Associates, Inc.*,[25.4] Abcon's default termination had been converted to a termination for convenience, Abcon submitted a convenience settlement proposal which was partially granted, Abcon appealed and the Board decided some, but not all, of the issues in Abcon's favor. On Abcon's EAJA request, the Board looked at each of the issues Abcon had appealed to determine whether the government's position in denying the claims was "substantially justified," which the Board defined as having "a reasonable basis in law and fact." The Board found that the government's position was not substantially justified on two of the four issues. To apportion the total fees and costs, the Board noted that Abcon recovered $693,962 of the total damage of $1,018,589, which was a recovery of approximately 68 percent. However, the Board declined to

[25.3] 83 Fed. Cl. 446 (May 21, 2008).

[25.4] PSBCA No. 5291, 2009 WL 775550 (Mar. 12, 2009).

award Abcon 68 percent of the total fees and costs incurred, based upon its analysis of the actual effort applied in the appeal to the various issues. "Although Respondent's [the government's] position regarding the $248,132 paid to subcontractors was not substantially justified, Respondent only lightly defended its position on that claim, and Appellant was required to do little to support its position, which the Board accepted. Appellant's initial and reply briefs reflected significant effort on the contract price cap, loss adjustment and profit issues, for which Appellant may not recover its fees and expenses. The value of the REAs was addressed at length in the reply brief and reply declaration, but less so in Appellant's initial brief. After reviewing the record as a whole, including Appellant's briefs, and estimating as best we can the legal work associated with the issues upon which Appellant did not prevail or on which Respondent was substantially justified and Appellant's relative success overall, we exercise our discretion on a jury-verdict basis and determine that Appellant's otherwise allowable EAJA attorney fees and expenses will be reduced by 50% notwithstanding its recovery of a higher proportion of its claim on a dollar basis." The same allocation was applied to the fees and expenses Abcon incurred in connection with the preparation and submission of its EAJA fee Application, including those incurred in replying to the government's opposition to the fee Application.

Page 218, add at end of note 28:

See also Orlosky Inc. v. United States, 68 Fed. Cl. 296 (2005), *appeal dismissed*, 180 Fed. Appx. 928 (Fed. Cir. Apr. 17, 2006) (court offered a "suggestion" to contractor with regard to whether it should apply for an award of attorneys' fees and costs under the Equal Access to Justice Act; although plaintiff obtained an award of delay damages and thus was qualified as a prevailing party in that it had secured a judgment on the merits, plaintiff was by no means blameless in its actions, in that it failed to inspect the worksite prior to beginning construction and its documentation of damages was inadequate; court noted that "[t]he spectacle of the Navy's studied ineptitude throughout the . . . project was matched only by plaintiff's maladroitness. Plaintiff failed to avail itself of the opportunity to view the site prior to making its bid. Its presentation of evidence exaggerated the dangers and problems it faced throughout the project, while the particulars relating to costs sustained were inadequate. The Government was more than substantially justified in defending against this lawsuit."). *But see* Application of W. L. Holbrook, AGBCA No. 2003-139-10, 2003 WL 23305323 (2003) (to determine whether the government's position had been substantially justified under the EAJA, the Board considered the evidentiary support provided by the contractor for each claim item, and the amount awarded by the Board in relation to the amount allowed by the government; the contractor was entitled to the attorneys' fees incurred in connection with the claim items as to which the contractor had submitted persuasive evidence and the government had allowed amounts much less than awarded by the Board).

Page 219, add at end of note 33:

; Karcher Envtl., Inc., PSBCA No. 4085, 02-1 BCA ¶ 31,787 (2002) (where the contractor was ultimately unsuccessful on claims totaling approximately 16 percent of the total amount in issue, any recovery of attorneys' fees and expenses for the period at issue would be limited to 84 percent of the incurred fees and expenses); Appeal of Donahue Electric, Inc., VABCA No. 6618E, 2008 WL 22070998 (2003) (contractor filed a claim for $132,000, alleging defective specifications, architect delays, and other additional costs; contractor prevailed only on the defective specifications claim, and was awarded $4,000; contractor applied to recover its attorneys' fees under the EAJA, submitting an itemization of the attorney's time that did not link the work to any particular aspect of the claim; Board held that in this situation, the fees and expenses would be apportioned based upon the contractor's ratio of success, and the contractor was awarded only a small fraction of the attorneys' fees it had sought to recover).

Page 219, add at end of note 34:

See also Baldi Bros. Constructors v. United States, 52 Fed. Cl. 78 (2002) (after plaintiff-contractor recovered only 55% of the damages it sought, the government urged the court to reduce plaintiff's total recovery of attorneys' fees by the same percentage; the court said, however, that "defendant's proposed mathematical approach, which predicates a plaintiff's fee award on the number of issues on which plaintiff prevailed, already has been soundly rejected. The ratio of successful claims to total claims simply need not correlate to actual expenses incurred in relation to any particular claim. The court thus may 'attempt to identify specific hours that should be eliminated, or it may simply reduce the award to account for the limited success'" (quoting from Hensley v. Eckerhart, 461 U.S. 424, 436-437 (1983)); a wide variety of factors should be considered in reaching the costs decision, including the conduct of the parties during trial; in this case, the court determined that a one-third reduction in the award of fees was warranted).

Page 220, add at end of note 39:

But see Application of Elrich Contracting, Inc., ASBCA No. 50867 (Aug. 7, 2002) (Board held that when an appeal is voluntarily dismissed after a favorable settlement agreement, the contractor is not a "prevailing party" under the EAJA, and cannot recover attorneys' fees).

Page 220, add at end of note 40:

See also Baldi Bros. Constructors v. United States, 52 Fed. Cl. 78 (Ct. Cl. 2002) (fees incurred in the preparation and filing of an EAJA claim are recoverable under the EAJA).

Page 220, add at end of section:

The rule is that a contractor can recover attorney's fees only to the extent those fees are incurred as contract administration costs, which includes preparations for negotiations with the government. A contractor cannot recover fees incurred for the purpose of bringing a claim against the government. These rules were again repeated in *Appeal of Bath Ironworks Corp.*,[40.1] where fees apparently incurred in preparing a claim where disallowed even though ongoing negotiations to settle the matter were still in progress.

The General Services Administration Board of Contractor Appeals has ruled that it lacks jurisdiction under the Equal Access to Justice Act to award attorneys' fees incurred in pursuing an ultimately successful appeal of a Board decision to the U.S. Court of Appeals. In *Herman B. Taylor Construction Co. v. General Services Administration*,[40.2] Taylor was appealing a default termination by the GSA on a contract for renovations to a federal building in El Paso, Texas. The Board denied Taylor's appeal. Taylor appealed the Board decision to the U.S. Court of Appeals for the Federal Circuit. The Court of Appeals reversed the Board decision and remanded the matter to the Board. The Board promptly granted Taylor's appeal and converted the default termination to a termination for convenience of the government. Taylor filed a timely application with the Board for appeals costs, which included the attorneys' fees incurred in the successful appeal to the U.S. Court of Appeals. The Board ruled that it could not award attorneys' fees or other costs incurred in a proceeding before a judicial body.

In *Appeal of David Boland, Inc.*,[40.3] a prevailing party's application for appeal costs under the Equal Access to Justice Act was ruled upon by the Veterans Affairs Board of Contract Appeals. In this matter, the contractor was the prevailing party, and the government was disputing portions of the contractor's applications for fees charged by its attorneys, paralegals, scheduling consultants, and legal consultants. The government asserted that paralegal time, which had been billed to the contractor at $110 per hour, should be paid only at the actual cost to the law firm, not at billing rates. After receiving evidence that the average billing rate for experienced paralegals in the area was $125 to $145 per hour, the Board found that the $110 hourly rate billed to the contractor was reasonable and that the contractor was entitled to the recovery of those costs. The Board acknowledged that this holding was different than in Armed Services Board of

---

[40.1] ASBCA No. 54544, 2006 WL 1148812 (Apr. 21, 2006). *See also* Application under the EAJA of Kostmayer Constr., LLC, ASBCA No. 55053, 2009 WL 3785181 (Oct. 30, 2009) (contractor that successfully appealed its termination for default was entitled to recover attorneys' fees and costs incurred by the contractor in connection with that appeal, but could not recover attorneys' fees or expenses incurred by the contractor in defending subcontractor/supplier lawsuits, or such fees and expenses incurred by the contractor's surety in negotiating a completion contract with the government and in assisting in the defense of the subcontractor/supplier lawsuits).

[40.2] GSBCA No. 12961 (2001).

[40.3] VABCA No. 5858E, 2003 WL 294373 (Jan. 31, 2003).

Appeals cases, which permit only actual costs to the law firm. The government also questioned the reasonableness of the charges by the contractor's scheduling consultant. The Board found that the government had paid its own scheduling consultant considerably more than the contractor had to evaluate the same matter, and the charges were reasonable and could be recovered by the contractor. The government further questioned charges by legal consultants to the contractor for providing expertise in government contract litigation and mock trial services. The government asserted these charges were duplicative and should not be allowed. The Board ruled the services were not duplicative and were reasonably needed, so it permitted recovery to the limit of the EAJA statutory rate of $125 per hour.

Unlike attorneys' fees, which "must" be awarded to EAJA eligible plaintiffs, no such entitlement exists as to expert fees and other costs; the award of such costs is entirely within the court's discretion.[40.4]

§ 10.04 ATTORNEYS' FEES ON MILLER ACT CLAIMS

Page 220, add at end of note 42:

See also Contractors Equip. Maint. Co., Inc. v. Bechtel Hanford, Inc., 150 Fed. Appx. 585 (9th Cir. (Wash.) 2005) (the "American Rule" governs the award of attorneys' fees in federal court in Miller Act cases; under the American Rule, attorneys' fees "are not ordinarily recoverable in the absence of a statute or enforceable contract providing therefor"; in this case, the trial court erred in awarding attorneys' fees when the relevant contract did not expressly provide for such an award).

Page 221, add at end of note 45:

See also, e.g., Scandale Associated Builders & Engineers, Ltd. v. Bell Justice Facilities Corp., 455 F. Supp. 2d 271 (M.D. Pa. 2006) (the plaintiff-subcontractor was entitled to relief under the Pennsylvania Contractor Subcontractor Payment Act, 73 Pa. Stat. Ann, § 501, *et seq.*, for amounts allegedly due the plaintiff as a result of delays and the contractor's breaches on a federal construction project; plaintiff's claim was not preempted by the Miller Act, but rather a claim under the state statute could be brought in addition to the Miller Act claim); Rogers & Willard, Inc. v. Harwood, No. 2007 WL 2684542 (Ala. Ct. App. Sept. 14, 2007), *rehearing denied* (Nov. 2, 2007), *cert. denied* (Aug. 8, 2008) (the appellate court reversed the trial court's determination that the contractor was not entitled to

[40.4] *See* Baldi Bros. Constructors v. United States, 52 Fed. Cl. 78 (Ct. Cl. 2002) (expert's testimony was "reasonably necessary" to pursuit of plaintiff's claim for delay damages, supporting recovery under Act, but only partial success warranted 33.3% reduction in recovery of claimed fees; Act did not support recovery of expenses of non-attorney employees of plaintiff or of non-expert witnesses).

attorneys' fees because both parties acted in a reasonable manner to protect their interests; under Alabama's Prompt Pay Act, Ala. Code §§ 8-29-1, *et seq.*, interest cannot be awarded if payment was withheld from the contractor based upon a "bona fide dispute," whereas attorneys' fees must be awarded to the party "in whose favor a judgment is rendered," regardless of whether there was a bona fide dispute; since the contractor recovered on its claim and the owner's counterclaims were denied, the contractor was entitled to recover its attorneys' fees).

§ 10.05 BAD FAITH EXCEPTION

Page 222, add at end of note 52:

See also Tupelo Redevelopment Agency v. Gray Corp., Inc., 972 So. 2d 495 (Miss. 2007) (attorneys' fees may be awarded on a *quantum meruit* claim under the Mississippi Litigation Accountability Act of 1988, Miss.Code Ann. §§ 11-55-1, *et seq.* and under the construction claim statute, Miss.Code Ann. § 31-5-57, for bad-faith conduct; in this case, the trial court did not abuse its discretion in awarding attorneys' fees to the subcontractor and against the general contractor and its surety when the evidence indicated that the general contractor knew that the subcontractor was entitled to the money, but withheld the money and continued to do so; in addition, the general contractor solicited and secured the subcontractor's efforts to persuade the owner to release the retainage, inducing the subcontractor to believe that it would get its money when in fact the general contractor had already assigned the entire retainage to its bank; also, the general contractor sought an equitable adjustment from the owner before trial in which it admitted that the subcontractor was due $458,158 for additional work, but it refused to pay the subcontractor this additional money "without substantial justification"); James Corp. v. North Allegheny Sch. Dist., 938 A.2d 474 (Pa. Commw. Nov. 30, 2007), *reargument denied* (Jan. 30. 2008) (under 62 Pa. Cons. Stat. § 3935(b), attorneys' fees may be awarded with regard to a public works contract if it is determined that the government agency acted in bad faith; in this case, the evidence indicated that the school district refused to tender payments to the contractor in bad faith, thus supporting the trial court's award of reasonable attorney's fees; Section 3935 further authorizes the award of a penalty of 1% per month if the withholding was in bad faith, although the contractor apparently did not seek to recover the penalty provided by the statute); Roofers Edge, Inc. v. Standard Building Co., Inc., 295 Ga. App. 294, 671 S.E.2d 310 (Nov. 17, 2008), *reconsid. denied* (Dec. 16, 2008) (subcontractor entitled to attorneys' fees under Georgia statute for bad faith, where contractor refused without explanation to pay for work performed, denied in its answer that a contract existed, asserted a counterclaim for breach of contract, and provided only the testimony of one witness who admitted that the subcontractor had performed the work under the subcontract, contended that the owner had withheld payment because some of the subcontractor's work was defective, and admitted he did not know the amount withheld and had no documentation to support the claim); Dick Anderson Constr., Inc. v. Monroe Constr. Co., LLC, 353 Mont. 534, 221 P.3d 675, 2009 MT 416 (Dec. 8, 2009) (Montana Supreme Court upheld the district court's confirmation of an arbitration award of attorneys' fees based in part upon the arbitration panels' finding that the owner, the non-prevailing party, acted in bad faith in asserting claims for defamation and fraud that were "totally devoid of merit"; court also rejected the owner's motion to modify the award of $331,982 in attorneys' fees to the correct amount of $221,982 based on a transcription error, because the owner failed to raise the issue within 90 days of receipt of the arbitration award as required by Montana statute).

Page 222, add to text after note 54:

A contractor also may be made to pay costs to the federal government if it submits a false claim. Thus, in *Larry D. Barnes, Inc. v. United States,*[54.1] the court found a contractor in violation of the Forfeiture of False Claims Act, 28 U.S.C. § 2514 ("claim against the United States shall be forfeited to the United States by any person who corruptly practices or attempts to practice any fraud against the United States in the proof, statement, establishment, or allowance"); the Contract Disputes Act Anti-Fraud provision, 41 U.S.C. § 604 ("If a contractor is unable to support any part of his claim and it is determined that such inability is attributable to misrepresentation of fact or fraud on the part of the contractor, he shall be liable to the Government for an amount equal to such unsupported part of the claim in addition to all costs to the Government attributable to the cost of reviewing said part of his claim"); and the False Claims Act, 31 U.S.C. § 3729 ("Any person who—(1) knowingly presents, or causes to be presented, to an officer or employee of the United States Government . . . a false or fraudulent claim for payment . . . is liable to the United States Government for a civil penalty of not less than $5,000 and not more than $10,000, plus 3 times the amount of damages which the Government sustains because of the act of that person"). The evidence indicated that the contractor's claim included amounts for knowingly unrecoverable lost profits, a non-existent work stoppage, and "added costs" for which no reasonable explanation was provided. Also, the contractor failed to verify its claim after being put on notice that several items were unfounded.

Page 224, add at end of section:

A contractor also may be able to assert a claim against a surety for vexatious refusal to pay on a bond. Thus, for example, a Missouri statute[60.1] allows a contractor to recover a penalty and attorneys' fees from a surety for vexatious

[54.1] 45 Fed. Appx. 907 (Fed. Cir. 2002).

[60.1] Mo. Rev. Stat. § 375.420.

refusal to pay, upon proof that the refusal was willful and without reasonable cause based on the facts that would have appeared to a reasonable person before trial. A paving subcontractor made such a claim against the general contractor's surety in *Missouri Department of Transportation v. Safeco Insurance Co. of America*,[60.2] and the trial court awarded damages of $143,894.78 for vexatious refusal to pay, and $111,715.50 for attorneys' fees. The judgment was reversed on appeal, however, because the evidence indicated that the principal presented a reasonable, if unsuccessful, defense.

§ 10.06 RECOVERABILITY OF COSTS OF PREPARING REQUESTS FOR EQUITABLE ADJUSTMENTS

Page 224, add at end of note 62:

See, e.g., Env't Tectonics Corp. v. United States, 72 Fed. Cl. 290 (July 31, 2006) (the plaintiff contractor alleged that as a consequence of having to file a certified Contract Disputes Act claim, it incurred $100,030.00 in claim preparation costs. Because these costs were alleged to have been incurred in connection with a prosecution of a claim against the government or in connection with an appeal of a claim against the government, they were dismissed by the court pursuant to 48 C.F.R. § 31.205-47).

Page 225, add at end of note 69:

See also Appeals of Fru-Con Constr. Corp., ASBCA No. 55197, 55248, 2007 WL 3265020 (2007) (after the Army Corps of Engineers changed the design of a poiree dam and requested that Fru-Con submit a request for equitable adjustment for the change, Fru-Con's subcontractor for the work, Noell, Inc., retained a law firm and a consulting firm to assist in the effort; after an extensive effort, Fru-Con and Noell submitted an REA for a price increase of $2.7 million, including $612,000 in consulting fees and $121,000 in attorneys' fees, and the REA was rejected by the Corps; on appeal, the Board first found that the design change resulted in Noell incurring direct costs of $30,000 and delay damages of $45,000; the Board then cited the *Bill Strong* case [49 F.3d 1491 (Fed. Cir. 1995)] for the proposition that consulting and legal fees incurred in seeking a negotiated settlement of a pending issue may be allowable as contract administration costs, and held that there is no requirement that the negotiations result in contract modification in order for the costs to be recoverable; however, the Board found that the costs in this case were not reasonable under the Federal Acquisition Regulations, based upon the absence of a detailed scope or budget for the services, the lack of billing detail reflecting what work was performed by which individual, and the

[60.2] 97 S.W.3d 21 (Mo. Ct. App. 2002).

apparent lack of oversight of the services by Noell; the Board applied the jury verdict method and awarded Fru-Con $65,000 for consulting services and $20,000 for legal services); Appeal of States Roofing Corp., ASBCA No. 55504, 2010 WL 337648 (Jan. 19, 2010) (Board found that attorneys' fees were incurred in preparing SRC's cost proposals and attempting to negotiate a settlement with the government, as the parties were still attempting to negotiate and had not yet reached an impasse, also citing the *Bill Strong* case; however, the Board disallowed the attorneys' fees based on its findings that (1) SRC normally included legal fees in its G&A expense, recoverable in its home office overhead rate, (2) SRC's treatment of legal fees as direct costs is inconsistent with its usual practice of treating them as indirect costs; and (3) although SRC acknowledged that the legal fees need to be transferred from the G&A pool to the contract as direct costs, it had failed to do so in the five years since SRC's claims had originally been denied by the contracting officer; and (4) SRC was therefore seeking a double recovery).

Page 227, add at end of note 77:

See also P.J. Dick Inc., VABCA No. 5597, 01-2 BCA ¶ 31,647 (2001), *aff'd in part, rev'd in part, and remanded*, P.J. Dick Inc. v. Principi, 324 F.3d 1364 (Fed. Cir. Apr. 7, 2003) (contractor was entitled to recover costs it incurred for the services of its schedule analysis consultant, who determined costs associated with government-caused delay, in light of contract provision requiring contractor to hire a consultant to perform schedule analysis using the critical path method); Appeal of International Bus. Sys., Inc., VABCA No. 6955 (2003) (Board recognized general rule that contractor cannot recover the cost of preparing a change order that is not adopted, on the theory that since the contractor is not required to prepare change order proposals, it essentially acts as a volunteer, and such costs are an overhead item; however, there are three exceptions where the contractor is permitted to recover change order preparation costs: (1) a strong element of government compulsion alters the traditionally voluntary nature of the effort; (2) the contractor goes to extraordinary efforts or incurs substantial costs beyond what would normally be expected; or (3) the proposed change is intended to correct a government error; here, the factual issues precluded the government's motion for summary judgment); P. R. Burke Corp. v. United States, 58 Fed. Cl. 549 (2003) (contract for improvement of a sewage treatment plant required that the plant remain in continuous operation during performance of the work; contract did not specify a particular sequence of work, but required that the contractor, Burke, submit a proposed construction schedule for Navy approval; Burke's proposed schedule was twice rejected, at which point the Navy issued a contract modification designed in part to address some of the sequencing issues the contractor was facing; Burke retained a scheduling consultant immediately after issuance of the modification and submitted a revised schedule, which was approved by the Navy; Burke sought to recover the scheduling consultant's fee under the FAR provision authorizing inclusion of professional and consultant service costs when pricing a contract modification; Navy's motion for summary judgment was denied on the grounds that Burke would be able to recover the consultant's fee if the evidence established that the scheduling consultant's services were used to reschedule changed work, rather than sequence work in compliance with the original contract requirements).

Page 228, add at end of note 78:

See also James Corp. v. North Allegheny Sch. Dist., 938 A.2d 474 (Pa. Commw. Nov. 30, 2007), *reargument denied* (Jan. 30. 2008) (the trial court erred in awarding the plaintiff contractor its expert witness fee expenses; although a Pennsylvania statute allows a contractor to recover expenses incurred in seeking recovery under a public contract when the government agency acted in bad faith, the act does not authorize an award of expenses when the expert's testimony concerns damages for acceleration, rather than the sums due directly under the contract).

Page 228, add before last paragraph of section:

When an REA is later converted to a claim, only those costs involved in preparation of the REA are allowable expenses of administering the change in the contract. In *Appeal of Advanced Engineer & Planning Corp.*,[78.1] the Armed Services Board of Contract Appeals ruled that the consultant fees incurred in preparing requests for equitable adjustment were allowable costs of contract administration, but the cost of revising the REA and converting it into a claim could not be recovered. This matter involved a Navy ship repair contract where the contractor negotiated a series of change orders. Most of the negotiations resulted in contract modifications; one did not and was revised by the contractor and certified as a claim. The claim was eventually settled but the parties could not agree on the recovery of the consultant fees incurred. The government refused to pay for the consultant fees on the basis that they had been used to prepare a claim. The contractor asserted that they had been incurred in an effort to negotiate resolution of the performance. The Board found that the portion of the fees related to the preparation of the initial REA were recoverable expenses of administering a change to the contract. However, the Board also found that after rejection of the REA by the government, that the parties reached an impasse, and the costs of revising the REA for certification as a claim was a claim prosecution effort, the costs of which could not be recovered.

[78.1] ASBCA No. 53366 (Jan. 21, 2003).

Page 228, add at end of section:

Claim preparation costs were awarded under the termination provision of a private contract in *Encon Utah, LLC v. Fluor Ames Kraemer, LLC.*[80] The trial court awarded the subcontractor, Encon, $50,000 in claim preparation costs under the termination clause of the subcontract. The contractor, FAK, challenged the award on the basis that it was against the clear weight of the evidence, because Encon's expert testified that the $50,000 figure for claim preparation was included "for analysis sake." The court upheld the trial court's award based upon its finding that FAK failed to meet its burden of showing that the testimony was insufficient to support the decision, noting that Encon's own expert testified that $50,000 in claim preparation costs was "appropriate," (which testimony was not mentioned in FAK's brief).

[80] 2009 UT 7, 2009 WL 172438 (Jan. 27, 2009), *reh'g denied* (June 24, 2009).

CHAPTER 11
PRESENTATION OF DAMAGES

§ 11.03 EXPERT ANALYSIS

Page 238, add at end of first full paragraph:

Even when expert testimony is presented, the expert's analysis will be subject to careful scrutiny by the court to determine whether it meets the standards of acceptability set forth in Federal Rules of Evidence 702 (and similar state rules of evidence), which requires a showing that: "(1) the testimony is based upon sufficient facts or date, (2) the testimony is the product of reliable principles and methods, and (3) the witness has applied the principles and methods reliably to the facts of the case." For example, the court in *United States ex rel. Greenmoor, Inc. v. Travelers Casualty and Surety Co. of America,*[1.1] rejected an expert's "measured mile" analysis [quoting the instant Treatise's definition] because the expert failed to calculate the traditional labor productivity ratios called for under the measured mile analysis and did not compare the amount of time the contractor spent on any given activity in the unimpacted and impacted phases of the project, despite the fact that the expert acknowledged that the work was nearly identical on the two phases, suggesting that a labor productivity ratio could have

[1.1] 2009 WL 4730233 (W.D. Pa. Dec. 4, 2009). *See also* Appeal of Packard Constr. Corp., 09-2 BCA ¶ 34234, ASBCA No. 55383, 2009 WL 2601247 (Aug. 10, 2009) (court rejected expert's opinion that contractor was entitled to 88 days of delay, listing numerous discrepancies between the facts cited in the expert's report and those reflected in contemporaneous project documentation); In re Electric Mach. Enters., Inc., 416 B.R. 801 (Bankr. M.D. Fla. Aug. 28, 2009) (court found general contractor's (HCC's) expert damages expert unreliable in opining that the subcontractor, EME, could have utilized a measured mile analysis in calculating its damages; the court stated "HCC's second expert, Mr. Nagorzanski, was retained to determine if a measured mile analysis could have been performed by EME. His analysis relied almost exclusively on information from HCC Senior Construction Manager Pete Milner and Project Manager Mike Sincavage and was generally not helpful to understanding the issues at hand. Although he testified that in his opinion EME and its expert could have performed a measure mile analysis, he did not perform one himself, despite having expended over $250,000 in expert consulting fees. (Trial Tr. 4842:23-4843:18.) Instead, he attempted to persuade the Court that a measured mile analysis could have been performed using multiple examples. (Trial Tr. 4842:23-4856:3.) EME was able to show, however, that each example was littered with questionable analysis and skewed reasoning and relied on data and information that failed to account for the problems EME encountered. It was clear from Mr. Nagorzanski's analysis that . . . he accepted at face value information the HCC personnel had provided him with little or no independent analysis. Thus, the Court gives little weight to the testimony or analysis of [HCC's expert]").

been calculated; instead, under the guise of the measured mile methodology, the expert compared the gross margin allegedly enjoyed by the contractor on the two phases, preventing the court from determining how, if at all, the contractor's claim for labor inefficiencies on the second phase of the project was altered).

A scheduling and damages expert witness was entitled to rely upon geotechnical information received from others in *MACTEC, Inc. v. Bechtel Jacobs Co., LLC.*[1.2] In that case, the subcontractor, MACTEC, sought to recover additional costs incurred to place added contour fill as a result of encountering unanticipated radiation hot spots in performing its subcontract to design and build a hydraulic isolation system for a Solid Waste Storage Area. In appealing the judgment of more than $3 million in MACTEC's favor, the general contractor, Bechtel Jacobs, contended that MACTEC's scheduling and damages expert witness, DuPree, was not qualified to testify about the engineering analysis necessary to evaluate MACTEC's claim. The court noted that DuPree relied upon MACTEC's engineers and other hearsay evidence to provide him the projected quantities of contour fill in MACTEC's bid as compared to the actual quantities of fill used. The court noted that F.R.C.P. Rule 703 expressly permits an expert to rely upon inadmissible facts or data in forming his opinions if the facts or data are of a type "reasonably relied upon by experts in the particular field. . . ." Finding that MACTEC submitted sufficient evidence to establish that the information relied upon by DuPree was routinely used by cost and scheduling experts testifying in construction litigation, and that Bechtel Jacobs was free to cross-examine all of DuPree's information sources, the court held that the district court did not abuse its discretion in admitting DuPree's testimony into evidence.

[1.2] 346 Fed. Appx. 59 (6th Cir. (Tenn.) Sept. 25, 2009).

CHAPTER 12
CLAIMS BY OWNERS

§ 12.01 INTRODUCTION

Page 241, add to end of section:

Owners sometimes assert claims that, at first impression, seem reasonable but on closer examination are inappropriate. For example, in *Pangea, Inc. v. General Services Administration,*[2.1] the GSA attempted to recover the savings on bond premiums to a contractor on a negotiated fixed price contract. In this matter, the contractor had negotiated a price for replacement of roofs of federal buildings in St. Louis. The GSA questioned costs for bonds listed in Pangea's proposals. Pangea stated it did not know the actual premiums and was estimating those amounts. GSA ultimately awarded Pangea two fixed price contracts. When the GSA learned that Pangea's actual cost for bond premiums was less than estimated, it unilaterally issued fixed price deductive changes against the contracts. Pangea appealed, asserting that the contracts were fixed price contracts. The government's argument was that under the "price reduction for defective cost of pricing" clause, the contract price could be reduced to reflect inaccurate or incomplete data. The Board rejected the government contention because the "estimated costs" submitted in proposals are not "cost and pricing data" and, therefore, cannot be "defective cost and pricing data" even when such estimates are inconsistent with actual costs incurred after award.

§ 12.02 FAILURE TO COMPLETE

Page 241, add at end of note 3:

See also Graham v. State, 2001 WY 5, 16 P.3d 712 (Wyo. 2001) (owner's measure of damages is the cost of completion of the unfinished structure less the cost avoided as a result of the substitute completion transaction; the contractor's willfulness in failing to complete the construction does not affect the amount of recovery, i.e., it does not warrant precluding the deduction of the cost avoided from the award); Driver Pipeline Co., Inc. v. Mustang Pipeline Co., Inc., 69 S.W.3d 779 (Tex. Ct. App., Feb. 13, 2002) (the owner must introduce proof that

[2.1] GSBCA No. 16688 (Sept. 29, 2005).

the contract price for completion of the project was reasonable for the work done; mere evidence of the amounts paid, without more, is no evidence that those amounts were reasonable); Erney v. Freeman, 84 S.W.3d 529 (Mo. Ct. App. 2002) (when a breach results from a combination of defective construction and a failure to complete the work, the owners' damages are calculated using the reasonable cost of reconstruction, repair, and completion in accordance with the contract; in the case at bar, the final contract price was $32,872, the owners paid the contractor $20,948, and they presented evidence that they paid $22,919.66 to complete the project; thus, given the contractor's breach by defective construction and his subsequent failure to complete the project because he rejected the options for completion and walked away from the project, the owners were entitled to a damage award in the amount of $10,995.66); Appeal of Gladwynne Constr. Co., VABCA No. 6598 (April 19, 2002) (the government has the burden of proving the amount of a deductive credit for incomplete punchlist work, and the proper measure is the cost of performing that work at the time of the failure to complete, plus an allowance for overhead and profit; the Board held that the $92,000 reduction in the contract price taken by the government was excessive, as it was based upon estimates prepared long after substantial completion; in addition, the government had performed much of the punchlist work, but did not base its calculation of the reduction on the actual costs incurred; finally, other government estimates included in a subsequent solicitation differed greatly from the estimates used to calculate the reduction; the Board reduced the credit to $37,000); Fru-Con/Fluor Daniel Joint Venture v. Corrigan Bros., Inc., 154 S.W.3d 330 (Mo. Ct. App. Oct. 19, 2004), *transfer denied* (Jan. 26, 2005), *transfer denied* (Mar. 1, 2005) (parties' contract made contractor responsible for cost of completing the work under its base contract, and cost of owner's change orders remained the responsibility of the owner; because owner did not distinguish between these two items, making it "impossible to know what portion of the takeover costs [were] [the contractor]'s responsibility, and what portion would be the [owner]'s responsibility," trial court could not award owner *any* damages for its takeover costs; although owner argued that it was not required by the contract to allocate its takeover costs, court held that contractor was not obligated to pay for unresolved change work, because owner did not separate those costs out); Mergentime Corp. v. Washington Metro. Area Transp. Auth., 2006 WL 416177 (D.D.C., Feb. 22, 2006) (if a termination for default is upheld, the owner is entitled to recover any increased costs occasioned in completing the work; to recover excess reprocurement costs, the owner must show that the reprocured services were the same as or similar to those involved in the termination, that it actually incurred excess costs, and that it acted reasonably to minimize the excess costs resulting from the default; once the owner has made this prima facie showing, the claimed amount will be sustained unless the contractor shows that the amount was excessive or unreasonable; in this case, excess reprocurement costs were calculated by taking the most recent pay estimate on the replacement contract and isolating those costs paid to the replacement contractor that related to the scope of work under the original contracts; this methodology revealed that $10,716,746 in costs were paid to the replacement contractor for the original contract work; the remaining contract balance for the contract at the time of termination, based upon the final pay estimate to the original contractor, was $2,724,160; thus, the amount recoverable by the owner in excess cost of reprocurement of the contract was $8,093,548); Hees v. Burke Constr., Inc., 290 Conn. 1, 961 A.2d 373 (Conn. Jan. 6, 2009) (when an owner receives a defective or incomplete building, any part of the price that is as yet unpaid is deducted from the cost of completion that is awarded to him; otherwise, the owner would be placed in a better position than full performance would have put him, thereby doubly compensating him for the injury occasioned by the breach; the proper measure of damages was to deduct the $16,472 balance from the $16,085 cost to complete, such that the owner actually saved money as a result of the contractor's breach, and judgment should have been rendered in the contractor's favor).

Page 242, add after first sentence in first full paragraph:

In *Frank Coluccio Construction Co. v. City. of Everett,*[3.1] the contractor appealed the amount of a jury's award of damages to the owner, alleging that differences between its contract and the completing contractor's were such that the costs of project completion were not properly assessed as damages. The court noted that an original contractor is not liable for the difference in cost between the original and a relet contract, unless the relet contract is the same as the original. In this case, however, the evidence was substantial that the differences in the contracts were a direct result of the original contractor's breach. Further, the court found that an owner must be given considerable latitude when forced to mitigate damages because of a contractor's breach—the effort to mitigate need only appear both reasonable and timely in the context of the time in which the decision was made. Based on these findings, the court affirmed the jury's award of the full cost of completing the original contractor's work, less the unpaid contract balance.

Page 243, add at end of section:

On a cost plus contract, an owner cannot normally recover the cost to complete if the contractor has been terminated. In *Schiro-DelBianco Enterprises, Inc. v. NSL, Inc.,*[4.1] the court ruled that the project owner on a cost plus contract could not recover the cost of completion from the terminated contractor. In this matter, two homeowners hired NSL to renovate an existing building. The contractor provided an estimated cost range, but the parties never entered into a fixed price contract. During the progress of the project, the homeowners made numerous changes to the work, and NSL submitted invoices that itemized and documented

[3.1] 104 Wash. App. 1046 (2001).

[4.1] 765 So. 2d 1087, 1087 (La. App. 4th Cir. 2000), *reh'g denied* (2002).

the expenditures including a 10 percent markup on labor and materials. These invoices were paid without objection through the sixth invoice. Upon submission of the seventh invoice, the homeowners refused to pay and locked NSL out of the job. An unpaid subcontractor sued NSL, and NSL then brought a third-party claim against the homeowners for the unpaid invoice. At trial, the court ruled that NSL was entitled to payment on the invoice, but offset that amount by a greater amount for the homeowners' cost of completing the renovation project. The Louisiana Court of Appeals found that the trial court apparently had believed that this was a fixed price contract, and that the owners' lockout had been justified. Instead, the appeals court ruled that the facts supported the existence of a cost plus contract and, as such, NSL could not be held liable for the costs of completing the work. The court noted that even in a cost plus contract, a contractor could be held liable for completion costs if the costs were to correct defective or improperly performed work.

It is imperative that the owner prove the amount of damages incurred as a result of the contractor's failure to complete the job with a reasonable degree of certainty. Thus, in *Cut Bank School District No. 15 v. Rummel*,[4.2] recovery was denied plaintiff School District in its suit against a contractor who failed to complete two contracts to effect repairs to steps and two sidewalks adjacent to a high school. When the contractor failed to complete the contracts on time, the district terminated the contracts and hired another contractor to complete the work. The School District then filed a complaint asserting that the contractor's failure to complete the projects by the due date was a breach of the contracts, and it requested monetary damages. The School District argued that sufficient evidence of damages it had incurred in the contractor's breach of the first contract was provided by the contractor himself when, on cross-examination, he was asked to give a rough estimate of what it would cost in materials and labor to complete the first contract project from the point at which he left it, and he responded, "I don't know off the top of my head . . . between three and 4,000, total, maybe." The School District presented no evidence of the actual cost to complete the project, because the School District had contracted with another construction company to repair the front steps and sidewalk using an entirely different method and materials. Thus, the only evidence relating to the District's damages for breach of the contract was the contractor's purely speculative statement at trial. Such speculation was clearly insufficient to prove damages to a reasonable degree of certainty.

With regard to the second contract, the School District presented testimony that it had employed two workers to complete the repairs to the sidewalk, resulting in expenditures of $224 for labor and $50 for materials. However, the contractor testified that after the contract was terminated, he had billed the District $1,276 for the work completed up to that point, representing the original bid of $1,500 less $224 as his estimate of what it would cost to complete the project. This $224

[4.2] 312 Mont. 143, 58 P.3d 159 (2002).

difference equaled the amount the School District subsequently expended for labor and, thus, the School District suffered no damages for the labor component of finishing the second contract. Moreover, the contractor testified that he offered to give the School District all the materials he had purchased for the project, but the School District refused to accept them. Had the District accepted the materials, it may have been unnecessary to incur the additional $50 for materials to complete the repairs to the sidewalk. Accordingly, the trial court's finding that the School District failed to establish damages with regard to the second contract was not clearly erroneous.

In *Merrill Iron & Steel, Inc. v. Minn-DAK Seeds, Ltd.*,[4.3] a contractor who failed to achieve substantial completion and defaulted was held by the court to forfeit all of the contract retention. Depending on the circumstances, this could be a harsh penalty. Normally when a contractor defaults, the project owners are only allowed to keep that portion of the retainage necessary to complete the work. In *Parem Contracting Corp. v. Welch Construction Co.*,[4.4] the Supreme Court of New Hampshire found that the retainage serves to protect the owner against incomplete or defective work, but is not intended to serve as liquidated damages in the event of a contractor default. In *TA Operating Corp. v. Solar Applications Engineering, Inc.*,[4.5] a contractor that did not furnish required lien waivers to the owner was awarded its retainage after the retainage was taken by the owner. In this matter, the owner certified that the contractor had achieved substantial completion, at which time the retainage was approximately $400,000. The contractor was provided with a punchlist of incomplete work items. After three months, the contractor had not completed the punchlist, but sued for breach of contract for the owner's failure or refusal to pay the retainage. The owner responded that the withholding of the retainage was justified because the contractor had never furnished lien waivers from its subcontractors. The court held that the owner could not use the lack of lien waivers to accomplish a complete forfeiture of the contractor's right to the contract retainage.

In *Stonehill-PRM WC I, L.P. v. Chasco Contractors, Ltd.*,[4.6] the parties entered into a GMP contract for $13 million for Chasco to construct a 156-unit student housing facility. Upon completion of the construction drawings, Chasco sought a change order in the amount of $17 million, contending that the parties had never agreed on a GMP. Stonehill rejected the request, and terminated Chasco before construction had commenced. Stonehill filed suit to recover its "expectancy damages" (i.e., "benefit-of-the-bargain" damages)—the difference between the value of the project had it been constructed in accordance with the

[4.3] 334 N.W.2d 652 (N.D. 1983).

[4.4] 512 A.2d 1104 (N.H. 1986).

[4.5] 191 S.W.3d 173, 2005 WL 712010 (Tex. Ct. App.-San Antonio Nov. 28, 2005), *reh'g overruled* (Feb. 8, 2006), *review granted* (Apr. 27, 2007).

[4.6] 2009 WL 349136 (Tex. App.-Austin Feb.11, 2009).

plans and specifications, calculated using appropriate rents, expenses, and prevailing capitalization rates for similar apartment structures, and the costs that Stonehill avoided. The trial court held that the proper measure of damages was the cost to complete the project that exceeded the costs that would have been payable to Chasco and, since no evidence of cost to complete was submitted by Stonehill, summary judgment was entered in Chasco's favor. The appellate court affirmed, finding that the contract specifically provided that in a termination for cause, to the extent the costs of completing work exceed the costs that would have been payable to the contractor except for contractor's default, the contractor shall pay the difference to the owner. The court found nothing that indicated this provision applied only if the owner chose to construct (or complete construction of) the project, and noted that this measure of damages was consistent with the common law measure utilized when there has been a "complete failure of performance." The court also found that the parties waived consequential damages under the terms of the contract, including losses of use, income, and profit.

§ 12.03 COST OF CORRECTING NONCONFORMING WORK

Page 243, add new note 4.1 after first sentence of section:

[4.1] *See, e.g.*, O & G Industries, Inc. v. All Phase Enterprises, Inc., 112 Conn. App. Ct. 511, 963 A.2d 676 (Feb. 10, 2009) (the owner contracted for installation of a steel roof system over a hockey rink, and, when the installed roof leaked severely, the owner contracted for a new rubber membrane roof that was placed over the existing structure; although the defendant roofing contractor argued that the trial court should not have awarded damages to the owner based on this "betterment" but should have awarded damages only for the cost of repairing the steel roof, the appellate court disagreed; the difference in value between what the owner contracted for and what it got was the full value of a properly constructed and installed roof; tearing down the roof to start over would have been economic waste; installing the rubber membrane was not an impermissible betterment, but rather, it was a reasonable and cost-effective way to remedy the defect in time for the upcoming hockey season).

Page 243, add new note 4.2 after third sentence of section:

[4.2] *See, e.g.*, Heine v. Parent Constr., Inc., 2009 WL 763534 (Fla. Dist. Ct. App. 4th Dist. Mar. 25, 2009) (although a home construction contract provided that "Contractor shall promptly correct Work" and that contractor "shall bear costs of correcting rejected work," it did not bar application of the economic waste doctrine to the calculation of damages for the contractor's breach of the contract; in this case, the remedy to correct the contractor's construction of the home at an elevation of 7.5 feet instead of the contracted-for 8.5 feet in a historic flood zone would have required the entire house to be torn down and rebuilt at a cost of $930,000, which exceeded the total contract price; under the economic waste doctrine, the proper measure of damages was the diminution in the value of the home, or $25,000).

Page 243, add at end of note 5:

See also Panorama Village Homeowners Ass'n v. Golden Rule Roofing Inc., 102 Wash. App. 422, 10 P.3d 417 (2000) (trial court did not err in allowing the owner to recover the cost of replacing defective roofs installed by the defendant contractor when evidence indicated that it would be cheaper to replace the roofs than to attempt a labor-intensive repair); Teramo & Co., Inc. v. O'Brien-Sheipe Funeral Home, Inc., 283 A.D.2d 635, 725 N.Y.S.2d 87 (2d Dept. 2001) (when the contractor substantially completes its contract but the owner is required to hire other contractors to correct problems caused by the contractor's poor workmanship, the appropriate measure of the owner's damages is the contract price less the cost of repairing the work improperly done); Mount Mariah Baptist Church, Inc. v. Pannell's Assoc. Elec., Inc., 835 So. 2d 880 (La. Ct. App. 2002), *reh'g denied* (2003), *writ denied* (La. 2003), (the appropriate measure of damages for breach of a building contract is the cost of repairing any defects or of completing the work; thus, when the owner presents evidence of the cost of completion of the work or correction of the defective work, the contract price may be reduced by that amount; in this case, the owner was also entitled to receive a credit of $14,300 because the contractor installed an asphalt shingle roof instead of the much more expensive metal roof called for in the original plans); TA Operating Corp. v. Solar Applications Eng'g, Inc., No. 191 S.W.3d 173, 2005 WL 712010 (Tex. Ct. App.-San Antonio Nov. 28, 2005), *reh'g overruled* (Feb. 8, 2006), *review granted* (Apr. 27, 2007) (when contractor has substantially performed its contract, the measure of damages ordinarily is owner's cost of remedy or repair); State *ex rel.* Stovall v. Reliance Ins. Co., 278 Kan. 777, 107 P.3d 1219 (2005) (state contracted for construction of an underground thermal piping system for a prison; "earthen trench" system installed by defendants was defective and had to be replaced with concrete trench system; defendants argued that concrete trench system was a "trade-up" to a better system than earthen trench system, and thus, damages payable to state should be limited to diminished value (alleged to be the difference between the value of the earthen trench system in its defective condition ($0) and its value without defects, which defendants contended was the $1.097 million *original* cost of the system), rather than the replacement cost; court, however, disagreed, noting that defendants had stipulated that earthen trench system had failed and was necessarily abandoned and replaced; also, concrete trench system had been installed at a cost less than would have been incurred if a new and identical earthen trench system had been constructed; thus state would not be gaining a windfall from being allowed to recover the cost of building the concrete trench system; court, however, limited this recovery to a cost not to exceed cost to build an earthen trench system as of the 1995 discovery date of the defect). *Cf.* Route 7 Mobil, Inc. v. Machnick Builders Ltd., 296 A.D.2d 809, 745 N.Y.S.2d 336 (3d Dept. 2002) (when construction has been completed, the general rule is that the proper measure of damages for the breach of a construction contract is the amount necessary to replace or cure the defective condition; the difference in value rule is applied only when it would be unfair to apply the general rule); Mergentime Corp. v. Washington Metro. Area Transp. Auth., 2006 WL 416177 (D.D.C., Feb. 22, 2006) (in a case involving construction of subway stations and connecting tunnels for the Washington, D.C. metropolitan area's Metrorail System, the general contractor was terminated by default, and, as a result, the owner incurred $234,815 in damages stemming from extra work to remedy the original contractor's deficient work, the court concluded that three-quarters of the responsibility for the problems causing the need for the extra work (flooding that caused damage to equipment) lay with the contractor's failure to control infiltration of water, while one-quarter of the responsibility lay with a flaw in the owner's design for waterproofing the system; accordingly, three-fourths of the damages paid to the subcontractor for water infiltration damage was chargeable to the contractor; in addition, after the termination, the owner expended more than 20,000 man-hours to clean up the site, installing a mile of safety fence to protect residents from the worksite hazards, removing almost 350 tons of scrap steel, and removing 350 tandem dump truck loads of trash; the cost of this effort, which was chargeable to the contractor, was $598,246). *But see* Country Village Homes, Inc. v. Patterson, 236 S.W.3d 413 (Tex. Ct. App. 2007), *review granted, judgment vacated, and remanded by agreement* (2008) (appellate court affirmed jury award to Patterson of $300,000 for the cost of repairing substantial defects in the new house built by Country Village, plus $250,000 in "stigma" damages for the reduction in market value of the home after all required repairs had been made; the Texas Residential Construction Liability Act (Tex. Prop. Code Ann. §§ 27.001 *et seq.*) permits a homeowner to recover "the reduction in market value, if any, to the extent the reduction is due to structural failure," in addition to the costs of repair, but only if the contractor has not made a reasonable offer of settlement or reasonably attempted to repair the defects; here, Country Village made an offer of settlement, which the jury found was not reasonable because Country Village excluded some of the defects from its offer to repair, and failed to satisfactorily make some of the repairs it agreed to make; Patterson's experts testified that the defects were structural in nature, including an undersized beam causing the second floor to sag, which required replacement of the entire second floor framing and a replacement roof; Patterson also presented expert testimony that the market value of the home, even after all repairs had been made, would be substantially reduced due to the reluctance of buyers to purchase a house that has undergone extensive repairs; although County Village's experts disputed the testimony of Patterson's experts, the court found that there was sufficient evidence to support the jury's award of stigma damages and cost of repair); Nichols Constr. Corp. v. Virginia Machine Tool Co., LLC, 276 Va. 81,

661 S.E.2d 467 (June 6, 2008) (the trial court did not err in awarding the plaintiff owner damages of $450,842 due to the defendant contractor's breach of a $140,000 contract to install a new roof on a building recently purchased by the owner for $200,000, despite the fact that the contract expressly excluded consequential damages; the owner's expert testified that the defective metal, standing seam roof would have to be removed and a new roof installed, and although the contractor contended that the plaintiff's estimate for replacing the defective roof would result in a windfall to the owner in that it "had contracted for a Chevy of a roof but wants that replaced with a Cadillac of a roof," the contractor did not cite any relevant authority and did not identify any evidence in the record that rebutted the accuracy of the estimate or established that the cost of repairs exceeded the economic value of the building; once the owner met its burden of establishing the cost of repair or replacement, the burden was on the contractor to establish that this cost was disproportionate to the value of the building and constituted economic waste; here, the contractor failed to meet that burden); John Thurmond & Associates, Inc. v. Kennedy, 284 Ga. 469, 668 S.E.2d 666 (2008) (homeowner sought to recover $751,632 for the cost of replacing floor joists to repair defects in JTA's performance of a $311,156 construction contract; trial court granted JTA's motion for a directed verdict on the grounds that Kennedy did not present the required evidence of the fair market value of the home after the requested repairs were made; the appellate court reversed, finding evidence of fair market value was not required, and the Georgia Supreme Court affirmed; the court stated that as a general rule, damages for defective construction are measured by the cost of repairing or restoring the damage, unless the cost of repair is disproportionate to the property's probable loss of value; however, cost of repair and diminution in value are generally alternative measures of recovery, and if the owner chooses to seek to recover on the cost of repair basis, evidence of fair market value of the improved property is not a necessary element of his claim of damages; the court refused to find that recovery is limited to the fair market value of the property after repairs are made, and held that since Kennedy offered evidence of the cost of repair and the trial court did not find cost of repair to be an inappropriate measure of damages, it was error to direct a verdict against Kennedy; a strong dissenting opinion stressed the lack of proportionality between the contract price of $311,156 and the cost of repair of $751,632, indicating that only the diminution in value measure of damages was reasonable in this case).

Page 243, add after second paragraph of section:

In *AgGrow Oils, LLC v. National Union Fire Insurance Co. of Pittsburgh*,[5.1] AgGrow awarded a contract to Ibberson for design and construction of an oilseed processing plant. The specifications included technical data and production guarantees for equipment manufactured by Anderson International. When the

[5.1] 276 F. Supp. 2d 999 (D.N.D. 2003).

completed plant failed to produce the quality and quantity of oil set forth in the production guarantees, AgGrow sued Ibberson, Anderson, and Ibberson's surety. Ibberson defended on the grounds that since AgGrow had included Anderson's technical specifications, Ibberson merely passed through Anderson's production guarantees to AgGrow. The court rejected Ibberson's position, holding that under the AIA A201 General Conditions document included in the contract, Ibberson warranted that the work, including the equipment, would conform to the contract requirements. Since Anderson's performance guarantees were a term of the design-build contract, Ibberson was responsible for compliance with the contract. The court held that Ibberson was liable for more than $2 million in corrective work and lost profit, and Anderson was jointly and severally liable for $900,000 of that amount, reflecting losses caused by the deficiency of Anderson's equipment.

Page 244, add after first paragraph:

On the other hand, it has also been held that once the owner has established the cost to remedy the defects, the contractor bears the burden of challenging this evidence to reduce the award, including providing the trial court with evidence to support an alternative award. In *Panorama Village Homeowners Association v. Golden Rule Roofing, Inc.*,[8.1] an action in which the owner sought to recover the cost of replacing defective roofs installed by the defendant contractor, the contractor failed to present any evidence of the diminution in value of the buildings or of the cost to repair the defects, and it did not challenge the reasonableness of the owner's estimate for the work. The court accordingly affirmed the trial court's award of the cost to replace the roofs.

Page 244, add at end of note 10:

See also, e.g., Sull v. Postan, 2003 WL 759186 (Ohio App. 2003) (the usual measure of damages in a home improvement case when the contractor fails to perform in a workmanlike manner is the cost of repairs, because the owner of the building is entitled to proper performance of the contract; however, in this case, the cost of repairs should have been offset by the amount that the homeowner failed to pay the original contractor for labor and materials expended on the job); Nichols Constr. Corp. v. Virginia Machine Tool Co., LLC, 276 Va. 81, 661 S.E.2d 467 (2008) (in the absence of proof of bad faith or a willful departure from a contract, a contractor held liable for breach of contract for defective construction is entitled to an offset for the balance due on the contract).

[8.1] 102 Wash. App. 422, 10 P.3d 417 (2000), *review denied* (Wash. 2001).

Page 245, add at end of section:

A contractor is not liable for the work of one of its subcontractors when the work at issue was performed directly for the project owner and not for the general contractor. In *Shufelberger Construction, Inc. v. Huddleston,*[13.1] Huddleston, the owner, contracted with Shufelberger to expand a motel. Significant disputes arose between Shufelberger and Huddleston. Huddleston refused to make final payment on the project, complaining of defects, one of which was that the grade of a handicap parking area did not comply with the Americans with Disabilities Act. Shufelberger asserted that the work involved had been done on a separate contract directly between Huddleston and the subcontractor and was not included in Shufelberger's contract scope of work. Huddleston acknowledged that the work in question was not within Shufelberger's contract, but argued that he had relied on Shufelberger to monitor the work outside the contract to assure compliance with codes and specifications. The court rejected the owner's argument, finding that since the work was not in Shufelberger's contract, Shufelberger had no implied duty to monitor the activities. In a related matter concerning defects in the electrical work, Shufelberger was found to have responsibility for monitoring the work of the electrician and was therefore responsible for defects in the work of the electrical subcontractor even though the electrical subcontractor was being paid directly by the project owner.

If the owner directs the contractor's means and methods of construction, the owner is responsible for resulting deficiencies in the contractor's work. In *Weimar v. Lyons,*[13.2] Lyons performed concrete work on Weimar's property pursuant to a fixed-price contract. Weimar verbally directed Lyons to perform additional work, including concrete sidewalks and caps on fountains. When Lyons advised he could not perform the elaborate forming required for the fountain caps within the time requested, Weimar agreed to have his own crew do the forming work. When Lyons was ready to pour the concrete, he informed Weimar that the forming had been improperly completed, and that the concrete pour should also be delayed because of the rainy weather. Weimar directed Lyons to pour the concrete that day, stating that he would "take responsibility." The court found that deficiencies in the sidewalk and the fountain caps were the result of pouring concrete in the rain, and that Weimar was not entitled to recover costs paid to another contractor to repair the deficiencies because Weimar had caused those deficiencies.

[13.1] 2004 WL 304324 (Cal. Ct. App., 3d Dist., Feb. 18, 2004) (unpublished).

[13.2] 164 P.3d 922, 2007 Mt. 182 (Mont. 2007), *on remand*, 2007 WL 5883133 (Mont. Dist. Aug. 7, 2007).

§ 12.04 COST OF DELAY

Page 245, replace first sentence of section with:

To assess delay damages against a contractor, an owner must establish that there was a delay to project completion. The burden is then upon the contractor to prove excusable delay to the project.[13.3] Any delays asserted by the contractor to be the responsibility of the owner may be concurrent with the delays for which the contractor is responsible.

Page 246, add new note 26.1 at end of item 15 on list:

[26.1] *See* Upper Occoquan Sewage Auth. v. Blake Constr. Co., Inc./Poole & Kent, 266 Va. 582, 587 S.E.2d 721 (Oct. 31, 2003) (the court noted that under Va. Code § 2.2-4335(C), a public body is protected against contractor delay claims that are false or without factual or legal basis by providing for recovery of litigation costs from the contractor; the statute provides: "A contractor making a claim against a public body for costs or damages due to the alleged delaying of the contractor in the performance of its work under any public construction contract shall be liable to the public body and shall pay it for a percentage of all costs incurred by the public body in investigating, analyzing, negotiating, litigating and arbitrating the claim, which percentage shall be equal to the percentage of the contractor's total delay claim that is determined through litigation or arbitration to be false or to have no basis in law or in fact"; in this case, the court denied the owner's application for costs under the statute, finding insufficient evidence of a determination within the meaning of the statute or a showing that the delay claims had no basis in law or fact).

Page 249, add new paragraph before first full paragraph on page:

Several types of owner claims were addressed in *Tennessee Gas Pipeline Co. v. Technip USA Corp.*[30.1] TGP contracted with Technip to construct improvements to a gas pipeline, with completion scheduled in 17 months. Due to delays caused by Technip, the project took three years to complete, and TGP brought a breach of contract action to recover damages caused by the delays, including damages more than $4 million in "project delay costs" for extended administration of the contract, almost $6 million representing loss of anticipated savings on the projected efficiency of the improved compressor components, and more than $6 million in loss of accrued interest on the funds TGP had invested in the project

[13.3] *See* Fru-Con Constr. Corp. v. United States, 43 Fed. Cl. 306 (1999), *on reconsid. in part*, 44 Fed. Cl. 298 (1999).

[30.1] 2008 WL 3876141 (Tex. Ct. App.-Hous. Aug. 21, 2008), *review denied* (2 pets.) (Sept. 25, 2009).

during the delay period. Technip argued that a contract clause precluding recovery of consequential damages for such items as loss of profits or revenue and loss of opportunity or use barred TGP from recovering any damages caused by delay. However, the court held that the clause did not exclude recovery of any direct delay damages (damages that result "naturally and necessarily" from the breach), and excluded only lost profits and loss of use that *also qualified* as consequential damages (damages that result "naturally, but not necessarily," from the breach).

The *Tennessee* court found that TGP incurred extended expenses for contract administration, including labor, travel, environmental contractors, TGP inspectors, supply of additional construction consumables, costs for hauling wastewater from the site, and services and utilities. Since all of these costs were the "Owner's Responsibilities" under the contract, the parties clearly contemplated that TGP would incur these costs throughout the project and that a delay in contract completion "naturally and necessarily" would cause these costs to be extended over a longer period of time. The court held these costs were thus direct damages, and not excluded under the consequential damages provision of the contract. With respect to the loss of accrued interest on the funds TGP had invested in the project during the delay period, i.e., interest TGP theoretically could have earned on its money (allegedly ranging from five to six percent) had it invested the funds it spent on this project in other investments during the delay period, the court found the lost use of money represented an indirect loss to TGP because any return that might be attributable to theoretical investments it might have made fell outside its contract with Technip. As such, this claim was a consequential "loss of use" claim that was precluded by the contract provision waiving recovery of all consequential losses. Finally, the court held that TGP's claim for loss of anticipated savings on the projected efficiency of the new compressor components was not a direct damage claim because it was too remote to be conclusively presumed to have been foreseen or contemplated by Technip as a consequence of its breach, and was similarly precluded by the consequential damages provision in the contract.

§ 12.05 LOST PROFITS

Page 249, add at end of note 32:

See Ambrogio v. Beaver Road Assocs., 267 Conn. 148, 836 A.2d 1183 (2003) (an oral surgeon sought to recover lost profits for breach of a contract for construction of his office; defective installation of flooring in one of the surgical rooms caused unsafe and unhealthy conditions, requiring plaintiff to close the room; court held that lost profits can be an appropriate measure of damages for breach of a construction contract when such damages were within the contemplation of the parties at the time they made the contract; whether the parties contemplated such damages is a question of fact ordinarily for the jury; thus, the trial court abused its discretion in this case by holding that lost profits were not within the reasonable contemplation of the parties at the time they entered into the contract). *Cf.* Teramo & Co., Inc. v. O'Brien-Sheipe Funeral Home, Inc., 283 A.D.2d 635, 725 N.Y.S.2d 87 (2d Dept. 2001) (trial court erred in awarding $21,000 in lost profits due to construction delay; owner's unsubstantiated claim that it lost business due to the delay in completing construction of the extension to its funeral home was too speculative to allow recovery); AgGrow Oils, LLC v. National Union Fire Ins. Co. of Pittsburgh, 276 F. Supp. 2d 999 (D.N.D. 2003) (owner was entitled to recover more than $2 million in corrective work and lost profits when the completed oilseed processing plant under a design-build contract failed to produce the quality and quantity of oil set forth in the production guarantees); Tennessee Gas Pipeline Co. v. Technip USA Corp., 2008 WL 3876141 (Tex. Ct. App.-Hous. Aug. 21, 2008), *review denied* (2 pets.) (Sept. 25, 2009) (in a breach of contract action brought to recover damages caused by delays in making improvements to a gas pipeline (scheduled completion in 17 months took three years), although the defendant contractor argued that a contract clause precluding recovery of consequential damages for such items as loss of profits or revenue and loss of opportunity or use barred the plaintiff owner from recovering any such damages caused by delay, the court held that the clause excluded only "lost profits" and "loss of use" that *also qualified* as consequential damages (damages that result naturally, but not necessarily, from the breach), and did not preclude recovery of lost profits and loss of use that constituted *direct* damages (damages that result naturally and necessarily from the breach); owner held entitled to recover as direct damages more than $4 million in extended field costs that owner was responsible for under the contract (e.g., construction and permanent power, storage and lay down areas, potable water, etc.); the court held the following damages were consequential and therefore not recoverable: almost $6 million representing the loss of anticipated savings on the projected efficiency of the new compressor components; more than $6 million in loss of accrued interest on the funds TGP had invested in the project during the delay period; almost $500,000 of backup generator costs and premature energization costs incurred due to the contractor seeking energization before it was necessary; and lost profits resulting from excessive blowdown reducing the amount of gas available for sale).

§ 12.06 OWNER'S CLAIMS AGAINST DESIGN PROFESSIONALS

Page 250, add at end of note 33:

See, e.g., Western Technologies, Inc., an Arizona Corporation v. All-American Golf Center, Inc., 139 P.3d 858 (Nev. Aug. 17, 2006), *reh'g denied* (Dec. 22, 2006) (a golf course developer that contracted for the construction of a nine-hole golf course brought this action against the general contractor, the architect, and the project's engineer and soil tester, alleging claims for breach of contract, breach of express warranty, negligence, and unjust enrichment, based on several constructional defects, primarily a defectively constructed retaining wall. After the general contractor and architect settled the claims against them, the developer obtained a judgment against the engineer solely based on defects in the retaining wall, and the court held that the engineer was entitled to an offset from this judgment for the settlement amounts paid by the other parties. However, because it was not clear how much of these settlements were attributable to the defective retaining wall, the court remanded the action to the trial court for such a determination).

Page 252, add at end of note 41:

But cf. C.H. Guernsey & Co. v. United States, 65 Fed. Cl. 582 (2005) (in the absence of an express agreement, an architect does not guaranty, imply, or warrant a perfect plan, or favorable or satisfactory results; thus, an architect's work can be inaccurate or imperfect without being an actionable deviation from the standard of care; in this case, fourteen days after the Army Corps of Engineers was notified of a possible design problem and twelve days after the architect was first notified of the issue, the architect proposed a solution, later adopted by the Corps, which allowed the project to be constructed; both the architect's expert and the government's expert agreed this solution was acceptable; if the Corps would have followed the architect's recommendation when it was first offered, the delay would have been approximately two weeks, not an unreasonable delay, given the fact that contract performance at that time already had been delayed ten days due to inclement weather; the court accordingly concluded that the delay caused by the architect was not unreasonable nor negligent and thus was not compensable).

Page 253, add at end of section:

A contractor also may assert a claim against an architect for indemnification when the architect's faulty design causes a delay in completion, and the contractor is subsequently held liable to the owner for liquidated damages. Thus, in *Ex parte Stonebrook Development, LLC,*[45] the contractor was required to perform additional work in a developer's residential neighborhood in order to repair some portions of the roads it had constructed. The contractor believed that all or part of its delay in performing the contract was a result of the architect's negligence. Although the architect argued that the contractor's claim was barred by the applicable statute of limitations because the action was not filed within two years of the contractor's completion of the project, the court hold that the action was timely because the claim for indemnification did not accrue until the contractor was held liable to the owner for the payment of liquidated damages.

[45] 854 So. 2d 584 (Ala. 2003).

In *Lanier At McEver, L.P. v. Planners And Engineers Collaborative, Inc.*,[46] the court was asked to determine the enforceability of a contract clause that purported to limited the liability of a civil engineering firm (PEC) to the owner (Lanier), the general contractor, all construction contractors and subcontractors on the project, and any third parties for any and all claims and expenses so that the total liability of PEC would not exceed its fee for services rendered. Lanier sued PEC for $500,000 for negligent design of the storm-water drainage system, and PEC's motion for partial summary judgment limiting it liability to $80,514, PEC's total fee for services, was granted and affirmed on appeal. The Georgia Supreme Court reversed, holding that the contract clause violated public policy as set forth in OCGA § 13-8-2(b) which prohibits any contractor from obtaining indemnification for its own sole negligence. Here, the contract clause purported to apply to "any and all claims" by third parties, thus shifting all liability above the fee for services to Lanier, no matter the origin of the claim or who was at fault. Thus, while a third party would not be precluded from suing PEC for any negligent actions in designing the storm-water drainage system, the clause at issue would have allowed PEC to recover any judgment amount entered against it from Lanier once the $80,514 threshold had been surpassed, including judgment amounts on third-party claims for which PEC was solely negligent. Such a clause was invalid under the Georgia statute.

A contrary result was reached in *1800 Ocotillo, LLC v. The WLB Group, Inc.*,[47] where the Arizona Supreme Court held that a contract provision limiting an engineer's liability to the amount of the fees paid for its surveying services did not violate the state's anti-indemnity statute, A.R.S. § 32-1159. The court found that only a provision completely insulating a party from liability for its sole negligence would violate the statute, whereas a mere limitation of liability clause was enforceable. On remand, the appellate court held that the limitation of liability clause was only enforceable if it was in fact bargained for, and that where, as here, the engineer's standard conditions containing the clause were virtually illegible, an issue of fact existed as to whether the parties bargained for the provision, thereby precluding summary judgment in the engineer's favor.

A limitation of liability clause was upheld under North Carolina law in *Mosteller Mansion, LLC v. Mactec Engineering and Consulting of Georgia, Inc.*[48] The contract between Mactec and the owner, Mosteller, for engineering services contained the following limitation of liability clause:

[46] 284 Ga. 204, 663 S.E.2d 240 (June 30, 2008), *reconsid. denied* (July 25, 2008), *on remand*, 295 Ga. App. 386, 671 S.E.2d 872 (Dec. 23, 2008).

[47] 219 Ariz. 200. 196 P.3d 222 (Nov. 3, 2008), *on remand* 2009 WL 1138049 (Ariz. Ct. App. Div. 1 Apr. 18, 2009).

[48] 190 N.C. App. 674. 661 S.E.2d 788 (May 20, 2008), *review denied*, 362 N.C. 473, 666 S.E.2d 124 (Aug. 26, 2008).

> To the maximum extent permitted by applicable law and for additional compensation of $10.00 from [Mactec], [Mosteller] hereby expressly agrees that the liability of [Mactec] . . . for any cause of action based upon breach of contract, strict liability, negligent professional acts, errors or omissions, or negligent misrepresentation arising out of or in connection with this Agreement and/or services provided or work product developed pursuant to this Agreement, shall be limited to the aggregate sum . . . of $50,000 or the total fees paid to [Mactec] by [Mosteller] under this Agreement, whichever is greater."

Mactec performed the necessary soil test borings, presented its findings, recommended foundations designs, and was paid $8,900 for its services. Several years later, Mosteller sued Mactec for more than $3 million in damages allegedly incurred as a result of unsuitable soils, asserting claims for breach of contract, negligence, professional negligence, and negligent misrepresentation. The court first determined that the law of North Carolina governed resolution of the tort claims, as this was the state in which the alleged tort was committed. (The court also found that the law of Georgia governed the contract claim since that was the stated choice of law under the terms of the contract. However, the court's decision that the limitation of liability clause was valid under Georgia law was based upon the lower court's decision in *Lanier*, above, which was subsequently overruled by the Georgia Supreme Court.) The court held that the limitation of liability provision was valid under North Carolina law, citing *Blaylock Grading Co. v. Smith.*[49]

Page 253, add new section:

§ 12.07 REDUCTIONS IN SCOPE THROUGH DEDUCTIVE CHANGES

Disputes over changes are not limited to changes that increase the contractor's price. Deductive changes, which are those changes that reduce the contract scope, and hence the contract price, can be extremely contentious. Typically, the owner is entitled to a credit for the reduced amount of work equal to the difference between the cost of performing the contract with the work included and the cost of performing the contract without the work included. Simply the owner is entitled to the contractor's savings in cost as a result of not performing the work. While this is a simple concept, determining what the work would have cost when it has not been performed can be difficult. It can become even more difficult when the originally estimated costs of performing the deleted work, and hence the amount included in the contractor's estimate, budget and contract price, are significantly different than the costs actually required to perform the now eliminated work.

[49] 189 N.C. App. 508, 658 S.E.2d 680 (Apr. 1, 2008), *review denied*, 362 N.C. 469, 665 S.E.2d 737 (Aug. 26, 2008).

On fixed price or lump sum contracts, the method commonly employed by contractors is to submit the estimated cost for the work not performed as the credit. Disputes may arise when either owners or contractors want to use previously submitted line item pricing, taken from either contract breakouts submitted with bids or from the Schedule of Values used for progress pay applications to determine the value of the work not performed. Line item prices, particularly those supplied for billing or progress payment purposes, do not necessarily reflect the actual cost of the work.

Two cases in which the Federal Government was unsuccessful in attempting to price deductive change orders using line item pricing from either pay applications or bid breakdowns are *Appeal of American Constr. and Energy, Inc.*[50] and *Appeal of J.A. Jones Constr. Co.*[51] In the American Construction case the government demanded a credit based upon the labor amount from the Schedule of Values American had prepared and used for progress payment purposes. That labor amount was more than twice the amount calculated by American using its actual costs for performing the work on that portion which had not been deleted. The Board ruled in favor of the contractor finding that the actual job cost records were presumed to be reasonable and should be used to compute the cost savings generated by a deductive change order. In the J.A. Jones case the Bureau of Reclamation had awarded a contract to Jones for a dam reconstruction project on the Salt River in Arizona. One of the line items in the contract called for furnishing and installing 5,400 linear feet of rock bolts, which Jones had bid at $130 per linear foot for a line item total of $702,000. Even though there were line items in the bid, the overall contract was a lump sum fixed price contract. The government subsequently deleted 3,060 linear feet of rock bolt from the contract and took a credit of $390,800 using the bid price of $130 per linear foot. Jones asserted that the credit should only be $89,512, the amount it would have paid its subcontractor to furnish and install 3,060 linear feet of rock bolts. Jones asserted that the manner in which it allocated profit and loss among its fixed price contract items was not relevant to the amount of the credit and that the credit had to be based on actual cost savings. The Board agreed with Jones and found that the fundamental principal underlying a deductive price adjustment is to leave the contractor in the same profit or loss position it would have been absent the deletion. Therefore, the pricing of a deductive change must reflect as closely as possible the actual cost savings to contractor. The contractor's entitlement to profit on deductive changes is discussed in § **8.11**.

Often, not allowing the line item pricings in a pay application to be the basis for credits works to the contractor's benefit since the line items typically have spread across them pro rata shares of jobsite general conditions and overheads as well as the contractor's overheads and profit. However, when work is

[50] ASBCA No. 34934 (Nov. 18, 1987).

[51] IBCA No. 3280 (Aug. 16, 1994).

deleted, typically the owner is entitled only to the cost savings and not the allocated general conditions, jobsite overheads and overheads and profits. The reason for this is that typically the contractor will have no savings in these items even though the overall work has been reduced.

Sometimes using the actual costs savings can result in unexpected results because of the manner in which pay applications are processed. In *Appeal of Cottman Mec. Contractors, Inc.*,[52] the unreliability of using pay application line items as a measure of value for deductive work is illustrated. In this matter, the government approved a progress payment for 99 percent of the work leaving a contract balance of only $5,711. After approving that contract pay application the government deducted a portion of the remaining work and took a credit for the cost of that remaining work of $17,788, more than three times the value of the amount remaining to be billed. The government was successful in arguing that because the credit it was entitled to was to be based on the saved cost, such a credit could exceed and did exceed the contract balance.

In unit price contracts, the pricing of deductive work appears to be simple. It is simply the contract value of the units not performed. However, when the size of the deduction becomes significant, this can work a significant hardship on the contractor as a result of the contractor not receiving the indirect costs that are spread over all of the original quantity of units. The treatment of large deductive changes on unit prices is discussed in more detail in § **15.03**.

[52] ASBCA No. 48882 (Feb. 16, 2000).

CHAPTER 13
LIQUIDATED DAMAGES

§ 13.02 PURPOSE OF LIQUIDATED DAMAGES

Page 257, add new note 1.1 at end of first sentence of second paragraph:

[1.1] S. Brooke Purll, Inc. v. Vailes, 850 A.2d 1135 (D.C. May 27, 2004) (party challenging enforceability of liquidated damages clause has burden of proving it is a penalty rather than an amount that might reasonably have been expected from a breach of contract *at the time of execution, i.e.*, burden is on owner to show that liquidated damages clause was disproportionate to contractor's *anticipated* damages in the event of a breach).

Page 257, add at end of note 2:

See also, e.g., A.G. Cullen Constr., Inc. v. State Sys. of Higher Educ., 898 A.2d 1145 (Pa. Commw. 2006) (a liquidated damages clause in a contract for the renovation of a state university building was enforceable when the evidence indicated that: (1) it was beyond dispute that delay damages in the complex construction would be difficult to prove accurately; (2) given the extent of the work involved in the project and the fact the contract to perform the renovation work exceeded $3 million, liquidated damages of $500 per day did not bear an unreasonable relation to the damages that might be expected to result from a breach; and (3) the contractor was an experienced contractor that dealt with the owner at arm's length—the record indicated that its officers understood the contract; under these circumstances, the liquidated damages provision did not constitute an unenforceable penalty). *Cf.* Appeal of Overstreet Elec. Co., Inc., ASBCA No. 53163, 01-2 BCA ¶ 31,470 (2001) (contractor's complaint alleged that liquidated damages provision of contract was unenforceable because at the time of contracting (1) the damages for possible delay were neither uncertain nor difficult to prove, and (2) the specified daily rate bore no reasonable relationship to any actual damages that might be incurred; these allegations stated a claim for which relief from the assessed damages could be granted, and the Board therefore denied the government's motion to dismiss); Idela Constr. Co., ASBCA No. 45070, 01-2 BCA ¶ 31,437 (2001) (in order to assess liquidated damages, the government must prove by a preponderance of the evidence that the contractor was in default, that the government did not prevent performance or contribute to the delay, and that the contractor was the sole cause of the days of delay; in this case, the contractor argued that liquidated damages were a penalty, but it failed to provide sufficient evidence to overcome the presumption that liquidated damages in a contract are reasonable); El Dorado Irrigation Dist. v. Traylor Bros., Inc., 2006 WL 38953 (E.D. Cal., Jan. 4, 2006) (under California law governing public works projects, a liquidated damages clause is enforceable unless the amount specified as recoverable is "manifestly unreasonable" under the circumstances existing at the time the contract was made; however, an earlier California decision held that "while liquidated damages must fit within the conventions of reason, they are not necessarily approximations of actual damage suffered"; thus, the instant court upheld a liquidated damages clause that resulted in an award of $191,000 to the owner, though the owner claimed that lost sales due to delay cost it approximately $2.4 million).

Page 258, add after carryover paragraph:

Liquidated damages are commonly asserted for late completion of a project. However, there is no requirement that liquidated damages be limited to damages for late completion. In *S. Brooke Purll, Inc. v. Vailes*,[2.1] the court enforced a liquidated damages provision that provided for payment to the contractor of 35 percent of the contract price in the event the owner cancelled the contract. In that case, the homeowner contracted for the renovation of a house at a fixed price. The contract had an express provision providing that if the contract was cancelled for any reason, the owner would pay the contractor, as fixed and liquidated damages, 35 percent of the full contract price. A dispute developed early in the project, and the owner terminated the contract and sued the contractor for return of its $5,000 advance deposit. The contractor counterclaimed for 35 percent of the contract price, more than $35,000, plus its attorneys' fees. The trial court found the liquidated damage provision an unenforceable penalty and not a valid liquidated damages clause, because the liquidated damages bore no relationship to the contractor's out-of-pocket costs. The appeals court reversed and explicitly adopted the rule that the party challenging the enforceability of a liquidated damages clause has the burden of proving that the amount constitutes a penalty, and that such a burden had not been met since the homeowner had introduced no evidence indicating that the costs and contractor's incurred lost profit would not be in the range of 35 percent.

A Michigan appellate court upheld a liquidated damages provision that allowed a price reduction if material samples did not meet specifications in *Angelo Iafrate Construction Co. v. Department of Transportation*.[2.2] The contract required that Iafrate submit samples of the asphalt binder to the DOT prior to performing the resurfacing of a highway, and that the DOT could take a 50% price reduction on the material or require removal of the installed asphalt if the samples did not conform to

[2.1] 850 A.2d 1135 (D.C. 2004).

[2.2] 2007 WL 3088577 (Mich. Ct. App. Oct. 23, 2007).

the specifications. The samples did not meet the specifications standards, and the DOT imposed the 50 percent price reduction. Iafrate contended that it was improper for the DOT to impose the price reduction, since it was undisputed that the asphalt actually installed met the contract standards. The court rejected Iafrate's claim, holding that the liquidated damages provision was not a penalty since the DOT suffered some actual damages due to additional testing that was required after the inadequate samples had been discovered.

A liquidated damages provision was upheld notwithstanding that the owner neither expected to incur nor actually incurred any damages as a result of the delay in completion of the highway project in *James Construction Group, LLC v. Louisiana Department of Transportation and Development.*[2.3] The contract provision at issue was headed "Disincentive for Late Construction" and provided for the imposition of "stipulated damages" of $10,000 per day for each day of late completion of the contract work. The contract stated that the stipulated damages were imposed not as a penalty, but in order to minimize construction duration and the impact on roadway users, and was based on the "daily road user costs," which consisted of "the average daily cost of interference and inconvenience to the road user." The contractor did not complete the work within the adjusted contract time, and the DOTD withheld $420,000 in stipulated damages. The appellate court affirmed the trial court's enforcement of the stipulated damages clause, finding that the contractor failed to meet its burden of proving that the stipulated damages "were so manifestly unreasonable as to offend public policy." The court found that the DOTD had the statutory duty to supervise and regulate roadways, and therefore had the authority to enter into an agreement with a contractor that provided for stipulated damages as a disincentive for late construction. The evidence established that the actual daily road user costs incurred by the motoring public during the period in question was $21,135, based upon a Federal Highway Administration program, and the contract rate of $10,000 per day was therefore not unreasonable. The court disregarded the fact that there was no evidence that any motorist sustained any actual loss or damage as a result of the delays in completion of the project and upheld the imposition of stipulated damages, noting that the contractor entered freely into the contract and cannot now claim that some other measure of damages should have been used.

Page 258, add at end of note 5:

See also, e.g., Wayne Knorr, Inc. v. Pennsylvania Dept. of Transp., 973 A.2d 1061 (Pa. Cmmw. May 14, 2009) (liquidated damages of $650 per day for the entire period from October 13, 2000 to August 8, 2001, which was the last day upon which "any physical work remains uncompleted" after substantial completion (the cut-off date under the contractual liquidated damages provision) constituted an "unreasonably large penalty that grossly exceeded PennDOT's (the government's)

[2.3] 977 So. 2d 989, 2007-0225 (La. Ct. App. Nov. 2, 2007).

cost of on site personnel" while the punchlist work was being completed; the court instead awarded the daily liquidated damages amount solely for those days on which Knorr was actually performing work).

Page 259, add at end of note 9:

; City of Rochester v. E & L Piping, Inc., 764 N.Y.S.2d 514 (2003) (court held that a contract provision assessing liquidated damages for failure to comply with a minority and women business enterprise requirement was unenforceable as a penalty, since the City had cited no actual economic damages it might incur as a result of a subcontractor's failure to comply with the requirement); Appeal of Valenzuela Eng'g, Inc., ASBCA No. 53936 (2004) (a liquidated damages rate, based upon the dollar value of the contract and the type of facility, came from the Navy's Contracting Manual and was held to be prima facie reasonable; contractor therefore had burden of presenting specific evidence that the rate was unreasonable and, having failed to do so, had no recourse); Eatherly Constr. Co. v. HTI Mem'l Hosp., 2005 WL 2217078 (Tenn. Ct. App., Sept. 12, 2005) (the trial court did not err in holding that a liquidated damages provision was a penalty and therefore was unenforceable where the court specifically found there was no proof in the record to support a finding that the liquidated sum agreed upon was a reasonable estimate of the damages to be incurred by the owner; there was a complete lack of evidence as to how this provision was negotiated and what foresight these individuals had when they entered into it as to what might be the potential harm; the best, if not only, evidence offered to support the contention that $500 per day was reasonable was that the parties "agreed" to the amount; although the parties' agreement to the amount is relevant, and it is a factor to be considered in order to determine whether the amount was a reasonable estimate at the time the parties entered into the contract, that evidence, standing alone, did not preponderate against the trial court's specific finding to the contrary); Hutton Contracting Co., Inc. v. City of Coffeyville, 487 F.3d 772 (10th Cir. (Kan.) Apr. 30, 2007) (the Tenth Circuit noted that the Kansas Supreme Court has evaluated liquidated damages only in prospective terms—whether the provision was reasonable "at the time of contract formation," although the Kansas cases have not definitively adopted the "single look" approach; however, the court did not need to determine this issue, as the contractor did not raise the argument in the district court; the court further found that the amount of damages actually incurred by the City was close to the amount of liquidated damages, such that the liquidated damages provision was reasonable even if a retrospective analysis was applied); Carrothers Constr. Co., L.L.C. v. City of S. Hutchinson, 288 Kan. 743, 207 P.3d 231 (May 22, 2009) (court stated the rule is that "the reasonableness of a liquidated damages clause in a contract deliberately entered into should be determined with regard to the conditions of the parties existing at the time the contract was executed, not from hindsight after the contract is breached, thereby rejecting contractor's argument that the reasonableness of a liquidated damages provision

should also be invalid if it bears no reasonable relation to the actual injury to the government resulting from the late completion"; noting the Hutton court's uncertainly as to the proper test under Kansas law, the Kansas Supreme Court specifically held that Kansas embraces "a prospective analysis as the sole basis for evaluating a liquidated damages provision in a contract; the court also rejected the contractor's argument that liquidated damages should not be assessed after the government took occupancy of the building, particularly where, as here, there was substantial work still to be completed at the time of occupancy); Highway Specialties, Inc. v. Montana Dept. of Transp., 351 Mont. 527, 215 P.3d 667, 2009 MT 253 (Aug. 03, 2009) (in Montana, a liquidated damages provisions is assumed enforceable unless the party opposing the provision establishes that it is unconscionable "as indicated by the nature of the bargaining process between the parties"; courts will consider whether the weaker bargaining party had no meaningful choice regarding acceptance of the provision, and whether the provision is within the reasonable expectations of, or is unduly oppressive to, the weaker party; the court found that in this case, contractors have an opportunity to discuss contractual terms with the MDT on an annual basis, and federal law required MDT to include the liquidated damages provision is HIS's contract; more importantly, the court found that the contractual terms were within HSI's reasonable expectations, because had previously executed numerous contracts with MDT containing similar provisions, and had triggered the liquidated damages provision in at least three of those contracts; further, the daily rate of $387 was not unconscionable, and the provision was therefore enforceable); Athens Generating Co., L.P. v. Bechtel Power Corp., American Arbitration Association Arbitration Award (Aug. 17, 2009) (arbitration panel held that liquidated damages of $49,000 per unit per date, totaling $26,950,000 on a $22 million EPC contract for a merchant power plant in Athens, New York, was not a penalty because the daily rate was a reasonable estimate of the damages Athens Generating might suffer from late completion at the time the parties entered into the contract; the fact that Athens Generating suffered significantly less actual damages was irrelevant; court also noted that Bechtel had assessed the same quantum of liquidated damages against its subcontractor, Siemens Westinghouse Power Corporation); Appeal of Weis Builders, Inc., ASBCA No. 56306, 2010 WL 602366 (Feb. 17, 2010) (fact that the government utilized a standardized form for determining the daily rate of liquidated damages did not render that rate unreasonable; the government is not required to determine liquidated damages rates tailor-made for each project, nor is it required to conduct an analysis prior to bidding of whether delay damages would be computable and measureable).

Page 259, add after second full paragraph:

Large construction contracts may have liquidated damages for completion of portions of the work. Application of the liquidated damages on these interim milestone dates can lead to disputes. Contractors frequently assert that if they meet the final completion date, it is unreasonable to assess liquidated damages for the early interim milestones. In *In re Pete Vicari General Contractor, Inc.*,[10.1] the Armed Services Board of Contract Appeals specifically enforced a contract provision for assessment of liquidated damages for failure to meet two interim milestone dates, even though the contractor met the final completion date. In upholding this assessment of liquidated damages, the Board found that the damages were different by phase and that there was a reasonable basis for both the damage amount and the interim milestones.

§ 13.04 IMPLEMENTATION OF THE CLAUSE

Page 264, add at end of section:

Oral agreements attempting to modify implementation of a liquidated damages provision will generally be held unenforceable. For example, in *Appeal of Trawick Contractors, Inc.*,[15.1] the contractor alleged that the Navy's administrative contracting officer had verbally agreed to settle the government's liquidated damages claim for $30,000 and would pay the balance of the retainage to the contractor in the amount of $68,000. Instead, the contracting officer charged the full $98,000 as liquidated damages, and issued a unilateral change order decreasing the contract price by that amount. The Board of Contract Appeals denied the contractor's claim, holding that an oral settlement agreement is unenforceable without a written contract modification reflecting the agreed-upon change in the contract price.

Where a subcontract passes through liquidated damages from the prime contract, the subcontractor cannot be held liable for liquidated damages unless the owner assessed liquidated damages against the prime contractor. In *Costello Construction of Maryland, Inc. v. J.D. Long Masonry, Inc.*,[15.2] the subcontract provided the "subcontractor shall be responsible for its proportionate share of liquidated damages . . . including all or a portion of any liquidated damages assessed by the Owner against the Contractor." The court found that this provision entitled the contractor to recover liquidated damages from the subcontractor only if the contractor is required to pay liquidated damages to the owner. Since the evidence established that the owner had not withheld any money from the contractor for liquidated damages and did not intend to assert its right to seek liquidated damages, the contractor could not recover liquidated damages from the subcontractor.

A unilateral modification to a liquidated damages provision was upheld in *Superior Steel, Inc. v. Woodrow Wilson Construction Co., Inc.*[15.3] Upon receipt of

---

[10.1] ASBCA No. 54982, 2005 WL 3150594 (Nov. 21, 2005).

[15.1] ASBCA No. 55097 (Feb. 23, 2007).

[15.2] 236 Fed. Appx. 877, 2007 WL 1857348 (4th Cir. (Va.) June 26, 2007).

[15.3] 2008 WL 4780248 (La. App. 1 Cir. Nov. 3, 2008).

the general contractor's subcontract, the president of Superior crossed out the provision allowing for liquidated damages for delay, placed his initials and the date next to the provision, and returned it to the WWCC. Nothing was said regarding the strike out, and Superior commenced work and received payments in accordance with the contract. WWCC withheld payment from Superior, asserting its right to assess liquidated damages against Superior, and Superior brought suit to recover the balance owed. The court held that although there had been conflicting testimony regarding what happened after WWCC received the amended contract, WWCC essentially acquiesced to the modification, such that there was no basis to assess liquidated damages against Superior. Further, even if the liquidated damages provision had not been deleted, the provision only permitted assessment of liquidated damages for delay, and only in the amount withheld by the owner. Here, the evidence established that the only amounts withheld by the owner for incomplete punch list items, none of which related to Superior.

A court has held that a claim for liquidated damages does not constitute "an occurrence" under a contractor's comprehensive general liability (CGL) policy in *Lyerla v. AMCO Ins. Co.*[15.4] The homeowner sued the contractor, Lyerla, for breach of contract, alleging defective work and failure to pay liquidated damages for late completion. Lyerla tendered the suit to his CGL carrier, AMCO, who denied coverage and refused to provide a defense. Lyerla settled with the homeowner, and sued AMCO for breach of the insurance contract. The court first held that although there is a division of authority as to whether defective work can constitute "property damage" caused by an "occurrence" within the meaning of a CGL policy, Illinois courts have generally reasoned that construction defects represent the natural and ordinary consequence of faulty construction, and therefore do not constitute an "accident" or "occurrence" under the policy. With respect to the liquidated damages claim, Lyerla argued that this constituted "property damage" because it sought to recover for "the loss of use of tangible property that is not physically injured," which is within the policy definition of "property damage." The court rejected this argument, holding that liquidated damages do not represent costs incurred by the owner for loss of use of tangible property, and are instead costs imposed on the contractor pursuant to the contract for failure to complete the project on time. Thus, the claims were not covered by the CGL policy.

[15.4] 536 F.3d 684 (7th Cir. (Ill.) Aug. 4, 2008).

§ 13.05 CALCULATING LIQUIDATED DAMAGES

[A] When Liquidated Damages Begin to Accrue

Page 264, add new note 15.5 at end of second sentence of section:

15.5 *See, e.g.*, Evan Johnson & Sons Constr., Inc. v. State, 877 So. 2d 360 (Miss. Mar. 4, 2004), *reh'g denied* (July 29, 2004) (trial court found that the completion date for the defendant/contractor was May 8, 1997, and the replacement contractor successfully completed the project on October 6, 1998; at the contractually specified rate of $231.81 per day, the 514 days of delay equaled $119,150.34 in liquidated damages properly assessed against the defendant). *See also* Rogers & Willard, Inc. v. Harwood, 2007 WL 2684542 (Ala. Ct. App. Sept. 14, 2007), *reh'g denied* (Nov. 2, 2007), *cert. denied* (Aug. 8, 2008) (the contractor, R&W, was contractually required to achieve substantial completion of the work not later than 200 calendar days "from the date of commencement," and provided for liquidated damages of $500 per day for every day the project is not substantially complete; the contract did not fix the "date of commencement," and R&W contended the commencement date was the date it obtained the building permit, whereas Harwood asserted it was the date the contract was signed; the court found that there was sufficient evidence to support the jury's finding that the commencement date was the date R&W obtained the building permit, such that R&W substantially completed within 200 calendar days and Harwood was not entitled to an award of liquidated damages).

Page 265, add new note 17.1 at end of subsection:

17.1 *See also* Brashear v. Richardson Constr., Inc., 10 P.3d 1115 (Wyo. 2000) (general contractor waived its right to rely on liquidated damages provision of a contract with its subcontractor when it allowed the subcontractor to commence work after the contractually specified liquidated damages date without requiring a change order or amendment to the contract).

[B] Extensions of Time

Page 265, add at end of note 21:

Cf. Hutton Contracting Co., Inc. v. City of Coffeyville, 487 F.3d 772 (10th Cir. (Kan.) Apr. 30, 2007) (a contractor is responsible for the unexcused performance failures of its supplier; thus, a contractor could not cite the contract's force majeure clause as a basis for avoiding liability to the owner for liquidated damages because of its supplier's delay in supplying necessary materials for the construction and the supplier's supplying defective materials, at least when the contractor does not assert that the supplier's failure was caused by a force majeure event; if a contractor is concerned about paying damages caused by a supplier's delay, it can protect itself by paying the supplier a higher price and obtaining a delay-damages clause in its contract with the supplier).

Page 266, add after third full paragraph on page:

Precisely what constitutes a weather delay and what makes a weather delay unforeseeable can be the source of considerable dispute. In *Commonwealth of Pennsylvania Department of Transportation v. Interstate Contractor Supply Co.*,[24.1] the court held that rain and snow in April in western Pennsylvania is not unusual and therefore should have been anticipated by the contractor; thus, the delay was not excusable. A New York court found that rainy weather is a contract risk faced by all contractors and therefore delays are not excusable.[24.2] Similarly, repeated snowfalls were found to be typical of Cincinnati winters and therefore the snow delay was not excusable.[24.3] The general rule was well-stated by the Board in *Appeal of B.D. Click Co., Inc.*:[24.4] "No matter how severe or destructive, if the weather is not unusual for the particular time and place, or if the contractor should have reasonably anticipated it, the contractor is not entitled to relief."

Page 266, add at end of note 25:

See also Dugan & Meyers Constr. Co., Inc. v. State of Ohio Dept. of Admin. Servs., 113 Ohio St. 3d 226, 864 N.E.2d 68 (Apr. 25, 2007), *on remand* 2007-Ohio-4141, 2007 WL 2405923 (July 19, 2007) (although the State apparently had actual knowledge of the need for time extensions due to multiple changes to the work, the court held that the contractor's failure to comply with the contractual requirement of written notice of a request for time extension within ten days after the occurrence of a condition necessitating a time extension constituted a complete waiver of the contractor's claim for time extension or for mitigation of liquidated damages); Mike M. Johnson, Inc. v. County of Spokane, 78 P.3d 161 (Wash. 2003) (contractor encountered telephone lines that were more shallow than indicated in the drawings and sent the county a letter stating the need to relocate the lines was delaying its work, and another letter indicating that the contractor expected to be compensated for the delay and the increased cost; county instructed contractor to comply with the contractual protest and claim procedure, which included the requirement of a written statement indicating the

---

[24.1] 130 Pa. Commw. 334, 568 A.2d 294 (1990).

[24.2] P.T. & L. Constr. Co., Inc. v. State of New York, 179 A.D.2d 850, 578 N.Y.S.2d 921 (1992).

[24.3] Blue Ribbon Remodeling Co. v. Meistrich, 97 Ohio Misc. 2d 8, 709 N.E.2d 1261 (1999).

[24.4] ASBCA No. 24586 (July 27, 1984).

dollar cost and the schedule impact of the protested work, and then a formal written claim including ten specific items of information; contractor did not comply with the contract requirements, but the contractor asserted it should not be precluded from recovering additional compensation because the county had actual notice of the claim, suffered no prejudice, and therefore could not enforce the contractual procedure; the Washington Supreme Court held that actual notice was not a substitute for compliance with the contractual claim procedure, and the contractor was barred from recovering on its claim); Winship Constr., Inc. v. City of Portland, 2008 WL 3867849 (Tex. App.-Corpus Christi Aug. 21, 2008) (since excusable delay would preclude the owner from assessing liquidated damages, and contractor submitted evidence that the owner agreed to extend the project completion date due to adverse weather but failed to do so, summary judgment in owner's favor was reversed).

[C] Multiple Causes for Delay

Page 267, add at end of note 26:

See also Sauer Inc. v. Danzig, 224 F.3d 1340 (Fed. Cir. 2000) (citing the rule that when "both parties contribute to a delay neither can recover damage, unless there is in the proof a clear apportionment of the delay and the expense attributable to each party"; in this case, because the plaintiff-contractor was able to prove that the government was responsible for only two days of excusable delay, the government was entitled to an award of liquidated damages for the delay period, with the exception of the damages attributable to those two days); Vicari v. United States, 53 Fed. Cl. 357 (Ct. Cl. 2002) (contracting officer deducted liquidated damages from contract price in the amount of $437 per day for each day that work was not complete beyond the contract completion date, as extended, for a total of $56,810 for 130 days; plaintiff's entitlement to a return of liquidated damages would depend on plaintiff's ability to establish excusable delay, citing *Sauer, Inc. v. Danzig*, 224 F.3d 1340, 1347 (Fed. Cir. 2000)); CEMS, Inc. v. United States, 59 Fed. Cl. 168 (Ct. Cl. 2003) (the court noted that if both parties contributed to a delay, neither can recover damages from the other, "unless there is in the proof a clear apportionment of the delay and expense attributable to each party" (citing *Sauer*); in this case, plaintiff argued that the several schedules it submitted were critical path schedules; however, these schedules did not provide the court with the ability to determine whether the alleged delays claimed by the plaintiff were on the critical path or whether concurrent delays also contributed to the delay on the project; plaintiff's delay analysis identified nine months of delay, but did not show that the days of delay asserted under the specific claims were based on much more than the witness' own estimates and speculation provided at trial; based on a review of the record, the court found that contractor did not carry its burden of establishing compensable delays; therefore, plaintiff was not entitled to recover liquidated damages withheld by the defendant); City of Westminster v. Centric-Jones Constructors, 100 P.3d 472 (Colo. App. 2003) (not released) (Centric-Jones was terminated by the City for alleged defects and delays in completion of a project for construction of a clearwell and pumping station almost two years after commencing the work, when most of the work was done; the City demolished and rebuilt the clearwell and the masonry walls of the pumping station and sued Centric-Jones to recover almost $2 million in liquidated damages for six years of delay; court found that the delay was caused in part by the City's decision to redesign the structures, including correction of errors by the original designers, and the City was precluded from recovering any liquidated damages since it failed to provide any basis upon which to apportion the delay between causes for which Centric-Jones was responsible and other causes); George Sollitt Constr. Co. v. United States, 64 Fed. Cl. 229 (Ct. Cl. 2005) (citing *Sauer, supra*, court stated that when apportionment of critical path delays is not possible in a government construction project, court cannot uphold retention of any liquidated damages by the government; in this case, critical path delays could *not* be apportioned between contractor and government with any certainty, and thus the trial court erred in assessing liquidated damages); Mergentime Corp. v. Washington Metro. Area Transp. Auth., 2006 WL 416177 (D.D.C., Feb. 22, 2006) (when delays are occasioned by the mutual fault of the parties, the court will refuse to enforce a provision for liquidated damages); ACE Constructors, Inc. v. United States, 70 Fed. Cl. 253 (Mar. 31, 2006), *aff'd,* 499 F.3d 1357 (Fed. Cir. Sept. 19, 2007) (when a delay is attributable to both an excusable and an inexcusable cause, liquidated damages will not be assessed for the period of that delay [*citing* Cibinic and Nash, *Administration of Government Contracts* at 1059 (3d ed.1995)]). *Cf.* Homer J. Olsen, Inc. v. Santa Clara Valley Transp. Auth., 2005 WL 3462739 (Cal. Ct. App., Dec. 19, 2005) (unpublished) (the trial court did not err in awarding liquidated damages even without an express finding that the contractor was the sole cause of the failure to complete the project on time; the contract allowed for an assessment of liquidated damages where the contractor did not complete the work in a timely manner; although the contractor argued that the owner had to show that the contractor was the sole cause of any delay, the applicable provision of the contract regarding liquidated damages did not so require, the court's conclusion that the owner was entitled to liquidated damages indicated that the court accepted the owner's evidence that the contractor was late in performing the work by the agreed-upon completion dates; the court apparently rejected the contractor's evidence that it was entitled to an extension to a different completion date; there was no basis for finding that the contractor would have been entitled to a time extension).

Cf. Quality Design and Constr., Inc. v. City of Gonzales, 977 So.2d 87, 2007 WL 4181286, 2006-2211 (La. Ct. App. 1st Cir. Nov. 28, 2007) (although the contractor contended that the trial court erred in awarding liquidated damages because the city's project engineer was responsible for a lengthy delay in resolving the issue whether brand name or equivalent products could be used on the project, there was no evidence challenging the validity of the liquidated damages provision or that the contractor did not meet the deadline for substantial completion of the project; the appellate court affirmed the award of liquidated damages by strictly construing the contract, without addressing the contention that the owner was responsible for the delay).

Page 267, add to end of note 28:

See also Sunshine Constr. & Eng'g, Inc. v. United States, 64 Fed. Cl. 346 (2005) (the court noted that the law on the apportionment of liquidated damages is unsettled, particularly with respect to sequential, as opposed to concurrent, delay; one line of sequential delay cases identifies a rule against apportionment, holding that when delays are caused by both parties to the contract the court will not attempt to apportion them, but will simply hold that the provisions of the contract with reference to liquidated damages will be annulled; another line of cases holds that liquidated damages may be apportioned in the instance of a sequential delay; because the more recent case law, including cases from the Federal Circuit, allows apportionment, the instant court held that apportionment of liquidated damages would be proper in the instant case); ACE Constructors, Inc. v. United States, 70 Fed. Cl. 253 (Mar. 31, 2006), *aff'd*, 499 F.3d 1357 (Fed. Cir. Sept. 19, 2007) (the court determined that the plaintiff-contractor should recover liquidated damages it was assessed for 151 of the 156 days that were charged by the government. The contractor averred that the delays in completing the project were not its responsibility, but rather were brought about by delays in the critical path that resulted from a differing site condition, improper specifications, and improperly imposed testing, and the court agreed with the exception of certain days that could not be adequately attributed by the contractor to government fault); *see also, e.g.*, R.P. Wallace, Inc. v. United States, 63 Fed. Cl. 402 (Ct. Cl. 2004) (plaintiff contractor was assessed $50,000 in liquidated damages for failing to complete renovations of a building by the appointed date; contractor then sought remission of the damages for "excusable delay," allegedly resulting from the contractor having been provided with defective window specifications; court noted that when a contractor seeks an extension of contract time for excusable delay, which will relieve it from the consequences of having failed to complete the work within the time allowed for performance, it has the burden of establishing by a preponderance of the evidence not only the existence of an excusable cause of delay, but also extent to which completion of the contract work as a whole was delayed thereby; when there are sequential delays—some delays attributable to the government and some to the contractor—they may be apportioned to determine the number of days that are compensable; in this case, court found that plaintiff was entitled to remission of liquidated damages for only 21 days, which, at $200 per day, amounted to a recovery of $4,200; in all other respects, said the court, plaintiff's claims simply were unsupported by the record or the law); GASA, Inc. v. United States, 79 Fed. Cl. 325 (Nov. 28, 2007) (plaintiff contractor alleged that but for delays by the Army Corps of Engineers, it would not have been assessed liquidated damages for fifty-four days, i.e., that it would have completed the contract within the contractually mandated 180 days (plus any extensions for weather-related delays beyond those contemplated in the contract) had the Corps issued the notice to proceed fifty-three days earlier; however, the evidence indicated that any delays due to work during months with adverse weather were addressed by the terms of the contract, and thus plaintiff could not argue that adverse weather affected its ability to complete the work within 180 days of the NTP; on the other hand, plaintiff could possibly show that the Corps delayed its work on one part of the contract for thirty-one days, and that this delay caused plaintiff to work beyond the 180-day period mandated by the contract; thus, plaintiff would be permitted to show that its liquidated damages assessment should be reduced by thirty-one days); Hutton Contracting Co., Inc. v. City of Coffeyville, 487 F.3d 772 (10th Cir. (Kan.) Apr. 30, 2007) (the court adopted the "modern view" that liquidated damages may be apportioned when there is evidence of delays by both parties and the damages are in fact divisible; the court thus rejected the contractor's contention that the City's breach of its duty of good faith and fair dealing in requesting unneeded repairs and failing to facilitate completion of cleanup-related tasks precluded it from any award of liquidated damages under Kansas law, and upheld the trial court's determination to reduce the amount of liquidated damages by the number of days the jury attributed to the City's breach); United States ex rel. Belt Con Constr., Inc. v. Metric Constr. Co., Inc., 314 Fed. Appx. 151, 2009 WL 458795 (10th Cir. (N.M.) Feb. 25, 2009) (the Tenth Circuit indicated that California case law suggests that California would not apportion concurrent delays, as opposed to sequential delays; the court did not base its decision on this, however, and instead held that the contractor, Metric, did not apportion delay among the owner, the contractor, and the subcontractor (Belt Con) in good faith, as required by the subcontract, since Metric had allocated all concurrent delay to the owner in a previous action, and now attempted to allocate the same delay to Belt Con; the court therefore refused to reverse the district court's decision to not attribute any of the delays to Belt Con).

[D] When Assessment of Liquidated Damages Stops

Page 268, add before last paragraph:

A contractor successfully asserted that once a building was available for beneficial use and occupancy, the government could not continue to assess liquidated damages because work remained involving trimming out and cleaning up of the project. In *In re Amigo Building Corporation*,[29.1] a contractor appealed an

---

[29.1] ASBCA No. 54329, 2005 WL 2001146 (Aug. 17, 2005).

assessment of liquidated damages on three grounds: (1) the rate of $575 per day was an unenforceable penalty; (2) the government inspector should have called Amigo's attention to deficiencies in the work as they were detected, rather than waiting until the end of the project; and (3) the work items that were incomplete at the deadline were mere punchlist items which would not prevent beneficial occupancy and did not justify assessment of liquidated damages. The government overcame the first two arguments by showing that the rate was reasonable and that the inspectors were performing their work for the protection of the government's interest, not the contractor's. The contractor, however, was successful in asserting that once the defects preventing occupancy of the building, in this case a fire alarm system, were remedied, liquidated damages should no longer be accrued while trimming and cleaning up was performed.

Page 269, add at end of note 31:

See also Evan Johnson & Sons Constr., Inc. v. State, 877 So. 2d 360 (Miss. Mar. 4, 2004), *reh'g denied* (July 29, 2004) (parties' contract gave the state the right (1) to terminate the contract for failure of the contractor to prosecute the work, or any separable part of it, with such diligence as would ensure completion within the time specified in the contract, or any extension given, (2) to then take over the work and see it to completion, and (3) to obtain "liquidated damages for delay, as fixed in the specifications or accompanying papers, until such reasonable time as may be required for the final completion of the work"; liquidated damages clause of contract provided for payments of $231.81 for each day of delay; trial court found that the contract completion date was May 8, 1997, and the replacement contractor successfully completed the project on October 6, 1998; at the contractually specified rate of $231.81 per day, the 514 days of delay equaled $119,150.34 in liquidated damages; contractor failed to contest the method of calculation of liquidated damages, and appellate court accordingly affirmed the award).

Page 269, add at end of note 34:

See also In re Roy Frischhertz Constr. Co., Inc., 2007 WL 3253143 (Bankr. E.D. La. Aug. 22, 2007) (although the owner on this public works project argued that it was entitled to recover liquidated damages from the time the project was supposed to be completed until the date the project was actually completed by another contractor, the court held that the damage period should run only until it was clear that the contractor's performance was no longer expected, i.e., when the contractor's attorney sent the government a letter indicating it was stopping work on the project, after which the government authority decided to finish the work itself).

Page 270, add at end of subsection:

In *Intermetal Fabricators, Inc. v. The Losco Group, Inc.*,[38.1] a general contractor terminated a subcontractor and hired a replacement to finish the work, then sought to recover liquidated damages from the original subcontractor for the period from when the project was supposed to have been completed to when the replacement contractor completed the job. The court held, however, that the general contractor was entitled to recover liquidated damages only for delays *attributable* to the subcontractor that exceeded the completion date. Although some or all of the delay between when the subcontractor was terminated and the steel work was finally completed might be attributable to the subcontractor, there was insufficient evidence to make that determination. For example, there was no evidence of whether the general contractor delayed in securing replacement subcontractors or whether those subcontractors delayed in completing their work. The only delay for which there was competent evidence to charge the subcontractor was the delay caused prior to its termination, and thus the general contractor could recover liquidated damages for this period only.

In *Appeal of Randolph & Co., Inc.*,[38.2] the Board ruled that the government could not assess liquidated damages after the contractor had substantially completed the project. Randolph contracted to raise an existing containment dike around a dredge spoil disposal area, but failed to complete the work in accordance with the contract schedule. The Board found that once the dike was capable of holding dredged slurry, the project was substantially complete as it was capable of being used for its intended purpose. Liquidated damages that the government had assessed after that point in time were therefore disallowed.

The government was held to be entitled to assess liquidated damages even though the government had continuous use of the facility throughout construction in *Appeal of William F. Klingensmith, Inc.*[38.3] The project was for phased modifications to a building at the National Institutes of Health, and the contract specified that the government would occupy the site and existing building during the entire construction period. The government assessed liquidated damages when the contractor failed to complete each phase of the project within the contract schedule. The Board rejected the contractor's argument that a liquidated damages provision is an unenforceable penalty when the government has continuous use of the facility, finding that the government could still anticipate actual damages as a result of late completion. The contractor further argued that the government's deletion of the contract requirement that the contractor maintain a CPM schedule constituted a waiver of its right to assess liquidated damages, since the absence of a CPM schedule prevented determination of responsibility for the late completion. The Board noted that the government deleted the requirement because it had

[38.1] 2000 WL 1154249 (S.D.N.Y. 2000).

[38.2] ASBCA No. 52957 (Nov. 6, 2002).

[38.3] ASBCA No. 52028 (Nov. 15, 2002).

lost confidence in the contractor's CPM schedule as a project control device, and ruled that there was no waiver of the right to assess liquidated damages. The Board found that the government could still use a CPM schedule, bar chart, or other method for tracking the progress of the work and apportioning responsibility for the delay.

If a contract does not contain a completion date, the owner will not be entitled to assess liquidated damages. Although decided in the context of an owner's claim for delay damages, the rationale of *Porrazzo Corp. v. Montan Corp.*[38.4] should be equally applicable to an owner's claim for liquidated damages. In the *Porrazzo* case, Porrazzo had two contracts with Montan, one for street grading and another for installation of curb gutters and street paving in a residential subdivision. Both contracts stated that time was of the essence, and the grading contract called for completion "ASAP." Neither contract indicated any specific completion deadline. Montan withheld payments, alleging delay in the completion of the contracts, and Porrazzo sued to recover the contract balances. The appellate court held that Montan could not assert any delay damages against Porrazzo: "In the absence of a completion date or performance schedule, there can be no delay damages because the damages cannot be measured." The court found that the contract provision that "time is of the essence" was meaningless when the contract did not provide a completion deadline, and that the requirement to finish the work "ASAP" was too vague to be enforceable. In addition, Montan failed to provide sufficient support for its contention that there was an implied "reasonable" date of completion.

[F] Determination of Amount of Damages

Page 271, add new note 39.1 at end of first paragraph:

[39.1] In *S. Brooke Purll, Inc. v. Vailes*, 850 A.2d 1135 (D.C. 2004), the court, as a matter of first impression, held that the party challenging the enforceability of a liquidated damages clause has the burden of proving that it is a penalty rather than an amount that might reasonably have been expected from a breach of contract at the time of execution. Thus, in this case, the burden was on the owner to show that the liquidated damages clause was disproportionate to the contractor's anticipated damages in the event of a breach.

Page 277, add at end of note 56:

See also In re Roy Frischhertz Constr. Co., Inc., 2007 WL 3253143 (Bankr. E.D. La. Aug. 22, 2007) (under Louisiana law, a person claiming liquidated damages

[38.4] 2003 WL 22925281 (Cal. Ct. App. 2003) (unpublished).

need not prove the actual damages incurred as a result of the other party's nonperformance, and liquidated damages may exceed actual damages; a liquidated damages recovery will not be modified by the court unless it is so manifestly unreasonable as to be contrary to public policy; here, the contract itself contained a liquidated damages provision specifying $500 per day for each day of delay, while the general conditions provided for an additional $500 per day for items such as extended architectural, engineering, or construction management fees and extended owner's overhead and personal expenses; the court found that $1,000 per day for the 92 days of delay would be manifestly unreasonable and against public policy, in light of the fact that the entire contract price was $242,000, such that liquidated damages at that rate would be approximately 38 percent of the contract price; the court held that the owner was entitled to liquidated damages at the rate of $500 per day); Zeer v. Azulay, 50 A.D.3d 781, 860 N.Y.S.2d 527 (2d Dept. Apr. 8, 2008) (when a liquidated damages provision is deemed enforceable, the measure of damages for breach will be the sum in the clause, no more, no less; if the clause is rejected as being a penalty, the recovery is limited to actual damages proven).

CHAPTER 14

CONTRACT CLAUSES THAT AFFECT DAMAGE CALCULATIONS

§ 14.02 CLAUSES THAT THE OWNER SHOULD INCLUDE IN ITS CONTRACT WITH THE GENERAL CONTRACTOR

[A] Indemnification

Page 281, add new note 1.1 at bottom of page:

[1.1] *See, e.g.*, Watral & Sons, Inc. v. OC Riverhead 58, LLC, 10 N.Y.3d 180, 855 N.Y.S.2d 49, 884 N.E.2d 1048 (Mar. 18, 2008), *reargument denied*, 890 N.E.2d 245, 860 N.Y.S.2d 482 (June 3, 2008) (the indemnification clause of a construction contract, requiring an excavation contractor to indemnify the owner for damages caused by the contractor's negligent acts, did not apply to require the contractor to indemnify the owner for damages allegedly sustained by a neighboring landowner when the contractor's backhoe struck and damaged an underground power cable that supplied electricity to the neighboring property; the cable was not where it was supposed to be, but had been relocated by others before the contractor began its work, and it could not be determined whether the person who had moved the cable was someone for whose acts the contractor was responsible).

Page 282, add to end of section:

The court in *Eatherly Construction Co. v. HTI Memorial Hospital*[1.2] held that an indemnification provision does not entitle an owner to recover attorneys' fees from a contractor in a direct action by the contractor against the owner. Rather, the indemnification provision applies only if and in the event a third party makes a claim based upon a breach of contract by the contractor for which the owner could be liable. Allowing an owner to recover attorneys' fees in an action by the contractor would produce an absurd result, for, if the indemnification provision applied, the contractor would be required to assume and conduct the owner's defense in an action in which the contractor was the plaintiff.

[1.2] 2005 WL 2217078 (Tenn. Ct. App. Sept. 12, 2005).

[B] Architect's Decision Clauses

Page 282, add new note 1.3 at end of first sentence of second paragraph, ending with "enforce such clauses as they are written":

[1.3] *See, e.g.*, Tribble & Stephens Co. v. RGM Constructors, L.P., 154 S.W.3d 639 (Tex. Ct. App. 2004) (construction contract provided that a subcontractor (1) agreed to perform its work "subject to the final approval of the Architect/Engineer"; (2) would receive payment after "acceptance and approval" of its work by the project architect, and (3) expressly accepted the "risk" that the "Owner may reject all or a portion of [the subcontractor's] work"; court stated that it is well established that such a "satisfaction clause," requiring performance by one party to be subject to the satisfaction of the other party, or a designated third party such as an architect or engineer, is enforceable; such clause will be upheld "unless it is shown that the arbiter of performance under the contract decided the matter due to fraud, misconduct, or such 'gross mistake' that it implies bad faith or the failure to exercise honest judgment"). *But see* Huen New York, Inc. v. Board of Educ., Clinton Cent. Sch. Dist., 890 N.Y.S.2d 748, 67 A.D.3d 1337 (App. Div. Nov. 13, 2009), *reargument denied*, 893 N.Y.S.2d 799, 70 A.D.3d 1519 (App. Div. Feb. 11, 2010) (holding that New York law rejects the notion that project architects are empowered to resolve delay damages disputes).

[C] Clauses Regarding Performance of Extra Work

Page 283, add at end of section:

In *Eaton Elec., Inc. v. Dormitory Authority of State of N.Y.*,[1.4] a contractor sought to recover delay damages allegedly resulting from substantial errors in the drawings and specifications issued by the owner, which required substantial corrections, redesigns, and modifications, and resulted in out-of-sequence work. The owner contended that the contractor's claim was not merely a delay claim, but rather fell within the definition of "Extra Work" under the contract. The owner argued that the contractor could not recover damages for extra work because it failed to comply with the notice provision that was specifically applicable to claims for extra work. The contractor argued, however, that it had been fully reimbursed for the costs of performing extra work, and it was seeking reimbursement for the increased costs and damages that it incurred in performing its original Contract work, specifically the impact costs that were attributable to delays, disruptions, and suspensions arising from the owner's defective plans and specifications, and to the owner's failure to provide a comprehensive coordinated

[1.4] 21 Misc.3d 1135(A), 2008 WL 5005264 (N.Y. Sup. Ct. Kings Co. Nov. 25, 2008).

design, needed corrections, the required project CPM schedule, and CPM scheduling reports and updates. The court agreed with the contractor, noting that although a contractor may be required to perform additional work on account of a delay, that expense does not necessarily constitute "Extra Work" as that term is defined in the contract; rather, delay damages and extra work damages are separate items of damages, particularly when, as here, the Contract provided separate provisions addressing Claims for Extra Work and Claims for Delay.

[D] Changes Clauses

Page 284, add new note 1.5 at end of subsection:

[1.5] *See, e.g.*, Doninger Metal Prods. Corp. v. United States, 50 Fed. Cl. 110 (Ct. Cl. 2001) (in order for a contractor to prevail on a changes clause claim for an equitable adjustment to compensate for increased costs of performance flowing from changes that altered the work to be performed under the contract, the contractor must establish that: (1) the contracting officer had the contractual authority unilaterally to alter the contractor's duties under the agreement; (2) any increased costs arose from conditions differing materially from those indicated in the bid documents; (3) such conditions were reasonably unforeseeable in light of all information available to the contractor; (4) the contractor's contract costs actually increased; and (5) the cost increases were the direct and necessary result of the change). *See also* Dugan & Meyers Constr. Co., Inc. v. Ohio Dept. of Adm. Servs., 113 Ohio St. 3d 226, 864 N.E.2d 68 (Apr. 25, 2007), *on remand*, 2007-Ohio-4141, 2007 WL 2405923 (July 19, 2007) (court held that a comprehensive changes clause provided the sole remedy available to the contractor for additional costs incurred due to changes required as a result of defects in the plans and specifications; court refused to find that plan changes resulting from such defects gave rise to a separate claim for delay based upon the *Spearin* theory of breach of an owner's impliedly warranty as to the accuracy of the plans and specifications).

Page 284, add to end of subsection:

Constructive changes will also be deemed subject to any changes clause in the contract. In general, if the owner requires the contractor to perform work or utilize materials that are beyond the scope of the contract documents, but fails or refuses to issue a formal change order, the contractor may recover the additional costs incurred due to the constructive change to the contract. For example, in *Metric Construction, Inc. v. United States*,[1.6] the court found that certain acts of

[1.6] 81 Fed. Cl. 804 (2008). *But see* Phoenix Corp. v. U. W. Marx, Inc., 64 A.D.3d 967, 881 N.Y.S.2d 714 (App. Div. July 9, 2009) (contractor could not recover overtime costs from the owner,

the Navy constituted constructive changes, while others did not. Metric entered into two contracts with the Navy to construct an airfield runway and a roadway on San Nicholas Island, California. The contract required that all material and equipment be delivered to the island by ocean-going barge, landing at either of two specified beaches. Metric bid the project planning to use a large barge that could only land at Daytona Beach, which was the same beach used by the Navy for its smaller barge. During the course of construction, in January 1999, the Navy installed a barge landing pontoon on Daytona Beach, and notified Metric that it was now required to use the pontoon instead of landing directly on the beach. Metric had been advised that the pontoon was not compatible with Metric's larger barge, and Metric ceased operations until the Navy provided a suitable landing site. Subsequently, Metric attempted to land its barge using the pontoon, but was only successful under certain limited conditions. Finally, in May 1999, the Navy granted Metric permission to again land its barge directly on Daytona Beach. The Navy failed to respond to Metric's request for equitable adjustment for additional costs, including delay costs, resulting from the Navy's direction to use the landing pontoon, but the court held that the Navy's action was a constructive change for which Metric was entitled to compensation. In doing so, the court rejected the Navy's argument that Metric's claim was solely a delay claim, for which Metric would not be allowed a profit.

Metric also contended that the Navy's multiple rejections of the asphalt placed on the runway constituted a constructive change because the finish the Navy wanted exceeded the specifications. However, the court held that the rejections were due to rock pockets in the asphalt, which were properly rejected under the contract. The court also found that the asphalt specifications were performance specifications, such that there was no implied warranty that all of the contractually-permitted methods of patching the asphalt would meet the specifications. Metric also asserted a claim of constructive change based upon the Navy's insistence that Metric salvage certain cable support rails it was removing, and then reinstall those rails. Although one drawing stated that Metric was to "reinstall cable support rail," other documents indicated that Metric was to remove "and dispose" of the rails. The Navy's actions were found to be consistent with the expectation that Metric was to re-install the existing rails only if the replacement rails did not timely arrive. As such, the Navy's direction to re-install the existing rails was a constructive change to the contract, and Metric was entitled to recover its additional costs.

---

even though the owner had requested the overtime and agreed to advance the contractor's payroll, due to the contract provision requiring all changes in writing; fact that the owner advanced the overtime payments under an oral agreement was of no relevance).

[E] Delay Clauses

Page 284, add new note 1.7 at end of fourth sentence of section, ". . . Article 8.3, does not preclude delay damages":

[1.7] City of Gillette v. Hladky Constr., Inc., 2008 WY 134, 196 P.3d 184 (Wyo. Nov. 14, 2008) (the contractor cited this Treatise for the proposition that Article 8.3 of the AIA General Conditions of the Contract for Construction does not preclude delay damages, and the court agreed, holding that Article 8.3 does not provide that an extension of time is the "exclusive remedy" available for delay, but rather that the remedies available under the contract are in addition to those remedies available at law; in this case, Article 8.3.1, which provided that if the Contractor were delayed at any time in the commencement or progress of the Work by an act or neglect of the Owner or Architect, then the Contract Time would be extended for a reasonable time, was not a "no damages for delay" clause, and thus the contractor was not precluded from recovering delay damages); Trocom Constr. Corp. v. City of New York, 51 A.D.3d 533, 859 N.Y.S.2d 41 (1st Dept. May 20, 2008) (contractor sued to recover early completion bonus it failed to earn as a result of the owner's interference with its work; court held that the contract's no-damages-for-delay clause did not preclude recovery, since the loss of an incentive bonus is not delay damages but is the loss of a pay item specifically included in the contract.

Page 284, add new note 1.8 after item 1 in list at bottom of page:

[1.8] *See, e.g.,* Daniel E. Terreri & Sons, Inc. v. Mahoning County Bd. of Comm'rs, 786 N.E.2d 921 (Ohio App. 2003) (no damages for delay clause was applicable to prevent the contractor from recovering delay damages in connection with the county's 16-month delay in issuing notice to proceed); Century-Maxim Constr. Corp. v. One Bryant Park, LLC, Tishman Constr. Corp. of New York, & Bank of Am., 886 N.Y.S.2d 70 (Apr. 7, 2009) (contractor was precluded from asserting acceleration claims for lost productivity against the owner when the owner refused to grant time extensions; the contract provided that the owner would not be liable "for any loss or damage sustained by the Contractor through delay caused by the Owner, Construction Manager, Architect or any other contractor, or by abnormal weather conditions, or by any other cause"; the court found that "delay damages include both the costs involved because it takes longer to complete a job or, alternatively, as in this case, the overtime and additional costs that are expended to compete the job on time"; the court also indicated that the contractor's reliance on the schedule attached to the contract could be considered unreasonable as a matter of law, since the contract provisions clearly stated that the schedule was subject to change based upon the progress of the work).

Page 284, add at end of note 2:

See also Triple R Paving, Inc. v. Broward County, 774 So. 2d 50 (Fla. Dist. Ct. App. 2000), *reh'g denied* (2001) (clauses providing for "no damages for delay," except in the case of fraud, bad faith, or active interference by the owner, are legal and enforceable; in this case, there was sufficient evidence that a design flaw in the bridge that the plaintiff contracted to construct for the defendant was withheld from the plaintiff, thus allowing the jury to determine whether fraud, bad faith, or active interference vitiated the no damages for delay clause); Clifford R. Gray, Inc. v. City Sch. Dist. of Albany, 716 N.Y.S.2d 795 (App. Div., 3d Dept. 2000) (it is well settled that, even if a construction contract contains "[a] clause which exculpates a contractee from liability to a contractor for damages resulting from delays in the performance of the latter's work," damages may still be recovered for (1) delays caused by the contractee's bad faith or its willful, malicious, or grossly negligent conduct; (2) uncontemplated delays; (3) delays so unreasonable that they constitute an intentional abandonment of the contract by the contractee; and (4) delays resulting from the contractee's breach of a fundamental obligation of the contract); Dennis Stubbs Plumbing, Inc. v. Traveler's Cas. & Sur. Co. of Am., 67 Fed. Appx. 789 (4th Cir. 2003) (not selected for publication) (diversity action applying Virginia law; court noted that the distinction between delay damages and active interference damages has long been recognized in the law; while there is no authority from Virginia directly on point, Virginia would likely recognize an independent claim for damages resulting from active interference that were not themselves delay damages); Alamo Community College Dist. v. Browning Constr. Co., 131 S.W.3d 146 (Tex. App. 2004) (when delays encountered by a contractor on a construction project were caused by the active interference of the owner, the owner was estopped from relying on its no-damages-for-delay clause); G.M. Harston Constr. Co., Inc. v. City of Chicago, 371 F. Supp. 2d 949 (N.D. Ill. 2005) (no damages for delay clauses are enforceable, but not if the delays were not within the contemplation of the parties or were of unreasonable duration or attributable to the owner's representative's inexcusable ignorance or incompetence; in addition, while delay costs include expenses incurred employees must be kept on the job when the work has been delayed, they do not include delays caused by changes in plans that require work to be done out of sequence or in an awkward fashion; in the instant case, the owner-city could not deny that it was well aware of the countless revisions of plans that disrupted and increased the contractor's work); RaCON, Inc. v. Tuscaloosa County, 953 So. 2d 321, 2006 WL 2089892 (Ala. July 28, 2006) *as modified on denial of reh'g* (Sept. 15, 2006) (the plaintiff-contractor was barred from recovering damages for the county's delays in relocating utilities by the contract's "no damages for delay clause". None of the recognized exceptions to enforcement of the clause applied. Although the plaintiff argued that the delay was "not contemplated by the parties," a provision of the contract expressly stated that the "County shall not be liable for damages or cost to [contractor] sustained due to any interference from utilities or appurtenances or from the operations of relocating the same". Nor did the contractor provide evidence that: (1) delays extended such an unreasonable length of time so as to amount to or to justify an "abandonment" of the contract—here, the period of damages under the utility-delay claim extended less than 30 days; (2) the defendant actively interfered with the work—although the contractor alleged that it repeatedly requested the county to relocate a gas pipeline, there were no facts to support a claim that the county "actively" interfered with the contractor's work; and (3) fraud or "bad faith"—there was no evidence to support such a claim); Trataros Constr., Inc. v. New York City Housing Auth., 34 A.D.3d 451, 823 N.Y.S.2d 534 (2d Dept. Nov. 8, 2006) (the trial court did not err in granting the plaintiff leave to amend its complaint to add a claim for delay damages because, although the parties' contract contained a no-damages-for-delay clause, such clauses may not be invoked to bar damages for (1) delays caused by the contractee's bad faith or its willful, malicious, or grossly negligent conduct, (2) uncontemplated delays, (3) delays so unreasonable that they constitute an intentional abandonment of the contract by the contractee, and (4) delays resulting from the contractee's breach of a fundamental obligation of the contract. Since the plaintiff alleged facts indicating that one or more of these recognized exceptions to the enforcement of the no-damages-for-delay clause might exist, the proposed cause of action could not, at this juncture, be considered palpably insufficient or patently devoid of merit); Guy M. Cooper, Inc. v. East Penn Sch. Dist., 903 A.2d 608 (Pa. Commw. 2006), *appeal denied*, 591 Pa. 706, 918 A.2d 748 (Mar. 1, 2007) (plaintiff-subcontractor could not recover delay damages from the owner in absence of proof that any exception to enforcement of the "no damages for delay clause" applied. The plaintiff contended that the owner was responsible for delays by its failure to oversee and control the General Contractor's work and by defects in the Architect's work; however, the owner was not responsible for the General Contractor's construction delays, because the General Contractor was an independent contractor; the owner was not responsible for any delays caused by the Architect's defective plans, because the plaintiff failed to present sufficient evidence of the Architect's failure to perform under its contract—the plaintiff's expert's report did not describe an architectural standard of care, it did not describe a breach of an architectural standard of care, and it did not identify drawings alleged to be defective or ambiguous); A.G. Cullen Constr., Inc. v. State Sys. of Higher Educ., 898 A.2d 1145 (Pa. Commw. 2006) (a "no damages for delay" clause could not be enforced to preclude a contractor from recovering delay damages in light of evidence that the owner caused the 31-day delay during which the plaintiff contractor was forced to suspend work. The owner failed to include provisions for lead paint abatement in the contract specifications despite the fact it was aware of the existence of lead paint at the project site. In addition, the owner failed to address the subject of lead paint despite its promise to do so in the notice to contractors); Tupelo Redevelopment Agency v. Gray Corp., Inc., 972 So. 2d 495 (Miss. 2007) (contractual no-damages-for-delay clauses are enforceable, though they are construed strictly against those who seek their benefit; Mississippi law recognizes four exceptions to enforcing a no-damages-for-delay clause, i.e., damages may be recovered for any delay that: (1) was not intended or contemplated by the parties to be within the purview of the provision; (2) resulted from fraud, misrepresentation, or other bad faith on the part of the one seeking the benefit of the provision; (3) has extended such an unreasonable length of time that the party delayed would have been justified in abandoning the contract; or (4) is not within the specifically enumerated delays to which the clause applies; the court noted that an owner's failure to grant extensions on a timely basis can reasonably be interpreted as active interference or bad faith and would justify a damages award, and there were issues of fact in this case that supported the trial court's denial of the owner's motion for directed verdict); Dugan & Meyers Constr. Co., Inc. v. Ohio Dept. of Adm. Servs., 113 Ohio St. 3d 226, 864 N.E.2d 68 (Apr. 25, 2007), *on remand*, 2007-Ohio-4141, 2007 WL 2405923 (July 19, 2007) (Ohio Rev. Code 4113.62(C)(1), adopted in 1998, after the parties in this case had entered into the contract at issue, declared no-damages-for-delay clauses void and unenforceable as against public policy "when the cause of the delay is a proximate result of the owner's act or failure to act"; the statute also declares void and unenforceable any other contractual provision that "waives any other remedy for a construction contract when the cause of the delay is a proximate result of the owner's act or failure to act); Cleveland Constr., Inc. v. Ohio Pub. Employees Ret. Sys., 2008-Ohio-1630, 2008 WL 885841 (Ct. App. Apr. 3, 2008), *appeal not allowed*, 119 Ohio St. 3d 1447, 893 N.E.2d 517, 2008-Ohio-4487 (Sept. 10, 2008) (the court held that Ohio Rev. Code 4113.62(C)(1), which invalidates any provision that "waives or precludes liability for delay . . . when the cause of the delay is a proximate result of the owner's act or failure to act," applied to a contract provision that disclaimed owner liability for acceleration and productivity damages; the jury awarded damages to Cleveland for loss of efficiency resulting from the owner's breach in failing to properly schedule and coordinate the project; the jury found that although the project was substantially complete within the adjusted project time, Cleveland had suffered labor inefficiencies as a result of out of sequence work, activity delay, coordination issues, and the project manager's failure to address issues impacting the schedule; the owner did not dispute these findings on appeal, but argued that Cleveland's claim was barred by the contract's no-damages-for-delay clause, which specifically precluded the recovery of damages for "any delay, interference, hindrance or disruption," including "costs of acceleration, consequential damages, loss of efficiency, loss of productivity, lost opportunity costs, impact damages, lost profits or other similar remuneration"; the court held that although Ohio Rev. Code 4113.62(C)(1) does not expressly apply to "acceleration," "loss of productivity" or other types of "inefficiency" claims, such claims are embodied in the concept of delay, and where, as here, there was evidence supporting a finding that the out-of-sequence work and acceleration resulted from owner-caused delays, the statute rendered the contract clause unenforceable and Cleveland was entitled to recover its acceleration costs and inefficiency damages; James Corp. v. North Allegheny Sch. Dist., 938 A.2d 474 (Pa. Commw. Nov. 30, 2007), *reargument denied* (Jan. 30. 2008) (under Pennsylvania law, exculpatory provisions in a contract cannot be raised as a defense when (1) there is an affirmative or positive interference by the owner with the contractor's work, or (2) there is a failure on the part of the owner to act in some essential manner necessary to the prosecution of the work; affirmative or positive interference sufficient to overcome a "no damages for delay clause" may involve availability, access or design problems that preexisted the bidding process and were known by the owner but not by the contractor; here, the clause was unenforceable because the District failed to act in an essential manner under the contract by failing to obtain the required permit, failing to issue a comprehensive sequencing schedule until four months after the project began, and refusing to adjust the project completion date); Commercial Elec. Contractors, Inc. v. Pavarini Constr. Co., Inc., 50 A.D.3d 316, 856 N.Y.S.2d 46 (1st Dept. Apr. 3, 2008) (subcontractor's allegations that work was delayed because contractor failed to provide temporary heat, made changes to the work, and failed to schedule the work of the different trades in an organized manner were not sufficient to fall within the exception that the delay resulted from the contractor's "gross negligence or willful misconduct"; subcontractor alleged "nothing more than inept administration or poor planning, and the no-damages-for-delay clause therefore barred the subcontractor's claim); Eaton Elec., Inc. v. Dormitory Auth. of State of N.Y., 21 Misc. 3d 1135(A), 2008 WL 5005264 (N.Y. Sup. Ct. Kings Co. Nov. 28, 2008) (under New York law, clauses in construction contracts that bar contractors from recovering damages for delay in the performance of the contract are valid and enforceable; however, the New York Court of Appeals has recognized four exceptions to the enforceability of such a provision, i.e., a no-damage-for-delay clause may not be invoked to bar the recovery of damages for "(1) delays caused by the [owner's] bad faith or its willful, malicious, or grossly negligent conduct, (2) uncontemplated delays, (3) delays so unreasonable that they constitute an intentional abandonment of the contract by the [owner], and (4) delays resulting from the [owner's] breach of a fundamental obligation of the contract"; in this case, the contractor submitted evidentiary facts sufficiently indicative of delays beyond the contemplation of the contracting parties, as well as evidence of a willful failure by the owner to perform its fundamental affirmative contractual obligations to coordinate, schedule, and progress the work, to raise a triable issue of fact as to the enforceability of the no-damage-for-delay clause). *Cf.* Huen New York, Inc. v. Board of Educ., Clinton Cent. Sch. Dist., 890 N.Y.S.2d 748, 67 A.D.3d 1337 (App. Div. Nov. 13, 2009), *reargument denied*, 893 N.Y.S.2d 799, 70 A.D.3d 1519 (App. Div. Feb. 11, 2010) (the lower court granted defendant Board summary judgment dismissing Huen's claim for delay damages on two contracts, on the grounds that Huen's notice of claim provided after completion of the work was untimely under the "Time Limits on Claims" provision of the contract that required notice of claim within 21 days of the occurrence of the event giving rise to the claim; a New York court of appeals reversed, but not on the issue of when the event giving rise to the claim occurred, as one would expect; instead, the court held that Huen's claim for delay damages sought relief "outside the scope of the contracts" because both contracts specifically precluded damages for delay, such that the notice provisions of the contract did not apply to claims for delay damages).

Page 285, add at end of note 3:

See also, e.g., FCI Constructors v. Foothill/Eastern Transp. Corridor Agency, 2002 WL 31525388 (Cal. Ct. App., Nov. 14, 2002) (nonpublished) (government agency significantly underestimated to general contractor the amount of soil on site that had to be removed to complete road construction project; thus, soil overage was not within contemplation of the parties at the time contract was signed, and by statute in California, a no damage for delay clause is inapplicable in such circumstances; furthermore, "California courts [have] generally held that 'no damage for delay' clauses in public contracts [do] not apply to delays arising from a breach of contract caused by the other party to the contract" (citing Howard Contracting, Inc. v. G.A. MacDonald Construction Co., Inc., 71 Cal. App. 4th 38, 83 Cal. Rptr. 2d 590, *reh'g denied* (1999)); Blake Constr. Co., Inc./Poole & Kent v. Upper Occoquan Sewage Auth., 266 Va. 564, 587 S.E.2d 711 (2003) (the court noted that although a majority of courts have recognized the validity of "no-damage-for-delay" provisions, some take a restrained view of such clauses because of their harshness; thus, as of 2002, at least 13 states had adopted legislation affecting "no damage for delay" clauses, and the courts of 22 states and the District of Columbia had recognized at least one judicial exception to such clauses (citing Alain Lecusay, *The Collapsing No Damages for Delay Clause in Florida Public Construction Contracts: A Call for Legislative Change*, 15 St. Thomas L. Rev. 425, 446 (2002)); Virginia is among the states that have enacted a statute limiting the use of "no-damage-for-delay" clauses; thus, Va. Code § 2.2-4335(A) provides: "Any provision contained in any public construction contract that purports to waive, release, or extinguish the rights of a contractor to recover costs or damages for unreasonable delay in performing such contract, either on his behalf or on behalf of his subcontractor if and to the extent the delay is caused by acts or omissions of the public body, its agents or employees and due to causes within their control shall be void and unenforceable as against public policy"; in the instant case, a "no-damages-for-delay" clause that attempted to further define and limit when damages could be recovered for owner-caused delay (only for bad faith, malice, gross negligence, or abandonment of the contract) was thus void and unenforceable under the statute); Martin Brothers Contractors, Inc. v. Virginia Military Institute, 277 Va. 586, 675 S.E.2d 183, 2009 WL 1026740 (Va. Apr. 17, 2009) (the public prime contract provided that the contractor could recover damages for unreasonable owner-caused delay through submission of a change order, while the change order provision allowed recovery of only certain site overhead costs and disallowed any home office expenses; the court held that these provisions violated Va. Code § 2.2-4335(A) because they were not a liquidated delay damages provision since they essentially barred recovery of most delay expenses that would normally be incurred by the contractor); Scoccolo Constr., Inc. v. City of Renton, 158 Wash. 2d 506, 145 P.3d 371 (2006) (under Washington law [Wash. Rev. Code § 4.24.360], no-damages-for-delay clauses in construction contracts are invalid as against public policy when the delay is caused by the contractee or "persons acting for" the contractee. In this case, a city contracted to widen a street from two to four lanes, necessitating the relocation of existing utility lines and power poles. Because the utilities were operating under franchise agreements with the City, which reserved to the City the power to require the utilities to relocate their facilities at their expense in order to accommodate construction projects undertaken by the City, the utilities were "persons acting for" the city-contractee); *In re* Roy Frischhertz Constr. Co., Inc., 2007 WL 3253143 (Bankr. E.D. La. Aug. 22, 2007) (under La. Rev. Stat. § 38:2216(H), a no damages for delay clause in a public contract is void if it purports to waive the rights of a contractor to recover damages for delay when such delay is caused in whole or in part by acts or omissions within the control of the contracting public entity or persons acting on its behalf; thus, the clause in the instant case was a nullity).

Page 285, add new note 3.1 after second sentence in first paragraph:

[3.1] *But see* United States v. Blinderman Constr. Co., 2000 WL 1308084 (N.D. Ill. 2000) (plumbing subcontractor on a contract to build the New Chicago Job Corps Center for the U.S. Department of Labor brought an action under the Miller Act to recover damages allegedly incurred as a result of delays caused by the general contractor; the court held that since the contractual no damages for delay clause was enforceable under the applicable state law, the clause prevented the subcontractor from recovering such damages).

Page 285, add at end of subsection [E]:

An owner should also consider including other provisions that limit a contractor's recovery of damages, such as a provision that the contractor waives any claim for damages to the extent that the total compensation and recovery would exceed the contract price. Although such provisions are generally enforceable, the owner's conduct in a particular case may render the provision inapplicable. For example, in *John B. Conomos, Inc. v. Sun Co., Inc.*,[3.2] Sun awarded a contract to Conomos to paint industrial piping at an oil refinery project. The contract provided that if Sun terminated the contract without cause, Conomos would be paid its costs incurred prior to termination plus profit on those costs. The contract also provided that Conomos waived any claim for damages to the extent the total compensation and recovery would exceed the contract price. During performance, Sun's inspector

[3.2] 831 A.2d 696 (Pa. Super. Ct. 2003).

insisted on a higher finish in preparing the surfaces of the pipes. Conomos contended this exceeded the specification requirements and stopped work. Sun terminated the contract without cause, and Conomos sued for damages. The trial court held that Sun breached the contract by insisting on surface preparation that exceeded the contract requirements, and that Sun's breach precluded Sun from enforcing the limitation of liability clause. The superior court reversed, holding that Sun could enforce the limitation of liability provision despite its own breach of the contract.

[F] Payment Clauses

Page 285, add at end of subsection [F]:

It also protects the owner against a claim from the contractor for an equitable adjustment after final payment has been made under the contract.[3.3]

The importance of the language of the release is demonstrated in *Metric Construction, Inc. v. United States*.[3.4] The contractor, Metric, had a potential claim during construction relating to the Navy's change in the required method of delivering equipment and materials to the island jobsite from a beach landing to a pontoon landing. Before Metric's claim was submitted, Metric and the Navy executed a change order deleting and adding certain work, and extending the contract time "due to batch plant fire, weather, etc." The change order further provided that:

> Acceptance of this modification by the contractor constitutes an accord and satisfaction and represents payment in full for both time and money and for any and all costs, impact effect, and for delays and disruptions arising out of, or incidental to, the work as herein revised.

The Navy contended that this change order operated as a waiver and release of Metric's pontoon claim, which arose prior to execution of the change order. Although Metric defended by establishing that the contracting officer verbally assured Metric that the change order would not effect a waiver or release of Metric's pontoon claim, the Navy asserted that Metric's reliance on such oral assurances was precluded by the parol evidence rule (which precludes evidence of oral statements that vary or contradict a written agreement). The court found, however, that the change order was patently ambiguous in its use of the terms "etc." and "the work as herein revised." Since a contractor is obligated to resolve

---

[3.3] *In re Tyree Organization, Ltd.*, ASBCA No. 53167, 01-2 BCA ¶ 31,480 (2001) ("final payment to the contractor by the government bars consideration of any claims for damages under the contract which are submitted subsequent to final payment . . . except those specifically excepted" (quoting from Mingus Constructors, Inc. v. United States, 812 F.2d 1387, 1391 (Fed. Cir. 1987))).

[3.4] 81 Fed. Cl. 804 (2008).

a patent ambiguity, evidence was permissible to show how the ambiguity was resolved, including parol evidence. The court noted that in addition to Metric's undisputed testimony regarding the contracting officer's statements, the evidence included a document written by a succeeding contracting officer after the change order was executed, wherein the officer stated "these are not the last of the claims [Metric] will be filing—I imagine the pontoon issue will be a doozie!!" Based upon the ambiguous language of the change order, and the additional evidence submitted by Metric, the court found that the change order did not constitute a waiver or release of Metric's pontoon claim.

In *Bell BCI Co. v. United States*,[3.5] the court rejected the owner's claim that contract modifications executed by the contractor, Bell, constituted an accord and satisfaction of Bell's cumulative impact claims. The modification with the broadest release language, Modification 93, provided that the parties agreed to the stated increase in the contract amount:

> as full and equitable adjustment for the remaining direct and indirect costs of [the addition of a sixth floor] and full and equitable adjustment for all delays resulting from any and all Government changes transmitted to the Contractor on or before August 31, 2000. . . . The modification agreed to herein is a fair and equitable adjustment for the Contractor's direct and indirect costs. This modification provides full compensation for the changed work, including both Contract cost and Contract time. The Contractor hereby releases the Government from any and all liability under the Contract for further equitable adjustment attributable to the Modification.

The court found that neither Modification 93 nor any of the other contract modifications included any government payment or other consideration to Bell for a disruption, cumulative impact, or labor inefficiency claim. Similarly, none of the modifications contained specific language waiving or releasing such a claim. The court noted that although the government had included the contracting officer on its witness list, she was not called to testify, and the court could therefore infer that her testimony would not have supported the government's position. Further, many of the events supporting Bell's cumulative impact claim occurred after Modification 93. As such, Bell had not waived or released its cumulative impact claims. On appeal, the Federal Circuit Court reversed the award on the grounds that Bell waived its delay claims in connection with certain modifications, and remanded to the lower court to determine which delays, if any, were not waived.

In contrast, the court found the contractor had waived its claims in *Addicks Services, Inc. v. GGP-Bridgeland, L.P.*[3.6] Pursuant to the payment provisions of the contract, the contractor, Addicks, submitted executed interim lien waivers

---

[3.5] 81 Fed. Cl. 617 (2008), *aff'd in part, vacated in part, remanded*, 570 F.3d 1337 (Fed. Cir. June 25, 2009), *reh'g and reh'g en banc denied* (Oct. 9, 2009), *on remand*, 72 Fed. Cl. 164 (Feb. 24, 2010).

[3.6] 596 F.3d 286 (5th Cir. (Tex.) Feb. 8, 2010).

each month to obtain monthly progress payments; the lien waivers stated that Addicks represented that the monthly payment received constituted full payment for all work performed as of the date of the waiver, and that Addicks waived any claim "for damages due to delay, hindrance, interference, acceleration, inefficiencies or extra work, or any other claim of any kind" as of the date of the waiver, "except as follows: _____." Addicks sued to recover damages for extra work and delay, and the owner's motion for partial summary judgment as to all damages allegedly incurred prior to the date of the last executed interim waiver was granted by the lower court. The appellate court confirmed, holding the fact that the owner would not permit Addicks to include extra work in its pay applications unless there was a signed change order did not constitute a course of performance whereby the owner waived enforcement of the releases in the interim waivers. The court also found that the language of the interim waiver did not evidence a mutual intent that each release applied only to the extent of the amount specified in the interim waiver as having been paid, or that the release applied only to "Work" as defined in the contract, and not extra work. Finally, the fact that the owner issued change orders for extra work that had been covered by previously executed interim waivers did not preclude the owner from enforcing the waivers as to remaining claims.

[G] Termination Clauses

Page 286, add at end of note 4:

See also Appeal of Kostmayer Construction, LLC, ASBCA No. 55053, 2008 WL 2345883, 08-1 BCA P 33869 (May 30, 2008) (the government's termination for cause was improper because it was based upon an inaccurate and incomplete analysis of the percentage of completion at the time of termination; the bar graph schedule utilized by the contractor included only pay items, thereby omitting a work item that was 25% of the total contract work and had already been completed; the government further erred in focusing on percentage of completion of compacted fill alone, when both compacted and uncompacted fill were critical; further, the government's own internal analysis of progress during construction reflected that the contractor was ahead of schedule; the government also failed to recognize the contractor's commitment of additional resources, which would have allowed the contractor to complete the contract work within the time allowed); Appeal of ALKAI Consultants, LLC, ASBCA 55581, 2009 WL 249763, 09-1 BCA P 34058 (Jan. 22, 2009) (termination for cause of contract to clean a digester at a wastewater treatment plant was improper where the contracting officer misunderstood the completion date to be June 1, 2006, rather than June 30, 2006, and ordered the contractor to demobilize on June 14, 2006 for failure to timely complete; court found that the contractor could have timely completed the work but for an unexpectedly high petroleum content in the digester and the government's failure to cooperate by making additional drying beds available; termination for cause was therefore converted to a termination for convenience).

Page 286, add at end of subsection:

If an owner is determined to have improperly terminated the contractor for cause, the termination will be considered a termination for convenience, which may preclude the owner from charging the costs to complete to the terminated contractor. For example, in *Appeal of Abcon Associates, Inc.*,[4.1] the United States Postal Service terminated Abcon's contract for default based upon delays in performing the work and paid Abcon's surety $2.7 million to complete the remaining $1.7 million of base contract work. The Court of Federal Claims found that Abcon was not in default at the time of termination, since Abcon had been entitled to time extensions pursuant to Requests for Equitable Adjustment that were denied by the Postal Service, and the termination was thereby converted to a termination for convenience. The contracting officer subsequently determined that Abcon could not recover any of the costs that had been submitted in the REAs because the sum of the payments made to Abcon and the surety exceeded the contract price. The Board of Contract Appeals reversed that decision, holding that the default termination became a convenience termination of the entire contract, such that there was no basis upon which to reduce the contract price limit by amounts paid for completion of the work. The Board further held that Abcon was entitled to recover costs that were submitted in the REAs even though the REAs did not comply with the requirements of the Contract Disputes Act. Since the termination for convenience clause required payment to the terminated contractor for all work performed before the effective date of the termination, to the extent the contractor was not already paid, Abcon was entitled to recover "its reasonable, allocable, and allowable costs, including costs related to unpriced changes, constructive changes, suspensions of work, differing site conditions, defective specifications, and even for some work performed that might not have complied in all respects with the contract."

[H] Termination for Convenience Clauses

Page 287, add new note 4.2 at end of subsection:

[4.2] *See, e.g.*, Avatar Dev. Corp. v. DePani Constr., Inc., 834 So. 2d 873 (Fla. App. 2002), *reh'g denied* (2003), *review denied sub nom.* DePani Constr., Inc. v. Avatar Dev. Corp., 848 So. 2d 1153 (Fla. 2003) (Florida court enforced a unilateral termination without cause provision, noting the distinction between

[4.1] PSBCA No. 5291, 2008 WL 53123 (Jan. 2, 2008).

unilateral termination, which only allows the contractor to recover for work performed, and termination for convenience, which generally authorizes payment of termination costs such as settlements with subcontractors, administrative expenses, and other indirect costs).

Page 287, add at end of subsection:

However, in *Jeffrey B. Peterson & Associates v. Dayton Metropolitan Housing Authority*,[4.3] the court held that although a termination for convenience clause is enforceable, it will not support termination for *any* reason. Rather, implicit in such a clause is a requirement that the termination decision be exercised in "good faith" and not constitute an "abuse of discretion." In this case, although the trial court failed to determine whether the defendant used bad faith or abused its discretion in terminating the plaintiff, the court's error was harmless in the absence of any supporting evidence of such conduct.

Similarly, in *RAM Engineering & Construction, Inc. v. University of Louisville*,[4.4] the court held that exercise of a termination for convenience clause is subject to the limitation of the implied covenant of "good faith and fair dealing," which applies to all contracts. Thus, although the government may terminate contracts for convenience, that right cannot supersede the good faith duty imposed under Kentucky law to do "everything necessary" to carry out the contract. That duty limits a contracting officer's discretion to terminate a contract for convenience and indicates that termination is justified only when there is a substantial "change of circumstances." In this case, no substantial change of circumstances was proven when the University itself was responsible for the situation it contended justified termination of the contract with plaintiff. "Relying on circumstances the University itself created simply is not grounds for termination under the changed circumstances standard." The court remanded for further consideration of whether the University acted improperly in terminating its contract with plaintiff.

In *In re Howell It Is*,[4.5] the U.S. Forest Service awarded a lump sum contract to Howell for monitoring 20 units of land in national forests in California. The specific units of land to be monitored were to be designated by the agency after contract award. The agency designated and paid for only 18 units, and the remaining units were assigned to other contractors. When Howell objected, the agency issued a termination for the convenience of the government, deleting two units of land. Howell filed a claim for the balance of the contract price. The Board ruled that since the notice of termination was issued after the deadline for contract completion, and the government provided no support for a retroactive termination for convenience, Howell was entitled to the remaining contract price for the two units, stating:

[4.3] 2000 WL 1006562 (Ohio Ct. App. 2000).

[4.4] 127 S.W.3d 579 (Ky. 2003), *reh'g denied* (2004).

[4.5] AGBCA No. 2003-137-2 (2003).

> To permit the use of the termination for the convenience clause under the given contract and facts, would change the contract into an indefinite quantity contract, containing risks different from those in the firm, fixed-price contract utilized. The Termination for Convenience clause is not to be used to reform the contract. This is not the situation where the Government encountered a true reduction in its overall requirements.

[I] Clauses for Delayed Completion

Page 287, add before last paragraph:

In *Merrillville Conservancy District v. Atlas Excavating, Inc.*,[4.6] the court held that a contract provision headed "Liquidated Damages" did not constitute a liquidated damages provision. In that case, the contract included the following provision:

> LIQUIDATED DAMAGES: Should the Contractor fail to perform the work within the period of time stipulated in the contract agreement, the Contractor shall pay to Owner, as liquidated damages and not as a penalty, all inspection and supervision costs and other expenses accruing to the Owner, but not to exceed $500 per calendar day of default, unless extensions of time granted by the Owner specifically provide for the waiving of liquidated damages.

The court held that this provision allowed the District to recover only its actual costs resulting from the contractor's delay in completion, with a cap of $500 per calendar delay. In order to effectively provide for liquidated damages, the contract must provide a set amount reflecting a reasonable forecast of actual damages, and that daily amount cannot vary.

§ 14.03 NEGOTIATING GENERAL CONTRACT TERMS AND SUBCONTRACT TERMS: GENERAL CONTRACTOR'S PERSPECTIVE

[D] Claims for Concealed Conditions

Page 291, add at end of note 7:

See also Metropolitan Transit Auth. v. Pyramid Constructors, Inc., 2001 WL 1382089 (Tex. Ct. App., Nov. 8, 2001) (unpublished) (contractor's right to recover damages from owner for breach of differing site conditions clause is not

[4.6] 764 N.E.2d 718 (Ind. Ct. App. 2002).

precluded by contractor's failure to pay subcontractor's invoices; owner's liability is directly to contractor, *i.e.*, it has no privity with subcontractor to allow it to contest subcontractor's right to recovery as a means to avoid owner's contractual liability to contractor); Southern Comfort Builders, Inc. v. United States, 67 Fed. Cl. 124 (Fed. Cl. 2005) (contractor was under contract with the National Aeronautics and Space Administration (NASA) to install heating, ventilation, and air conditioning (HVAC) equipment, along with the associated ductwork, wiring, and piping, in Mobile Launch Platforms (MLPs) for the NASA space shuttles at Kennedy Space Center in Florida; the contractor's discovery of lead-based paint on the decks of the MLPs constituted an unforeseeable differing site condition, as the contractor claimed, because there was no indication in the contract documents that the MLP surfaces contained lead-based paint, and a reasonable inspection of the MLP would not have revealed the presence of lead-based paint; however, because NASA compensated the contractor $38,839.32 through several contract modifications for the lead abatement work, which the contractor completed through a subcontractor, and the evidence indicated that this constituted full compensation for the work, the contractor could not recover additional damages in the instant action).

Page 291, add at end of note 8:

See also, e.g., George Sollitt Constr. Co. v. United States, 64 Fed. Cl. 229 (Ct. Cl. Feb. 23, 2005) (evidence before court did not show that contractor gave government notice of differing site conditions before adding extra work to the contract, as required by the Differing Site Conditions clause; nevertheless, in order for government to prevail in a case in which notice (of a differing site condition) has not been provided on a timely basis by the contractor, government has burden of proving that the untimeliness caused prejudice to its case; here, government showed that it *was* prejudiced by lack of timely notice of differing site condition, because contractor's solution may have been entirely unnecessary, or a lower-cost solution might have been preferred); Renda Marine, Inc. v. United States, 66 Fed. Cl. 639 (Fed. Cl. Jul. 28, 2005) (although FAR § 52.236-2(a) requires a contractor to establish as a threshold matter when attempting to prove that it encountered a Type I differing site condition that it "promptly, and before the conditions are disturbed, g[a]ve a written notice to the Contracting Officer" of the alleged differing site condition, the requirement that notice be "in writing," has been relaxed by the courts; rather, notice need not be in any particular form—it may be oral and given to the contracting officer's representative, and it may even be waived if the court finds that defendant had actual or constructive notice of the conditions encountered; when proceeding on a theory that the government had actual or constructive notice of a differing site condition, the contractor can recover if it proves that defendant was not prejudiced by the lack of written or oral notice; on the other hand, the government can defeat recovery by proving that it *was* prejudiced or disadvantaged by plaintiff's failure to give notice, and it can satisfy this burden by establishing that the passage of time obscured the elements of proof or that the defendant could have minimized the extra work and attendant costs if notice had been given). *Cf.* Ronald Adams Contractor, Inc. v. Mississippi Transp. Comm'n, 777 So. 2d 649 (Miss. 2000), *reh'g denied* (2001) (trial court erred in granting the defendant partial summary judgment with regard to the contractor's claim under a differing site conditions provision; although the clause mandated that the government be given written notice of unforeseen conditions, the defendant in this case arguably had *actual notice* as a result of its engineer's investigation and approval of extra work; the court remanded the action for the jury to determine (1) whether the contractor actually encountered a "differing site condition," and (2) whether the contract allowed the defendant's engineer to authorize additional compensation for extra work without the defendant Commission first executing a supplemental agreement and making an appropriate entry in its minutes); Appeals of Fuel Tank Maint. Co, LLC, ASBCA Nos. 54402, 54516, 2008 WL 2579747, 08-2 BCA P 33888 (June 12, 2008) (requirement of written notice of differing site condition will not preclude a valid claim where the government was otherwise aware of the operative facts and failed to establish that it was prejudiced by the absence of written notice; contractor gave written notice on two occasions that demolition of the concrete was "difficult," and advised the government that it supported its subcontractor's claim of "defective specifications" based upon the hard concrete; although the claim was actually a differing site conditions claim, the court found that the government had an opportunity to investigate the conditions at the site to the extent it was not already aware of them, and was therefore not prejudiced by the absence of the required notice); Koga Eng'g & Constr., Inc. v. State of Hawaii, 122 Haw. 60, 222 P.3d 979 (Haw. Jan. 14, 2010) (summary judgment in contractor's favor that it had not failed to provide the required notice should not have been granted; the contract allowed late notice of claim only if the state was not prejudiced, there was evidence that the state had been prejudiced since it had not monitored the contractor's costs, and that was an issue of fact that should have precluded summary judgment. *But see* Razorback Contractors of Kansas, Inc. v. Board of County Comm'rs of Johnson County, 227 P.3d 29 (Kan. App. Apr. 2, 2010) (contractor was precluded from asserting a differing site conditions claims based upon adverse weather due to contractor's failure to meet the requirement of written notice of the claim within 30 days after the start of the event giving rise to the claim; although the contractor advised the owner of the wet surface conditions in a number of project meetings in September through December 2004, and requested and received a time extension in February 2005 based on the adverse weather, the contractor did not submit a written request for additional compensation based on weather until June 2005, which clearly did not meet the contractual notice requirements; the court rejected the contractor's argument that actual notice to the owner was sufficient, declining to create an "actual notice" exception).

Page 292, add at end of note 9:

See, e.g., CEMS, Inc. v. United States, 59 Fed. Cl. 168 (Ct. Cl. 2003) (the purpose of a differing site conditions clause is to shift the risk of adverse subsurface or latent physical conditions from the contractor, who normally bears such risk under a fixed-price contract, to the government; however, such a clause does not shift all unanticipated risk in a project's site conditions to the government; the government bears only those risks that encourage "more accurate bidding"; those risks are shifted to the government so that contractors will not add to their bids the cost of assessing whether adverse subsurface conditions exist or the cost of confronting such conditions if and when they are encountered; in this case, involving construction of a bicycle path, the contractor established differing site conditions because the contractor encountered ongoing and pervasive seepage that kept the subgrade wet, preventing or impairing compaction and grading; moreover, a status report for the bicycle path project stated that during excavation, "natural springs were encountered," and an inspector noted in his daily logs that there was "extreme saturation" of the existing soils; based on the evidence in the record, the court found the plaintiff encountered a Type I differing site condition [subsurface or latent physical conditions at the site which differ materially from those indicated in this contract], and awarded the contractor the additional costs incurred in addressing the differing site condition); Baldi Bros. Constructors v. United States, 50 Fed. Cl. 74 (Ct. Cl. 2001) (in order to succeed on a claim for differing site conditions, the contractor must "promptly . . . give a written notice to the Contracting Officer" of the differing conditions before the conditions are disturbed, as provided in FAR § 52.236-2; moreover, the contractor is charged with notice of the information appearing in contract documents, such as field logs, boring samples, and topographical maps, while the Government is liable for damages attributable to misstatements of fact (in a contract or specifications) that are representations made to the contractor); Rapid Demolition Co., Inc. v. State of New York, 54 A.D.3d 921, 864 N.Y.S.2d 503 (App. Div. 2d Dept. Sept. 23, 2008), *leave to appeal denied*, 22 N.Y.3d 714, 901 N.E.2d 763, 873 N.Y.S.2d 269 (Jan. 13, 2009) (bridge demolition contractor was denied recovery for a differing site condition even though the actual thickness of the concrete deck overlay on the bridge was substantially greater than depicted in the contract documents; the contract contained the standard provision requiring the contractor to inspect the site, and further provided that the contractor would make no claim against the DOT by reason of any representations; the contract drawings depicting the overlay contained a note stating that the drawings were not based on actual field conditions; the court found that "even a visual inspection of the concrete overlay would have revealed its true thickness;"). *See also* Hazlehurst Lumber Co., Inc. v. Mississippi Forestry Comm'n, 983 So. 2d 309, 2008 WL 975077 (Miss. Apr. 10, 2008), *reh'g denied* (June 19, 2008) (where contract provided a data sheet containing a "100 percent inventory" listing the number and size of the timber to be removed, the contractor could not recover for losses incurred when the actual tree count was substantially less than stated on the data sheet, since the contract contained a provision disclaiming the accuracy of the data sheet and requiring the contractor to inspect the site and make its own determination as to the amount of timber to be removed).

Page 292, add at end of note 10:

See also, e.g., Trucco Constr. Co., Inc. v. Columbus, 2006-Ohio-6984, 2006 WL 3825262 (Ohio Ct. App. 10th Dist. 2006) (in order to recover under either a differing site conditions clause or the *Spearin* doctrine, a contractor must show that the contract contained an affirmative representation regarding the subsurface physical condition that forms the basis of the claim. In this case, the only representation on which the contractor based its claim was an engineer's estimate that dewatering would comprise one percent of the total cost of the job. However, a dewatering cost estimate, without more, does not constitute an affirmative representation about the conditions that will be encountered on the site. Thus, the contractor was unable to satisfy the first element of its differing site conditions claim, and summary judgment was properly granted against it).

[E] Extra Work Clauses

Page 292, add new note 10.1 at end of last sentence in section:

[10.1] Compliance with contract notice requirements is important in recovering costs of extra work. *See* Barclay White Skanska, Inc. v. Battelle Memorial Institute, 262 Fed. Appx. 556, 2008 WL 238562 (4th Cir. (Md.) Jan. 29, 2008) (the district court erred in finding that the contractor's written statement that it was considering filing a claim for delay was inadequate notice under the contract; evidence indicated that the contractor sent its last payment application to the owner, indicating its position that it was owed $13,426,444.72 for the entirety of the contract, and when the contractor received the check and final payment letter, it responded by rejecting the check and indicating it was of the position that the owner owed more money under the contract; the final payment application and subsequent letter were sufficient to fulfill the written notice requirement).

§ 14.04 CLAUSES THAT THE GENERAL CONTRACTOR SHOULD INCLUDE IN THE SUBCONTRACT

[B] Incorporation by Reference Clauses

Page 293, add new note 10.1.1 at end of section:

[10.1.1] *But see* Industrial Window Corp. v. Federal Ins. Co., 565 F. Supp. 2d 513 (S.D.N.Y. July 16, 2008) (subcontract provided: "This Agreement specifically incorporates by reference herein all of the Contract Documents, including, but not limited to, the Plans and Specifications issued by, [sic] and the provisions and terms of all existing, or issued during the course of this Agreement, standard details, standard documents, standard drawings, and all applicable provisions which govern the installation and operation of all work"; court held that this clause was not sufficiently clear and unequivocal to meet the requirements under New York law for incorporating the prime contract's alternative dispute resolution procedure); Industrial Window Corp. v. Federal Ins. Co., 609 F. Supp. 2d 329, 2009 WL 921120 (S.D.N.Y. Apr. 6, 2009) (same); Waldner Consulting, Inc. v. Miller Contracting, Inc., 152 Wash. App. 1015, 2009 WL 2942657 (Wash. App. Sept. 15, 2009) (subcontract provided that the prime "Contract, conditions, specifications, schedules and addenda are incorporated herein," and further specifically incorporated the prime contract's definition of the "Work" and certain other provisions; court held that the subcontractor's claims were not time-barred by the prime contract's requirement that all claims be instituted within 180 days after substantial completion of the work; the subcontract did not evidence the parties "clear intent to incorporate all the provisions of the prime contract," and that a subcontract provision requiring the parties endeavor to negotiate and settle any contract disputes would be inconsistent with the 180-day provision). *See also* Encon Utah, LLC v. Fluor Ames Kraemer, LLC, 2009 UT 7, 2009 WL 172438 (2009), *reh'g denied* (June 24, 2009) (the prime contract, which was incorporated into the subcontract, provided that damages upon termination for convenience were limited to the value of the work performed, whereas the subcontract's termination for convenience provision contained no such limitation; the court rejected the contractor's argument that the prime contract should govern, finding that the prime contract's provision applied exclusively to the relationship between the owner and the contractor, whereas the subcontract's clause applied exclusively to the relationship between the contractor and the subcontractor. There was thus no conflict between the two provisions, so it was irrelevant that the subcontract stated that the prime contract took precedence over the subcontract in the event of conflict).

[D] Indemnification Clauses

Page 293, add new note 10.1.2. at end of first sentence in first full paragraph:

[10.1.2] *See* Brooks v. Judlau Contracting, Inc., 898 N.E.2d 549, 869 N.Y.S.2d 366 (Oct. 21, 2008) (partially negligent contractor held entitled to enforce an indemnification provision in the subcontract, but only for that portion of the damages attributable to the subcontractor's negligence; contractor would not thereby obtain indemnification for its own negligence, which was precluded by statute).

Page 294, add new note 10.1.3 at end of second sentence in first full paragraph:

[10.1.3] *See* Crawford v. Weather Shield Mfg., Inc., 44 Cal. 4th 541, 187 P.3d 424, 79 Cal. Rptr. 3rd 721 (July 21, 2008) (where a subcontractor agreed to defend and indemnify the general contractor, the subcontractor was obligated to defend the contractor against claims alleging construction defects arising from the subcontractor's negligence, even though the subcontractor was ultimately determined not to have been negligent and the subcontract gave the contractor the right of indemnity only if the subcontractor was negligent; the court based this holding both on a California statute that imposes a duty to defend upon every indemnitor, and on the subcontract language that confirmed that duty; the court held that the duty to defend arose immediately upon the indemnitee's tender of the defense of pending claims, and disapproved decisions holding that the duty to defend arose only if the indemnitor became liable for indemnity; the court noted that a newly revised California statute (Cal. Civ. Code Section 2782) prohibited an indemnitee from ultimately bearing defense costs to the extent the indemnitor is found negligent, but this statute was not retroactive).

[G] No Damages for Delay Clauses

Page 295, add new note 10.2 at end of example of no damages for delay clause:

[10.2] Another example of a no damages for delay clause may be found in the court's decision in J.A. Jones Constr. Co. v. Lehrer McGovern Bovis, Inc., 89 P.3d 1009 (Nev. May 19, 2004), *reh'g denied* (Aug. 26, 2004), *reconsid. en banc denied* (Nov. 4, 2004). In that case, the court held the following no damages for delay clause to be valid and enforceable:

> Should Contractor [plaintiff subcontractor] be obstructed or delayed in the commencement, prosecution or completion of the Work, without fault on its part, by reason of: failure to act, direction, order, neglect, delay or default of the Owner, the Architect/Engineer, Construction Manager, or any Other Contractor employed upon the Project; by changes in the Work; fire, lightning,

> earthquake, enemy action, act of God or similar catastrophe; by Government restrictions in respect to materials or labor; or by an industry-wide strike beyond Contractor's reasonable control, then Contractor shall be entitled to an extension of time to perform the Work which shall be equal to the time lost by reason of any or all of the causes aforesaid. . . . Contractor expressly agrees not to make, and hereby waives, any claim for damages, including those resulting from increased labor or material costs, on account of any delay, obstruction or hindrance for any cause whatsoever, whether or not foreseeable and whether or not anticipated including but not limited to the aforedescribed causes, and agrees that the sole right and remedy therefor shall be an extension of time, provided the requisite condition as to written claim has been met.

Page 295, add new note 10.3 after first sentence of last paragraph on page:

[10.3] *Cf.* Ohio Rev. Code § 4113.62(C)(1):

> Any provision of a construction contract, agreement, or understanding, or specification or other documentation that is made a part of a construction contract, agreement, or understanding, that waives or precludes liability for delay during the course of a construction contract when the cause of the delay is a proximate result of the owner's act or failure to act, or that waives any other remedy for a construction contract when the cause of the delay is a proximate result of the owner's act or failure to act, is void and unenforceable as against public policy.

In Inland Waters Pollution Controls, Inc. v. Marra/Majestic Joint Venture, 2009 WL 700773 (N.D. Ohio Mar. 13, 2009), the court held that the parties could negotiate limitations on delay-related damages without running afoul of § 4113.62(C)(1). Thus, the parties' agreement that the general contractor could receive up to $4,400,000 as compensation for any future claims that might arise could not, "by any stretch, be fit into the letter or meaning of 'no-damages-for-delay-clauses' prohibited by § 4113.62(C)(1)."

Page 296, add at end of note 11:

See also Bovis Lend Lease LMB Inc. v. GCT Venture, Inc., 6 A.D.3d 228, 775 N.Y.S.2d 259 (1st Dept. Apr. 13, 2004) (while clauses in construction contracts exculpating parties from damages for delay in performance are generally valid and enforceable, such clauses may not be invoked to bar damages for (1) delays caused by the protected party's bad faith or its willful, malicious, or grossly negligent conduct; (2) uncontemplated delays; (3) delays so unreasonable that they constitute an intentional abandonment of the contract; and (4) delays resulting from breach of a fundamental obligation of the contract; in this case, plaintiff's evidence opposing summary judgment raised material issues of fact concerning applicability of three of the four exceptions: evidence was submitted to indicate that the delays were so unreasonable (two-and-a-half years), and the changes in the contracted work so dramatic (value of the work performed was more than twice the original contract price), that triable issues of fact were raised as to whether delays went beyond contemplation of contracting parties, or whether delays were so unreasonable that they constituted an intentional abandonment of the contract; in addition, the fact that appellants allegedly allowed tenant-requested design changes to continue unabated, thereby increasing the scope of the subcontractor's work and preventing completion in a timely fashion, raised an issue as to whether delays were caused by bad faith and/or willful and grossly negligent conduct on appellants' part); Metropolitan Steel Indus., Inc. v. Perini Corp., 6 Misc. 3d 1002A, 2004 N.Y. Slip. Op. 51698U (June 14, 2004), *aff'd*, 23 A.D.3d 205, 803 N.Y.S.2d 549, (App. Div. 1 Dept. Nov. 10, 2005) (no damages for delay provision must be enforced unless the party seeking the delay damages can establish that the delays were not contemplated at the time of the subcontract and were caused by another party's breach of a fundamental obligation expressly imposed by the subcontract, bad faith, willful misconduct or gross negligence); J.A. Jones Constr. Co. v. Lehrer McGovern Bovis, Inc., 89 P.3d 1009 (Nev. 2004) (the following exceptions to enforcement of a no damages for delay clause aid in enforcing the implied covenant of good faith and fair dealing that exists in every Nevada contract and essentially forbids arbitrary, unfair acts by one party that disadvantage the other: (1) delays so unreasonable in length as to amount to project abandonment; (2) delays caused by the other party's fraud, misrepresentation, concealment, or other bad faith; and (3) delays caused by the other party's active interference; court, however, rejected an exception for "delays not contemplated by the parties at the time they entered into the contract," because, knowing that unforeseen delays can occur, parties can bargain accordingly, *i.e.*, subcontractor can protect itself from the risk of unforeseen delay simply by adjusting its bid price in recognition of the potential additional costs or by refusing to accept such a provision in the contract); MacQuesten General Contracting, Inc. v. HCE, Inc., 296 F. Supp. 2d 437 (S.D.N.Y. 2003) (exculpatory language that purports to preclude damages for all delays resulting from any cause whatsoever are not read literally; even with such a clause, damages may be recovered for: (1) delays caused by the contractee's bad faith or its willful, malicious, or grossly negligent conduct, (2) uncontemplated delays, (3) delays so unreasonable that they constitute an intentional abandonment of the contract by the contractee, and (4) delays resulting from the contractee's breach of a fundamental obligation of the contract; in this case, there was evidence bringing the case within at least two of these exceptions—first, much of the delay in proceeding with the project was attributable to the discovery of unanticipated rock that impeded foundation work, and second, the general contractor was tardy in producing revised architectural and shop drawings which, in turn, inhibited the subcontractor from performing its work; accordingly, the subcontract's no-damages-for-delay clause did not bar an award of delay damages; the court remanded for a new trial on damages because the proof presented by the subcontractor in support of its claim for delay damages was legally insufficient); S.N. Tannor, Inc. v. A.F.C. Enters., Inc., 276 A.D.2d 363, 714 N.Y.S.2d 273 (1st Dept. 2000) (general contractor was entitled to the protection of the subcontract's no damages for delay provisions because the delays it caused the subcontractor were not (1) the product of willful, malicious, or grossly negligent conduct; (2) uncontemplated; (3) so unreasonable as to constitute an intentional abandonment of the contract; or (4) the result of a breach of a fundamental obligation of the contract; rather, the conduct of the general contractor alleged to have caused the complained-of delays and extra work amounted to no more than inept administration and thus fell within the subcontract's exculpatory provisions); Landis & Gyr Powers, Inc. v. Berley Indus., Inc., 298 A.D.2d 435, 750 N.Y.S.2d 82 (2d Dept. 2002) ("It is well established that no-damage-for-delay clauses commonly included in construction contracts are enforceable unless the claimed delays were not contemplated by the parties at the time they entered into the contract or the delay damages were the result of the contractee's intentional wrongdoing, gross negligence or willful misconduct"; in this case, plaintiff-subcontractor failed to raise any factual issue that the delays were not contemplated by the parties, or that the general contractor's conduct was intentional, willful, or grossly negligent; thus, summary judgment dismissing the cause of action was properly granted); Kiewit Constr. Co. v. Capital Elec. Constr. Co., Inc., 2005 WL 2563042 (D. Neb., Oct. 12, 2005) (no damages for delay clauses are generally enforceable because, given that one of the main purposes of construction contracts is to allocate the risks of construction among the parties, no damages for delay clauses are used to assign the risk of delays, for whatever cause, to one of the contracting parties, with the assumption that the party bearing the risk has bargained for a price that covers the burden of carrying the risk; a clause becomes unenforceable only with proof of concealment, misrepresentation, fraud, bad faith, or malicious intent; in the absence of proof of any such conduct in the instant case, a subcontractor's pre-acceleration claim for damages was barred by the valid no damages for delay clause in its contract with the general contractor); U.S. *ex rel.* Tennessee Valley Marble Holding Co. v. Grunley Constr., 433 F. Supp. 2d 104 (D.D.C. 2006) (under Maryland law, a literal enforcement approach to no damages for delay clauses is applied, pursuant to which an unambiguous provision precluding damages for delay will be enforced regardless of whether the type of delay was contemplated by the parties. Thus, in the instant case, the plaintiff contractor could not recover even if it did not understand the word "delay" to encompass a postponement in furnishing field verifications); Scandale Associated Builders & Engineers, Ltd. v. Bell Justice Facilities Corp., 455 F. Supp. 2d 271 (M.D. Pa. 2006) (there was a genuine issue of material fact whether a no damages for delay clause could be enforced to bar recovery by a subcontractor or whether the exculpatory provision could not be raised as a defense because either (1) there was an affirmative or positive interference by the contractor with the subcontractor's work, or (2) there was a failure on the part of the contractor to act in some essential matter necessary to the prosecution of the work. The plaintiff subcontractor provided a non-exclusive list of twelve alleged acts or omissions by the contractor, including such items as earthwork delays resulting in a shut down for approximately two months, change in performance conditions, re-sequencing of work areas, and failure of the contractor to properly supervise and coordinate the work of all subcontractors. The contractor argued, on the other hand, that the subcontractor's allegations were unsupported by the record and that the subcontractor and other actors caused some of the delays, that the subcontractor was not precluded from working during the earthwork shutdown, and that, in fact, the subcontractor continued to construct footings during the alleged shutdown); The Law Co., Inc. v. Mohawk Constr. & Supply Co., Inc., 2010 WL 973032 (D. Kan. Mar. 16, 2010) (under Kansas law, agreements limiting liability are valid and enforceable so long as they were "fairly and knowingly entered into and if not in violation of other provisions of law"; the no-damages-for-delay clause in the instant case provided that an "extension of time shall be Subcontractor's sole remedy for delay," except when the delay was intentionally caused by the owner or prime contractor, and that changes in scope or suspension of the subcontractor's work would not be deemed intentional interference; the subcontract further provided that the subcontractor "recognizes that revisions will be made to the Schedule and agrees to comply with such revisions without additional compensation" and "Subcontractor agrees to make no claims against Contractor or Owner should the Schedule not be strictly adhered to"; the Subcontractor, Mohawk, contended that the no damages for delay clause should not apply in this case because actions of the owner, Law, represented a "fundamental breach" of the subcontract, citing three New York cases finding that such a breach was an exception to no damages for delay clause; the court held that even if the "fundamental breach" exception were adopted in Kansas, the contractor's delay in furnishing materials and the out-of-sequence work that resulted did not indicate that the eight-month delay "completely frustrated project completion," and therefore did not constitute a fundamental breach; the court refused to recognize an exception for delays "not contemplated by the parties," and found that the delay in this case was not an "unreasonable" delay; the court held that the subcontract precluded the subcontractor's recovery of delay damages, was freely entered into and was not unconscionable, and was therefore valid and enforceable under Kansas law); Commercial Electrical Contractors, Inc. v. Pavarini Construction Co., Inc., 856 N.Y.S.2d 46 (1st Dept. Apr. 3, 2008) (court noted a no-damages-for-delay clause is unenforceable if the delays were caused by the contractor's bad faith or its willful, malicious, or grossly negligent conduct; were uncontemplated; were so unreasonable that they constitute intentional abandonment of the contract; or resulted from breach of a fundamental obligation of the contract; the subcontractor alleged that the work was delayed between 8 and 20 months because the contractor failed to provide temporary heat as planned, permitted sugarblasting of the concrete walls with high pressure water when the subcontractor was scheduled to perform electrical work, and failed to schedule the work of the different trades in an organized manner; the court found that the alleged conduct did not fall within any of the exceptions to enforceability of the no-damages-for-delay cause; although the contractor's conduct constituted "inept administration or poor planning," it did not amount to gross negligence or willful misconduct; further, it was foreseeable that there would be changes in the work and delays of the type alleged, and the contract included a procedure to deal with delays; finally, the delay alleged was not long enough to qualify as abandonment of the contract); Mafco Elec. Contractors, Inc. v. Turner Constr. Co., 2009 WL 807469 (D. Conn. 2009), *aff'd*, 357 Fed. Appx. 395 (2d Cir. (Conn.) Dec. 21, 2009) (no-damages-for-delay clauses, though valid, are strictly construed against the party seeking relief from liability; the law of both Connecticut and New York recognizes four situations where such clauses will not be enforced: (1) delays caused by the contractee's bad faith or its willful, malicious, or grossly negligent conduct, (2) uncontemplated delays, (3) delays so unreasonable that they constitute an intentional abandonment of the contract by the contractee, and (4) delays resulting from the contractee's breach of a fundamental obligation of the contract); court granted summary judgment to the general contractor on the grounds that there was no genuine issue of material fact, and the delays for which the subcontractor sought to recover did not fall within any of the exceptions; appellate court did not reach the issue, as it affirmed on the basis that the subcontractor waived its claims by executing change orders that stated they included compensation for delays); U.S. f/u/b Gurtz Electric Co. v. Gilbane Building Co., 2008 U.S. Dist. LEXIS 81217 (N.D. Ill. 2008) (subcontract limited damages for delay to cases of: (1) owner or general contractor's (Gilbane's) active interference; and (2) defective plans and specifications; subcontractor Gurtz sought $2 million of delay damages based on Gilbane's providing defective plans and specifications; demanding that Gurtz perform work different from, or in addition to, the work required under the subcontract; interfering with Gurtz's reasonable access to the project and otherwise delaying and disrupting Gurtz's ability to work on the project; failing to cooperate with Gurtz; and failing to properly schedule or coordinate its other subcontractors and suppliers in a manner which would permit Gurtz to perform its work in a timely and efficient manner; Gilbane moved to dismiss those portions of the claim seeking recovery for actions not identified in the subcontract limitations clause, arguing that the judicially-created exceptions to no-damages-for-delay clauses did not apply to the subcontract because it merely limited damages for delay, rather than excluding them; the court rejected Gilbane's argument, finding that the subcontract provision was overly restrictive because it would prevent Gurtz from recovering for delays caused by Gilbane's mismanagement of the subcontractors working on the project and Gilbane's failure to cooperate with Gurtz—"actions which may not fall within the Limitations Clause but nonetheless prevented Gurtz from substantially completing its work by the GSA's deadline"; as such, the additional exceptions established by

Illinois courts were applicable, such that Gurtz could recover damages attributable to: (1) delay "not within the contemplation of the parties"; (2) delay of "unreasonable duration"; and (3) delay attributable to "inexcusable ignorance or incompetence ofthe engineer"; the court held that Gurtz's allegations fell within these exceptions and the ones set forth in the subcontract, and denied Gilbane's motion to dismiss); Acme Contracting, Ltd. v. TolTest, Inc., 2008 WL 1990780 (E.D. Mich. 2008), *aff'd in relevant part, rev'd in part on other grounds*, 2010 WL 1140997 (6th Cir. (Mich.) Mar. 24, 2010) (contract provisions that bar, limit or waive delay damages that are caused by the owner or contractor are unenforceable under Ohio Rev. Code § 4113.62; the subcontract between TolTest and Acme provided that Acme would only be entitled to extra compensation for suspension, delay, or acceleration if such compensation was specifically allowed and paid to TolTest by the general contractor; the contract between the general contractor and TolTest, which was incorporated into the subcontract, stated that an "extension of time shall be the sole and exclusive remedy of Contractor for any such delays or suspensions, but only to the extent that a time extension is obtained from the Owner," and that "No claims will be accepted for costs incurred due to delays caused by others except to the extent that such delays exceed four (4) months"; the court held that because the subcontract as a whole precluded, limited, or waived liability for delay, even when the cause of the delay was a proximate result of the general contractor's actions or failures to act, the provisions were void and unenforceable and did not preclude recovery of delay damages by the subcontractor in this case).

Page 296, add at end of subsection:

For example, in *Burt Welding & Automotive Repair, Inc. v. U.W. Marx Inc.*,[11.1] the plaintiff, the subcontractor on a construction project in which it agreed to install structural steel and precast concrete panels, alleged that because the defendant, the general contractor, failed to properly coordinate delivery of the

[11.1] 272 A.D.2d 737, 707 N.Y.S.2d 548 (3d Dept. 2000). *But see* Mecca Constr. Corp. v. All Interiors, Inc., 2009 WL 3416426 (Mass. Super. Ct. 2009) (subcontract contained the following no damages for delay clause: "Subcontractor agrees it shall have no claim for money damages or additional compensation for delay, no matter how caused. For an increase in the time required for performance of this subcontract not due to fault of the subcontractor, the sole and exclusive remedy shall be only such extension of time as allowed to the general contractor by owner"; court denied the owner's motion for summary judgment, finding that a genuine issue of material fact existed as to whether subcontractor's claim due to "hindrances" caused by the contractor's failure to coordinate subtrades resulted in out-of-sequence work and a loss of production were precluded by the delay provision, particularly as the subcontractor finished its work on time; the court held that "at least some of plaintiff's damages here are alleged to be separate and distinct from any delay damages, but rather to be the result of damage to plaintiff's property and increased labor and other costs required to complete the job on time in light of the hindrances plaintiff allegedly encountered. . . . [T]o the extent that plaintiff can prove damages which are separate and distinct from any delays, recovery is not barred by the "no-damages for-delay" clause of the contract").

precast concrete panels to the job site, the subcontractor's cranes were idle much of the time and, consequently, it was unable to perform the subcontract in a "continuous integrated fashion," allegedly resulting in damages. In an attempt to avoid the legal consequence of a no damages for delay provision, the subcontractor brought a breach of contract action, arguing that three typewritten pages attached to the subcontract required the general contractor to sequence the delivery of the precast panels in such a fashion as to permit their efficient erection. The court held, however, that the provision did not supercede the unequivocal no damages for delay provision. Rather, it only served to establish that delays relating to these conditions were specifically contemplated by the parties at the time they entered into the subcontract, a factor reinforcing the applicability of the no damages for delay provision. The court concluded that regardless of the subcontractor's efforts to characterize its claim as one for breach of contract, it was quintessentially a claim for delay damages, precisely the type of claim that the no damages for delay clause was intended to bar.

In *Costello Construction of Maryland, Inc. v. J.D. Long Masonry, Inc.*,[11.2] the subcontract provided that the contractor had the right to direct the manner in which the subcontractor performed the work, and that the subcontractor would work overtime or increase crews and equipment at no cost to the contractor "unless and only if the costs therefore are paid by the Owner for the subcontractor's behalf." The subcontract further provided that a time extension "shall be the sole and exclusive remedy of the Subcontractor for delays or suspensions caused by Contractor." The court found that the subcontract thereby precluded the subcontractor from recovering monetary damages from the contractor, even for delays caused by the contractor, unless the owner agreed to pay the costs. Since the owner had not paid any costs relating to the alleged delay, the court affirmed the district court's grant of summary judgment to the contractor on the subcontractor's claim for delay damages.

A Colorado appellate recognized the enforceability of a no-damages-for-delay clause in *Tricon Kent Co. v. LaFarge North American, Inc.*[11.3] The subcontract contained a provision entitling the subcontractor, Tricon, to a time extension for delay or interference caused by the owner, the contractor, or other subcontractors, but precluding Tricon from recovering damages except to the extent the contractor recovers from the owner for such delays. Noting that the majority of jurisdictions have upheld no-damages-for-delay clauses, the court held that such clauses are valid and enforceable in Colorado, "but they are to be strictly construed against the owner or contractee." Tricon contended that the contractor actively interfered with Tricon's work, and the court recognized active interference as an exception to the enforcement of the no-damages-for-delay clause; the court stated that "a plaintiff contractor or subcontractor claiming active interference on the part of the defendant owner or contractee needs only to show that the

[11.2] 236 Fed. Appx. 877, 2007 WL 1857348 (4th Cir. (Va.) June 26, 2007).

[11.3] 2008 WL 1902514 (Colo. Ct. App. May 1, 2008).

defendant committed an affirmative, willful act that unreasonably interfered with the plaintiff's performance of the contract, regardless whether it was undertaken in bad faith. However, we further conclude that, while it is unnecessary to show bad faith or reprehensible conduct, active interference requires more than a simple mistake, error in judgment, lack of total effort, or lack of complete diligence." Tricon submitted evidence at trial that the contractor: (1) failed properly to schedule, sequence, and coordinate Tricon's activities on the project; (2) ordered Tricon to proceed with its work knowing that another subcontractor had not completed its work; (3) threatened Tricon with a claim for liquidated damages if it did not perform the out-of-sequence work; and (4) knew Tricon needed two lane openings for efficient performance of its work, yet failed to provide it with open lane access. The court held that this evidence was sufficient for the jury to find that the contractor actively interfered with Tricon's work, which entitled Tricon to the award of damages for delay.

The Montana Supreme Court found that a provision requiring the subcontractor to perform "as directed" by the contractor had the effect of a "no damages for delay" clause. In *Keeney Construction v. James Talcott Construction Co., Inc.*,[11.4] Keeney's subcontract provided that Keeney, would work "as directed" by Talcott, the general contractor. During the project, Talcott and the owner negotiated an expanded scope of work and an extended completion schedule. Although the changes did not alter Keeney's scope of work, they did affect the timing of Keeney's work. Keeney asserted a claim against Talcott for damages for delay, arguing that the "as directed" language could not be construed as a disclaimer of Talcott's responsibility for its own breach of contract or negligence, as such a provision would be contrary to Montana law. The Montana Supreme Court disagreed. The court noted that the subcontract did not incorporate any schedule or completion deadline for Keeney's work, and held that the "as directed" language gave Talcott full discretion to schedule Keeney's work, thereby precluding a claim for delay damages. The court said the provision was not contrary to Montana law, as it did not relieve Talcott of all liability.[11.5]

No-damages-for-delay clauses are generally enforced in California. For example, in *Harper/Nielsen-Dillingham Builders, Inc. v. United States*,[11.6] the subcontract between the general contractor, Harper, and its subcontractor, KCI, on a federal housing project included a no-damages-for-delay clause limiting the subcontractor to an extension of time for any delays caused by Harper or the government. Although such clauses are not contained in federal contracts, the government would not be liable to the general contractor for delay damages if

[11.4] 45 P.3d 19 (Mont. 2002), *reh'g denied* (2002).

[11.5] *But see* Blake Constr. Co., Inc. v. C.J. Coakley Co. Inc., 431 A.2d 569 (D.C. App. 1981) (court held that an "as directed" provision did not give the contractor the right to direct out-of-sequence work or to otherwise actively interfere with the subcontractor's performance).

[11.6] 81 Fed. Cl. 667 (2008), *appeal dismissed*, 2009 WL 981976 (Fed. Cir. Jan. 29, 2009), *reconsid. denied*, 2009 WL 1227719 (Fed. Cir. May 4, 2009).

the general contractor had no liability to the subcontractor for delay damages, under the *Severin* doctrine.[11.7] When KCI suffered delays caused by one of the government's separate contractors, it asserted a pass-through claim against the government, arguing that no-damages-for-delay clauses are not favored, and that the delays were not contemplated by the parties. The court held that the clause in this case was unambiguous and was enforceable, as a matter of law, as an "iron-bound" bar against liability for delay-related damages, as the only statutory exception to enforceability (Cal. Public Cont. Code Section 7102, involving contracts with state and local agencies) did not apply to subcontracts between private parties on a federal project. The court further found that, even if additional exceptions might be allowed under California law, the evidence established that the delays in this case where known to exist prior to execution of the subcontract, such that the delays were specifically within the contemplation of the parties.

New York courts come to similar results. In *Premier-New York Inc. v. Travelers Property Casualty Corp.*,[11.8] a subcontractor was unsuccessful after asserting five separate grounds in an attempt to overcome a no-damages-for-delay clause. Premier was the roofing subcontractor to Tratoros, one of multiple co-prime contractors on the project. Prior to executing the subcontract, Premier received a bar chart "sample" schedule from Tratoros, which Premier asserted it relied upon in preparing its bid. Although the subcontract stated that the subcontractor might have to work out of sequence, and that Premier waived claims for additional costs due to delays, disruptions, acceleration, or work that was re-sequenced, rescheduled, or interrupted, Premier asserted a claim against Tratoros for delay damages, arguing that delays caused it to incur additional costs in re-sequencing the work and obtaining access to key facilities. Premier first contended that the no-damages-for-delay clause was inapplicable because Tratoros fraudulently induced Premier to submit a lower bid based upon a misrepresentation of the schedule for the project. The court rejected this argument, finding that a "sample" schedule is a forward-looking document subject to change, and is therefore not a material fact upon which a subcontractor can reasonably rely. The court also found that Premier provided no evidence to support its contention that the no-damages-for-delay clause did not apply because Tratoros acted with bad faith, which required proof of something more than active interference, such as willful or grossly negligent misconduct. The next exception raised by Premier was that the delays were not contemplated at the time the subcontract was executed. The court stated this exception applied only when the delays were "wholly unanticipated," requiring proof that the delays at issue were not reasonably foreseeable and were not mentioned in the contract. In this case, the court found that where

---

[11.7] Severin v. United States, 99 Ct. Cl. 435 (1943), *cert. denied*, 322 U.S. 733 (1944) (allowing a subcontractor's claims to be asserted against the government, even though there is no privity of contract, as long as the contractor who is in privity with the government is potentially liable to the subcontractor and brings the claim on behalf of the subcontractor).

[11.8] 20 Misc. 3d 1115(A), 867 N.Y.S.2d 20 (July 8, 2008).

there are multiple co-prime contractors on a project, the risk of inactivity or poor performance by the other co-primes is foreseeable. Similarly, a general contractor's inept administration of the contract, including poor planning and scheduling, is reasonably foreseeable and, in this case, was specifically addressed in the subcontract. The court also rejected Premier's argument that the no-damages-for-delay clause was inapplicable because Tratoros breached a fundamental contractual obligation by re-sequencing the work. Under the subcontract, Tratoros had the right to change the schedule, so the sample schedule was not an affirmative obligation that could be breached. Premier's fifth argument to avoid the no-damages-for-delay clause was that Tratoros was paid delay damages by the owner, and the subcontract permitted Premier to recover delay damages in that situation. The court found that since the delay damages that were recovered by Tratoros had nothing to do with Premier's work, but related to a different subcontractor, Premier could not recover delay damages.

Another no-damages-for-delay clause was upheld in *Worth Construction Co., Inc. v. TRC Engineers, Inc.*[11.9] In that case, the owner agreed in the prime contract to make the property available to the general contractor, TRC, by a date certain. The subcontract provided that, in the event the property was not made available to TRC by that date, Worth could recover only its costs of demobilization and remobilization, not to exceed $60,000 and $40,000, respectively, and $300,000 in the aggregate. The property was not timely made available, and Worth sued to recover delay damages, but did not allege any demobilization or remobilization damages. The court rejected Worth's argument that the no-damages-for-delay clause was unenforceable because the delay was uncontemplated and breached a fundamental obligation of the subcontract. The court found that a delay in the owner making the property available was clearly contemplated, since the subcontract provided a remedy for such delay, and that TRC did not have an obligation under the subcontract to make the property available by a date certain.

[H] Payment Clauses

Page 296, add at end of subsection:

Some courts recognize a difference between pay-when-paid and pay-if-paid contractual clauses. Under a pay-when-paid clause, a contractor's obligation to pay the subcontractor is triggered upon receipt of payment from the owner. Most courts hold that this type of clause means only that the contractor's obligation to make payment is suspended for a reasonable amount of time for the contractor to receive payment from the owner. Thus, a pay-when-paid clause is a timing mechanism only; it does not create a condition precedent to the obligation to

[11.9] 55 A.D.3d 388, 865 N.Y.S.2d 95 (N.Y.A.D. 1 Dept. Oct. 16, 2008).

make payment, and it does not expressly shift the risk of the owner's nonpayment to the subcontractor. On the other hand, under a pay-if-paid clause, receipt of payment by the contractor from the owner is an express condition precedent to the contractor's obligation to pay the subcontractor. A pay-if-paid provision in a construction subcontract is intended to shift the risk of the owner's nonpayment under the subcontract from the contractor to the subcontractor. In many jurisdictions, courts will enforce a pay-if-paid provision only if the language is clear and unequivocal. Thus, courts will hold that a pay-if-paid provision does not create a condition precedent if the provision is ambiguous.

In *Mid America Construction Management, Inc. v. Mastec North America, Inc.*,[11.10] the court held that the following contractual clause was a pay-if-paid provision: "[A]ll payments to Subcontractor by Contractor are expressly contingent upon and subject to receipt of payment for the Work by Contractor from Owner, even if . . . the Primary Contract is on a 'cost plus' or other reimbursement basis requiring the Contractor to pay subcontractors prior to being reimbursed by Owner." This provision contained the necessary conditional language to make the owner's payment to the general contractor a condition precedent to the general contractor's obligation to pay the subcontractor. Instead of using timing-related terms like "until," which are indicative of a pay-when-paid clause, the agreement used phrases that were clearly conditional, such as "expressly contingent upon" and "subject to." While the agreement could have been made more explicit, the agreement's "failure to say all that it might have said" was not enough to call into doubt the intent of the contracting parties. Because such clauses are enforceable under Texas and New Mexico law, the states whose law was to be applied pursuant to the contract's choice-of-law provision, the defendant general contractor in the instant case was not obligated to pay the subcontractor for the work that the subcontractor performed under the subcontract agreement unless and until the owner paid the general contractor for that work.

[11.10] 436 F.3d 1257 (10th Cir. (Okla.) Feb. 8, 2006). *See also* Universal Concrete Products Corp. v. Turner Construction Co., 595 F.3d 527 (4th Cir. (Va.) Feb. 19, 2010) (clause that the contractors obligation to pay the subcontractor "is subject to the express condition precedent of payment therefor by the Owner" was an enforceable pay-when-paid clause, and subcontractor could not recover payment from the contractor until the contractor received payment from the owner; *[the court was apparently treating the provision as a pay-if-paid clause]*). *But see* Sloan Company v. Liberty Mutual Ins. Co., 2009 WL 2616715 (E.D.Pa. Aug. 25, 2009) (provision stated final payment to the subcontract "shall be made within thirty (30) days after the last of the following to occur, the occurrence of all of which shall be conditions precedent to such final payment. . . . (6) Contractor shall have received final payment from the Owner for the Subcontractor's Work"; court held the language was insufficient to demonstrate an intent to shift the risk of nonpayment onto the subcontractor, and the provision was therefore a pay-when-paid clause; thus, even though the contractor never received "payment from the Owner for the Subcontractor's Work," the contractor was required to make payment to the subcontractor).

In *Hugh O'Kane Electric Co., LLC v. Mastec North America, Inc.*,[11.11] the court held that under New York law, a pay-if-paid clause—a provision in the subcontract making its obligation to pay the subcontractor "expressly contingent upon and subject to" its own receipt of payment from the owner for the subcontractor's work—was void as against public policy. However, the subcontract contained a Florida choice-of-law clause, and in Florida such provisions are enforced. A New York court will enforce a choice-of-law clause as long as the law chosen has a reasonable relationship to the agreement and does not violate a fundamental public policy of New York. The court then concluded that because such provisions were acceptable in New York for a considerable period of time, the current prohibition against such provisions is not a deeply rooted tradition of the state. Accordingly, the provision would be enforced by the court.

In *Lakin Enterprises v. Sebastian*,[11.12] Lakin was the general contractor on two projects owned by Bachrach Clothing, Inc., and entered into subcontracts with Sebastian to install fixtures on the project. Both subcontracts provided that payment to the subcontractor would be made "by Owner." The second subcontract further provided: "Payments are subject to the Contractor receiving payment from the Owner and is a condition precedent to the Contractor's obligation or its Surety's obligation to pay Subcontractor, its suppliers, labor, etc." Bachrach went bankrupt when Sebastian was owed $1,120 on the first subcontract, and $26,070 on the second subcontract. The court found that Sebastian was entitled to payment by Lakin under the first subcontract, since the language "by Owner" provided only for how the payments would be processed, but did not condition Lakin's liability upon payment by the Owner. In contrast, the second subcontract expressly madepayment by the owner a "condition precedent" to Lakin's liability for such payment. Since Lakin did not receive payment from the owner, Lakin was not liable to Sebastian for payment.

A contractor or subcontractor is generally required to sign a partial release upon receipt of payment from the owner or general contractor, and a final release upon receipt of final payment. Such releases will generally be upheld, and will bar the assertion of claims that existed at the time the release was signed. For example, in *Kenneth Hantman, Inc. v. The Whiting-Turner Contracting Co.*,[11.13] the subcontractor on a Navy project, Hantman, complained on several occasions during construction that a Navy Inspector was interfering with its work, although Hantman did not indicate at the time that it was incurring any delays or additional costs as a result of such interference. Hantman executed all partial releases and the final release upon payment by Whiting-Turner, as required by the subcontract, and did not enumerate any claims or circumstances that could give rise to any future claims against the Navy in the space provided on each of the releases. Thirteen months after final payment, Hantman sought to assert a claim against

[11.11] 19 A.D.3d 126, 797 N.Y.S.2d 45 (1st Dept. June 2, 2005).

[11.12] 2009 WL 428491 (Tex. App.-Dallas Feb. 23, 2009).

[11.13] 2008 WL 4072591 (E.D. Pa. Sept. 2, 2008).

the Navy for damages resulting from the Navy Inspector's interference, and Whiting-Turner sponsored the claim. When Whiting-Turner refused to sign an affidavit submitted by Hantman to the effect that Whiting-Turner did not believe the releases barred Hantman's claims against the Navy, Hantman withdrew its claim, and brought an action against Whiting-Turner for breach of contract and of the implied duty of good faith and fair dealing based on Whiting-Turner's alleged withdrawal of Hantman's claim and its acquiescing in the Navy Inspector's conduct. Whiting-Turner contended that such claims were barred by the releases executed by Hantman. After trial, the court held in favor of Whiting-Turner, finding that the releases were valid and enforceable, and that Whiting-Turner did not waive the release provisions by forwarding the claims to the Navy, nor was there a mutual mistake as to the validity of the releases (although there may have been a unilateral mistake on Hantman's part).

[I] Termination Clauses

Page 297, add at end of subsection:

In *Abra Constr. Corp. v. 112 Duane Associates, LLC,*[11.14] the court rejected a subcontractor's attempt to calculate its damages from wrongful termination using a percentage-of-completion method. The court found that this method could be used only if Abra, the subcontractor, established substantial completion of the contract as a whole. Here, the subcontract was terminated when Abra had only been on the job for two months. In addition, Abra attempted to obtain the benefit of the percentage completion of other subcontractors for which Abra did not pay. The court held that the trial court properly calculated the value of the work performed by using Abra's payroll records, adding reasonable percentages for labor burden, overhead and profit, and adding to that figure the amount of proven cost of Abra's materials that had been stipulated by the parties.

[J] Termination for Convenience Clauses

Page 297, add note 11.15 at end of 1st sentence of subsection:

[11.15] *But see* Questar Builders, Inc. v. CB Flooring, LLC, 410 Md. 241, 978 A.2d 651 (Md. Aug. 25, 2009) (contractor's ability to exercise a termination for convenience clause in the subcontract was subject to the implied obligations of good faith and fair dealing, as the ability of the contractor to terminate the subcontract "on a whim" would render the subcontract illusory and unenforceable).

[11.14] 59 A.D.3d 263, 873 N.Y.S.2d 574 (1st Dept. Feb. 19, 2009).

Page 297, add at end of subsection:

The language of the termination for convenience clause must be carefully worded to ensure it meets the contractor's intent, as the placement of a single comma can drastically change the meaning of a provision. In *Encon Utah, LLC v. Fluor Ames Kraemer, LLC*,[11.16] the subcontract provided that in the event of Encon's termination for convenience, Encon could recover:

> the actual costs of all such Work satisfactorily executed to the date of termination, plus an allowance for reasonable overhead and profit on such costs incurred prior to termination (but not to exceed a pro rata portion of such Contract Price for such Work based on the percentage of Work properly completed to the date of termination), together with reasonable costs occasioned by such termination and not previously paid for, less such sums as [Encon] has already received on account of the Work performed. In no event shall total payment to [Encon] exceed the Contract Price [of $6,842,342].

The contractor, FAK, argued that the pro rata cap applied to both actual costs and the overhead and profit, such that Encon's total recovery could not exceed the value of the work completed at the time of termination, which Encon had already been paid. The court rejected this argument, based in large part on the punctuation of the applicable provision. The court identified three types of costs mentioned in the clause—actual costs, overhead and profit, and costs occasioned by termination—each of which was set off by commas. Since the pro rata cap was included within the portion that related solely to overhead and profit, the cap did not apply to the other two categories of costs. Thus, if there had been another comma immediately prior to the parenthetical containing the pro rata cap, the cap would have applied to the first two categories of costs, rather than just the second category.

[K] Choice of Law and Choice of Forum Clauses

Page 298, add to end of note 12:

See also Mid America Constr. Mgmt., Inc. v. Mastec N. Am., Inc., 436 F.3d 1257 (10th Cir. (Okla.) Feb. 8, 2006) (when subject matter jurisdiction is based on diversity of citizenship, federal courts look to the forum state's choice-of-law rules to determine the effect of a contractual choice-of-law clause; under the law of the forum state in this case, Oklahoma, a contract is governed by the laws of the state where the contract was entered into *unless otherwise agreed and unless contrary to the law or public policy of the state where enforcement of the contract is sought* because in this case the parties agreed to be governed by the laws

[11.16] 2009 UT 7, 2009 WL 172438 (Utah Jan. 27, 2009), *reh'g denied* (June 24, 2009).

of Texas and New Mexico, the court was required to determine whether the application of those states' laws to the interpretation of the subcontract agreement would violate the law or public policy of Oklahoma as expressed in the state's constitution, statutes, or judicial records; the court concluded that the subcontract agreement's pay-if-paid clause would be enforceable under both Texas and New Mexico law, and enforcing the clause would not yield a result in violation of the law or public policy of Oklahoma; the court thus applied Texas and New Mexico law in interpreting the subcontract agreement and its pay-if-paid clause).

[L] Arbitration Clauses

Page 298, add new note 12.1 at end of subsection:

[12.1] *See, e.g.*, Dunn Indus. Group. Inc. v. City of Sugar Creek, 112 S.W.3d 421 (Mo. 2003) (contract contained a broad arbitration provision that mandated arbitration of "[a]ny controversy or claim arising out of or relating to [the] contract"; this language clearly applied to a claim for damages for a contractor's "failure to timely complete the contract" and for its "failure to properly perform and coordinate the construction work"; although the subcontractor argued that a change order freed it from its obligation to arbitrate, the court disagreed, holding that the change order did not modify or rescind the arbitration provision in the construction contract but rather preserved the parties' agreement to arbitrate as well as other unspecified rights or remedies that were not inconsistent with that obligation).

Page 298, add to end of subsection:

Some states enforce arbitration provisions only if they are clear and unequivocal, such that a mere incorporation of a prime contract that contains an arbitration provision into a subcontract that does not may not be sufficient to bind the subcontractor to arbitration. For example, in *Industrial Window Corp. v. Federal Insurance Company*,[12.2] the contract between the owner and Hill International, the construction manager, contained a clear and unequivocal clause requiring a detailed alternative dispute resolution (ADR) procedure for all disputes between the owner and Hill. Hill then entered into a contract with Beys General Construction Corp. to act as general contractor on the project, and this contract specifically incorporated the owner/Hill contract, to which Beys agreed to be bound to the same extent as Hill was bound. Finally, Beys entered into a

[12.2] 565 F. Supp. 2d 513 (S.D.N.Y. July 16, 2008). *But see* DB Acoustics, Inc. v. Great River Contractors, LLC, 2010 WL 1375319 (Iowa App. Apr. 8, 2010) (supplier to a subcontractor was compelled to arbitrate in accordance with the requirements of the prime contract and the subcontract, notwithstanding that supplier had no written agreement with the subcontractor).

subcontract with Industrial Window Corp. (IWC) to install a curtain wall system, and the subcontract specifically incorporated the owner/Hill contract. IWC incurred additional costs after its initial plan to install the curtain wall was rejected and, after its request for a change order was denied, IWC refused to submit its claim to the ADR procedure set forth in the owner/Hill contract. IWC instead filed suit against Federal, the surety who issued Beys' payment bond. The surety contended that IWC was required to follow the ADR procedure in the prime contract, but the court rejected this argument. Under New York law, an ADR agreement "must be clear, explicit and unequivocal and must not depend upon implication or subtlety." The court found that the Beys/IWC contract did not exhibit a clear intent to submit all disputes to any ADR procedure, nor did it mention the ADR provision in the owner/Hill contract. In addition, even if the ADR provision had been properly incorporated into the Beys/IWC contract, the provision would be too ambiguous to enforce, as it applied by its terms only to disputes between the owner and Hill, and therefore did not clearly indicate what disputes, if any, between Beys and IWC were intended to be subject to the ADR procedure. The court also found that since the owner/Hill contract specifically required that all subcontracts contain a provision that disputes under the subcontract would be submitted to the ADR procedures set forth in the owner/Hill contract, it was apparent that a subcontractor would not be bound to the ADR procedures without such a provision.

Subsequent to this decision, Federal filed a third-party complaint against Beys, and Beys filed a fourth-party complaint against Hill. Hill then moved to dismiss Beys' complaint on the grounds that Beys was required to follow the ADR procedure in the owner/Hill contract. The court in *Industrial Window Corp. v. Federal Insurance Company*[12.3] followed the same rationale as in the previous decision in finding that the Hill/Beys contract did not indicate a clear intent that Beys be bound by the ADR procedure in the prime contract. Hill argued that Beys should be judicially estopped from denying that it was bound to the prime contract's ADR procedure, since Beys submitted affidavits in support of Federal's motion in the 2008 case, stating that Beys expressly contemplated that disputes under the subcontract would be resolved in accordance with the prime contract's ADR provision. The court rejected this argument, finding that judicial estoppel would apply only if the court had adopted Beys' inconsistent position, but the court did not rely on Beys' affidavits in its earlier decision.

Page 299, add new subsection at end of § 14.05:

[N] Scheduling Clauses

The general contractor should ensure that a provision is included in the subcontract giving the contractor the right to schedule the work.

[12.3] 609 F. Supp. 2d 329, 2009 WL 921120 (S.D.N.Y. Apr. 6, 2009).

However, a scheduling clause may not give the contractor the unfettered right to change the schedule without regard to its impact on the subcontractor's work. For example, in *New Design Construction Co., Inc. v. Hamon Contractors, Inc.*,[12.4] NDCC was the paving subcontractor on two highway projects for which Hamon was the general contractor. Hamon's initial phasing plan, upon which NDCC based its bid, was for sequential construction of the five bridges for the project. The subcontract required NDCC to "prosecute the work undertaken in a prompt and diligent manner whenever such work, or any part of it, becomes available, or at such other time or times as [Hamon, the contractor] may direct." During construction, Hamon abandoned its plan to work sequentially, and instead constructed the bridges simultaneously. Hamon withheld almost $1 million of contract funds from NDCC, asserting substandard paving and entitlement to liquidated damages for delayed completion. Hamon defended against NDCC's breach of contract claim to recover the withheld funds by asserting that the subcontract gave Hamon the absolute right to direct the timing of NDCC's work. The court noted that the prime contract required Hamon to develop a critical path method schedule and a phasing plan describing the projects' work. The court also found that the implied covenant of good faith and fair dealing required that Hamon not abuse its discretion in directing the timing of NDCC's work. The court held that Hamon breached the subcontract by failing to incorporate its re-sequencing plan into the critical path schedule, and upheld the trial court's award to NDCC.[12.5]

In contrast, in *Keeney Construction v. James Talcott Construction Co., Inc.*,[12.6] Keeney's subcontract did not contain a completion date, but provided that Keeney would "complete the work of this Subcontract as required by job progress or within the following time limits: As directed by James Talcott Construction, Inc." During the project, Talcott and the owner negotiated an expanded scope of work and an extended completion schedule. Although the changes did not alter Keeney's scope of work, they did affect the timing of Keeney's work. Keeney asserted a claim against Talcott for damages for delay, arguing that the "as directed" language could not be construed as a disclaimer of Talcott's responsibility for its own breach of contract or negligence, as such a provision would be contrary to Montana law. The Montana Supreme Court disagreed. The court noted that the subcontract did not incorporate any schedule or completion deadline for Keeney's work, and held that the "as directed" language gave Talcott full discretion to schedule Keeney's work, thereby precluding a claim for delay damages. The court said the provision was not contrary to Montana law, as it did not relieve Talcott of all liability.

[12.4] 215 P.3d 1172, 2008 WL 2522306 (Colo. Ct. App. June 26, 2008).

[12.5] *See also* Blake Constr. Co., Inc. v. C.J. Coakley Co. Inc., 431 A.2d 569 (D.C. App. 1981) (court held that an "as directed" provision did not give the contractor the right to direct out-of-sequence work or to otherwise actively interfere with the subcontractor's performance).

[12.6] 45 P.3d 19 (Mont. 2002), *reh'g denied* (2002).

§ 14.05 CLAUSES THAT THE SUBCONTRACTOR SHOULD INCLUDE IN ITS SUBCONTRACT WITH THE GENERAL CONTRACTOR

[A] Incorporation by Reference

Page 299, add new note 13.1 at end of last sentence in subsection:

[13.1] *But see* URS Group, Inc. v. Tetra Tech FW, Inc. and Foster Wheeler Environmental Corp., 181 P.3d 380 (Colo. 2008) (applying New Jersey law, the court found that although the subcontract did not contain a differing site conditions clause, such that the subcontractor would normally bear the risk of differing site conditions, the prime contract contained a differing site conditions provision which was incorporated by reference into the subcontract; the court held that the subcontractor could therefore recover additional compensation for differing site conditions).

[C] Indemnification Clauses

Page 300, add at end of subsection:

In *Summit Contractors, Inc. v. General Heating & Air Conditioning, Inc.*,[13.2] the court held that a waiver of subrogation clause was not inconsistent with an indemnification clause in the contract between a contractor and a subcontractor, nor was the waiver of subrogation clause in violation of public policy. The waiver of subrogation clause provided, in pertinent part, that the contractor and subcontractor waived all rights against each other for damages caused by fire, to the extent covered by property insurance, and also provided that "[a] waiver of subrogation shall be effective as to a person or entity even though that person or entity would *otherwise* have a duty of indemnification, contractual or otherwise, did not pay the insurance premium directly or indirectly, and whether or not the person or entity had an insurable interest in the property damaged" (emphasis supplied). The contract's indemnification clause provided: "To the fullest extent permitted by law, the Subcontractor shall indemnify . . . Contractor . . . from and against losses . . . arising out of or resulting from performance of the Subcontractor's Work . . . attributable to . . . destruction of tangible property (other than the Work itself). . . ." The court held that the "otherwise" language included in the waiver of subrogation referred back to the provision regarding indemnification for damage to property *other than the Work itself.* In other words, even though the subcontractor was required to fully indemnify the contractor for damage to

[13.2] 358 S.C. 410, 595 S.E.2d 472 (2004).

the property of others, the contractor waived subrogation for damage to *the construction site* to the extent covered by property insurance. There thus was no conflict within the waiver of subrogation clause.

[F] Changes Clauses

Page 302, add at end of subsection:

In the absence of an express provision in a subcontract for pricing change orders, the subcontractor may be limited to the amount the project owner paid the prime contractor for the subcontractor's work. In *Fox v. Mountain West Electric, Inc.*,[13.3] Fox subcontracted with Mountain West to furnish and install alarm devices on a project for Lockheed Martin, and Fox commenced work without a signed subcontract. Lockheed Martin made a number of changes to the fire alarm system. Fox submitted prices for the changed work to Mountain West, who then proposed change order pricing to Lockheed Martin. Mountain West then presented Fox with a proposed subcontract that called for a pass through of subcontract change order compensation, and Fox refused to sign the subcontract. At trial, Fox testified that he considered his prices firm, consistent with the fixed-price nature of the subcontract and the prime contract. However, the court held that there was an implied contract using the industry's standard flow-down method of compensation for change orders, rather than a series of fixed price contracts between Mountain West and Fox.

[13.3] 52 P.3d 848 (Idaho 2002).

Page 304, add new Chapter 15 before Appendixes:

CHAPTER 15
UNIT PRICE CONTRACTS

§ 15.01 INTRODUCTION

Unit price contracts are contracts that are based, in whole or in large part, on unit prices, frequently with estimated quantities of each unit.[1] Contracts for heavy and civil construction, particularly highway and utility work, are often put out for bid and priced using a schedule of unit prices and estimated quantities. Even lump sum contracts may contain some items that are based on unit prices. Issues often arise when the estimated quantities in the contract on which the contract price is based vary significantly from the actual quantities performed. A body of law has developed to determine when the owner or the contractor is entitled to a price adjustment under these circumstances, depending upon whether the contract contains a variation in quantity provision concerning such price adjustments or if it is silent on this issue.

§ 15.02 UNIT PRICE CONTRACTS GENERALLY

If work or material is contracted on a unit price basis, a given unit is established (such as one cubic yard of dirt or one linear foot of pipe) and a price is set for each unit (*e.g.*, $2.20 per cubic yard of unclassified excavation). The bid and contract price are based upon an estimated number of units. The estimated quantities are generally determined by the owner of the project (or by the engineer on the owner's behalf), and the specific work covered by each unit is frequently defined either in a standard specification or in the specific specification. The contractor bids a unit price for each item. The overall bid price is based upon the total of the estimated quantity multiplied by the unit price. Each unit price has to contain the variable cost for performing a unit of work as well as a share of the contractor's non-specific costs, such as general conditions costs (jobsite overhead), overhead, and profit. Changes in quantity are generally stated to be based upon the unit prices bid. Small changes in quantity frequently involve limited additional cost. However, significant changes in quantity or significant changes in the means, methods, and manner of performance can result in significant cost changes in the cost to perform and significant changes in the revenue received by the contractor.

---

[1] *See, e.g.*, Prunty Constr., Inc. v. City of Canistota, 2004 SD 78, 682 N.W.2d 749 (June 9, 2004) (court defined a "unit price," or "unit bid," contract as one in which the contractor submits a price per unit for each of the various categories involved; this type of contract is used when final quantities of work cannot be determined with accuracy until final completion; clearest indication that a contract is a "unit bid" contract is from the advertisement for the bid and the bid itself; in this case, city's Advertisement for Bids used unit prices for the major items necessary for the projects to be bid, and for each of the items, there was an "estimated quantity" column, a "unit" column (measurement), a "unit price" column, and a "total price" column; further, bid form itself indicated that it was a unit bid contract; court therefore concluded, based upon the language of the document, that contract was a unit bid contract, not a lump sum contract as argued by the city).

The definition of what is included and not included within a specific unit can become a matter of extreme importance when there are significant changes in either the quantities or in the means, methods, and manner of performance. For example, a unit price for drilling and shooting rock may need to include the additional cost of handling the shot rock produced by the drilling and shooting if there is no other unit covering those costs. A small increase in the number of holes being drilled and shot may have a minor effect on costs. However, a significant increase in these quantities may have a major impact on the contractor's costs of performance. The contractor may be unable to obtain additional compensation for some of those costs if the unit definitions require the removal of all of the shot rock produced by the drilling and blasting as part of an excavation unit price but the contractor has not included those costs in calculating its unit price.

Ambiguities in what was included in unit-priced line items were at issue in *Lebanon Valley Landscaping, Inc. v. Town of Moriah.*[2] Lebanon Valley contracted with the Town to replace a water distribution and sewer collection system for 79 homes. The contract provided that Lebanon Valley would install an estimated 200 sanitary service connections at the price of $395 per unit, along with an estimated 2,000 feet of six-inch house service lateral pipe at $21.50 per lineal foot. During construction, the Town decided not to convert certain duplex residences from two-service per home lines to single-service connections, which necessitated the addition of 70 sanitary service connections. The contract price was adjusted by change order based upon the $395 unit price. Lebanon Valley eventually sought payment for 4,901 lineal feet of six-inch lateral pipe, which the Town denied on the basis that the six-inch pipe referred to in the contract would have been required only for the conversion from two-service to single-service connections, which conversion was eliminated by change order. As such, any six-inch pipe that Lebanon Valley actually installed was part of the sanitary service connection and was therefore included in the $395 unit price for each connection for which Lebanon Valley received full payment. The court found in favor of the Town, citing the contract provision that each sanitary service connection is "to include pipe as specified," and contract drawings containing illustrations which appeared to indicate that the sanitary service connection included six-inch pipe. The testimony of the Town's engineer and its supervisor were consistent with the Town's position, and Lebanon Valley's complaint was therefore properly dismissed.

A contracting officer's determination as to what was included in an indefinite delivery/indefinite quantity (IDIQ) contract was rejected in *Appeal of HITT*

---

[2] 50 A.D.3d 1407, 857 N.Y.S.2d 749, 2008 WL 1820696 (N.Y. App. 3d Dept. Apr. 24, 2008). *See also* Appeal of R. L. Bates General Contractor Paving & Assocs., Inc., ASBCA No. 53641, 2009 WL 5111784, (Dec. 16, 2009) (contractor agreed to perform out-of-scope work under its unit price contract; the court held that since the contractor was not obligated to accept the out-of-scope-work, but agreed to perform it under its contract, the unit prices of the contract were applicable).

Contracting, Inc.[3] The Department of Defense awarded an IDIQ contract to HITT to perform construction and renovation work at the Pentagon on an as-needed basis. The contract contained a voluminous attachment setting forth descriptions and agreed-upon prices for more than 300 scheduled line items. The DOD was entitled to order supplies and services through the issuance of task orders including scheduled and/or non-scheduled line items, with the parties negotiating a price for any non-scheduled items. One task order set forth work to be performed to renovate a mail-handling trailer, including a scheduled line item of "Engineering Services" for design of a fire alarm system, and further stated that it included no non-scheduled line items. Upon completion of the design for the fire alarm system, HITT submitted a proposed modification for the cost of installing the fire alarm system, which was rejected by the contracting officer on the grounds that such installation was a part of the task order. HITT appealed, and the Board found that since the installation (as opposed to the design) of a fire alarm system was not included as a scheduled line item in the contract, and the task order stated it included no non-scheduled line item, the task order could not have included installation of a fire alarm system. As such, HITT was entitled to recover the costs incurred in installation of the system.

The determination of how units are to be calculated for the purpose of payment is extremely important in unit price contracts. Disagreements over the measurement of units are not uncommon. In *In re CKY, Inc.*,[4] the contractor's method of unit measurement was rejected. The Army Corps of Engineers had awarded a unit price contract to CKY for rehabilitation of the levy. One unit price covered stone protection. Another covered installation of soil embankment. The specification stated that payment was to be made by the cubic yard for fill placed "as specified in this section." Specification also provided that "materials for filling the voids in the stone protection . . . will be measured for payment by the cubic yard . . . as specified in this section. . . . No measurement for payment will be made for the embankment materials used to fill in the voids within the stone protection." The contractor used embankment materials to fill voids in the stone protection and requested payment for that soil fill based on the cubic yards of material placed, asserting that the specification was, at best, latently ambiguous. The Board rejected the contractor's contention and held that the express payment provision was clear and unambiguous.

Absent a contract provision allowing the unit prices to be renegotiated for quantity changes, the general rule is that a contractor or an owner cannot require a unit price to be renegotiated simply because of a quantity change. For example, in *DeFoe Construction Corp. v. Beame*,[5] the owner of the project was not entitled to reduce the unit price for cement grout when the quantity required greatly increased over the estimated quantity. The contract included a set unit price for

[3] ASBCA No. 55758, 2008 WL 4467183, 08-2 BCA P 33971 (Sept. 16, 2008).

[4] ASBCA No. 54181, 2005 WL 1385134 (June 6, 2005).

[5] 75 Misc. 2d 309, 347 N.Y.S.2d 626 (1973).

"Neat Cement Grout" at $.50/lb with an estimate of 10,000 lbs. Upon commencement of the work, it was found that the method originally planned would not be appropriate or feasible, and the owner authorized extra work that required 131,412 lbs. of Neat Cement Grout. The owner contended that the payment for this extra work should be at $.50/lb, for the first 20,000 lbs. and $.23 per pound for the remainder of 111,412 lbs. Article 26 of the contract provided: "Extra work for which there are applicable contract unit prices will be paid for at such unit prices. Where there are no applicable contract unit prices . . ." the amount shall be computed by a specified formula. The court held that since there was a set contract unit price for the cement grout and since there was no agreed change of that amount, the contractor was entitled to be paid for the 132,412 lbs. at the contract price of $.50 per pound.[6]

The risks that a contractor on a unit price contract without a quantity adjustment clause takes when certain units bear a disproportionate amount of overhead and profit is illustrated in *Appeal of Oneida Constr., Inc./David Boland, Inc. Joint Venture.*[7] In this matter the joint venture of Oneida and Boland had a contract with the Air Force for resurfacing a runway. Two of the contract line items were unit priced and two line items were fixed price. As a result of a design change by the government a deductive change order was issued eliminating, in its entirety, one of the unit priced items. That unit price item had carried a disproportionate amount of the overall profit and home office overhead. The contractor claimed that the credit for the deduction of this unit price work should not include the overhead and profit component but only the actual cost estimated for that work. The government asserted that the contract unit price governed the credit unless the contractor could show that as a result of the deletion there was an increase in the performance cost of the remaining work. The Board agreed with the government finding that the contractor by carrying a disproportionate amount of overhead and profit in the unit price work assumed the risk associated with a deductive change.

---

[6] *See also* Kingsley v. City of Brooklyn, 78 N.Y. 200 (1879) (owner was not entitled to reduce the contract price when, at the owner's direction, the piles were driven to shallower depths than anticipated). *But see* In re Redondo Constr. Corp., 411 B.R. 89 (Bankr. D.P.R. Aug. 31, 2009), *amended in part on other grounds*, 424 B.R. 29 (Bankr. D.P.R. Feb. 11, 2010), *stay pending appeal granted*, 2010 WL 1286849 (Bankr. D.P.R. Mar. 30, 2010) (where material specified was a 90-foot pile, which required the use of a splice to weld two shorter piles and the purchase of a steel point to protect the pile during installation, and differing site conditions prevented the piles from being driven deeper than 60 feet, payment to the contractor based upon linear feet of piles driven resulted in an underrun, such that the contractor was unable to recover the cost of the splices and steel points; contractor was entitled to recover these costs under the differing site conditions clause of the contract).

[7] ASBCA No. 47914 (Dec. 8, 1994).

In certain cases, an increase in quantity may be so substantial that it becomes a "qualitative" increase for which the contractor may seek additional compensation. In *Tufano Contracting Corp. v. State*,[8] the contract called for construction of 28 temporary road detours, whereas more than 120 detours were actually constructed. The court found that an increase of this magnitude was not within the parties' contemplation and was qualitative, thereby entitling the contractor to recover on a time and material basis for all detours in excess of the 28 contemplated in the contract.[9]

In *Perini Corp. v. United States*,[10] Perini was the general contractor on a dam construction project. The contract provided for payment of $.40 per unit of water pumped from the worksite, with an estimated quantity of 625,000 units. Upon completion of the contract, Perini had pumped 7,425,681 units, and the government sought a downward adjustment in the unit price of $.40 under the Changed Conditions clause of the contract. The court first noted that the cases that have applied the Changed Conditions article to substantial variations from the quantity estimated in the contract have done so on the basis that such a material deviation was not reasonably foreseeable. Those cases dealt with special situations where: (1) the contractor could not have verified the estimated quantities from the contract documents and his investigation of the site; (2) the contractor had no opportunity to investigate the conditions at the site or for other reasons had the right to rely on the government's estimate or (3) both parties labored under a mutual mistake as to the accuracy of the government's estimates. Since the government contended that this was a situation of mutual mistake, the court found that the test to be applied in this case was whether the parties, from the information available to them, should reasonably have expected a material variation in the contract estimates of the water that would have to be pumped. The evidence established that both parties should reasonably have anticipated that a substantially greater quantity of water would have to be pumped than the amount estimated by the government, and that Perini did in fact expect such an overrun and relied on its own appraisal of the situation in submitting its bid. The court held that since the facts of this case established that a material variation from the erroneously computed estimated quantities was foreseeable, the government was not entitled to an equitable adjustment in the contract unit price under the Changed Conditions clause.

In *Pavers, Inc. v. Board of Regents of the University of Nebraska*,[11] the unit price contract contained the following provision:

---

[8] 269 N.Y.S.2d 564 (1966), *aff'd*, 309 N.Y.S.2d 355 (1970).

[9] *See also* Saddler v. United States, 287 F.2d 411 (Ct. Cl. 1961) (contractor was entitled to increased costs plus 10 percent overhead when the amount of earth required to complete a levee embankment increased by almost 100 percent, on the theory that this was a cardinal change to the contract entitling the contractor to an equitable adjustment in the contract price).

[10] 381 F.2d 403 (Ct. Cl. 1967).

[11] 276 Neb. 559, 755 N.W.2d 400 (Sept. 12, 2008).

> **7.1.4** If unit prices are stated in the Contract Documents or subsequently agreed upon, and if quantities originally contemplated are so changed in a proposed Change Order or Construction Change Directive that application of such unit prices to quantities of Work proposed will cause substantial inequity to the Owner or Contractor, the applicable unit prices shall be equitably adjusted.

During construction, it became apparent that the University's quantity estimates for soil disposal and seepage water removal/disposal were substantially understated, and Pavers notified the University of the quantity overruns. The University directed Pavers to proceed with the work. Upon completion of the work, Pavers sought payment of $1.7 million, which include approximately $1 million for the additional quantities of soil (8,000 tons versus an estimated 1,400 tons) and seepage water (173,900 gallons versus an estimated 1,200 gallons), utilizing the unit prices in the contract. The University refused to pay the amount requested, and instead paid Pavers a total of $379,337, which the University claimed was fair and equitable for all of the work performed. The trial court found that the University failed to meet its burden of showing that the equitable adjustment provision was applicable, but the court then applied a "total cost method" to adjust the amount owed to the difference between Pavers' total costs of $1.3 million and the $379,337 paid by the University. Both parties appealed, and the Nevada Supreme Court held that since the trial court determined that the University had not met its burden of proof to entitle it to an equitable adjustment of the unit price, the trial court had no basis to award anything other than the full amount sought by Pavers, which was based upon the contractual unit price. The court noted that the University could have sought an equitable adjustment to the unit price as soon as it became aware of the large quantity overruns, but instead directed Pavers to proceed and then sought to adjust the price. The court found there was nothing in the contract that "permits the University to unilaterally reduce the unit prices in the contract after the work has been performed."

The contractor will likely be held to the prescribed unit price if the contract specifically sets forth different unit prices for different quantities of work or materials. For example, in *Depot Construction Corp. v. State*,[12] the contract required the contractor to excavate 600 cubic yards at a set price, and provided that excavation in excess of that amount would be paid at $22 per cubic yard. Although the contractor actually excavated more than 2,900 cubic yards (almost five times the estimated quantity), the contractor was precluded from recovering any increase in the $22/cubic yard unit price.

Where the contractor is terminated, the unit prices of the contract generally govern and the contractor is not entitled to a price adjustment. In *Appeal of Ideker, Inc.*,[13] a contractor who was terminated on a unit price dredging contract

---

[12] 278 N.Y.S.2d 363 (1967).

[13] ENGBCA Nos. 4389 and 4602, 87-3 BCA (CCH) ¶ 20,145 (1987).

complained that the unperformed work was the highest profit margin work and that it should be compensated for the lost profits. The Board ruled that the unit prices governed, and the contractor was not entitled to the additional profit allegedly carried in the unperformed units of work.

In *Appeal of Manis Drilling*,[14] the contractor had an unbalanced bid in which one or more bid items carried less than their proportionate share of overhead and profit, and others carried more than their share. The government deleted 91 percent of the cement requirement and 100 percent of the sand and exploratory drilling requirements under the contract, and the contractor sought an equitable adjustment to the contract price. The contractor argued that it should not be bound to the unit prices in its estimate on the basis that its cement estimate included additional costs not related to the cement work. The Board rejected this argument, stating: "It is clear that appellant's costs and profit under the contract were affected not only as a result of the termination, but also as a result of appellant having assigned dollar values to line items in its cost proposal in such a manner as to create an unbalanced proposal. We recognize that the practice of submitting unbalanced bids in the construction industry is not uncommon. While a contractor may legitimately unbalance its bid as a bidding technique, it does so at its own peril and must accept the consequence that deletion of separately priced items might affect its profit (or cost) structure."

A contractor cannot use an unbalanced bid to take advantage of an obvious error in estimated quantities in the bid documents. In *Dugan Construction Co., Inc. v. New Jersey Turnpike Authority*,[15] the contractor submitted a lump sum bid of $1.7 million for remediating polluted groundwater at 17 wells, which included unit prices of $4 per gallon for removal and disposal of the engineer's estimate of 2,200 gallons of hazardous wastewater, and $50 per gallon for removal and disposal of the engineer's estimate of 55 gallons of non-hazardous wastewater. The contract required that the contractor notify the Authority of any apparent ambiguities or errors in the contract documents, and provided that changes involving an increase of more than 25 percent of a projected quantity would be subject to a negotiated price. About two weeks before commencing work, Dugan obtained a proposal of $57,000 from a subcontractor to perform the wastewater removal work, which the subcontractor estimated would involve the removal of 255,680 gallons of water. Dugan had the subcontractor perform the work without prior notice to the Authority of the dramatic variance in estimated quantities, and demanded that the Authority pay Dugan more than $9.5 million for removal of approximately 200,000 gallons of non-hazardous wastewater at the contract unit price of $50 per gallon. The appellate court noted that there was evidence that Dugan knew of the mistake in estimated quantities when it put its bid together, and that it deliberately unbalanced its bid. The court held that regardless of any

[14] I BCA No. 2658 (1993).

[15] 398 N.J. Super. 229, 941 A.2d 622 (N.J. Ct. App. Feb. 29, 2008), *cert. denied,* 196 N.J. 346, 953 A.2d 764 (July 15, 2008).

intentional wrongdoing in preparing the bid, Dugan's failure to notify the Authority of the increased quantities prior to performing the work was "unconscionable and violated the duty of good faith and fair dealing that is inherent in every contract," thereby justifying a reformation of the contract. The court found that the value of the extra work performed was $52,330, based upon the amount Dugan actually paid its subcontractor, and entered judgment in Dugan's favor in that amount.

If a bid protester seeks to challenge a competitor's unbalanced bid, the protestor must also show that the government's quantity estimates were inaccurate. In *Matter of Cherokee Painting, LLC*,[16] there was no dispute that the low bidder on a unit price government contract, Wind River Construction, submitted an unbalanced bid, as four items were significantly overstated and 18 items significantly understated. The disappointed bidder, Cherokee, challenged the "best value" award to Wind River on the grounds that the unbalanced bid posed a risk to the government that could cost additional funds during the life of the project. The Board rejected the protest, finding that there is generally little risk that the government will pay unreasonably high prices as a result of an unbalanced bid unless the government's quantity estimates were inaccurate. Here, Cherokee did not assert, nor was there any evidence to suggest, that the estimated quantities were inaccurate, and Cherokee's protest was therefore denied.

In *Appeal of Minehole Closure Consultants*,[17] the bid schedule for emergency reclamation work at a mine in Iowa consisted of unit-priced line items with estimated quantities of work, and the unit prices were required to include overhead and profit for the work involved. The contract documents stated that although bids would be evaluated based upon the total of the line item prices, the actual quantities of work would be determined during construction, and a fixed, lump sum price would be established for the entire contract. Minehole was awarded the contract as the low bidder. During performance of the work, the government determined that low slump grout would not be used to fill the shaft, and prepared a contract modification reducing the total bid price by the bid schedule's line item price for low slump grout. Minehole refused to sign the modification, contending that a reduction of that magnitude would increase its overhead rate and reduce its profit on the contract. The Board ruled in Minehole's favor, finding that this was essentially a deductive change to a fixed-price contract, and that prices from the bid schedule are not determinative in that situation. The Board held that the government was entitled to a price reduction for only the direct, out-of-pocket costs the contractor would have incurred if it had performed the deleted work. The contractor would thereby fully recoup its overhead expenses on the project and retain its profit expectations.

---

[16] GAO No. B-311020.3 (2009).

[17] IBCA No. 4306-4307/2001 (2004).

In *Rumsfeld v. Applied Cos., Inc.*,[18] the government awarded Applied an annual requirements contract for supply of refrigerant storage cylinders, with an estimated quantity of 119,495 units. Although the government determined prior to award that the purchased quantity would be only about 10 percent of the RFP estimate, it failed to notify Applied of the anticipated variation in quantity prior to the award. After award, the government notified Applied of the revised estimate, and ordered 11,000 units. Applied requested a substantial increase in the price per unit. The parties could not agree on a modification, and the government then terminated the contract for convenience before delivery. On Applied's claim for an increase in the unit price, the court held that Applied was entitled to recover the reasonable value of the work performed, which may include an equitable adjustment to the price per cylinder to reflect the change in quantity, plus reasonable profit.

The contract unit price is not always applicable in a breach of contract situation. In *G. B. Boots Smith Corp. v. Cobb*,[19] Smith, the general contractor for a highway project, entered into a contract with Cobb to purchase "all fill dirt" for the project. The agreement estimated the quantity of fill dirt at 550,000 cubic yards at a unit price of $.40 per cubic yard. After removing and paying for 440,000 cubic yards from Cobb's property, Smith purchased an additional 262,000 cubic yards from another source. Cobb filed suit to recover the contract price for the additional cubic yards, asserting that the contract was a "requirements contract." The Mississippi Supreme Court agreed that this was a requirements contract under which Smith had agreed to purchase all fill dirt for the project from Cobb. The court held, however, that Cobb was not entitled to the unit price for the fill Smith had purchased from another source, and could only recover the difference between the contract unit price and the current fair market value of the additional fill.

A lump sum contract may not be adjusted by unit costs for changes in quantity, unless permitted by a specific contract provision. For example, in *Randall & Blake, Inc. v. Metro Wastewater Reclamation District*,[20] the $2.7 million contract for the South Platte River Improvements Project contained a lump sum bid of $1.4 million for construction of a new reaeration structure, with the remainder of the work to be paid on a unit price basis. The contractor was able to use excavated material as bedding for the rip rap throughout the project, including at the reaeration structure, rather than having to purchase and import bedding material as anticipated. The District sought a unit price reduction to reflect the cost savings the contractor realized from not having to purchase the bedding material. The district court found that the contract was a unit price contract, and the District was therefore entitled to the price reduction. The appellate court reversed, finding that the contract

---

[18] 325 F.3d 1328 (Fed. Cir. 2003), *cert. denied*, 124 S. Ct. 462 (2003).

[19] 860 So. 2d 774 (Miss. 2003), *reh'g denied* (2003).

[20] 77 P.3d 804 (Colo. App. 2003).

specifically provided that the work on the reaeration structure was to be bid, performed, and paid on a lump sum basis, and the District was therefore not entitled to any unit price credit.

When work is priced on a unit price basis, whether it is to be paid on a unit price basis can be the source of dispute. In the matter of *Bender, GmbH v. Secretary of the Army*,[21] a contractor with a fixed price contract was found to have performed work on a change order on a unit price basis and hence was limited by the actual units of work performed. In this matter, the Army awarded a fixed price contract to the contractor, Bender, to clean and close a sewage treatment plant. After the contract was awarded, the Army learned that some of the sludge was contaminated with heavy metals and required Bender to remove that sludge. Bender proposed to remove 430 cubic meters of sludge at a price per cubic meter. This proposal was accepted. The contract modification stated that the modification would be funded and definitized based on the price proposal and disposal certificates provided by the contractor. After completion and acceptance of the work, the Army discovered that Bender had disposal certificates for only 229 cubic meters of heavy metal—contaminated sludge and demanded a refund for the cost of 201 cubic meters of sludge removal. The contractor argued that since the contract was on a fixed price basis, so was the modification. The Army argued that the language of the modification indicated a unit price work scope. The U.S. Court of Appeals for the Federal Circuit found that it was a unit price contract and the Army was justified in revoking its final acceptance to recover the overpayment to the contractor.

Quantity estimates in a unit-price contract do not constitute guarantees of the minimum quantities of work without specific contract language to that effect. In *Fusion Bonding Coating Systems, Inc. v. Regional Steel Corp.*,[22] the steel subcontractor on a Caltrans bridge construction project subcontracted the epoxy coating of the reinforcing steel for the project to Fusion Bonding (FBC) and Fletcher. FBC's subcontract stated approximate quantities of different configurations of rebar that would be coated at specified unit prices. Attachments to the subcontract required FBC to "provide adequate [resources] to comply with the project schedule," and stated that the purchase order "outlines the minimum requirements required by [FBC] to insure that FBC can comply with Caltrans Special Provisions. . . ." After a lengthy project delay caused by the owner, FBC and Fletcher submitted new proposals for the remaining epoxy coating work. Although Regional did not specifically agree to FBC's increased unit prices on the rebar coating, Regional paid the increased prices on the relatively small amount of rebar FBC coated after the delay. However, Regional sent the bulk of the rebar to Fletcher, which agreed to coat the rebar at lower unit prices. FBC sued Regional for

---

[21] 126 Fed. Appx. 280, 2005 WL 643357 (Fed. Cir. Mar. 21, 2005).

[22] 2009 WL 163730 (Cal. App. 1 Dist. Jan. 26, 2009) (unpublished/noncitable).

breach of contract in failing to provide the approximate quantities of work specified in the subcontract. The court affirmed the trial court's entry of summary judgment in favor of Regional, holding that FBC's subcontract did not contain a guarantee that the estimated quantities would be provided to FBC. The court distinguished cases where the subcontract evidenced an intent that the subcontractor would perform all of the subject work necessary for the project. Here, FBC was one of two subcontractors retained to perform the work, with no specified minimum or maximum amount of work to be allocated to either subcontractor. The court noted that the subcontract provision requiring FBC to provide adequate resources to comply with the project schedule suggested that FBC was expected to place some reliance on the estimated quantities, but was insufficient to convert the estimate into a guaranteed minimum. Further, the existence of a provision for adjustment of the unit price if the actual quantities varied more than 25% from the estimate also supports a finding that the estimate was not a guaranteed minimum. Finally, the fact that FBC submitted new unit prices to Regional after the delay indicates that the parties were no longer operating under the original agreement, such that Regional was certainly free at that time to redistribute the work among its two subcontractors depending upon the price each agreed to charge for the same work.

Similarly, in *ABC Paving Co. v. Washtenaw County Road Commission*,[23] the court rejected a contractor's argument that it was entitled to additional compensation as a result of actual quantities being less than estimated quantities. ABC was the general contractor on a project to replace a water main and a portion of a three-lane road. Under the contract, ABC would be paid a higher unit price for removal of 13,700 square meters of material that was more than 130 mm thick ("pavement"), and a lower unit price for removal of other material ("soil"). The actual amount of "pavement" was far less than estimated, and the amount of "soil" was more than anticipated. ABC sued the owner to recover additional compensation at "pavement" removal rates, essentially arguing that the stated contract amount was a guaranteed minimum. The court noted contract stated that the quantities shown were "approximate only and are subject to either increase or decrease. . . ." In addition, the MDOT standard specifications, incorporated into the contract, provided that the quantities appearing in the list of bid items were "estimated" and "may be increased, decreased, or deleted," and that the contractor will be paid for the "actual quantities of work performed. . . ." The court held that since ABC was admittedly paid in full for the work actually performed at the rates set forth in the contract, no additional compensation was due.

In a rather novel attempt to avoid the unit price agreed upon in the contract, a contractor attempted to rescind the contract in *Schipper Constr., Inc. v. American Crystal Sugar Co.*[24] Schipper was awarded an earthmoving contract for the

[23] 2008 WL 4605929 (Mich. App. Oct. 2, 2008).

[24] 2008 N.D. 226, 758 N.W.2d 744 (N.D. Dec. 16, 2008).

maintenance of two dikes, stating estimated quantities of "up to" 67,000 cubic yards and "up to" 85,600 cubic yards, respectively, at the unit price of $3.25 per cubic yard. The owner paid the invoice for 45,000 cubic yards at the first dike in full, but withheld a portion of the invoice for the 50,000 cubic yards at the second dike, claiming that Schipper had actually moved no more than 70,000 cubic yards on both dikes. Schipper then sent the owner a final billing requesting approximately $200,000 based on the time and materials spent on the projects, which the owner refused to pay. Schipper filed an action seeking compensation based on theories of breach of contract or, alternatively, *quantum meruit* following a rescission at law. Schipper contended that it rescinded the contract through two letters to the owner, which calculated what the project would have cost on an hourly basis, and asserted the owner had grossly misrepresented the quantities for both phases of the contract. The court found that neither letter stated a clear, unambiguous, and unequivocal intention to rescind the contract, particularly as one of the letters contained an itemized billing, and held that the district court did not err in dismissing Schipper's rescission claim.

§ 15.03 VARIATION IN QUANTITIES CLAUSES

Many contracts contain provisions that specify under what, if any, circumstances a party can seek an adjustment in the unit price of work or material. If the contract specifically provides that a change in quantity will not result in a change of unit price, neither the owner nor the contractor is entitled to an adjustment in the unit price when the quantity increases or decreases. For example, in *Camarco Contractors, Inc. v. State*,[25] the contractor claimed that it lost profits due to changes in the contract reducing the amount of sheathing required for the support of trenches where pipe was being installed. The contract provided: "The Engineer reserves the right to increase or diminish any or all of the above mentioned quantities of work or to omit any item, as he may deem necessary, and such increase or decrease of the quantities given for any of the items shall not be considered as sufficient grounds for granting an increase in the unit prices bid." The court found that the contractor was thereby precluded from seeking recovery for the variation in quantity.[26]

Many form contracts contain provisions governing changes in quantity. For example, AIA Document A201-2007, Standard General Conditions, contains the following provision:

---

[25] 305 N.Y.S.2d 207 (1969), *modified on other grounds*, 323 N.Y.S.2d 434 (1971).

[26] *See also* Farub Found. Corp. v. City of N.Y. 49 N.Y.S.2d 922 (1944) (where the contract provided that the estimated quantities set forth in the contract were in no way guaranteed and they would not be made the basis of any claim in the event that they should not correspond with the final quantities, contractor could not recover for greatly increased unit cost when the city used only 13 percent of the estimated materials).

> 7.3.4 If unit prices are stated in the Contract Documents or subsequently agreed upon, and if quantities originally contemplated are materially changed in a proposed Change Order or Construction Change Directive so that application of such unit prices to quantities of Work proposed will cause substantial inequity to the Owner or Contractor, the applicable unit prices shall be equitably adjusted.

EJCDC C-700 (2007), Standard General Conditions, Section 11.03(D) provides that either party may make a claim for an adjustment in the contract price if:

1. the quantity of any item of Unit Price Work performed by Contractor differs materially and significantly from the estimated quantity of such item indicated in the Agreement; and
2. there is no corresponding adjustment with respect to any other item of Work; and
3. Contractor believes that Contractor is entitled to an increase in Contract Price as a result of having incurred additional expense or Owner believes that Owner is entitled to a decrease in Contract Price and the parties are unable to agree as to the amount of any such increase or decrease.

Some contracts contain clauses that specify that an adjustment in unit price will be permitted if the actual quantities vary by more than a certain percentage of the estimates quantities. These provisions are known as Variation in Estimated Quantities (VEQ) clauses, and are common in government road construction contracts. For example, the Montana Standard Specifications for Road and Bridge Construction (2006), Section 104.02.3, provides as follows:

> If the alterations or changes in quantities significantly change the character of the work under the contract . . . an adjustment, excluding anticipated profit, will be made to the contract. . . . The term "significant change" applies only to the following circumstances. . . .
>
> B. When a major item of work, as defined in Subsection 101.03, is increased in excess of 125 percent or decreased below 75 percent of the original contract. Any allowance for an increase in quantity will apply only to that portion in excess of 125 percent of the original contract item quantity, or in the case of a decrease below 75 percent, to the actual amount of work performed.
>
> C. When an item of work, not defined as a major item in Subsection 101.03, is increased in excess of 150 percent or decreased below 50 percent of the original contract. Any allowance for an increase in quantity will apply

> only to that portion in excess of 150 percent of the original contract item quantity, or in the case of a decrease below 50 percent, to the actual amount of work performed.

The Montana Specifications further prohibits any allowance for change in quantities except as provided in Sections 109.03 "for any increased expense, loss of expected reimbursement, or loss of anticipated profits suffered or claimed resulting either directly from such alterations or indirectly from unbalanced allocation of among the contract items of overhead expense and subsequent loss of expected reimbursements or from any other cause."[27]

The Nebraska Standard Specifications for Highway Construction (2007) allows contract adjustments for "significant changes in the character of work," which are deemed to apply when:

> "(1) The additional work differs materially in kind or nature from the work included in the original proposed construction; or (2) A major item of work, defined as an item whose total original contract cost exceeds 10 percent of its original group total amount, is increased in excess of 125 percent or decreased below 75 percent of the original contract quantity. Any allowance for an increase in quantity shall apply only to that portion in excess of 125 percent of the original contract item quantity, or in case of a decrease below 75 percent, to the actual amount of work performed."[28]

Except as allowed in Sections 104 and 108 (contract termination), the Department will make no pay adjustment or allowance for the Contractor's:

a. Increased operating expense.
b. Loss of expected reimbursement.
c. Loss of anticipated profit.[29]

The Colorado Standard Specifications for Road and Bridge Construction are virtually identical to the Nebraska Specifications with respect to variations in quantity, and most states have similar provisions.

The existence of a VEQ clause generally reduces the number of disputes that arise concerning variations in quantity. However, even with a VEQ clause, recovery may be denied if the increased cost of performing the additional units was not caused by the variation in quantity. In *Victory Construction Co. v. United States*,[30] the court held that the party seeking an adjustment under the VEQ clause must show that there are cost differentials between the estimated quantity

---

[27] Mont. Standard Specifications for Road and Bridge Construction § 109.03 (2006).
[28] Nebraska Standard Specifications for Highway Construction § 104.02.2.c. (2007).
[29] *Id.*, § 109.04.
[30] 510 F.2d 1379 (Ct. Cl. 1975).

and the overrun or underrun quantities, and that the adjustment "will be confined in amount to such cost differentials as are directly attributable to a volume deviation greater than 15 percent from stated contract quantities." The *Victory* decision was followed in *Foley Co. v. United States,*[31] holding that without a showing that there are cost differentials between the estimated quantity and the overrun or underrun quantities due solely to the volume deviation, no adjustment to the contract price may be made.

In *Appeal of S & T Enterprises,*[32] S & T entered into a contract with the Forest Service to repair the spillway of a dam in Oregon. One of the line items was for shotcrete, with an estimated quantity of 34 cubic meters, which S & T bid at $235 per cubic meter. The contract also incorporated the standard VEQ clause, authorizing an equitable adjustment to the unit price if the actual quantity varied more than 15 percent from the estimated quantity. S & T applied 52.2 cm of shotcrete at an actual cost of more than $500/cm. S & T sought an equitable adjustment in the unit price for the overrun quantity of 13.1 units, but the Board denied the claim on the basis that there was no evidence that the increased cost of performing the overrun units was caused "solely" by the quantity overrun itself. Here, the Board found that S & T merely underbid the work.

In *P.R. Contractors, Inc. v. United States,*[33] the contractor sought to recover overhead, profit, bond, and taxes it claimed were incurred as a result of its reliance on the original contract estimates. The contract contained a VEQ clause which allowed for an equitable adjustment when the quantity of a unit-priced item varied by more than 15% from the estimate, and the actual quantities of semi-compacted and uncompacted fill were less than 85% of the quantities estimated in the contract. The VEQ clause specifically provided that any equitable adjustment "shall be based upon any increase or decrease in costs due solely to the variation above 115 percent or below 85 percent of the estimated quantity." The court noted that the VEQ clause precludes an equitable adjustment on anything other than the contractor's "costs," and found that the contractor provided no documentation that its claimed costs for overhead, bond or taxes increased due to the lesser quantity of fill it supplied. Since the contractor failed to demonstrate either increased costs or any nexus between its alleged increased costs and the under-run, the court held that the contractor could not recover under the VEQ clause.

---

[31] 11 F.3d 1032 (Fed. Cir. 1993). *See also* Appeal of KiSKA Constr. Corp.-USA and Kajima Eng'g & Constr., Inc., ASBCA No. 54613, 2009 WL 585935 (Feb. 19, 2009) (contractor was entitled to payment for the quantities that exceeded the estimate by more than 15% at the contract unit price, but was not entitled to an equitable adjustment of the unit price since it failed to show it incurred any increased costs as a result of the variation in quantity).

[32] AGBCA No. 2001-159-1 (2003).

[33] 76 Fed. Cl. 621 (2007), *aff'd*, 2008 WL 1734281 (Fed. Cir. Apr. 14, 2008).

Some courts have held that if a quantity variation does not come within the purview of a VEQ clause, an appropriate adjustment can be made under the differing site conditions or changed conditions clause of the contract. In *Morrison-Knudsen Co. v. United States*,[34] the contract contained a VEQ clause allowing for adjustment of unit prices only if the actual quantities varied from the estimated quantities by more than 25 percent. The variation in quantity of borrow was less than six percent, but the contractor was required to haul the borrow a much greater distance than anticipated, and the contractor sought a unit price adjustment under the changes clause of the contract. The court noted that courts generally limit the application of quantity variation clauses to "reasonable" quantity variations, pricing large or abnormal variations resulting from differing subsurface conditions under the standard differing site conditions or changes clauses. In contrast, "a change in such circumstances is compensable under the Changes clause if the extra costs so incurred differ materially from the costs reimbursed through unit-price payments." The court permitted the contractor to recover all additional costs arising from the variation in quantity of borrow under the contract changes clause, based upon its finding that the change in borrow pit location caused the contractor to incur extra costs that were not anticipated within the unit price.

The differing site conditions clause may also apply, rather than the VEQ clause, in cases where the cost of additional units varies greatly from the contract price, no matter the reason for the increase. In *United Contractors v. United States*,[35] the estimated quantity of excavation was 20,000 cubic yards at a unit price of $3.00/cubic yard. The actual quantity excavated was 25,077 cubic yards. The contractor sought an increase of $1.50 in the unit price for the entire 25,077 cubic yards under the changed conditions clause of the contract, based upon the discovery of unanticipated groundwater. The Board denied the contractor's claim on the grounds that the contract's VEQ provision precluded recovery. The VEQ clause required completion of the work at the specified unit price even when performance involved quantities greater or less than the estimated quantities, unless the actual quantity of work performed under any item varied from the estimated quantity by more than 25 percent. In the event of such a variation, renegotiation of the unit price was permitted only for the actual quantity of work in excess of the estimated quantity plus 25 percent. The Board noted that the actual quantity was only 77 cubic yards in excess of the estimated quantity plus 25 percent, and held that this variation was negligible and not enough to call for a renegotiated unit price. The Court of Appeals reversed, noting that:

> The [VEQ] clause is a ready vehicle for adjusting, with a minimum of haggling, the compensation received by contractors who are called upon in the course of performance to do, within limits, more or less work than could be estimated. But we have held that clauses of this type do not control when

---

[34] 397 F.2d 826 (Ct. Cl. 1968).

[35] 368 F.2d 585 (Ct. Cl. 1966).

> the cost of doing the extra work greatly differs from the stated unit-price because of factors not foreseen by either party. In that event, the Changed Conditions clause comes into play and overrides the Special Condition.[36]

The appellate court held that the amount of the adjustment should be determined by the Board.

[36] *Id.* at 601. *See also* Continental Drilling Co., ENGBCA No. 3455 (1975) (a material variation, not reasonably foreseeable, between the quantity of work set forth in the contract and that actually done is a differing site condition within the purview of the differing site conditions clause; a VEQ clause has no effect on this legal principle when, as in the present case, the cost of doing the work differs significantly from the unit price in the contract); Loftis v. United States, 76 F. Supp. 616 (Ct. Cl. 1948) (when the actual cost of unit price work differs greatly because of unforeseen factors, repricing is proper whether or not VEQ limits have been met; the repricing may apply not only to the overrun/underrun quantity, but may also include some or all of the original estimated quantity); Ray D. Lowder, Inc. v. North Carolina State Hwy. Comm'n, 217 S.E.2d 682 (N.C. App. 1975) (contractor who removed 259,000 cubic yards of undercut excavation on contract estimating removal of 12,000 cubic yards was entitled to recover additional costs under the changed conditions provision of the contract, as the variation in estimated quantities clause was not solely applicable).

TABLE OF CASES

References are to sections.

B

C

E

I

J

M

N

O

P

Q

R

T

Y

Z

INDEX

References are to sections.

E

H

I

J

L

M